W9-BWX-727

Dad,

In thanks for
all your love + support
during my MBA days!

Love,
Andrew
8/16/84

THE MIAMI YEARS
1809 - 1984

End papers:
Front, Miami in McGuffey's Time
Rear, Miami University in 1984

ALSO BY WALTER HAVIGHURST

Pier 17

The Quiet Shore

Upper Mississippi (Rivers of America)

The Winds of Spring

No Homeward Course

The Long Ships Passing

Land of Promise

Signature of Time

George Rogers Clark: Soldier in the West

Annie Oakley of the Wild West

Wilderness for Sale: The First Western Land Rush

Vein of Iron

The Heartland

Proud Prisoner

Voices on the River

Three Flags at the Straits

Alexander Spotswood: Portrait of a Governor

River to the West

Ohio: A Bicentennial History

The Dolibois Years

IN COLLABORATION WITH MARION BOYD HAVIGHURST

Song of the Pines

High Prairie

Climb a Lofty Ladder

THE MIAMI YEARS

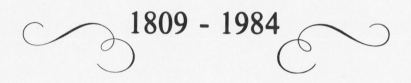

1809 - 1984

BY

WALTER HAVIGHURST

*The sweetest path of life leads
through the avenues of learning.*
—David Hume

G. P. PUTNAM'S SONS, NEW YORK

Copyright © 1958, 1969, 1984 by Walter Havighurst

All rights reserved. This book, or parts thereof, must not be reproduced in any form without permission. Published simultaneously in the Dominion of Canada by Longmans Canada Limited, Toronto.

175th Anniversary Edition

Library of Congress Catalog Card Number: 69-18179

PRINTED IN THE UNITED STATES OF AMERICA

Revised printing by Oxford Printing Company

CONTENTS

Part Three
OUR MIAMI: 1968-1984

Twenty pages of illustrations will be found following page 224.

PART ONE

OLD MIAMI

1809-1873

Chapter I

BEGGAR ON HORSEBACK

O N THE 14th of February, 1811, a worn traveler, six weeks
out from Cincinnati, arrived in Washington on a lame
horse. In the rude new city just emerging from the Maryland
forest he splashed through mud and alder swamps and drew
up at the cluster of boarding houses around the half-built
Capitol. There he found the two Ohio senators, Alexander
Campbell and Thomas Worthington.

He introduced himself—the Reverend John W. Browne,
native of Bristol, England, preacher to the Paddy's Run con-
gregation in Butler County, Ohio, more recently editor of the
weekly *Liberty Hall* in Cincinnati. Now he was beginning a
tour of the East to raise a building fund for the Miami University.

The Senators were aware of the Miami University; its
foundation and location had been repeatedly discussed in the
Ohio General Assembly. To the fund they donated twenty
dollars each, and they were joined on the subscription list
by other Western congressmen.

Cheered by this beginning, Browne took his tired horse to
a livery stable and went to call on President James Madison.
Senator Campbell led him over the stone footway bordering
the muddy gash of Pennsylvania Avenue, with wood and

coal carts lurching past, to the new sandstone executive mansion. In the President's office the University agent was presented to frail, pale, precise James Madison.

Madison heard the appeal but his dark eyes were restless. Troubled by touchy relationships with England and France, the noisy Warhawks in the new Congress, and dissensions within his cabinet, he had little mind for an unbuilt college in the western wilderness. When Browne presented the subscription list, the President pursed his stubborn mouth, shook his white-wigged head, and went back to the vexing problems of foreign commerce.

Still hopeful, Browne approached the Secretary of War, William Eustis, and the Treasury Secretary, Albert Gallatin. He was refused by both. Then he called on Vice-President George Clinton. The crusty old New Yorker, whose nephew would build the Erie Canal, took time to ask a question: What was this Miami University, and where did it come from?

It was a tangled question which would take a long time to answer, even if the financial agent knew. There were no college buildings, no faculty, no students—only a township of wild land (the Reverend Mr. Browne was ready to sell lots, on his own speculation) whose revenues would support the prospective institution. There was a Board of Trustees; Browne had their names along with a plat of college lands among his papers.

One of the trustees was Daniel Symmes, a nephew of Judge John Cleves Symmes who was now living in illness, debt, and despair on a great bend above the Ohio River. Early in this year, 1811, enemies had set fire to Judge Symmes' house at North Bend and burned his jumbled land records. He was a scorned man on the frontier; settlers called him "the greatest land-grabber on the face of the earth" and the government considered him a trespasser on the public domain.

Yet Judge Symmes had come West in the brave year of

1788 with high hopes and generous aspirations. A big, buoyant man who had been chief justice of New Jersey and a member of the Continental Congress, he was as near a founder as Miami University had; his contract with Congress for the purchase of the land between the two Miami rivers entailed the granting of a township to endow a college. An Act of Congress, on May 5, 1792, signed by George Washington, declared that the granted township should be located with the approval of the Governor of the Territory northwest of the Ohio River and forever held in trust to erect and support an academy.

The most valuable land in the Symmes Purchase was the thirty miles of frontage on the Ohio River, and the most valuable of that was the land across from where the Licking leads south into Kentucky. Give Symmes credit for a generous intention: he first proposed to reserve a college township as nearly opposite the mouth of the Licking as an entire township could be formed. This Township 3 of the First Entire Range was withheld from sale and was marked on Symmes' map as the college township; it now embraces the northern suburbs, from Mount Airy to Glendale, of modern Cincinnati. But when Symmes asked Congress to reduce his proposed purchase from two million to one million acres, he seems to have assumed that he relinquished the grant of a college township. So he erased the entry and promptly sold the choice township. When the Territorial Legislature convened in 1799 Symmes was asked about the college tract. He then offered to reserve Township 2 of the Second Fractional Range (the ranges are irregular because of the curving Ohio River), which embraces the western suburbs of Cincinnati. But Governor Arthur St. Clair found conflicting claims on this township; Symmes had forgotten that he had sold half of it to his colleague Elias Boudinot back in 1788. So the college township was still a promise only.

Finally, on March 3, 1803, two days after Ohio attained statehood, Congress granted one complete township to be located in the District of Cincinnati under direction of the Ohio Legislature; if no township within the Symmes Purchase were offered in five years, then a township from federal lands was granted the State of Ohio to be held in trust for the establishment of a college. No township was offered, since no unentered township remained between the two Miami rivers.

On April 15, 1803, the Ohio Assembly passed an act to provide for the locating of a college township and appointed three commissioners to choose the land. That summer Jeremiah Morrow and William Ludlow splashed through creeks of Butler County and selected a wild township on Four Mile Creek; it was not yet called Oxford Township. For five years deer and foxes roamed the college lands. At the end of that waiting period the 23,000 acres became the possession of the State of Ohio, in accordance with the Act of Congress of March 3, 1803, to be held in trust to support a college.

So, in 1809, with its land grant finally and irrevocably made, the college could be legally created. On February 17th, with "An Act to Establish the Miami University," the Ohio General Assembly gave a name and a charter to the institution. The Legislature appointed a board of fourteen trustees and delegated three commissioners to select a college site. In that summer of 1809 two of them met at Lebanon in Warren County and chose a campus of forty-one acres, offered to the future college by Ichabod Corwin, at the western end of the town of Lebanon. On the trunk of a witness tree they slashed M.U.V., to mark the location of the first college building.

That forty-one acres of rolling woodland was never crossed by campus paths; it became the Lebanon cemetery. For many years the white oak with its slowly healing initials shaded the grave of eloquent Tom Corwin, Ohio governor and senator and United States minister to Mexico.

Lebanon, a prosperous and attractive frontier town, seemed a good location for a college. But because one of the

commissioners was absent when the site was chosen, the
Legislature rejected the choice. Lebanon wanted the college;
so did Cincinnati, Dayton, Hamilton, and Yellow Springs.
Probably as a compromise the Ohio General Assembly on
February 6, 1810, directed the trustees to lay off a town to
be called Oxford in the college grant and to select a campus
site within the college lands. So the wild college township,
without a road leading into it, with a few pioneer settlers
and a score of squatters living on the creek banks, took an
ancient academic name, and surveyors hacked their way into
the forest.

The Board of Trustees, now enlarged to twenty members,
met on March 26th in Hamilton (population 260) and appointed a committee of five to select a tract one mile square
for the college town. On March 29th, after tramping for two
days through the woods along Four Mile Creek, which was
also known by the musical Indian name Tallawanda, the
committee chose the site of Oxford, 640 acres of forest on a
rounded hill crest. With auspicious foresight they reserved
fifty-six acres at its eastern end for the "University Square"
and forty acres in the northeast corner for "Botanical Gardens." In May, in Hamilton, came the first land sale, eleven
in-lots going for an average of twenty dollars, and eight four-
acre out-lots at five dollars an acre. Bidders on the township
land paid no purchase price but took a perpetual lease to
their land, paying an annual rent of six per cent of the auction price to the University treasurer. The Board of Trustees
had a trickle of money coming in.

The trustees were young men; more than half were in their
thirties. A college was a new order to them. Just two had
diplomas, James Shields from the University of Glasgow and
Daniel Symmes from Princeton. One other, the Reverend
Joshua Wilson, had attended Transylvania College in Kentucky. The rest were little informed on academic matters but
strenuously experienced in Indian fighting, surveying, land-
seeking, town-planning, frontier legislation, and commerce.

Around the bare table was concentrated a formidable body of pioneer character and experience.

At the head of the board sat John Bigger, a native of Pennsylvania who had settled on wild lands in Warren County. A shrewd, practical, weather-burned man, he was twenty times elected to the Ohio General Assembly; he was defeated for the governorship of Ohio in 1826, but one of his sons became governor of Indiana. Taking the secretary's notes in his firm clear hand was James McBride, a robust and versatile young man of twenty-three. He had little schooling but a wide-ranging mind and lively sense of history. As a pioneer merchant he rode the trails of the Miami country, trading merchandise and measuring Indian mounds and earthworks.

Lean, lined Benjamin Whiteman was a veteran of the border wars. He had crouched in the canebrakes with Daniel Boone, fighting off Shawnee raids on the Kentucky stations; he had scouted with Simon Kenton, marched to defeat in Harmer's campaign and then to victory with General Wayne at Fallen Timbers. He became a brigadier general in the War of 1812. D. H. Morris, a native of New Jersey, was one of the first white men ever to see the dark woods and bright prairies of western Ohio. He had been a soldier and hunter in Harmer's expedition; after the Treaty of Greenville in 1795, along with two other young bachelors he took a homestead on Freeman's Prairie in the wilds of Miami County. John Reily, of Virginia, had taught the first school in western Ohio; between terms he fought Indians in the Mill Creek Valley, ran a pack-horse trade to Fort Hamilton, and helped to bury the dead after St. Clair's defeat in 1791. James Shields, born in the North of Ireland, educated at Glasgow University, had cleared a farm in the depths of Butler County and reared twelve children there; after nineteen years in the Ohio Legislature he became a member of Congress. Dr. Stephen Wood, a neighbor of John Cleves Symmes at North Bend on the Ohio, was a physician, farmer, and justice of the peace; for a time he had been treasurer of the Northwest

Territory. In his log house above the river, in 1795, he had married Symmes' daughter Anna to lean young Captain William Henry Harrison. Colonel William Ward, in white linen and black broadcloth, was a big land-owner from Greenbriar County, Virginia; long-striding Simon Kenton had guided him to western Ohio where the shrewd colonel laid out the town of Urbana in the rich land above King's Creek. General James Findlay, pioneer soldier, settler and merchant, had opened the first store in Cincinnati; now, in 1810, he was Cincinnati's mayor.

This body of frontier men, with their horses stamping at the hitching rack, were establishing a university. In time the township lands would be settled and the college fund would grow. But they were not content to wait. Already they had adopted a seal "figuratively representing the sun of literature and science rising over the mountains of ignorance and superstition." Meeting in Cincinnati in June, 1810, they employed the Reverend John W. Browne as college "missionary," to solicit contributions. He was to have a salary of fifty dollars a month and expenses, out of the donations received. The trustees hoped that his success would entitle him to be called "the friend and father of our institution."

In the national capital Missionary Browne got no money from Vice-President Clinton, but he did get some more questions. "What have your own Ohio neighbors done? Have the trustees themselves, and the inhabitants of the State, shown no examples of generosity?" The trustees had pledged a total of $800 in loans for college "apparatus," but Mr. Browne did not know it. He must have been glad to get away.

Browne's next prospect was Senator John Pope of Kentucky. This sympathetic Westerner did not find it convenient to contribute cash, but he offered books—a five-volume set of Plowden's *History of Ireland*. Likewise Joel Barlow, impressive poet and patriot, just appointed minister to France, suggested that many men who would not be disposed to give money might be persuaded to give books. Here began a new

turn in Browne's campaign. The application for both books
and money, he reported to the trustees, "would promote
each," and either response would answer a valuable purpose
for the university. Barlow examined his own library and
handed down ten big volumes.

So, with "a new spring to my mind," as he reported,
Browne pushed on to Baltimore, where he collected a trunk
full of books and a little cash. In Baltimore, tempted by some
educational equipment, he spent $57 from his cash contribu-
tions for more books along with "a neat small pair of Globes."
Delaware proved to be poor territory; the take from two
weeks' solicitation amounted to $22 and thirty-five assorted
volumes.

It was high summer when Browne jogged into New Jersey.
This was Judge Symmes' state, where he had first publicized
the Miami lands, and Browne kept a watch for speculators
or prospective settlers; he had bid in, without any payment,
sixteen lots in Oxford Township. But he was even less successful for himself than for the college. He found no takers
and all his leases were finally forfeited.

In this summer the Ohio Valley lay slumbrous, rich and
green. A great silence hung over it, as in time unmeasured.
But at a few points there rose a purposeful din. Under the
hills of Pittsburgh the first steamboat of the West was building, with a creaking of ropes and a clatter of hammers, on
the trampled riverfront. In Cincinnati wagons rumbled on
the landing, trees crashed down on upper Broadway, herds-
men drove hogs and cattle through the streets. Thirty miles
north in the deep woods of Oxford Township sounded the
steady thud of ax and mallet. One hundred fifty dollars had
been appropriated from the college funds and a log schoolhouse was building; it rose in a ragged clearing where Brice
Scientific Hall now stands. Surveyors were lining out the
streets that would bound the campus. The first log houses
were spreading along the stump-dotted High Street. In the
"University Grove" stood a broad low Indian mound, cov-

ered with foot-thick maple trees. Once this campus had been
a ceremonial place, seed gourds rattling, voices rising and
falling, dark faces gleaming in the firelight. Now a school
was growing there.

Mr. Browne had that solid schoolhouse to refer to as he
went on through New Jersey. In Trenton, where in 1787 John
Cleves Symmes had issued a glowing circular inviting pur-
chases of Miami Valley land, he collected some seventy dollars and a hundred books. At Princeton, President Samuel
Stanhope Smith received him politely and donated five dollars. Somewhere in New Jersey there were investors in
Symmes' Purchase. Browne wrote that he meant to "find out
such persons . . . and ply *them* pretty closely." But nothing
came of that.

In October he sailed up the Hudson in a new steamboat.
Albany, he learned, had a town ordinance prohibiting all
solicitation, but he went ahead, explaining, "I came to beg,
and beg I must." Collections were small. Then in hard winter
weather he pushed on to New England. In Salem he com-
peted with a campaign for missionaries on the Island of
Borneo; appeals to three congregations yielded three hundred dollars and some books. In Boston he hoped for a
thousand dollars, but the Bostonians showed little interest in
an unborn western college. He called on Governor Caleb
Strong, a large land-owner in Ohio, but got nothing. Out at
Quincy old President John Adams gave him two books and
a ten dollar bill. A final appeal at New Haven, where he was
pleasantly received by President Dwight of Yale, yielded
$161.50.

With this, Browne closed his subscription list. Sending a
wagon-load of books to Cincinnati, he traveled west by
stages. He reached Cincinnati "after a very fatiguing journey" on the 3rd of August, 1812.

A few weeks later, while on a preaching mission in Cler-
mont County, Missionary Browne guided his horse to a ford-
ing place in the Little Miami River. The water was high and

he missed the crossing. Alone in the woods on a summer day the tired, far-traveled Englishman was drowned.

His report to the University trustees had not been made, and it was twelve years before the final accounting. Meanwhile some of the books he had acquired were selected for the college library; the rest were sold at auction in Cincinnati. With the books was found a barrel of "Spanish whiting" (whitewash) which the trustees pondered over and finally sold. During his travels Browne had sent to the trustees some seven hundred dollars, and the sale of books netted another three hundred. A sum of $217.62 was due from Browne's estate, but it seemed undesirable to press that claim. Mr. Browne's mission had not made him the "father of the institution," as the trustees had hoped.

One March day in 1937 a visitor to the University called at the office of President Alfred H. Upham in Benton Hall. He was Samuel L. Stokes of Bethesda, Maryland, a grandson of the Reverend John W. Browne. The visitor presented to President Upham an envelope containing Mr. Browne's long-delayed report on his mission, his credentials and account book. He had found his grandfather's papers in an attic trunk where they had rested for more than a hundred years. Mr. Stokes had married a Miami graduate, Marie Hirst of the class of 1904.

During the summer of 1812 axes were thudding in the college forest. The Indian mound on the site of present Stoddard Hall was leveled and two acres were cleared for a university campus. But there was no building fund. By 1815 the costs of surveying, a set of office books, and the building of a log schoolhouse had used up all the college funds except $143.35. James McBride calculated that the 23,000 acres of college land, most of it yet unleased, was worth $56,000, which at the six per cent rental would bring an annual income of about $3,400. It was years before the land rents reached that revenue.

Meanwhile the trustees were scattered. During Browne's

return journey from the East war had been declared with England. Two weeks after his arrival in Cincinnati, Detroit was surrendered to the British and the whole Northwestern frontier seemed threatened. Land sales ceased—in the college township as elsewhere. Some of the University trustees went into the regular army; others served in the militia. Secretary James McBride built a flatboat in Hamilton, loaded it with flour, whisky and apples, and began a trading trip to New Orleans. In Oxford brush and brambles crept over the two-acre clearing in the college square.

Quite naturally the Oxford settlers began to doubt that they would ever have a university. In 1814 James McBride, having returned from a profitable journey to New Orleans, prepared "An Address to the Inhabitants of the Miami College lands," assuring them that the site of the Miami University had been permanently established, "and on the banks of the Four Mile has been planted the stake where the Miami University will stand immovable till time shall be no longer."

More than that, he gave a glowing account of the University's prospects: "The present arrangement which has been made for the disposition of the lands belonging to the Miami University is such, that when the lands are all disposed of it must afford a greater income to the University than any other seminary of learning in the United States is at present endowed with, and I trust the time is fast approaching, and now not far distant, when we shall behold a splendid college, whose stately spires tip the clouds and whose surrounding country bespeaks the industry and happiness of its inhabitants, where but a few years since the bark covered hut of the savage was the only mark of human improvement. And where, late the howling of the beasts of prey and the war whoop of the Indian were the only sounds which broke upon the ear of the wandering traveler, I trust we shall meet with the most polished of society. And on that same spot shall we meet with the youth assembled from various quarters of the world, to learn the arts and become acquainted with rhetoric and belles lettres. Astonishing change! But it is a change which every circumstance warrants us in expecting. And now, Oh! ye friends of literature and science, now is the time to extend your fostering hand to cherish and protect this institution of learning, which is to give a character and feature to your sons and your grandsons to the fortieth generation. . . ."

To this prophecy he added the practical reminder that in the college township an honest citizen "can procure himself a farm and settle himself comfortably without advancing one cent; he can have the use of money forever by paying the interest—true, this small sum of interest will have to be paid yearly, and for a few years until his cabin is comfortably enclosed and his land improved he may meet with some inconveniences: but some inconveniences we must expect to surmount in all situations in life. Recollect that in a few years these lofty poplars and walnuts which at present cover the face of the township will disappear or be converted into houses and inclosures for your fields; land which is now valued at three dollars per acre will sell for forty or fifty. The lot for which you pay fifteen or eighteen dollars per annum you can rent for an hundred. Such is the way you will be enabled to settle yourselves so as to live comfortably and happy, and in this way you will be enabled to acquire wealth without advancing any capital."

He concluded his long address—which was published in Hamilton in July, 1814—with the earnest trust that "the almighty being who rules the destiny of mortals here below would protect with his guardian power this infant institution."

As yet there was nothing but the primeval forest to protect. When peace came in 1815 Miami University was in the sixth year of its corporate existence, and still it had no college building, no faculty, no students. One of its newly-appointed trustees, Dr. Daniel Drake of Cincinnati, declared: "That it will attain to the rank of a second-rate college . . . where it is now fixed, no well-informed person has the courage to predict." Over the campus hung the forest silence, with wild turkeys roosting in the trees and fox-eyes gleaming in the dark.

Chapter II

FOUNDATION STONE

IN THE YEAR 1818 crews of Irish shovelmen began digging the Erie Canal, the first Great Lakes steamship paddled between Buffalo, Cleveland and Detroit, and the National Road from Baltimore reached the Ohio River at Wheeling. Illinois became a state, and George Rogers Clark, desolate and forgotten, died at Locust Grove outside of Louisville. In that year a woman named Nancy Hanks Lincoln died at Pigeon Creek, Indiana, and eight-year-old Abe Lincoln whittled pegs for her coffin. At St. Mary's, Ohio, a council of Shawnee, Wyandot and Ottawa chiefs signed a treaty for their last shrinking reservation lands in the Ohio country.

On the Miami campus in the summer of 1818 workmen were pounding a roof on a three-story brick structure called Franklin Hall; it was the first part of the building later called Old Main and still later Harrison Hall. Watching the job was James Maxwell Dorsey, superintendent of construction. A slight, middle-aged man with sloping shoulders, a high forehead and a bony nose, he looked like a college professor except for the restless eyes behind his steel-rimmed glasses.

Dorsey was a man of several minds—surveyor, soldier, teacher, business manager, philosopher, reformer. He had come to Oxford in 1810, when there was only a trail through the forest, and the next year he became the town's first teacher, opening a "Select School" in the new log building on the University grounds. In December, 1811, Dorsey ran a partition across the eighteen-by-thirty-foot room. He lived in one end with his family and taught the township scholars just beyond the wall.

Seven months later, in June of 1812, war was declared with England and the school door closed. Master Dorsey became Major Dorsey, commanding the "Old Battalion," four companies of volunteers from Butler and Warren counties. They served on the Northwestern border, scouting the Maumee and upper Wabash valleys and guarding the settlements from Indian attack.

When the war was over Dorsey came back to Oxford, which was little changed in his absence. But change was coming. In the spring of 1816 the University trustees hired him to measure and clear the ground for a college building. A good ax- and mattock-man, Dorsey chopped brush out of the previous two-acre clearing and leveled a foundation site. On April 10th, with a carpenter and two stone-masons standing there in the half-leafed forest, James Dorsey laid the first stone "eighteen or twenty inches below the surface of the ground."

For two years that structure, the eventual West Wing of the Center Building, was under construction, at a cost of $6,167, paid from the college land rents. James Dorsey kept an eye on the brick work—the bricks were baked of clay taken from the leveled Indian mound southeast of the building—but his mind was ranging.

The frontier was hospitable to ideas as well as to men. Already into the Ohio Valley had come new religious and social doctrines. There was a flourishing Shaker community near Lebanon, Ohio, and a colony of German Pietists on the Wabash at Harmony. Others would come with their revolutionary social orders. New lands stimulated new thoughts.

In 1816 James Dorsey and William Ludlow, president of the Miami University trustees from 1810-13, organized the "Rational Brethren of Oxford." This society, incorporated on Christmas Day, 1816, proposed to hold land and engage in manufacturing, all its members sharing in ownership and being provided for, each according to his needs, out of the common funds. It would admit any landholder of abstemious habits whatever the value of his land and any mechanic, with or without land, who was disposed to contribute virtue and habits of industry; all members would receive one share in the common property. Both Dorsey and Ludlow owned land south of present Chestnut Street along Collins Run; they expected their society to do a business in pot and pearl ashes and in agricultural goods, and perhaps in fruit trees, as William Ludlow had a nursery on Collins Run and a larger one—120,000 trees—on Mill Creek.

In later and less spacious times University trustees would blanch at Socialism, but Ludlow and Dorsey breathed the air of a new country. With a few of their Rational Brethren they discussed the organization of Oxford Township around the University—education being essential to a rational society —as a Socialistic community. "Equal good and happiness of all is to be the object of our Association"; the college would serve to improve useful knowledge and encourage freedom of inquiry.

These airy ideas never took root in the township soil. No substantial number of Oxford residents joined the Rational Brethren, though Ludlow's older brother, Colonel Israel Ludlow, who was Symmes' principal surveyor and the founder of Cincinnati, Dayton, and Hamilton, listed some lands with the association. Apparently no other trustees shared the rational hopes and enthusiasms of Ludlow and Dorsey. There was more Calvinism than Socialism in the college that opened in 1824. Oxford was orthodox from the start.

For James Dorsey, the search for social perfection led away from the college township. His life veered in a new direction when the astonishing Robert Owen came to America in 1824 and addressed the United States Congress about his plan to establish an ideal community on the Wabash, to which men of all nations were invited. "Here in the heart of the United States," he declared, "that Power which governs and directs the Universe . . . permits me to commence a new empire of peace and good-will to men, founded on other principles and leading to other practices than those of present or past." Robert Owen, a slight, soft-spoken man with steel-rimmed spectacles sliding down his nose, looked like a wandering schoolmaster, but he meant to change the world. In Scotland he had transformed a desolate mill town into a happy, clean and prosperous community, increasing the profits of the Lanark mills while he improved the lives of their workers. Now on the American frontier he saw a vaster theater in which to try his plan of social reform. In New Harmony there would be no rich or poor, no owners or exploiters, no oppressors or oppressed; all would be free and equal citizens of a New Moral World.

For three years, while he served as treasurer of Miami University, James Dorsey corresponded with Robert Owen. To the Wabash community flocked reformers, zealots, educators, some brilliant Socialists, more homeless eccentrics and still more fanatics and revolutionists. In 1827 Dorsey resigned his Miami office and went to New Harmony to supervise the school system. By then the bloom was gone from the great experiment. The Wabash community was deep in discord and Owen was about to return to London. He left the general direction of the community to "Mr. Dorsey, late treasurer of Miami University, in whose steadfastness, integrity, ability and disinterested devotion to the cause I have full confidence."

Dorsey watched New Harmony dim and dwindle. He had missed the short-lived excitement of the New Moral World on the Wabash; now he was left to liquidate Owen's lands, and to send their proceeds to New York and London to support Socialist newspapers.

The foundation he had laid for Miami University was more lasting. That first college building, completed in 1818 and named Franklin Hall, received attention as far away as Philadelphia. On June 12, 1819, the *Philadelphia Register and National Recorder* described it as "a large building of brick; it contains twelve rooms, one of which is occupied as a library, another as a meeting house, the other ten are occupied by the students of whom last session there were twenty-two."

The University trustees appointed one of their own members, James Hughes, to teach the school. It was not yet a college but a grammar school, with beginning courses in Latin and Greek. A frontier college had to prepare its own students.

James Hughes, Presbyterian minister from Pennsylvania, came to Ohio as a missionary to the Wyandot Indians on the Sandusky River. He was appointed to the Miami University Board of Trustees in 1815, and three years later was named by the board to teach the University school. Soon after his arrival he organized the Oxford Presbyterian Church, using the college building for its meeting place, and he served as its pastor along with his schoolmaster's duties. A rather handsome, slender, unworldly man, he appears in his silhouette portrait, with hair clubbed back and a string bow tie in his collar. He lived in the old log building on the site of Brice Hall, where James Dorsey had lived and taught in 1811; a second story was added for the Hughes family in 1818. Assisting him as schoolmaster was a scholarly German, Nahum Myers, recently arrived from Prussia. He came to teach Hebrew and to learn English, a combination which must have been hard on the schoolboys.

The Miami University grammar school opened on November 3, 1818, with twenty-one students. They were assigned rooms in the new college building and took board with Oxford families at $1.50 a week. They paid a tuition fee of $5 a session. Two terms were scheduled, winter and summer, with vacation at planting season in April and harvest time in October. A list of seventeen rules required attendance at morning prayers and Sunday worship and prohibited drunkenness, gambling, unnecessary noise, and the patronizing of any tavern or other public place. Each student was required to study composition and public speaking in addition to his classical course.

Meanwhile James Dorsey was leasing more of the college lands and supervising a new and larger construction. In 1820 work began on a three-story addition to Franklin Hall, adjoining it on the east. With large rooms and high ceilings, so that its three stories rose above the older wing, it was designed as "the center and principal building of the Miami University"; and it stood until 1958 as the central portion of Harrison Hall. It was then the oldest existing Miami building, as the west wing was completely rebuilt after the Civil War. The new Center Building was four years under construction; it was finished in 1824 at a cost slightly over $15,000. It was capped with a cupola—there were no towers until after the Civil War. It was whitewashed soon after completion and periodically until 1870 when all the campus buildings were painted red.

The combination of the Center Building and its Franklin Hall wing, together to be called Old Main, was an impressive college building for the time. It was noted in the *New Hampshire Patriot and State Gazette* that the trustees of Miami University had expended a large sum of money in the erection of a costly building. "Something magnificent and splendid appears to be their object," wrote the editor, who went on to observe that "for many years the edifice of Dartmouth College consisted of logs, piled one on top of another and dovetailed together in the usual manner at the corners. . . . In this humble and rude little temple, President Wheelock the

elder, commenced a course of classic instruction." To the
Yankees it seemed that, with such a building as the Miami
edifice, the West was putting on airs.

One of the rules governing the grammar school required
an annual examination of students by a committee of the
Board of Trustees. This practice was continued until the
Civil War; with monotonous regularity the examining committee attested to the intellectual progress of the students
and to standards of scholarship which were a credit to the
institution. But in April, 1821, after two and a half years of
operation of the grammar school, the examining committee
was not satisfied. They recommended that the school be
closed. Perhaps the illness of Mr. Hughes—he died a few
weeks later of typhoid fever—influenced their action. But
there was also a financial angle: expenditure for the grammar
school was draining the college income. At any rate after
five sessions the school disbanded. Meantime construction
continued on the Center Building, and the trustees labored
with the land rentals and land forfeitures. While Dorsey was
occupied with collecting rents, and with the plans of the
Rational Brethren, workmen on the new building moved
their families into quarters on the lower floor. When they
were evicted, the disgruntled bricklayers retaliated with a
slowdown.

Then came a real problem. Early in 1822 a group of Cincinnati politicians proposed that Miami University be moved
from Oxford Township and merged with Cincinnati College.

Here was that question again: Where should the Miami
University be situated? Assigned to the Symmes Purchase,
to be endowed by a township there, it was now developing a
campus on its own grant outside the Purchase. When in 1810
the Ohio Legislature established the University on its new
lands, there was disappointment and protest in Cincinnati.
The resentment had smoldered for a dozen years.

Cincinnati had bad luck with its own college-founding.

The first try was met by a natural disaster; a nearly-completed college building was blown down by a spring tornado in 1809. Five years later a Lancastrian school was opened at Fourth and Walnut streets, but its utilitarian course did not satisfy people who wanted a classical college. In 1819 the Lancastrian school was re-chartered as Cincinnati College.

Meanwhile the existence, in prospect at least, of Miami University thirty-five miles away vexed some of the citizens of Cincinnati. In 1814 they made a legislative effort to move Miami University to within the Symmes Purchase. Though the attempt failed, it was not forgotten. An article in the *Western Spy,* a Cincinnati weekly, in October, 1817, referred scornfully to Miami University as "our college in the gloom of the beechwood flats, where the footsteps of enlightenment and liberal patronage cannot penetrate, and from whence not a ray of science will be reflected for a century." Miami University had a small but increasing income and was dedicated to the advancement of literature and science; it was just what Cincinnati wanted. So the debate grew. The *Hamilton Advertiser,* arguing for the University's Butler County location, stated that Cincinnati was too full of paper-money maneuvering and houses of ill fame to be a fit place for a college. To that, Isaac G. Burnet of Cincinnati replied: "The amenities of a large town [Cincinnati with 7500 people became a "city" in 1819] have generally a refinement about them which improves the mind."

On January 10, 1822, a proposal was made to the General Assembly and a bill was introduced to move Miami University to Cincinnati. An appeasement clause called for the retaining in Oxford of an "Oxford Academy" which could use the existing University buildings and ten acres of ground and would receive one-eighth of the income from the college lands. Such an academy, had it not promptly died, would have become a preparatory school for the Miami University removed to Cincinnati.

The bill provoked one of the most strenuous debates in
the early years of the Ohio Legislature. The House of Representatives argued it until the winter darkness fell; then by
candlelight the debate went on. To legal and practical arguments the Cincinnati group added the flat statement that
"the school in Oxford has not succeeded and cannot assist in
the education of the present population." The opposition was
led by Captain Joel Collins, pioneer settler of Oxford, surveyor of the township, ex-Indian fighter, and long-time friend
of Miami University. He succeeded in delaying action until
the Butler County men could organize their defense.

In Oxford, alarmed at this threat to the town's only enterprise and its sole future, residents held a public meeting.
With James Dorsey presiding, they formed a committee to
publicize the injustice and impolicy of removing Miami University, and they sent to Joel Collins for an account of the
struggle in the Legislature. In his reply Collins stated that
many legislators were prejudiced against the lessees of school
and college lands generally, the lands having failed to realize
expected profits, and that "it was the policy of the Cincinnati
College to continue to make those unavailing efforts to ob-
tain the funds from Oxford, and thereby retard the progress
of the Miami University, by fixing on the public mind that
it is not permanently established at Oxford." He concluded,
however, with an assurance that the present effort to move
the site of the University had failed.

To strengthen their defense for the future, the Oxford residents elected doughty James McBride to the House of Representatives. McBride prepared a long speech—nine thousand
words on the complicated history of the college grant and
the establishing of Miami University, followed by six thousand words of orderly, detailed, closely-reasoned argument
against its removal. In addition to legal reasoning on the
validity of contracts, he argued on moral grounds that the
rustic setting derided by the Cincinnati group was better

than an urban site for a university. "I had rather send my son to a seminary of learning provided there were able professors, even though it should be *immersed in the gloom of the Beech Woods,* as the (Cincinnati) gentleman will have it . . . than to send him . . . where he would be exposed to the temptations and vices which are always prevalent in large cities. . . . It is not in the dust of a merchant's shop, or amidst the din of mechanics' hammers, much less at a theatre, a tavern, or a grog-shop that the classics can be read with most advantage."

This formidable speech was never delivered, as the bill for the University's removal was not re-introduced.

With both Collins and McBride in the Legislature and Miami trustees alert for any new action, the threat to Miami University was diminished—though it would appear again, briefly, fourteen years later. Now, with a new cheerfulness, Dorsey collected land rents in the college township and watched the progress of the Center Building, and the Board of Trustees discussed the choosing of a University president.

In 1824 James Dorsey was elected treasurer of Miami University, taking an office whose duties he had partially filled for some years past. It was a busy job, dunning defaulters, leasing and re-leasing tracts of farm land, keeping the records of rent and disbursal. But these practical matters did not dim his dream of a rational society where men could have perfect freedom, equality and brotherhood. In 1827 he went to New Harmony, and disillusionment. After six years he came back to Ohio, settling first at Greenville, and later in Piqua where he died in 1857. His name and his memory would linger at Miami University. From 1854 to the closing of Old Miami in 1873 his son, G. Volney Dorsey, prominent in Ohio medicine and politics, sat on the Miami Board of Trustees, and his great-grandson, William Wilson Wood, served as a trustee in the 1940's.

In his own declining years James Maxwell Dorsey watched the progress and achievement of Miami University. It had not become a center of Rational Brethren, but its graduates were in the colleges, the pulpits, the legislatures of America, and in foreign embassies from Bolivia to Russia. Sometimes James Dorsey must have remembered the foundation stone he had laid, on an April morning, in the empty forest.

Chapter III

INAUGURAL PROCESSION

ON A WINDY AUTUMN NIGHT in Edinburgh in 1801 a rangy, rawboned young theology student chanced to meet on a street corner an American churchman who was recruiting Presbyterian ministers for careers in America. As a result of this meeting Robert Hamilton Bishop and his young bride sailed for America in the fall of 1802. In New York Bishop was assigned to the Presbytery of Kentucky—"then the extreme of the far West," he noted with satisfaction. On his way he stopped at Chillicothe, Ohio, where he found the town buzzing with talk of a constitutional convention. He had arrived in Ohio at the hour of its statehood.

For a year the rugged Scotchman preached to frontier congregations in Kentucky and Southwestern Ohio, traveling on horseback to scattered settlements on the river banks and in forest clearings. In the ardor of young manhood he had come to a new land, a land which kindled his mind and emotions. "Kentucky and the Miami Valley appeared to me to be not only the garden of America, but the garden of the world, and were fixed upon my mind not only to be filled with a dense population, but to be the center of influence to the future states and future nations of the Mississippi Valley."

In 1804 at Transylvania College in Lexington, Kentucky, the oldest college west of the Alleghenies, he became professor of moral philosophy, logic, criticism and belles-lettres. During twenty years there he also taught natural philosophy, history, mathematics and astronomy. He was a tall but not a narrow man.

In those years Lexington was the literary capital of the West. Bishop's colleagues included the jurists Henry Clay and John Breckenridge, the distinguished physician Daniel Drake, the versatile editor Amos Kendall, and that far-wandering gypsy-scientist Constantine Rafinesque. Among these scholars and discoverers Bishop took an equal place; in fact, his students ranked him at the top. His learning, his magnetism, his profound and lofty earnestness they never forgot. "Clay at the bar, or Bishop in the pulpit" they considered the *ne plus ultra* of human greatness. One of his students was Jefferson Davis, who in later years remembered Bishop as "a man of large attainments and very varied knowledge." Francis Preston Blair, pre-eminent Jacksonian editor, wrote that Professor Bishop was one of the best teachers he had ever known. The height of his mind, these students knew, was matched by the breadth of his humanity. After a college riot which President Holley could hardly cope with, one of the rioters said, "Mr. Bishop could have done it. We may respect Dr. Holley, but we love Mr. Bishop."

In the fall of 1824 three dusty youths on horseback clattered into Lexington and inquired the way to Robert Hamilton Bishop, then vice-president of Transylvania. They brought letters to him from their families in Abbeville, South Carolina. Bishop welcomed them to Transylvania, but said that he would not be there much longer. "I am going over the river," he explained, "to establish a college in the woods, in Ohio."

"Then," declared the boys, "that is where we are going."

They rode on to Oxford and were in the chapel when President Bishop met the first students of Miami University, looking over the bare square room and beginning, "My young friends—"

In the previous spring when the Center Building was nearly completed a committee of the Board of Trustees had begun a search for the first president of the college. One member of the committee had been a student under Bishop at Transylvania, another knew him through activities of the Presbyterian Church. At a meeting on July 6, 1824, the University trustees elected Robert Hamilton Bishop as Miami's president. On September 14th he rode into Oxford, tied his horse to a campus tree, and in the library "chamber" of the new Center Building presented to the trustees a formal acceptance. It concluded with a quietly optimistic view of the University's future: "From the situation and resource of the Miami University the public are authorized to expect that within a reasonable period it shall be an extensive public blessing."

He looked at the president's "mansion," the old log school where Dorsey had taught the first Oxford students; it now had a second story, and Bishop suggested that it be white-washed outside and in and that a sitting room be added. Then he rode back to Kentucky for his family. They came through the colored woods of October in a two-horse wagon —his wife, eight children ranging from three years to nineteen, and Nellie, a Kentucky slave girl, who was working out her freedom. They found the president's log house freshly covered with weatherboard and painted red; a stable stood near it to the west. That family filled the house to overflowing.

Since the appointment of President Bishop the trustees had announced in nearby newspapers the opening of Miami University on the first day of November, 1824. There would be two sessions, November through March, May through September. Tuition $10 a session in the college, $5 in the grammar school. Board $1 a week. Rooms in the college were free except for a $5 fee for "servant hire." The total of a student's expense was $93 for the year.

At the start, however, Miami University offered an opportunity to students who could not pay fees. In the trustees' records appears a resolution—"that five students, should that number apply and produce satisfactory evidence of their inability to discharge the fees of tuition, and of their goodness of character, shall receive instruction in any department of the university without paying tuition fees for the first year that the college shall be in operation." A year later they agreed to waive tuition for eight superior students in return for one hour per day as tutors.

For the opening of the college there were twenty students —four seniors, three sophomores, five freshmen, eight in the grammar school. More came in the spring, piling out of muddy wagons to be greeted by tall, lean President Bishop at the college door. At the end of the first year the roll of students numbered sixty-eight. Coming from various backgrounds and without uniform schooling, they ranged from ten-year-old boys to stalwart young men of thirty. The ten freshmen varied from twelve to twenty-three years. Together this assorted class recited their Greek and Latin, algebra, modern geography and Roman history. They lived together in the college rooms and were subjected to the same regulations. "Every student, except at recitation or lecture, shall remain in his room during study hours, which shall be regulated by the faculty." No wonder there were outbreaks.

On the ground floor of the old wing was the president's office and the secretary's rooms, with two classrooms across the hall. The Center Building contained the chapel, later the Towers Theatre, a library room and recitation rooms. The advertisements had stated: "The college already possesses a library comprising a collection of many rare and valuable works in various departments of literature and science, to which additions will be made from time to time." The library was open only a few hours a week and students were not allowed to take books away. A few years later the rule was liberalized: "Only the Senior class shall be allowed to take books from the library."

A whitewashed fence enclosed four or five acres around the college building, a campus denuded of forest but dotted with stumps. The fence kept out stray hogs and cattle, except as restless students led a cow into the chapel room or threw a sheep into a classroom or dormitory window. A muddy path, the original "Slant Walk," led diagonally from the college building toward the distractions of the village. Town and gown were inimical in the early years, and the faculty contended with the saloonkeepers of High Street. A well just north of the college building provided water and a trodden path led eastward to a privy in the woods. The main entrance of the building faced south—the town was expected to grow in that direction—and a double row of spindly poplar trees led to the south campus fence. Much of the native forest—too much of it—had been cleared. The poplars were the first re-forestation.

Daily schedule called the students to a study period at 5 A.M. Except for meals followed by two "exercise periods" they were assigned to study and recitation until the evening prayers. Classes were summoned by a trumpet, as President Bishop considered a bell an extravagance. He preferred to spend money for books and apparatus.

In the first faculty President Bishop, professor of logic and moral philosophy, had two colleagues. William Sparrow, educated at Trinity College, Dublin, had the chair of ancient languages. John Annan, of Dickinson College in Pennsylvania, was professor of mathematics. Bishop's salary was $1000 plus the use of a house and garden. The other two salaries were $500 each.

In the business of getting the college organized and going there had been no ceremony, but when the first winter was past the trustees arranged a fitting inaugural for the first president. On March 30, 1825, Robert Hamilton Bishop,

D.D. (he had just received the honorary doctorate from Princeton) was formally installed in office.

At eleven o'clock on that bright spring morning the convocation formed at the Methodist Church, the pioneer church of Oxford, and marched down High Street through the campus gate and over the path to the college door. A brass band led the procession. The committee were dubious about the fitness of women in this ceremony, but they arranged— "should any female attend"—to have them march together, first the unmarried, dressed in white, then the matrons. They were followed by the students of the University, marching according to their classes. Next came the University secretary, the treasurer, the collector, then the trustees, finally the president of the board and the three members of the faculty.

The procession, two abreast, arrived duly at the south door of the college where the column halted, facing inward, and the line of march reversed, those in the rear marching between two files and into the chapel room.

"Suitable odes" were sung by a choir. There were three prayers, two addresses, the charge to the president, and finally Dr. Bishop's inaugural address.

Some of the speaking was high-flown: "Here, lately a wilderness, has the sun of science begun to dawn. Within these consecrated walls is now erected a standard, around which the sons of the *south and west* are rallying to receive that instruction which will make them the lights and safeguards of our beloved country. Here the ancient wisdom of sciences, the morals and religion of the sacred scriptures, will invite, amuse, improve and reform the youthful mind."

Some of it was monitory: The president, charged with the instruction of the youth placed in his care, was to "watch over their morals, train them to regular habits, and imbue their minds, as far as human exertions can effect, with the meliorating influence of our holy religion."

President Bishop's own words were sturdy, warmed with measured optimism, and shrewdly prophetic: "All things con-

sidered, our situation this day is, perhaps, as encouraging as
that of Oxford, in old England, was in the days of Alfred, or
that of Cambridge, in New England, not two hundred years
ago.

"Not sixty years ago all the country west and south of the
Allegheny mountains was a wilderness. There are now in that
region nine states and three territories, and a population of
not less than three millions.

"Twenty years ago the state of Ohio was just organized
with a population of not more than forty thousand. In 1792
Volney describes Cincinnati as not much superior to an Indian village. We have now a population of upward of 600,000;
and we have farms, and cities, and manufacturing establish-
ments, which vie with those of the oldest states in the Union.
Other sixty years hence, and the population and improvements will, in all probability, be extended to the Pacific
ocean.

"We are, my friends, in the good providence of God, a part
of this mighty nation. The institution which we are now organizing is one of the outposts of her extended and extending
possessions. Only a generation hence, and what is now an
outpost will be the center."

The band played again while the convocation streamed
out into the thin spring sunlight. The first college ceremony
had ended.

Chapter IV

SHADOW OF A MAN

T HE PRESIDENT'S ROOM FACED SOUTH, looking across the college yard to the old road from Hamilton and the solid woods beyond. Here, filling large pages in his gnarled and knotty hand, Robert Hamilton Bishop wrote out chapel talks and sermons, lecture notes on moral philosophy and logic, annual reports to the trustees. And here he sometimes wrote a column for the University magazine begun in 1827.

It was President Bishop, probably, who noted the stream of movers passing through. On an October day in 1828 the rumble of wagon wheels drew his eyes to the window and his mind to the great migration. "To a person who has never witnessed it," observed the *Literary Register,* "the tide of emigration which sets in regularly every fall would be incredible. The *Indiana Journal* says that from twenty-five to thirty families pass through Indianapolis daily, on their way to the Wabash and other western settlements in that state. We have not had an opportunity of counting the average number of families that pass through this place daily; but it really seems to us that from morning till night 'moving waggons' are hardly out of sight. They form an almost continuous line with their waggons, their stock and their children, jogging along at their leisure with great cheerfulness."

A few weeks later the *Literary Register* reported of Oxford, "The inhabitants are from various countries, from England, and Scotland, and Ireland, and from most of the Atlantic states." They too, and Robert Hamilton Bishop included, were part of the migration that was finding its future in a new land. Oxford was a frontier town ringed by the stubborn forest. The township maps showed a few creeks winding through wild land marked only by scattered sawmills, grist mills, Indian mounds. For the village's five hundred residents there were six stores, three taverns, a harness shop, a tanyard, a livery stable, some log and some frame houses. All spring the Oxford air was hazed with smoke from the clearings; sometimes candles were lit at noon because the sky was dark from brush and forest fires. The High Street merchants sold axes, ox-yokes, log chains, grubbing hoes. The town had a few well-bred families; the rest were a raffish lot. More than a muddy campus path separated town and college.

In this frontier village Robert Hamilton Bishop meant to develop a university. Its first catalogue, published in 1826, concluded with a paragraph thanking those who had "thus far encouraged an infant institution" and assuring them that "every possible exertion will be made to make the Miami University in all its departments a public and common good."

A university seal had been adopted in 1826, showing an open book, a globe and a telescope, all surmounted by a sturdy motto *Prodesse Quam Conspici*—"To Accomplish Rather Than to be Conspicuous." A year earlier thirteen students had formed the Erodelphian Literary Society, and twelve others had organized the Union Literary Society. Together the rival orders bought a movable press in Cincinnati, carted it over the rough roads to Oxford, and set it up in the college building. In June of 1827 they published their first periodical, the *Literary Focus*, aiming to produce a magazine of educational value for themselves and the community. It failed within a year, but was promptly followed by a new effort, the weekly *Literary Register*, published by Professors

Bishop, Annan and McGuffey and students from the two societies. This periodical, broader than the *Focus*, offered current news, essays on literature and science, and items of local interest. On January 17, 1828, appeared an account of a Butler County hog weighing 1260 pounds whose owner, having exhibited the prodigy in towns on the Ohio River, planned to take it to the eastern cities "to show the Yankees what kind of hogs we raise in Ohio." The same issue contained a poem "from the pen of a young Quaker Shoe-maker living in Haverhill, Massachusetts—John Greenleaf Whittier." The college weekly was relating the East and West to each other.

In 1829 William W. Bishop, the oldest of the president's six sons, bought the literary societies' press. For a few years he carried on a publisher's business and a book store, chancy ventures in a frontier town. Debt overtook him while he was building a house on the stump-dotted lane hopefully called High Street. He went West, like the movers in their creaking wagons, to a career as editor and publisher in Missouri and Illinois, leaving his father to discharge his debts. With patience and penury President Bishop paid off the obligations and completed the first house beyond the north fence of the campus. In 1836 he moved his family into it, and wore his own path to the college building. He lived there during his uphill years, vexed by financial troubles, contending with the saloon-keepers of Oxford, dissension in his faculty, and opponents of his liberal views. But he never doubted the role and the future of Miami University. It had lighted the old lamps of learning and piety in a new country.

At its opening in 1824 the college offered only the traditional classical course, leading to the A.B. degree. This remained the core of the college, but very early the curriculum was broadened and extended. In 1825 a new "English Scientific Department" offered modern languages, applied mathematics and political economy as training for the practical professions; the course led to a certificate rather than to a diploma. This second curriculum was begun in the year that George Ticknor's pamphlet argued the claims of the sciences and the modern languages at Harvard, and two years before a non-classical "parallel course" was provided at Amherst College. President Bishop was abreast of educational philosophy in the East.

In 1827 the trustees proposed a law school at Miami, but Governor Trimble of Ohio discouraged a request for state funds for its support. Some members suggested that part of the college lands be sold outright to raise money for a law professor and a law library, but the board was not persuaded.

In 1829 the *Literary Register* announced the opening of a Theological Department and a Farmer's College. President Bishop's accents sound clearly in the statement: "We are the servants of the community, and it is our wish to make Miami a common good to all classes of men." The farmer's college was not an agricultural course but a three-year academic program for farm boys. "Literary and scientific knowledge is no longer to be the exclusive property of a few professional men," wrote Bishop with an awareness of what a century later would be called general education. "It is to become the common property of the mass of the human family." The farmer's college required neither Latin nor Greek but included the more "modern" studies in the existing curriculum.

In 1830 the trustees proposed to establish a medical department to be located in Cincinnati. Daniel Drake, a former colleague of Bishop at Transylvania and the foremost physician in the West, was named its dean and instructed to select his faculty. He chose a distinguished list of six doctors and announced the opening of the department in the fall of 1831. Then came the opposition. Because of legal complications and Cincinnati rivalry, the Miami Medical School never enrolled a student or conducted a class. An appropriation from the Ohio Legislature enabled the floundering Cincinnati medical college to reorganize and to hire the entire faculty which Drake had gathered.

The theological department was a more successful story. In 1828 the two Lane brothers in Cincinnati gave funds to establish a seminary for the training of ministers of the New School; Ebenezer Lane later lived in Oxford, on the site of The Pines, and gave the grounds for the Oxford Female College, now Fisher Hall. Originally Lane Seminary was to have both a literary and a theological department, but with Bishop's influence the literary department was soon transferred to Miami; that is to say, students destined for theological study at Lane Seminary were encouraged to take preliminary college work in Oxford. For ministerial students Miami offered classes in Hebrew and systematic theology, in addition to the college courses. From Miami in the early years went a steady stream of Presbyterian ministers. The old Oxford Presbyterian Church, on the corner of Church Street and Campus Avenue, the "mother church of ministers," was for thirty years a resounding center of doctrinal controversy.

Most of the Old Miami faculty were ordained Presbyterian ministers; many of its trustees were Presbyterian clergymen and laymen; until 1885 all the presidents were Presbyterian divines. President Bishop, a national leader in the church, was chairman of a committee which awarded Presbyterian scholarships to college students. In the 1830's the Presbyterian Education Society sent scores of students to Miami and contributed nearly two thousand dollars in the form of scholarships. Though Miami University was created by the Federal Congress and established by the State of Ohio, it could not have been more Presbyterian if founded by John Knox.

The situation in Miami was not unique; in these years the Presbyterian Church dominated state-created colleges in North Carolina, South Carolina, Kentucky, Tennessee, and Indiana. In 1834 Indiana Methodists demanded appointment of a Methodist professor in the state university. Samuel Bigger (son of the president of the Miami University trustees in 1810), a member of the Indiana Legislature, declared there was "not a Methodist in America with sufficient learning to fill a professor's chair if it were tendered to him." Samuel Bigger became governor of Indiana in 1840, but the Methodists took credit for defeating him two years later.

With its several courses of study—classical, theological, and English and scientific—Miami was responding to the needs of the new country. Many pioneer communities had a dislike for "colleges, pianos and Yankees," and "Yankee college" was a doubly damned term. Miscalled the Yale of the Early West, Miami was not a foster child of the East but a true product of the frontier, with character and identity of its own.

In 1826 Professor Sparrow had resigned his chair of ancient languages to become vice-president of Kenyon College. In his place came young William Holmes McGuffey, just graduated from Washington College in Pennsylvania, riding into Oxford with Latin, Greek and Hebrew texts bulging out his saddle bags. He moved into the college building, taking a room next to Professor Annan on the second floor. Shortly after his arrival the brick cupola on the roof collapsed. The crash sent McGuffey to his window, but a workman told him not to jump. In the spring vacation of 1827 McGuffey and Annan took a horseback tour through Butler County, riding along the raw new ditch of the Miami and Erie Canal. Back in Oxford the two colleagues, with some students swinging axes beside them, chopped and burned out stumps on the south campus. With his backwoods upbringing McGuffey was no stranger to an ax.

That summer McGuffey married Harriet Spining, niece of an Oxford merchant, taking her to board in the only brick house on South Main Street, at the corner of Collins. The next year saw the beginning of their own brick house on Spring Street, across from the south gate of the campus. Here McGuffey began work on his Readers.

In 1828 came buoyant, hearty John Witherspoon Scott, professor of sciences, and his young wife from Philadelphia. Scott, with a recent M.A. from Yale, came direct from a chair at Washington College, where McGuffey had been a student. But these two colleagues, totally unlike in character and temperament, were soon at swords' points in Miami. In 1831 Scott built a handsome brick house on High Street across from the gate of the slanting campus path. Here in 1832 was born his daughter Caroline who twenty-one years later became the wife of Benjamin Harrison.

In 1829 students moved into a newly-completed dormitory, officially named Washington and Clinton Hall but commonly called the Northeast Building; it is now Elliott Hall. A three-story plain brick building, it was built for $7,000, part of it borrowed. The rooms were heated with iron stoves; the boys could buy firewood in the village or look for it in the forest at their door. For kindling, there was the woodwork in their hall; in 1833 President Bishop reported half the doors of the building gone and the stair rails hacked and whittled. Rooms were rent-free. A student furnished his own bed, chairs, table, usually adding cooking utensils and a box of provisions.

By 1834 enrollment reached 234, the faculty had grown to seven, and more living space was needed. The building committee proposed a row of two-room cottages, with central chimneys, at intervals of a hundred feet in the college grove. Fortunately that idea was discarded and a second dormitory, "plain, substantial and neat" like the first, was completed in 1835 at a cost of $9,500. President Bishop suggested naming it Harrison and Shelby Hall, proposing to recognize William Henry Harrison, the son-in-law of Judge Symmes and author of the Harrison Land Act which encouraged settlement of the public lands, and Isaac Shelby, twice governor of Kentucky and one of the original trustees of Transylvania College. In coupling their names he must have meant to memorialize their joint achievement in the War of 1812, when Shelby led four thousand volunteers to join General Harrison in the invasion of Canada. But the name was not adopted; the new hall became the Southeast Building. It is now Stoddard Hall. It was opened in 1835 to junior and senior men, each student to have "an apartment to himself" —a luxury now long past. The other hall housed two and three students in a room.

Three years later, in 1838, a small science laboratory, no larger than a classroom, was built for $1,250. It stood southwest of the Center Building, near the present Bishop Hall, being kept at that distance for fear of fire. This building, "Old Egypt" as generations of students called it, finally burned in 1898. By 1838 there were the Center Building with its west wing, the two residence halls, and the science laboratory; these comprised the campus buildings throughout the five decades of Old Miami, until the college closed in 1873.

There was, however, one other structure, the remains of which persist on the campus now and occasion surprisingly little wonder. A hundred feet from the front door of Bishop Hall is a sandstone pier, three feet high and two feet square. A close look, which few have taken in the past half century, shows it scored with initials of students long gone from Miami and a fading inscription:

Designed in 1834
and erected in 1838
by John Locke, M.D.

This is the remnant of the second astronomical observatory in the United States.

American astronomy began in 1830 when a scientist at Yale carried a five-inch telescope to a college steeple and observed Halley's Comet before word of it came from observatories in Europe. The first observatory in the United States was built at Williams College in 1836, and the next effort came in Ohio. In 1836 John Locke, an ingenious professor in the Cincinnati College of Medicine, designed a stone pier for the mounting of a small transit telescope. This primitive observatory he sold to Miami before the year was over, and Professor Scott set it up on the treeless south campus. The old stone pier still shows one of the iron fastenings which supported the transit.

In the spring of 1838 a small frame house was built over the stone pier, but it didn't last. On winter nights when a student's fire was sinking that shed began to go. It was all gone by 1840, and the transit was moved into Old Egypt nearby. However, in Loomis' *Practical Astronomy*, published in 1855, the Miami Observatory is listed—at Lat. 39° 30′ N., Long. 84° 46′ W.—along with the other observatories of the world.

From the old dorms a path led to the college well just north of the main building. A wooden bucket on a rope, stiff-frozen in the winter, supplied water to be carried in a pail to a student's room. A candle flickered on the table and red sparks sifted to the ash-pan under the stove. Outside was the forest darkness, with an owl hooting from a hollow tree.

Through the chilly dusk students tramped to boarding clubs or to private homes in town. The first dining room, the "University Inn," was opened in the South Dormitory in the late 1840's. But some couldn't afford that.

In the autumn of 1832 Benjamin Chidlaw left a log cabin home in Delaware County, Ohio. After five days' walking he trudged up the hill to Oxford and presented his school record to President Bishop. From fifty dollars in his wallet he paid tuition, furnished his room, bought his books and engaged "real good fare" at a dollar a week. At the end of a month his wallet was shrinking and he joined with a classmate in "keeping bachelor's hall." They bought corn meal and potatoes for 12½ cents a bushel, meat at 1¼ cents a pound, and as an occasional extravagance a big loaf of bread for 6¼ cents at Lathrop's bakery. "I never enjoyed better health," he wrote, "or greater facilities for study." For the rest of the year he lived on 32 cents a week.

Here is another, gloating over his snug, possessive life in Old North, and not fussy about his English: "I have just light my lamp, and drawed my table up near the fire, and locked

my door, and commenced to wright. I wish you were here to
see me as I sit here writing. There is my cuboard and desk
in one corner by the door, and here is my bed standing behind me with one end of it against my desk. Just at the other
end of my bed, stands my high table at which I stand and
study when I am tired sitting, and next to that in the other
corner at one side of my chimley lays my little pile of wood,
just in the other corner at the other side of my chimley is my
clothespress, potato box, etc., etc., under my bed lies a big
pile of apples which old man Swan brought me in the other
day. They are first-rate. And finally just before me my fire
burns up very bright, but above all I have got a first-rate
chicken on boiling which I bought yesterday already cleaned
for the pot. It is now boiling and it smells so good that I can
hardly wright. What a feast I will have just now!!"

Students soon left their mark on the buildings. In 1833 a
trustees' committee reported: "The new edifice [North Hall]
has been much injured . . . the stairs and woodwork generally have been much cut and damaged and the glass much
broken." In 1835 Joel Collins was made superintendent of
the University, and from that time breakage declined. Collins
arranged repair of the campus fences, graveling of the paths,
and he rented out some campus pasture lots—which kept the
grass down and brought in fifty dollars a year. Meanwhile
he asked the faculty to inspect the students' rooms (each of
the professors took one day of the week) and to set up a
system of fines for splitting or sawing wood in the buildings,
breaking doors, railings or furniture, defacing walls or breaking glass.

The college life was primitive, but it was not provincial.
Along with boys from the Miami Valley there were students
from Illinois, Iowa, Mississippi, and the Carolinas. For a year
or two a group of young Osage Indians from Arkansas lived
in the west wing and studied Latin, algebra and Roman history in the grammar school; Dr. Bishop had brought them to
Miami under a home missionary program.

Though the college was remote it was not removed from the vital currents of the time. For thirty years the question of slavery was a ferment on the campus. In 1832 Miami students formed an Anti-Slavery Society and paraded by torchlight through the village streets. In the Literary Halls they debated abolition and colonization, and in the columns of their magazine they argued about nullification and states' rights. President Bishop was a leader in the abolition movement and in liberal theology, but his faculty was divided. In the mid-1830's Professor Albert T. Bledsoe, who would become assistant secretary of war for the Confederacy, interrupted his lectures on calculus to argue that the federal constitution was subordinate to the sovereign states. Professors McArthur and MacCracken, two stubborn Scots, asserted Calvinism against Bishop's milder doctrines. The Miami students lived in the midst of great issues.

To a traveler on horseback or a family in a mover's wagon, Miami must have looked idyllic—the whitewashed buildings against the forest trees and boys lounging around the campus well. A college always looks serene, while its strains and tensions go on, generation after generation. Old Miami on its hill crest has had stress and strife, quarrels and controversies, and never more bitter and ugly than in the 1830's when its fame was growing through the West.

The students, Northern and Southern alike, were agreed on one point: they shared "a universal and most intense feeling of admiration and revering esteem for Dr. Bishop." This tall, lean, early-rising, porridge-eating, religious, argumentative but tolerant man had a sense of humor to balance his sense of duty. That balance gave him ease, directness and simplicity. College students, for all their lack, can detect pretension. In this man they sensed a simple greatness, and they honored him. It has never been easy to please a college faculty or a student body. Bishop endured many troubles, but he had the trust and admiration of his students.

Still, they were students, young, restless, sometimes reckless. They took the muddy path to the village and the High Street bar rooms. Vainly Bishop pled with the proprietors to close their doors to students, and the trustees petitioned the Ohio Legislature to outlaw the sale of liquor in Oxford. Not till 1882 did Ohio law provide for local option in a college town, and not till 1905, in President Guy Potter Benton's time, did Oxford banish its saloons.

The trustees' examining committee reported regularly on the academic side—"a pleasing progress of improvement in literature and science . . . reflecting credit on the Institution, the gentlemen that conduct its instruction, and the capacities and attention of the young gentlemen."

But Bishop was troubled about other capacities of the students. In 1832, the college catalogue stated that certain proprietors in Oxford were ensnaring students by the sale of groceries—hard drink; it added that students patronizing these places of cheating and dissipation would be dismissed and the names of the proprietors publicly circulated. Two years later Bishop threatened to publish a "History of Retailing Ardent Spirits in Oxford"; the book would contain an account of "Groceries and Tavern Keepers" and the "Biography of a few of the most distinguished Young and Old men, who have been ruined for time, and in all probability for Eternity also, by frequenting the Groceries and Bar-rooms which have been in Oxford."

Then came the outbreak of 1835. In January, Francis Carter, a hot-headed youth from Alabama, was expelled on three counts: continued idleness and neglect, instances of intoxication and profanity, and riot at a grocery. On March 13, John Caperton was dismissed "for using improper language to one of the Professors at the close of a recitation." Three days later came a shooting-and-stabbing in the college building: George B. Haydon of South Carolina was expelled for discharging a pistol at Calvin Miller of Mansfield, Ohio, and the wounded Miller was expelled for attacking Charles Telford with "cowhide and dirk." With that, the eruption

subsided—for a while. In July four students were expelled
for disorderly conduct and in August three Southern students
were sent home for "riotous proceedings in the town of Oxford." Eleven expulsions in one year; it was a blow for the
ten-year-old college.

President Bishop believed in freedom and student responsibility. "The general principle of the government of the
institution is: that every young man who wishes to become
a scholar and expects to be useful as a member of a free
community must at a very early period of life acquire the
power of self-government." Now, needled by McGuffey, the
faculty decided to clamp down. On Christmas Eve, 1835
(there was no Christmas recess until after 1837), a group of
the best students in the college were charged with disorder;
according to Scott their offense consisted of "making a very
trifling noise" near the door of North Dorm. The first faculty
vote was for severe discipline, only Bishop dissenting. Mc-
Guffey exulted, but some of his colleagues changed their
minds and the students went free. Already jealous of Bishop's
authority and prestige, McGuffey began a prolonged attack
upon the president. Professor Scott, Bishop's strong ally, believed that McGuffey was not only a fomenter of discord but
a hypocrite as well—calling for harshness in faculty meetings
and courting student favor outside. "I have myself observed
a very great difference between the tone assumed by Mr.
McGuffey respecting a young man in secret Faculty session,
and when the young man was present before us. In the one
case it has sometimes been harsh, laconic, and denunciatory
in the extreme;—in the other smooth as oil."

Political and theological differences increased the faculty
tension. McGuffey was pro-Southern and a Calvinist, and
Bledsoe, a Virginia man who came to the Miami faculty by
way of West Point, endlessly argued for states' rights. In
1836 both of them resigned, McGuffey to become president
of Cincinnati College and Bledsoe to practice law in Illinois;

years later, after the Civil War, the two were colleagues again on the faculty of the University of Virginia.

In Cincinnati in 1836 there developed a new effort to divert the income of Miami University to Cincinnati College. Whether McGuffey was involved is not clear. But as head of Cincinnati College he did advise parents not to send their sons to Miami "where it was more likely they would be made Drunkards and Gamblers than good Scholars."

In March, 1836, Bishop reported "a year of peculiar trial and difficulty." He had been ill—"nearly lost the use of my right side and scarcely knew what it was to have a good night's rest." Professor Armstrong had died after a painful illness; his Latin, Greek and Hebrew classes were added to the tasks of the already torn and burdened faculty. A number of students had turned out to be "uncommonly disorderly." Later that year Bishop moved from the campus cottage into the new house on High Street. He must have hoped for a new turn, but his eight years there were years of trial and frustration.

The year 1836 brought no student violence and no special damage to the building, though Superintendent Collins reported that a college backhouse "worth $50 or 60 dollars" was set on fire and destroyed. At graduation time, in September, two outside men sat with the faculty in the final examination of the seniors. They reported: "That an efficient and well directed system of instruction has been pursued in the University,—2nd, That the System of government and discipline is such as to promote order and preserve and increase a kind and mutually good understanding between the faculty and the students." They found the college in an excellent state of scholarship, morality and discipline.

In 1839 Old Miami reached its peak enrollment—250 students from thirteen states. Larger than Princeton and Columbia, it was surpassed in enrollment by only three American universities: Harvard, Yale and Dartmouth. Its alumni had already made the college famous, and the seven-man faculty, augmented by ten lecturers and tutors, was the strongest teaching staff in the West. But there were new lines in President Bishop's face. New tensions divided the faculty and cleft the Board of Trustees. The old dispute over discipline still smoldered, but it was not discipline that caused the discord. It was doctrine.

Along with the struggle to tame wild land there was an intellectual struggle in the West—the long contest between tradition and reform, between Calvinism and free will. One of its arenas was the Presbyterian synods of the frontier, where Old School and New School fought their stubborn battle. Bishop strove for peace; in 1838 he published, with a group in Oxford, the periodical *Western Peacemaker and Monthly Religious Journal.* "Malice and guile and hypocrisy and evil speaking are the great heresies," he wrote. "They are to be found among both the old and new school men—and they have produced and cherished all our other difficulties and evils." He refused to align himself with either Old or New School agitators, and it cost him the support of both camps.

At Miami, Professors McArthur and MacCracken were rigid Old School men, who attacked the doctrinal laxness of Bishop and Scott. In addition to his faculty chair MacCracken was pastor of the Oxford Presbyterian Church. He was expected to resign from the faculty, but the resignation did not come. Wrote Scott in his earthy style, "I am informed that he has declared his intention . . . to continue until fall (1840). It is very sweet to suck two teats yielding $800 per annum each, and who would not hang on until choked off?"

While the Miami boys played hop, skip and jump on the south campus and studied the Trojan Wars, the war of doctrine was swirling around them. In 1838 young Henry Ward Beecher appeared before the Oxford Presbytery as a candidate for ordination, and was blocked by rigid Professor McArthur. The next year Lyman Beecher, liberal head of Lane Seminary, came at Bishop's invitation to speak in the college chapel. A group of students, prompted by MacCracken and McArthur, tried to break up the meeting. But Beecher preached, calling for tolerance and freedom and the spread of enlightenment ("If in our haste to be rich and mighty we outrun our colleges," he had declared, "the battle for liberty is lost"). More than that, he stayed on for a fortnight in Oxford, talked to a hundred students and won most of them to his liberating views.

The other struggle, not entirely outside the theological warfare, was over slavery. Bishop had joined the lists early. During his years at Transylvania he had organized in Lexington sabbath schools for Negroes, an activity which drew criticism from political and Presbyterian leaders. Soon after his arrival in Oxford he helped to organize a branch of the American Colonization Society, which aimed at a gradual freeing of slaves and transporting them to a colony in Africa. With Bishop's encouragement Daniel Christy of Oxford became a Colonization agent. William McLain, Miami 1831, was a long-time officer of the society.

During the early 1830's the anti-slavery movement went like a wind through the West. In 1833 at Lane Seminary a rule prohibited discussion of the inflammatory subject; as a result three-fourths of the students left Lane and went to Oberlin where they became the first student body of Oberlin College. Later in that year a new band of theological students entered Lane Seminary and despite the trustees' ruling proposed a public discussion of slavery. The great debate went on for eighteen nights, students marshaling the economic, ethical and religious arguments for abolition. A few months later a group of Miami students formed an anti-slavery society. One of its leaders was James G. Birney, Jr., son of the abolitionist candidate for the presidency of the United States. Along with other activities the Oxford band circulated *The Philanthropist*, the anti-slavery newspaper published by James Birney, Sr.

To the Miami faculty in 1835 came Albert T. Bledsoe

with his outspoken states' rights views. McGuffey encouraged
Bledsoe though he voiced no opinions of his own. After Mc-
Guffey's departure in 1836 Bishop tried to replace him with
Thomas E. Thomas, a recent Miami alumnus who had become a leader in the anti-slavery movement. But the opposition was too strong; Miami had close connections with the
South and there were strong Southern feelings in the Board
of Trustees. With the support of Professor Scott, Bishop
worked for an anti-slavery stand in the local Presbyterian
Church. He came under increasing criticism for his views
both in theology and the slavery question.

In 1840 a committee of the trustees inspected the college
buildings and made a glum report: "We find the old West
Wing greatly wanting in repairs, and the condition of the
rooms occupied by the Students in this wing very dirty, and
the committee feel it their duty to state that the habit in-
dulged in by the Students of *Urinating* out the College windows is a disgraceful nuisance. . . . If no other means can be
adopted to prevent the evil, the committee would recom-
mend that the Superintendent fill up the lower part of the
windows by a brick wall." But soon they forgot that nuisance
in a harder problem.

A year before, in 1839, the board had ruled that sectional
and sectarian doctrines should not be taught in the University. But no resolution could stay the winds of doctrine, and
Bishop was not a man who could remain silent in times of
crisis. Through the long still summer of 1840 a storm hung
over the Miami campus.

President Bishop must have felt that he was being weighed;
his report in August gave an accounting of his entire sixteen
years at the head of the University. It was a grave, affirma-
tive, quietly gratified report. ". . . During the last ten years
the Junior Class in Miami University has been as far advanced as the Senior Class in any other Western College. . . .
Superior advantages are not always to be enjoyed by Eastern
Colleges. Nor unless we shall be very unfaithful to ourselves

in the West are they to be enjoyed long. . . . The strength of the American empire in population and wealth and intelligence is very soon to be in the great valley. . . . The graduates of Miami University have already come into contact in Theological Seminaries and law offices and in active life with the best Colleges in the East, and have not suffered in character by the contact. Nor have we any disposition to allow that any of the fourteen classes which we have sent forth are inferior either in talent or useful attainments to any class of the same years from any college in the Union." By 1840 there were ten colleges in Ohio, and Miami was clearly pre-eminent among them.

This review of a notable record did not ease the present tension. All the faculty except stubborn John W. Scott resigned, and a committee of the trustees sat in conference with Bishop. From that conference came Bishop's resignation as president and his demotion to a chair of history and political science at a salary of $750, lower than that of his colleagues.

To the presidency the trustees elected John C. Young, president of Centre College at Danville, Kentucky; he was a leader among Old School Presbyterians and very nearly a defender of slavery. Young declined the office, and while Bishop remained acting president, the trustees chose George Junkin, president of Lafayette College, a militant Old School hunter of heretics and a pro-slavery man.

When Junkin arrived in Oxford, Scott took a hard look at him and wrote: "We have just this day had a glimpse of our President elect, the redoubtable Dr. Junkin. Bah! I suppose there is no doubt he will transfer his Catapulta and Battering ram here to the west, to defend orthodoxy in and about Miami University. . . . The little champion seems on sight to dwindle down to a very moderate measure. The truth is, after seeing him my mind has been struck still more forcibly with the wart of generosity with which Dr. Bishop has been treated; and especially the absurdity of putting him as a

Professor under the Presidency of such a man—a Sampson under a pigmy."

Bishop remained for four years, teaching his classes and cooperating with his successor, while the college dwindled and student disorders increased. Controversy grew and Junkin was surrounded with dissatisfaction and strife. When he resigned in 1844 the trustees met in Lebanon, away from the agitated campus. In an effort to clear the air, believing that "a change is called for," they removed Bishop and Scott from the Miami faculty.

Bishop was then seventy, with "no property whatever." Alumni protested the removal of Miami's two best men "against whom nothing can be alleged, but the liberality of their religious sentiments and their opposition to slavery." Scott put it more bluntly: "If Junkin [the trustees' man] had to go, Dr. Bishop and Professor Scott would have to go too." And so it stood.

In the fall of 1845 Bishop and Scott went to Cary's Academy, newly organized as Farmer's College, a few miles out of Cincinnati. It had been founded by Freeman G. Cary, a Miami graduate of 1832 and one of Bishop's favorite students. Here at College Hill, Robert Hamilton Bishop spent the twilight of his life, ten peaceful, harmonious and useful years. In 1849 Scott returned to Oxford to head the Oxford Female Institute, but Bishop stayed on, "the beloved Father" of Farmer's College. A group of Miami alumni built for him a cottage on the college grounds. There he lived in the clear evening after the stormy day, teaching history and writing in his *Recollections and Reflections* his own eventful history which had led from the moors of Scotland to the arena of American religious and political strife.

He had devoted students at Farmer's College. Among them were Murat Halstead who became editor of the Cincinnati *Commercial*, and Benjamin Harrison who followed Scott to Oxford, being in love with his daughter, and was graduated from Miami in 1852. On leaving Farmer's College

Ben Harrison wrote to his venerable professor, "Having for some years enjoyed the benefits of your instruction and being now about to pass from under your care, it would be truly ungrateful were I not to return my warmest thanks for the lively interest you have ever manifested in my welfare and advancement in religious as well as scientific knowledge. . . . Though I shall no more take my accustomed seat in your classroom I would not that this separation should destroy whatever interest you may have felt in my welfare. But whenever you may see anything in my course which you may deem reprehensible, be assured any advice which may suggest itself under whatever circumstances or on whatever subject, can never meet with other than a hearty welcome."

In 1855 after a brief illness Bishop prepared to go to his classes. "A recitation or two," he told his wife, "would do me more good than all the doctors." But he died without leaving the cottage, and his wife died two weeks later. They were buried in an unmarked grave on a leafy slope behind the college. For years returning alumni at Commencement season marched in silence past the Bishop grave.

In Oxford he left no burial place but a college strong enough to stand through troubled years to come. He left the Bishop House, under great walnut trees across from the campus, and he left his son Robert Hamilton Bishop, Jr., who would be "Old Bobby" to later generations of Miami men.

In 1841 in Concord, Massachusetts, Ralph Waldo Emerson wrote: "An institution is the lengthened shadow of one man," and in that year Robert Hamilton Bishop was removed from the president's office. But as long as it should last Miami University would bear the stamp of this gaunt, grave, kindly man who stood before his students, saying "My young friends—"

Chapter V

PRIMER FROM A GREEN WORLD

LATE IN THE YEAR 1825 two riders jogged into Oxford from the Hamilton road and pulled up at the Center Building. Down from the saddle slipped a man and a boy, William Holmes McGuffey and his eleven-year-old brother Aleck. The unknown new professor carried a bag of books and a roll of clothing to a room on the second floor of the West Wing. He was twenty-five years old, about to be graduated *in absentia* from Washington College, Pennsylvania, and ready to begin his career. Forty years later his name would be as familiar as the alphabet.

Six months before, President Bishop of Miami University, on a speaking tour in the Ohio Valley, had heard of a zealous young teacher in a country school outside of Paris, Kentucky. The school, it was said, was in a smoke-house, but the scholars came early and stayed late. Bishop was interested in such a teacher. He found a serious young man with a high broad forehead, a big homely nose and deeply lighted eyes. He was teaching reading, writing and figuring, but on his plank desk were texts in Latin, Greek and Hebrew. Bishop offered him the chair of ancient languages at Miami University at a salary of $600.

One of eleven children of a Scotch-Irish farmer who had settled in New Connecticut (northeastern Ohio) and chopped out his own road to the village of Youngstown, McGuffey had struggled for an education. It was hit or miss, at home or during brief periods in rural schools, until his formal education began when he was eighteen. But by that time his hungry mind had stored away whole chapters, verbatim, from the Bible. He got to college at twenty and between terms he taught school in the frontier settlements. Now with news of appointment to a college faculty he rode home. A few weeks later, with his young brother beside him, he clattered off for Oxford, three hundred miles across the state of Ohio. Miami had a grammar school where Aleck could prepare for the course in college.

At Miami Alexander McGuffey, promptly named "Red," became a great tree-climber and broad-jumper in the college yard and a notorious swimmer, splasher and ducker in the deep hole in Four Mile Creek; a few years later he was a leading declaimer and debater in the Literary Halls. Meanwhile Professor McGuffey was married to the niece of an Oxford merchant and ordained into the Presbyterian ministry. He preached on Sundays, alternating between the college chapel and rural congregations within horseback range of Oxford. In 1833 he moved his wife and two small daughters into their new brick house across from the south gate of the campus.

Every morning Professor McGuffey walked the path, where the Library now stands, to the college and climbed to his classroom in the southwest corner on the second floor. There was a determined elegance in his garb; a silk stovepipe hat and a suit of glossy black bombazine, a shiny paper collar and a black bow tie. Long-necked, intent and humorless, with a leathery skin and a farm boy's big hands, he did not look easy in that dress. But he was at home in the classroom. His mind was clear, orderly, exact; his language ready and precise. He treated abstract and complex ideas in

concrete and simple terms. One of his literary masters was
the succinct Alexander Pope.

McGuffey was zealous, ambitious and resourceful. Before
breakfast he met students in his study for practice in elocu-
tion and forensics. Between classes he gathered neighbor-
hood children to test the appeal of simple poems and stories.
In his study stood a revolving eight-sided desk, made by
himself, in his own woodshed, with eight pie-shaped drawers
—just right for filing word lists, spelling rules, reading exercises and selections. The young professor was compiling a
series of school books.

From his terms of teaching McGuffey knew the somber
lessons which introduced children to the wonder of the
printed page. The famed *New England Primer* (five million
copies printed since 1690) began with the bedrock of Calvin-
istic theology—"In Adam's Fall, we sinnèd all." McGuffey
was sufficiently Old School in the pulpit, but like the children
in his schoolrooms he had grown up in a new green world
—a world of creeks and woods and meadows, of dogs and
horses, sheep and cattle, orchards, pastures and farmyards.
Already he had published a "Treatise on Methods of Reading." As he walked the campus path he pondered the teaching of children in the new and spacious West.

In the strenuous Revolutionary period the leading American textbook was *Webster's Elementary Speller.* It contained
a lengthy moral catechism, a series of moral fables, a collection of readings in prose and verse, and word lists ranging
from "bag" to "equiponderant." Thousands of this "Blue
Back Speller" came over the mountains, packed with the
pots, pans and pails in the movers' wagons. The one notable
school book between the *New England Primer* and McGuffey's Readers, it was also the family anthology and encyclopedia.

By 1830 Lexington, Louisville and Cincinnati were centers
of a new Western book trade. Printers had brought movable
presses over the mountains and down the river; publishers

saw bright prospects in a bookless country. Soon Cincinnati took the lead, with a stream of almanacs, farm manuals, spelling books (including a new edition of Webster), school readers, testaments and hymn books pouring from the presses. Their business was served by the high cost of freighting books across the mountains and by the sectional consciousness of the new country. "Western books for Western people" was a persuasive slogan.

A second floor room on lower Main Street in Cincinnati housed the small firm of Truman and Smith, publishers of *Ray's Arithmetic* and a few other elementary school books. Winthrop B. Smith had an idea for a series of eclectic readers and he looked for an educator to compile them. In 1833 he proposed the series to Catherine Beecher, daughter of the president of Lane Seminary and sister of the future author of *Uncle Tom's Cabin*. Miss Beecher was preoccupied with higher education for women—she had opened in Cincinnati the Western Female Institute—and declined the task. Probably it was she who suggested a professor at Miami University; through the activities of a pioneer teachers' association, the Western Teachers' College Institute, McGuffey was acquainted with the Beechers. Smith soon made a contract with McGuffey for the publication of six books—a primer, a speller, and four readers—for which the compiler would receive royalty payments of $1,000. No one could foresee that the series would make the fortune of Winthrop Smith and of a whole series of publishers who followed him.

Before the first meeting with Truman and Smith, McGuffey had filed in his octagonal desk a sheaf of pages beginning "A is for Ax." Now he took the manuscript to one of his students, Welsh-born Benjamin Chidlaw, asking him to make a careful copy for publication. Chidlaw was living on 32 cents a week, cooking porridge and potatoes on his stove in the Northeast Building. At his study table he copied out the *Primer*, and McGuffey paid him five dollars for the job.

The *First* and *Second* readers were published in 1836; the

Primer and the *Third* and *Fourth* readers followed in 1837. To the selections were added questions, rules of pronunciation and exercises in spelling—an apparatus in which Catherine Beecher collaborated. By 1843 the series was selling half a million copies a year.

In 1844 appeared *McGuffey's Rhetorical Guide*, an anthology of English and American literature compiled for a fee of $500 by Alexander McGuffey. The great tree-climber was then a leading Cincinnati lawyer, the son-in-law of Dr. Daniel Drake and a warm friend of the Beecher family, and he soon grew bored with the fame of the McGuffey Readers. The *Rhetorical Guide* bore the name "A. H. McGuffey" which was close enough, especially in English script, to "W. H. McGuffey" to be accepted as coming from the same hand. A revision of the series in 1853 added the *Rhetorical Guide* to the set as the *Fifth Reader*. With selections from the great historians, orators, novelists, essayists and poets, it became the most famous Reader of all. More than a school book, it was a literary storehouse for family reading and a portable library for ambitious youths in a nearly bookless country.

The enlarged series swept southward and westward into thousands of new school districts as settlement spread. By 1860 sales of the Readers passed two million copies a year. When Cincinnati could not fill the orders, other publishers were licensed to produce the McGuffey series: Clark, Austin, Maynard and Company in New York; Lippincott and Company in Philadelphia; Cobb, Pritchard and Company in Chicago. After the Civil War the Methodist Book Concern in Nashville published huge editions for distribution in the South. In the second half of the nineteenth century the proprietors became successively W. B. Smith and Company; Sargent, Wilson & Hinkle; Wilson, Hinkle & Co.; Van Antwerp, Bragg & Co.; and finally The American Book Company.

The Gilded Age was a golden age for the McGuffey publishers who rode the wave of American expansion. The Readers went West in freight wagons and with emigrant caravans; traders packed them into Indian reservations; they turned up in sod schoolhouses on the prairie, in cow towns on the plains and mining camps in the Rockies and the Sierras. Between 1870 and 1890 the series sold sixty million copies. They were the basic schoolbooks in thirty-seven states. Except for New England, where they never got started, the McGuffey Readers blanketed the nation.

In the 1890's the texts were translated into Spanish, and American imperialism carried them into the thatch-roofed schools of Puerto Rico and the Philippines. A Tokyo edition, with alternate pages in English and Japanese, was used in schoolrooms under the shadow of Fujiyama.

After 1900 the business dwindled, and by 1920 the time of the Readers was past. But a new phenomenon was beginning. Change comes swiftly in America, but memory lingers. In the headlong twentieth century people recalled the old district school and the dog-eared Readers. From West Virginia to California McGuffey clubs sprang up. Groups of old residents held McGuffey reunions and retired schoolmasters formed McGuffey societies. A National Federation of McGuffey Societies met annually on the Miami campus, a congress of piety and remembrance. They recalled the lessons of long ago—the boy who cried Wolf! Wolf!; Mr. Toil and Hugh Idle; Try, Try Again; Harry and the Guide Post; the Honest Boy and the Thief. They told and retold how young William Holmes McGuffey walked six miles to recite Latin to his tutor, how he memorized poems, orations and whole books of the Bible. They wrote odes to the great educator "whose classroom was a nation" and sang hymns to his memory. On the centennial of the first publication of the Readers they dedicated a memorial statue in the west courtyard of McGuffey Hall. In the warm slow summer under the Oxford trees they relived wintry days in the red schoolhouse where the jolly old pedagogue "tall and slender and sallow and dry" opened to them the safe, sure, pious guidance of the eclectic Readers. The doubt and confusion of the 1930's increased their wistfulness for the simpler past.

In 1932 Henry Ford, the man who had done most to change McGuffey's America past recognition, issued a facsimile edition of the 1857 series and moved McGuffey's log cabin birthplace to his museum at Dearborn, Michigan, beside the Ford laboratories. Collectors were bidding up the prices of the earliest McGuffeys—one hundred, two hundred, three hundred dollars for a tattered *Primer* or *First Reader*. By that time McGuffey meant the horse and buggy days, the Saturday night bath, the creak of the kitchen pump and the woodbox behind the stove, the lost American innocence and piety. He had become a myth as American as Uncle Sam and as homespun as linsey-woolsey.

In 1830 when young Professor McGuffey began filing selections in his eight-sided desk, the West was a bookless country but there was strenuous competition for the school trade. Eastern publishers sent barrels of books in canal barges and Conestoga wagons to the western market, while the new western publishers turned out textbooks of their own. In 1838 Samuel Worcester of Massachusetts filed suit against McGuffey and his publishers for plagiarism of the Worcester series of Readers. The court found that certain of McGuffey's selections duplicated selections in the Worcester series, and awarded damages of two thousand dollars to the eastern publisher. The McGuffey set was promptly reissued in a "Revised and Improved Edition," with new selections replacing the disputed ones. In defense of McGuffey, Catherine Beecher said that Truman and Smith had sent to Oxford seven volumes of contemporary school readers, to aid him in making up his texts. Inevitably, she inferred, there were duplicate selections.

Fifteen sets of school readers were published in America between 1820 and 1841, but for some reason, or reasons, the McGuffey series ran away with the race.

Perhaps the clue is in the first lesson—"A is for Ax." While children learned those letters the ax was ringing in every clearing, it was hewing logs for cabins and schoolhouses, it was changing the mid-continent. Thud, thud, thud—in the sound of the ax the future of America was beating like a pulse. The picture showed a boy not as tall as the ax-helve leaning against a stump. It was a real ax, from the child's real world, the rough-hewn, hopeful, equalitarian world of the Jacksonian West. After ax came box, cat and dog; nut, ox and pig; vine, wren and yoke—all homely and familiar things. The lessons were alive with children at work, at play, at school; boys with hoops, kites, skates; girls with dolls, sleds and jumping ropes. Reading could be fun.

It was also morality. The selections were shrewdly eclectic moral lessons attuned to the mixed people of the Ohio Valley and the expanding nation. They contained enough Puritanism to satisfy transplanted Yankees, enough Cavalier manner to fit the attitudes of the South, enough practical optimism to appeal to ambitious Scotch, German and Irish settlers, and enough assurance of the material rewards of virtue to gratify all. Reading itself was described as a means to morality. Said a narrator in the *Second Reader:* "I hope my young readers will not forget this story. I know you must study hard, if you wish to learn to read; but the boys and girls who cannot read must go through the world like the man on his journey. They will never know whether they are on the right road or the wrong road."

The books were vigorously Western, but that has always been a relative term and it did not limit their market. The life they pictured and the ethic they advanced had an almost nation-wide appeal. Yet in certain ways they were keyed to the newer country beyond the Appalachians. In the *Fourth Reader* an essay by Daniel Drake stated a belief which the books themselves were serving: "Measures should be taken to mould a unified system of manners out of the diversified elements which are scattered over the West. We should foster western genius, encourage western writers, patronize western publishers, augment the number of western readers, and create a western heart." McGuffey's texts were an immeasurable influence in creating a common mind and heart among the mingled strains that peopled the Ohio Valley and surged on to the farther West.

The Readers pictured a land where opportunity is open to all—all who will soberly and steadily pursue it. Scores of lessons repeated the gospel of success; each new Reader put it in stronger terms. In the *Second Reader* little Frank learned that the sands in the hour glass and the hands of the clock never waste a minute; they keep at work as steadily as time itself. Said the *Third Reader:* "The road to wealth, to honor, to usefulness and happiness is open to all, and all who will may enter upon it with the almost certain prospect of success." And the *Fourth Reader:* "Gypsies are a class of people who have no settled place to live in, but wander about from spot to spot and sleep at night in tents or barns. We have no gypsies in our country, for here every person can find employment of some kind, and there is no excuse for idlers or vagrants." Even the treasure-trove of literature, the *Fifth Reader,* ended on the familiar note: "God Blesses the Industrious."

Here was the spreading myth of democratic, practical, middle-class America: work, strive, persevere, and success will follow. Virtue is its own reward, more precious than riches, but the virtuous become rich also. George, in the *Second Reader,* having confessed to breaking a merchant's window with a snowball, felt happy for doing what was right. But the story is not over. The merchant took honest George into his employ, with the happy outcome that "George became the merchant's partner and is now rich."

Industry is the watchword in the McGuffey books. "The idle boy is almost invariably poor and miserable," said the *Third Reader.* "The industrious boy is happy and prosperous." Lazy Ned, who wouldn't pull his sled uphill, died a dunce. Mr. Toil "had done more good than anybody else in

the World." The lessons contained no wonderers or wander-
ers, no pilgrims or seekers, no rebels, reformers or dissenters;
but endless examples of practical ambition and prosaic success. They were certainly monotonous, but they reflected
and upheld the unimaginitive values of an acquisitive people.
"One doer," ended the story of little Amy with her empty
berry pail, "is worth a hundred dreamers."

Yet along with this dutiful morality, the Readers contained
selections of simple charm and of lasting literary worth. Once
past the two-syllable limits of the *Second Reader,* the scholar
met Hawthorne, Irving, Bryant, Longfellow, Whittier, Dick-
ens, Lamb, Goldsmith, Milton, Shakespeare. The *Fourth
Reader,* on a present junior high school level, had color and
vitality; few of its selections have gone bad. The *Fifth* and
Sixth readers were mature, varied and discriminating anthologies of poetry and prose. These volumes were read in the
family circle, at church socials and grange suppers, as well
as in the schoolroom. They were cherished by scholars long
after school days were past. Hamlin Garland, who read them
on the prairies of Iowa and South Dakota, wrote in *A Son
of the Middle Border:* "I wish to acknowledge my deep
obligation to Professor McGuffey, whoever he may have
been, for the dignity and grace of his selections. From the
pages of his Readers I learned to know and love the poems
of Scott, Byron, Southey, Wordsworth, and a long line of
English masters. I got my first taste of Shakespeare from the
selections which I read in those books." Many other nineteenth century Americans have expressed the same gratitude.

While his name and a kind of fame went across the country, McGuffey kept on with his academic labors. After ten
strenuous years as a college president, first at Cincinnati
College and then at Ohio University, he began in 1845 a long
term of teaching at the University of Virginia. Declining the
presidency of Miami in 1854, he stayed there till his death in
1873. To the undergraduates he was "Old Guff," teaching
moral philosophy and living quietly in Pavilion 9, while his

textbooks made ten millionaires. Unlike the diligent lads in the Readers he did not get rich. A story says that each year at Christmas time the publishers sent him a barrel of hams.

His son-in-law Andrew Dousa Hepburn came to Oxford in 1868. He served as the last president of Old Miami; after New Miami opened in 1885 he became the chairman of its English department and the dean of its College of Liberal Arts. He brought back to Oxford McGuffey's second daughter, who had been born across from the south campus gate, and McGuffey's old eight-sided desk. For years the desk served as a reading table in the old library room in the main building; it was appropriate there, as young Professor McGuffey had been also Miami's first librarian. Now it rests in the McGuffey Museum, along with seven hundred copies of the Readers in their many editions.

Chapter VI

VOICES ON THE THIRD FLOOR

FRIDAY, as it has always been at college, was the day to wait for. Recitations closed at noon, and already the boys were restless. An hour after dinner, dressed in their best jackets with a rose—three folds of silk ribbon—pinned on the left lapel, they climbed the steep stairway of Old Main. At the third floor landing they separated, Erodelphians with the red rose going into one door, members of the Miami Union, wearing the white rose, into the other. The doors were closed. At the pound of the gavel the buzz of voices died. The Literary Halls came to order.

Around the whitewashed room they sat, responding to roll call, hearing the minutes and the communications, casting their votes for new members, honorary members, library assessments, anniversary and exhibition speakers. Sunlight slanted in the tall south windows, glinting on the glass-front bookshelves, gleaming on the fluted columns that framed the president's rostrum, warming the classic bust in the archway under the carved motto "Scientia, Eloquentia et Amicitia." It was their room, their library, their incorporated Society.

Friday afternoon was for the reading of compositions and declamations. For two hours the walls rang with Paul's De-

fense of Agrippa, The Roman Soldier, Apostrophe to Mont
Blanc, The Trial of Warren Hastings, The Traveler at the
Sources of the Nile. The room filled with distant times and
places while shadows lengthened on the floor. As long as
memory lasted the Hall would bring back pictures of the
stately ruins of Rome, the strewn field at Waterloo, Napoleon
in exile and Empedocles on the slopes of Etna. Following the
criticism and summaries, the gavel rapped again. The Society
was adjourned till early candlelight.

Friday evening was for debate. Then the Hall was a
spacious high-ceiled forum, the speakers' shadows moving
on the walls and the room filled with disputation. Was Brutus
Justified in Killing Caesar? Was the French Revolution Beneficial to Mankind? Should a Republic Support a Standing
Army? Would Colonization Benefit the Negro? Should the
Government Grant Public Lands to Railroads? Should Congress Assist in the Abolishing of Slavery?

After the speeches and rebuttals, the summations and
judgment, the candles were put out. In midnight darkness
the members groped down the breakneck stairs. A scuffle of
footsteps on the path, voices under the stars, then the doors
banged in the old dorms. In cold rooms smelling of apples,
wood and cowhide boots the debaters went to bed, their
minds still burning with the great questions in the Hall.

"No professor," said Henry Mitchell MacCracken, Miami
1857, chancellor of New York University, "was so valuable
to many a student as was his Literary Society; no classroom
was so attractive as his Literary Hall; no wit or humor more
talked of than that which flashed out during the attrition of
Society debates. No position was so sought as an appointment to be one of the four speakers at the annual Exhibition."

These youths were preparing for careers in the law, the
ministry, and teaching. The Literary Halls were their bench,
their pulpit and their classroom.

In 1825, the second year of Miami University's operation,

the two societies were founded. On November 9th, in the second week of the term, thirteen students formed the Erodelphian Literary Society. The coined name shocked McGuffey's sense of linguistic rightness, but the organization got off to a fast start. Before November was past the society had inducted officers, begun the collecting of a library, heard the inaugural address of their first president, and held a debate on the question: "Is the reading of novels and romances productive of moral and intellectual improvement?" On December 14th another group of students, meeting in Professor Annan's classroom, organized the Union Literary Society "for the cultivation of the moral and intellectual faculties of the mind and for . . . mutual benefit." Robert C. Schenck, its first secretary, noted that Caleb Blood Smith was among the first petitioners for membership. Years later these two would be colleagues again, working for the nomination of Abraham Lincoln at the Republican convention in Chicago; soon afterwards Schenck was commissioned brigadier general in the Union army, and Smith served in Lincoln's cabinet as Secretary of the Interior.

In the spring of 1826 President Bishop assigned permanent quarters to the societies, Erodelphians taking possession of the southwest room on the third floor of the Center Building and the Union moving into the southeast room. Both groups furnished their halls with carpeting, sturdy arm chairs, library cases and cabinets for the display of scientific collections. President Bishop encouraged them in the enlarging of their libraries, the publication of their periodicals, the celebrating of their anniversaries, and in their self-government.

During the next decade the societies secured incorporation from the state, thus acquiring an independence which troubled certain of the trustees and the faculty. But Bishop reported in the uneasy year 1836 that "the Societies have from the beginning been remarkably well conducted, and as a means of intellectual and moral improvement are equal to at least two professorships." By that time the societies had

launched Miami's first literary periodicals, held annual public
"Exhibitions" and acquired collections of books more extensive than that of the University library.

Each year the two halls vied for new student members and
also for honorary members from a distance. By 1835, the
Erodelphian roster included the names of Washington Irving,
John Quincy Adams, Henry Clay, Andrew Jackson, Lyman
Beecher, Daniel Webster, James Madison, and Robert Dale
Owen. Honorary membership in the Union had been ac-
cepted by some of the same eminent men and many others.

The furnishing of the halls was a matter of rivalry for
many years, but the sharpest contest came when the societies
were young. In 1830 the Union sprang a triumphant surprise,
exhibiting on its wall a full-size oil portrait of President
Bishop. With careful secrecy they had engaged Horace
Harding, a western painter, and persuaded Bishop to sit for
him. Now the craggy president, his strong and kindly features lighting a shadowed canvas, his hands holding an open
book of logic, looked on at all the Union declamations and
debates. It was a tribute to the man all Miami students revered, and a triumph over the rival society.

Week after week the Erodelphians discussed what they
could do, and their unhappy decision was to engage the same
artist to paint another portrait of the president. It was all
but voted when little Charlie Anderson, a sophomore from
Louisville, who would be governor of Ohio in years to come,
took the floor. This, he declared, was a thing *not to do*—to
have in all the University and town of Oxford but two oil
paintings, and those two of the same subject, by the same
artist, hanging in the same place in two halls parted by a
narrow passage. The Erodelphians agreed; it was a poor
idea. But what else?

Then Charlie Anderson remembered something. Passing
through Cincinnati on the way to Oxford he had been fascinated by the wax figures in D'Orfeuille's Western Museum
on lower Main Street. The artist who had caught those

images could make a life-like bust of President Bishop—a classic head to occupy the niche above the rostrum—"to be a witness of all our future proceedings." Anderson's proposal fired the spirits of the Erodelphians. Soon a committee of three boarded the stagecoach for Cincinnati. After a fresh look at D'Orfeuille's wax figures they asked for the man who had made them.

The artist was Hiram Powers, and they found him in his studio on Fifth Street. As Governor Anderson recalled, fifty-five years later: "Powers himself met us in his muddy apron with his hands also clay-covered. . . . I thought then and I think now that he was, taken all together, the handsomest man I ever saw. . . . We at once told him our business. Powers said in his modest manner that he would make our bust for one hundred dollars and would mould it or else have it moulded into plaster for five dollars more. Although our sub-scription fund was only some twenty-five dollars we promptly closed the contract."

The Presbyterian Synod convened that year in Cincinnati, with Robert Hamilton Bishop as moderator. Into its meetings slipped a dark-eyed, handsome man with lean strong hands and clay-caked fingernails. Hiram Powers sat through the long synod sessions, studying the subject of his first commis-sioned bust. Before the year was over the strong, lean, kindly features of President Bishop looked down from between the fluted columns in the Erodelphian Hall.

Fifteen years later Charles Anderson on a tour of Italy met Powers in his famous studio in Florence. When Anderson referred to the sculptor's first commission in frontier Cincin-nati, Powers' dark eyes lighted. "What?" he said, "Dr. Bishop of Oxford. Were you of that committee of boys? Yes, to be sure. How could I forget you?"

By that time another Powers figure, done in the Florentine studio, had found a place in an older college. The classical "Proserpine" occupied a niche at the entrance to the Christ-church College Library in Oxford, England.

On his return from Italy, Anderson brought another artist to Oxford to make a mould of the Bishop bust. In the process the original was destroyed, but a bronze copy was returned to the Erodelphians. Almost a century later, when memories of the 1830's had faded at Miami, President Raymond M. Hughes led Dr. Robert Hamilton Bishop IV, Miami '03 and director of the Lakeside Hospital in Cleveland, up the long stairs to the third floor of the Main Building. There, decorated with a German mustache and serving as a doorstop, was the Bishop head, still arresting in its strength and dignity. Dr. Bishop took the battered bust to Cleveland and had it freshly cast by the artist Gorham. Now it occupies a window niche at the foot of a curved stairway in Constance Mather Bishop's home at Arrowhead Farm outside of Cleveland. Its duplicate, presented to Miami at the 1924 Commencement, rests over the reference desk in the Library reading room, "a perpetual witness" to the changing stream of Miami students.

Another rivalry between the Halls concerned the programs for their Exhibitions. In the fall of 1834 the Erodelphian Society, observing its ninth anniversary, was addressed by a Byronic-looking lawyer, orator and reformer from South Carolina. Thomas Smith Grimke spent a week in Oxford, with the whole college gathering around him. Two weeks later, journeying to Columbus, he was stricken with cholera and died in a farmhouse on the way. In Oxford the Erodelphians wore bands of mourning and hung his portrait on their wall, and years after his death his Erodelphian address was read by millions. In 1843 Alexander McGuffey, compiling selections for the *Rhetorical Guide,* recalled the stirring oration he had heard ten years before in the Erodelphian Hall. In the Reader he used five paragraphs of Grimke's "The Natural and Moral Worlds," reprinted from the collected *Erodelphian Lectures:* "The same God is the author of the invisible and visible worlds. The moral grandeur and beauty of the world are equally the products of his wisdom and goodness, with the fair, the sublime, the wonderful of the physical creation. What indeed are those but the outward manifestations of his might, skill and benevolence? What are they but a glorious volume, forever speaking to the eye and ear of man, in the language of sight and sound, the praises of its author?" So the idealism that was kindling the minds of Emerson and Carlyle came to the schoolboy in the *Fifth Reader,* as it had come to the members of Erodelphian Hall.

Other speakers at the societies' exhibitions included Lyman Beecher, Alexander Campbell, Daniel Drake, Thomas Ewing, John J. McRae and Edward Deering Mansfield.

In 1829 the Union Society announced that General William Henry Harrison would speak at its anniversary. Harrison was just back from his short term as United States minister to Colombia, and illness prevented his appearance. He sent regrets through his son, Carter Bassett Harrison, a leading member of the Union Hall.

Among John Cleves Symmes' disappointments was the death of his two sons in infancy. But he saw five grandsons romping through the Harrison farmhouse at North Bend. Twelve years after his death the youngest of them, Carter Bassett Harrison, enrolled in the college created by Symmes' Purchase.

Carter Harrison was a remote heir to Virginia aristocracy and a direct heir to the frontier West. He was born at Vincennes on the Wabash while his father was marching against the Indians at Tippecanoe. All the currents of the West washed around his boyhood. His oldest brother, John Cleves Symmes Harrison, was the federal land agent at Vincennes. His brother William Henry was married to Clarissa Pike, whose father had discovered the source of the Mississippi and had explored the Rocky Mountains of Colorado. His adventurous and wayward brother Benjamin (uncle of President Benjamin Harrison) went on a trapping expedition with old Jim Bridger to the Big Horn Mountains and was later captured by Mexicans in Texas. His sober brother John Scott

Harrison ran a farm, like countless Western settlers, at North Bend, Ohio.

In 1826, Carter Harrison came to Miami, which had not opened in time for his brothers. The next year his father was appointed minister to the Republic of Colombia, and young Carter, seventeen, packed up for a trip to South America as his private secretary. That Christmas they spent in the sleepy Venezuelan port of Maracaibo; then began a five-week trek by mule-train to the remote high capitol of Bogota. It was a year of revolution for Colombia and of revelation for Carter Harrison.

Recalled by President Jackson, Harrison came home to North Bend, with a pet macaw in a cage and some exotic shrubs to set out on the Ohio. In Cincinnati the general and his son were honored at a four-hour banquet in the fantastic hall of Mrs. Trollope's bazaar; that evening there was the first talk of Harrison for President of the United States.

That fall Carter Harrison returned to college. He found a new dormitory on the campus and a student body of 130 men. Over a bushel of apples around a wood-burning stove, he had tales to tell—the capture of a privateer in the Lee-ward Islands, a diplomatic ball with girls from twenty na-tions, revolutionaries smuggling rifles from the Bogota arsenal, emerald mining in the high Andes, a swirling flat-boat journey down the Magdalena River, spies and conspira-tors in the old walled town of Carthagena. Among all the voices that haunt Elliott Hall, Carter Harrison's is one to remember.

Some of the lines in old General Harrison's face were put there by his sons. Three of them were spendthrift and way-ward and overfond of whisky. Carter was the youngest, the sunniest, the most promising. When he left Miami in 1833 he studied law in the Cincinnati office of Robert C. Schenck, his comrade in the Union Literary Society, and he helped his troubled father conduct the Court of Common Pleas. In 1836 he married a Hamilton girl and opened an office in Hamilton.

But he never found the measure of his talents. Three years later, at twenty-eight, he died.

One of his friends in the Union Society wrote his obituary, including a college attitude that has not changed. "He was not so much a student as a general reader, preferring the standard works of prose and poetry of ancient and modern times to the technicalities and seeming uselessness of many of the class books. His mind was chaste and clear and richly stored with knowledge. While in college he sustained himself in the high rank to which he rose, and when we separated we foretold for him no common career."

No common career was ahead of his friends in the Literary Halls. From them came a governor of Ohio, a governor of Iowa, a president of a Mississippi college, two founders of Wabash College, a mayor of Cincinnati, an editor of the *Western Citizen,* a railroad president, missionaries to Oregon and Syria, and United States ministers to Brazil, Russia, and England. The ambassador to England was Robert C. Schenck —lawyer, congressman, general, diplomat, and an author too; while in London he wrote a little book with a couplet on its title-page:

> Put not your trust in Kings and Princes,
> Three of a kind will take them both.

His *Rules for Playing Poker* introduced an American card game to England and brought upon him, General Schenck said, "the wrath and reprehension of many good people in America."

No common career is what President Bishop foresaw for his students, and he supported all their mimic trials and combats in the Literary Halls. During the 1830's they enjoyed a heady freedom, and in that decade they had their greatest influence and distinction. With warm approval Bishop described the societies as "pure democracies . . . and miniature representations of the two Houses of Congress of the different state legislatures."

But with President Junkin's arrival the atmosphere changed. On April 10, 1841, at the beginning of the spring term, a young Erodelphian named Charles Hardin, who would become governor of Missouri thirty-five years later, wrote a letter lamenting the death of the nation's president —William Henry Harrison—and noting the arrival of a new president at Miami. "Dr. Junkin comes to Oxford today or Monday. We look for something extra. Few new students have come in yet. The teachers in college number eight now. We have a professor who teaches all living languages from Indian to Chinese." The identity of this universal linguist is not clear, but the "something extra" which was looked for from Dr. Junkin, by the trustees at least, was an exercise of discipline.

President George Junkin was a short, positive, strong-tempered man with a tight mouth and habitually-clenched hands. He disapproved of the free and easy ways of Miami undergraduates. In an evening chapel service he had a quarrel with an usher who was a member of one of the Literary Halls; when the fellow-members rushed in, President Junkin retreated barely in time to avoid a riot. In his first sermon in Oxford he denounced the Methodist Church for its crudities in logic ánd theology, starting a denominational quarrel in the village. The *Western Christian Advocate* editorialized: "Miami University is no place for Methodist students who desire to enjoy their religious privileges," and the University enrollment dwindled. On a summer evening in 1841 the students broke up a lecture on penmanship in the chapel—as Governor Hardin recalled, "We cheered him so much that we 'inadvertently' broke all the lamps, disorganized all the benches and stoves, including the writing-master who departed through a window and has not been seen since." It was a restless college into which the new president was formally inaugurated on the 11th of August.

On that warm summer day the academic procession marched from the college gate down the "slanting path" and past the Center Building to the grove where the Beta Bell Tower stands. There in the forest shade before "a vast concourse of people" President Junkin delivered his inaugural address. Its subject was "Obedience to Authority," and it proposed a strong rule in place of the paternal and democratic regime of his predecessor. "Every good school," the new president declared, "is a monarchy," and he promised an administration of firm discipline under moral law.

Soon after this strong stand some Oxford joker sent to the *United States Gazette* in Philadelphia a report of Dr. Junkin's death. Before Junkin could protest, his family was receiving letters of condolence and two funeral sermons were prepared by clergymen who had been his former associates. He went on attacking Methodists and abolitionists, but he was already dead as an effective Miami president.

In 1842 the Junkin regime adopted a set of "Laws of Miami University for the Government of the Faculty and Students." These rules, an expression of Junkin's belief in legislative morality, included some unrealistic provisions: "Every applicant for admission shall furnish written evidence to the Faculty that he sustains a good moral character, which shall be kept on file by the President. . . . Every student upon admission shall sign his name in the Matriculation Book under a written pledge to obey the laws of the Institution. . . . Ten hours per day (except for Saturdays) shall be devoted to study and recitations. Their particular distribution shall be announced by the Faculty at the opening of each Session."

The humorless rules for deportment of students have become humorous to later generations: "The students are to consider themselves as young gentlemen associated for the purpose of improvement. . . . They are to treat the President, Professors and other instructors on all occasions with profound respect. . . . No student shall wear about his person pistol, dirk, stiletto or other dangerous weapon. . . . Every student shall be required to observe a religious and becoming deportment on the Lord's Day. . . . The Faculty are authorized and enjoined to break up any and every combination that may be found to resist the government of the College.... Any student who shall send or accept a challenge to fight a duel . . . shall be immediately expelled from College. . . . No student shall during term time attend any ball, dancing school, theatrical exhibition, horse race or any other place of similar resort. . . . Any student engaged in putting off fireworks or other combustible matter on the College premises shall be punished according to the nature of his offence. . . . All behavior inconsistent with comfort and good order shall be considered as misdemeanors and visited with suitable penalty."

Despite these laws, or because of them, the Miami of the 1840's was a restive place. The three Junkin daughters enjoyed a popularity with Miami men that did not touch their father; and though it is not necessary or important that a president be popular, he must be respected. "Our little warlike Dr.," Professor Scott called Junkin, and he added, "This same little Sir Hudibras is rather a hard case to get along with." The students found it so. They muttered about a "reign of terror," and resistance grew. In the spring of 1844 all the sophomores refused to attend class because of their dislike for a certain textbook. On a summer night after the first mowing of the campus the chapel was filled with hay. In the morning while the students watched from the edges of the room President Junkin worked his way around to his desk and conducted the service as usual, except for a lengthy reference to "transgressors" in his prayer. When a returning student who had been in trouble with the president was placed on the Commencement program of the Miami Union, the faculty threatened to deny graduation to his sponsors. An apology saved them their degrees, but it was also a defiance, still questioning "whether the faculty had the right to interfere." The seniors talked of cutting the name of President Junkin from their diplomas.

The monarchy had failed, and there was no regret when

Dr. Junkin left Oxford in the fall of 1844. He was no better liked by the townspeople than by the students. When Joel Collins fenced off the upper part of the campus to keep village cattle out of the college "commons," the villagers blamed Junkin. "The president is putting on airs," muttered one cattle-owner, who took an ax, battered down the fence, and let his cows in to graze on the Miami grass.

From Oxford President Junkin went back to the presidency of Lafayette College. Four years later he became president of Washington College at Lexington, Virginia. There he taught his classes and directed the college for thirteen uneasy years. He was still a fighter, equally opposed to abolition and to secession. In the tense April of 1861, he denounced states' rights and upheld the bonds of the Union. When he found a rebel flag over his classroom he dismissed his students and resigned from the college. Leaving a married daughter in Lexington (her husband would soon be known to the world as "Stonewall" Jackson) he drove his own carriage 350 miles through the border turmoil to Philadelphia. During the war he talked, condoled and prayed with wounded soldiers in the military hospitals. He was writing an exhaustive commentary on Paul's Epistle to the Hebrews when he died in 1868.

To the Miami presidency in 1845 came Erasmus D. McMaster; he had been president of Hanover College in Indiana. A towering, white-haired bachelor with courtly manner and distant eyes, he was totally different from President Junkin. In political belief he was an ardent free-soil man. The divided trustees had chosen an abolitionist to succeed a defender of slavery; it was the opposition's turn.

President McMaster had a prodigious learning and phenomenal memory. To the students his learning became a legend: he knew the whole of Butler's *Analogy*, every chapter, page and paragraph verbatim; he could take the place of any absent professor and without a textbook hear a recitation in conic sections or the *Iliad;* he never brought a book or paper into the classroom. Yet this long-haired scholar could not remember the names of Miami students or understand their natures.

But he could not fail to see the growing contest between the Literary Halls and the faculty. In the middle of May, 1845, the Miami Union elected as its anniversary speaker Robert Dale Owen, educator, reformer, and member of Congress, from New Harmony, Indiana. At its next meeting the secretary read a letter from the University faculty, reminding the hall of the regulation requiring the members to submit the names of speakers for all public occasions. The faculty would doubtless have approved Congressman Owen; they were merely affirming a principle.

Voices rose on the third floor. Both societies asserted their independence of the University. Their anniversaries, though now held during Commencement week, were not a University exercise; let the faculty direct the Commencement, the societies would conduct their own reunions. As the August Commencement approached the tension grew. Goaded by their alumni, the halls clung to their independence, while the faculty insisted on control of the college. In a meeting of faculty and society representatives the students were urged to submit the names of speakers for the approaching Commencement exhibitions, with assurance that they would be approved. For seven hours the members of the Miami Union argued the question, finally voting down this compromise. The Erodelphians made the same defiance. The deadlock lasted through three years—the years of the Snow Rebellion and of the growth of the *sub rosa* Greek letter fraternities.

At last a new generation of students gave in to the adamant president and faculty. In the subdued, half-empty college after the Snow Rebellion of 1848 there was no more fighting spirit. Finally Ardivan Rodgers, secretary of Erodelphian and one of the founders of Phi Delta Theta, handed the president the name of a proposed speaker, asking for approval. The Union then submitted its names, and the long struggle was past. Everyone was relieved, except the alumni—who like all alumni wanted to preserve the college life, even the strife, that they remembered.

Past also was the full strength and influence of the Literary Halls. They would carry on for many years, but in the enlarging shadow of the new Greek letter societies—which the halls had prepared for. Certain touches of fraternity organization had marked the societies from the beginning: the wearing of the "rose," the pride in their meeting rooms, the secrecy of their constitutions and of "the proceedings of the Hall." Members had been recruited in the fraternity way. Three freshmen boarding the stagecoach for Oxford in the fall of 1839 found there a group of upper-class members of the Miami Union. Before they saw the college yard the new students had agreed to join the Union Society. In that year twenty members of the Union organized an eating club. Alumni members contributed to the society funds and returned to the society reunions. In and out of college the members felt bound by ties of the closest friendship. *Amicitia* was carved over the Erodelphian rostrum, and the inscription on the graves of three members buried in the student cemetery was *Vale, mi frater.*

The Old Student Burying Ground was at the far corner of the University land, half a mile through the forest from the college yard. It was a sylvan half-acre, on the present site of number eight green of the Miami golf course, where a broad white oak still shades the grassy knoll. Of the score of students buried there before 1850, several were members of Erodelphian and their graves were tended by the society.

For students far from home in a time of little transportation, their comrades in the Literary Halls took the place of family. Like brothers they cared for them in illness, watched at their dying, arranged their funerals and placed monuments on their graves. In the spring of 1841, John Jamison of Ross County, Ohio, died of measles. In the summer of 1844, John W. Smith, a freshman from Oxford, Mississippi, died of dysentery. In the winter of 1846, Joseph Little of Indiana, a high-ranking senior just a few weeks short of graduation, died of smallpox. These three were buried with Erodelphian monuments to mark their graves.

In a remote small college a death touched them all. "No faculty meeting was held or other regular college business transacted in consequence of the death—" is a familiar minute in the faculty records. After a funeral service in the chapel, members of the literary societies formed a line and marched, with the faculty and other students, through sunlight and shadow to the burial ground. In summer there were wildflowers to cover the coffin, in winter only the frayed silk badge of the society.

In 1852 the Oxford Cemetery was opened on the hill across Collins Run, and the student graves were moved to the University lot in that new burial ground. They stand there still, among the graves of Miami presidents and professors, three weathered obelisks bearing the Erodelphian seal and the inscription *Vale, mi frater*. For many years on Memorial Day in the radiant Oxford spring, the Erodelphians marched to the cemetery and left fresh roses on the graves.

In the 1830's, the literary societies were the only student organizations. By 1850 new activities were coming: a cricket club with the wicket fixed where Irvin Hall now stands, gymnastic exhibitions in a third floor room next to the Literary Halls, campus baseball teams—the "Moundbuilders" of present Stoddard Hall competing with a team from the North Dormitory. But Friday was still the climax of the week, with voices ringing in the third floor halls. When Old Miami closed its doors in 1873, the societies' records were stored in their library shelves; the shades were drawn, the doors locked, and the keys entrusted to Professor McFarland until the college should open again.

When New Miami began its first term in 1885, the literary societies reorganized. But things were not the same. The old halls were shabby, the pictures faded on the walls, the carpet mottled under the cracked and leaky ceiling. The sound of declamation and debate was lost in other voices—cries of class rivalry in the Tower Rush, cheering from the football field, the chanting of the black-robed Dekes carrying their coffin by torch-light through the grove, the midnight songs of the fraternities. The Greeks were dominant now, and up under the roof a few students patiently debated the questions of Chinese immigration, the eight-hour working day, and public ownership of the railroads.

When the Alumni Library was opened in 1910, the societies transferred their books to the University and surrendered their halls for use as classrooms. For some years the organizations held on, encouraged by their alumni, but their time was past. In the 1920's they adjourned their final meetings and gave their bulky record books to the university librarian. The last Erodelphians were graduated in 1924, ninety-nine years after the society's founding. In 1928 a note in the *Miami Student* stated that the Miami Union was dissolved.

Now the third floor is silent on Friday nights and no one visits the three worn gravestones on the hill. But the portrait of Bishop hangs in the Sesquicentennial office, his bust looks over the reading room in the Library, and some calf-bound books in the library stacks still carry the yellowed bookplates of the Literary Halls.

Chapter VII

FORTUNES OF THE GREEKS

I N 1841 the Board of Trustees passed a resolution: "Resolved that the faculty be requested to require every student of the institution who is known to be connected with a Secret and invisible Society . . . to withdraw from it forthwith . . . and that it is hereby declared to be unlawful for any student in future to become a member . . ." Fifty years later Miami was known abroad as the "Mother of Fraternities." Of some 4,000 fraternity chapters in the United States and Canada in 1958, one in every ten had its origin on the Miami campus. One sixth of all members of Greek letter fraternities belong to societies founded at Miami University.

Fraternity founders have a compulsion which follows them through college and beyond. They know a secret, having made it for themselves, which they need to share. In the early years they enjoyed the opposition of the college trustees, faculties and other students. So the orders grew.

In 1835 Samuel Eells, a recent graduate of Hamilton College and a founder of Alpha Delta Phi, came west to Cincinnati and joined the law firm of Salmon P. Chase. It was a busy office, but Eells did not forget the claims of Alpha Delta Phi. When William S. Groesbeck, just graduated from Miami, became a law clerk in the firm, Eells talked to him about a national college society aimed at developing *the entire man* —moral, social and intellectual. Groesbeck liked the idea, and Eells turned from the paper work on his desk to initiate a new member into Alpha Delta Phi.

Groesbeck then wrote to some of his friends at Miami. Soon Charles Telford and John Temple took the stagecoach to Cincinnati. In a hotel room in the old Dennison House at Fifth and Main streets, they were inducted into the society. That fall, 1835, the two initiates organized the Miami chapter of Alpha Delta Phi, the first fraternity west of the Alleghenies.

It was an entirely secret society at first, but by mid-winter, with nine members, the fraternity came out of hiding. They turned in a notice at the morning chapel service, and President Bishop made a kind of history by announcing the weekly meeting of the "Alpha Delta and Phi" society. A few days later the nine members appeared with large badges on their lapels—and the whole campus turned hostile.

The next Friday afternoon voices clashed and clamored in the third floor Literary Halls. After strenuous discussion both the literary societies voted to exclude members of the new fraternity. As though a Greek brotherhood were not enough, the Alpha Delta Phis organized their own literary society, the Miami Hall. Then began a see-saw struggle between the Literary Halls and the fraternities, a struggle confused by the resemblance between the two orders—the fraternities met for declamation and essay reading and they held public anniversaries and exhibitions. To outsiders the fraternity seemed an organized group within the literary society, seeking to control it. Finally in 1842 the Union Society merged with the splintered Miami Society, forming the Miami Union with no exclusion of fraternity members, and in 1846 the Erodelphian Society opened its doors to the Greeks. By that time it was possible to see a difference between the forensic activities of the halls and the closer ties of friendship, formalized by oath and ritual, that bound the members of fraternities. De-

spite the political tensions of the time, the fraternity groups
were not sectional; both Northern and Southern students
wore the first Greek badges.

One of the loudest protests to the appearance of Alpha
Delta Phi came from John Reily Knox, president of the Union
Society. Yet he had a strong sense of the ties of friendship
within that group—"one shall be to another as a brother and
the name of Union Literary shall be the shibboleth of love."
Soon he was busy founding the closer brotherhood of Beta
Theta Pi, the first of the Miami Triad of fraternities. Knox
had been reading a book about secret organizations in the
Middle Ages, their knightly vows and pledges, but the original aim of his six associates seems to have been merely to
offset the influence of Alpha Delta Phi in the literary societies.

In a room in the West Wing on August 8, 1839, John Reily
Knox gathered eight men and proposed a secret organization.
Their next meeting was held in the Union Hall; as president
of the society Knox had keys to the room. There a constitution was framed, a badge adopted, and four men were initiated into the Beta Theta Pi Association.

For seven years Beta Theta Pi remained a *sub rosa* organization; not till 1846 did the members emerge publicly on the
Miami campus. By that time they were a national fraternity.
Although the founders had not planned to extend the fraternity to other colleges, a second chapter had been planted at
Cincinnati College in 1840. In 1843, a chapter was organized
in the Harvard Law School, and another chapter at Princeton. Then the fraternity spread north and west, to the University of Michigan and to Indiana University. Wooglin's
Clan was growing, not by activity of the original Miami
group but by propagation from the other chapters. The national organization kept Beta Theta Pi alive when the Miami
chapter was suspended after the Snow Rebellion of 1848.

In the mid-1840's President McMaster was having troubles.
Controversy over the Mexican War divided the college, and

epidemics of smallpox and cholera made it uneasy. The long quarrel between the faculty and the fraternity-ridden literary societies hung over the campus like a cloud. It was a restive, smoldering college.

One summer night some students drove twenty-three cows from the campus (the grounds had been opened again to the village live-stock) into the college chapel. Next morning the janitor got the cattle out and cleaned the floor, but at chapel time the room smelled like a stable. Dr. McMaster read the scripture, preached a brief and earnest sermon, and closed with prayer. Then he made a sarcastic comment about Miami students who were at home only in the barnyard and should have stayed there. It was not the way to win students or to keep them.

In 1847 the enrollment fell to 137. To attract more students the trustees tried to add new departments of study. They asked the Ohio Legislature for $40,000 to support a chair of agriculture, a chair of law and a law library—request denied. Then in the first days of 1848, came the famous and almost fatal Snow Rebellion. It began with some students coming home from a Wednesday night prayer meeting in a village church.

The day of January 12th was hushed and beautiful—snow falling through the silent woods, covering the campus paths, whitening the streets of Oxford, steadily deepening in the college yard. Dusk came early and yellow lamplight gleamed from the college windows. Snow was still falling when a dozen boys trudged into town to attend the prayer meeting. When they came back the snow had ceased and the campus lay white and still. It was a mild night, the snow damp and fluffy. Someone began rolling a snowball—toward the dark doorway of the Main Building.

Quickly the idea grew. A dozen huge snowballs rolled into the dark hallway. They came to rest against the chapel door and the doors to the recitation rooms. Finally the outer door was closed and the last white barricade was rolled against it, from inside. The students groped up the creaking stairs and slid down a rope from a second story window. They went to their dormitory rooms and slept soundly, with a good night's work behind them. They had been to prayer meeting and had barred the master out.

In the morning Job, the colored janitor, crossed the trampled yard by lantern light and found the door barricaded. He climbed the rope dangling from an upper window and after an hour's labor he got the doors open. Students and faculty filed through the snow-banked hallway for a late chapel service. Professor Moffatt, a gentle classicist who wrote poems about his rambles in Scotland, thought it amusing, but towering President McMaster was in a towering rage. From the chapel platform he announced that the guilty students would be uncovered and expelled; he was determined to make Miami "a decent college." So he fanned the smoldering defiance.

That night, with snow still melting, a larger crowd gathered in the slushy yard—new hands along with the prayer-meeting party of the night before, one of whom said he might as well be hung for an old sheep as a lamb. They went to work—"with greater determination, excesses and success" the trustees later noted. First they nailed up all the doors and windows of the recitation rooms. They carried in the whole University stock of fuelwood—twenty cords, one report said —and banked it against the doors. Then came old stoves, planks, tables and benches, and that bristling mass was cemented with some tons of soggy snow. They left a solid barricade across the main hall.

The next morning no chapel bell sounded, for the bell had been carried down from the roof and dropped in the college cistern. There were no recitations; the college was sealed tight as a fortress. The janitor got in, after breaking a window in Professor McArthur's room. He broke down the door with an ax and began the formidable task of opening the hallway. That was on Friday. It was Monday when the faculty got in.

That week there were no recitations, but the students were called in, one by one, for questioning and discipline.

In a change of weather the slushy snow had frozen rigid, and while they waited summons the students kept a cordwood fire blazing at the east end of the building. As a boy went into the courtroom he was cheered by the crowd. If he came out suspended or dismissed they carried him over the icy campus on their shoulders.

In the second floor courtroom some students confessed and some denied participating in the rebellion, but none would implicate any other. So the trial dragged on until the students sent in a list of forty-six names of the "guilty." These boys refused to apologize for wrong-doing or to make any promises for the future. The harried faculty made a general expulsion and offered to readmit any students who would acknowledge their error. Still defiant, the expelled students hired a brass band and marched through the village. They packed their trunks, sold their supplies of wood and apples, and said goodbye to Old Miami.

It was a disheartened college that dragged through the radiant Oxford spring. The senior class was reduced from twenty to nine, the junior class from twelve to five. Only the preparatory classrooms were full.

The Greeks had been leaders in the rebellion ("Put not your faith in any Greek," Euripides had said) and they were dispersed now. All the members of Alpha Delta Phi were expelled or quit the college in sympathy and disgust. Two Betas were left to graduate that summer. Three of the expelled Betas went to Centre College, Kentucky, and started a Beta chapter there. Not till 1852 was Beta Theta Pi revived at Miami.

That fall sixty-eight students clumped through the half-empty halls. The literary societies were at an ebb; not a lone Greek was left on the campus. In that void a new fraternity appeared.

On the desk in his room in the North Dorm Robert Morri-

son had a small corked bottle of "snow water," saved from
the pile of melting snow in the Main Building corridor. That
next winter he thought of bygone days at Miami, when
secrets, plans and rivalries were in the air. On the night after
Christmas, 1848, while college was recessed and most of the
students were at home, Morrison called five men into his
room and shared with them his dream of a new fraternity
called Phi Delta Theta.

The six founders soon initiated others, including three
sympathetic members of the faculty. In an atmosphere of
good feeling the fraternity outgrew the capacity of Morrison's
room. For some months Phi Delta Theta met in two divisions. Alpha and Beta chapters, of ten men each, gathered
separately in dormitory rooms, recitation rooms, and in fine
weather in Lane's woods above the Tallawanda with sentries
posted.

A new climate had come to the college with President Anderson in 1849. A liberal, humane, broadly-experienced man,
he brought to his office a natural directness of speech and
action. That summer it was reported to the trustees that conditions were again disgraceful in the dorms—"stoves and
stove-pipes broken up and destroyed, doors and windows
broken." The new president made a new start, bringing the
faculty closer to the students than they had been since
Bishop's time. Professor Matthews moved into a rent-free
apartment in North Hall; later Professor Elliott lived there,
lining the walls with pictures of Greek monuments and temples. When David Swing, graduated in 1852, joined the
Miami faculty in 1853, he lived in dormitory rooms. To that
apartment he brought his bride, Elizabeth Porter, the daughter of an Oxford physician. A member of Phi Delta Theta, he
had fraternity boys around him—even after he bought a
frame house on Collins Street and Campus Avenue. Years
later that house was occupied by Phi Delta Theta and still
later by Delta Upsilon.

As a part of the new sweep President Anderson asked R.

H. Bishop, Jr. ("Bobby Bishop" in the 1850's; "Old Bobby" to later generations in Miami) to keep a Dorm Book. Sample entry:

Room No. 1, North Door, Eastern Building—rent per session $5.00. Furnished with an open-sided stove with an elbow and four joints of pipe, a lock and key to the door furnished by myself, a pair of tongs and shovel, 3 lights of glass partially injured in front window, balance in good repair. I am to return the said room and furniture at the close of the session in the same good condition in which I received it.

Signed_____

The Dorm Book states semester rents of $3 or $5 for a single room, and carefully describes the stove installed— open-sided stove, box stove, sheet iron air tight stove, oval stove, air tight fancy stove, small cooking stove. Some rooms were equipped with a wood box and one had "a desk somewhat out of repair." This room, in the third story of the West Wing, was occupied rent-free by a "bellman," who also had free tuition for ringing the college bell.

Except for heating apparatus the students furnished their own quarters, usually buying the room's contents from a predecessor and selling to the next occupant. In 1848, M. R. Shields of Paddy's Run sold to freshman David Swing his furnishings—two chairs, one table, a stand and pitcher, a cot and quilt—for $3.50. After faculty members moved into the halls, the Dorm Book shows an abrupt decline in damage to the rooms and furnishings.

In this new atmosphere of harmony and cooperation, President Anderson and his son became members of Phi Delta Theta, and chapter sessions were as earnest as the weekly faculty meetings. When serious Ben Harrison arrived in 1850, a transfer student from Farmer's College in Cincinnati, he became the nineteenth member of the fraternity. Soon he and David Swing persuaded the rest to take the pledge against use of alcohol. Members who fell off the wagon were reprimanded in chapter meeting. After a stormy session Gideon McNutt and two other offenders were expelled from the fraternity. Three sympathizers left with them. A few months later, early in 1852, a member of Delta Kappa Epsilon from Yale came to Oxford for a visit and fell in with McNutt and his friends. The visitor, Jacob Cooper, saw here a likely group of Dekes and proceeded to initiate them; the Kappa chapter was established at Miami on March 2, 1852, with six original members and six more added before the year was out.

Two years later the trivial question of electing a poet for the Erodelphian Society divided the Dekes right down the middle, six on one side and six on the other. Leader of the loyal six was Whitelaw Reid of Xenia, Ohio—destined for fame as a Civil War correspondent, newspaper editor, and diplomat. Leader of the opposition was Benjamin Piatt Runkle, who would become a Civil War general, newspaper editor, and clergyman. The final strained meeting of the twelve members was held in February, 1855, in Reid's room in present Stoddard Hall. Four months later, meeting in Ben Runkle's room over a drug store on the village square, the six rebels formed the Sigma Chi fraternity—at first named Sigma Phi. By this time it was an accepted idea that a fraternity should spread. Said the Sigma Chi constitution, drafted by Ben Runkle at his student's desk, "The fraternity shall consist of chapters which may be established in such places as the Fraternity may deem fit." The Miami Triad was complete.

It was the custom of the Greek societies to "meet around" in the rooms of the members. As they grew larger and stronger, they needed a fixed meeting place. In 1861 the Dekes rented a chapter room, reached by a steep and crooked stairway, in the northeast corner of the third floor of the North Dorm. They furnished and decorated this chapter hall, put a double lock on the door and painted the windows with their coat of arms. On winter nights when the Dekes were in session colored lights gleamed up among the leafless trees. It was the first fraternity hall in Oxford.

After the Civil War the Dekes occupied the third story of a business block on High Street. A long narrow room, thirteen feet by fifty-five, it looked like an over-size Mahomet's coffin. Down its long open rear stairway the members carried the coffin for their torchlight procession through the town and campus. That long hall has not been a chapter room since Miami closed in 1873, but the Greek K (Kappa chapter) and DKE still mark the third floor gable across from the office of the *Oxford Press*.

After the Civil War came the Miami chapter of Delta Upsilon. Founded at Williams College in 1834 as an "anti-secret society," DU had become another social fraternity, with nine chapters scattered from Vermont to Ohio. It flourished here from 1868 to 1873 and was revived in the New Miami in 1908.

On a raw March day in 1906, a group of independent men climbed the stairs to the old Miami Union Hall to form a "Non-Fraternity Association," and a new fraternity was in the making. Befriended by Dean E. E. Brandon and led by William H. Shideler, who would have a long and influential career in Miami's geology department, this group organized as "Fre-no-com," its name derived from the initial syllables of two proposed names "Miami Friends" and "Miami Comrades" linked by two letters from "Non-fraternity." Slight changes made it the more classical-sounding "Phrenocon Association," which acquired a house, began rushing new members, and published a magazine which opposed an anti-fraternity bill under discussion in the state legislature; the magazine was edited by Joseph M. Bachelor, who after twenty years in a New York publisher's office would spend the latter part of his career in the Miami English department. Phrenocon had spread to six other colleges before it adopted a genuinely Greek name. In 1916 the National Phrenocon Association became Phi Kappa Tau, completing the familiar evolution of a non-fraternity group into a fraternity. On its fiftieth anniversary in 1956, Phi Kappa Tau installed its seventy-first chapter, at Long Beach State College, California.

The twentieth century brought coeducation to Miami, and coeducation brought sororities. Delta Zeta was founded at Miami in 1902 by a group of girls with the encouragement of President Benton. To start a new order, rather than petition one already formed, was in the Miami tradition. During the next two decades, while it spread to other colleges, Delta Zeta was joined at Miami by Delta Delta Delta, Chi Omega and Alpha Omicron Pi, and by the 1930's a dozen sororities had installed Miami chapters. Like the old literary societies they first met in classrooms. But the new women's residence buildings included sorority suites, leased to the societies, which became the halls for chapter meetings, teas, receptions and parties. Now the long first-floor corridors of Hamilton, Richard and Center halls are lined with Greek names and clamorous with women's voices.

By 1910, Miami fraternity groups were living in their own houses scattered around the campus. When the University offered leases of campus land for a "fraternity place" on lower High Street, Phi Delta Theta built a memorial chapter house in 1909. Soon it was joined by DKE and Sigma Chi. After the first World War, Delta Tau Delta and Sigma Nu built houses on Tallawanda Road, facing the old Botanical Gardens. There a new fraternity row developed, with Phi Kappa Tau, Delta Upsilon and Sigma Alpha Epsilon building the first houses on a fraternity square. In 1956, Phi Delta Theta moved from the original fraternity row to a new house on Tallawanda, while academic buildings edged into the deep woods on the south side of High Street.

Now, with all freshmen living in campus halls and fraternity membership deferred to the sophomore year, a student belongs to Miami University before he belongs to a fraternity. But the twenty fraternities, housing some five hundred men, have a secure place in the New Miami. At the fiftieth anniversary of Phi Kappa Tau, President Grayson Kirk of Columbia University recalled the value of group identity during his student years at Miami. Some colleges, he said, can remain small enough to include all students in a single kinship. Some can develop a House Plan, like Harvard's, or a College Plan, like Yale's, within the enlarging university. Others, like Miami, support a fraternity system, where a student can belong closely to a group, diverse and yet coherent, within the larger community of the campus.

The centennial anniversaries of the Miami Triad were events beyond the farthest dreams of anyone in Old Miami. In 1939, the Beta Theta Pi convention assembled under the campus trees and dedicated the peal of bells in the Beta Bell Tower. In 1948, a Phi Delta Theta assembly gathered at the campus gate, dedicating a general headquarters building on the site of Professor Scott's historic residence and presenting to Miami University the Robert Morrison Seminar Room in Upham Hall. In 1955, the Sigma Chi pilgrimage marched up High Street to the site of the founders' room and presented to the University a memorial scholarship fund. These fraternities, with two hundred thousand members, looked back to the little bands of men in Old Miami who had pledged themselves together—"one for all and all for one."

Chapter VIII

MORNING PRAYERS AND
MIDNIGHT REVELS

IN THE SPRING of 1849, President McMaster resigned. He had presided over a dwindling college, and the four years past must have seemed a long term to him. As his successor the trustees chose the Reverend Thomas Stockton of Cincinnati. When Stockton declined, the *Cincinnati Daily Dispatch* reported: "The presidency of Miami University has absolutely gone begging." (Miami has always endured a grudging and purblind press in Cincinnati.) On the next try the trustees got a good man indeed, the Reverend William C. Anderson of Dayton, a brother of Charles Anderson, Miami 1833, who later became governor of Ohio. Anderson was chosen in June; two months later the letter found him in a mountain resort in Austria where he was recovering from an illness. Perhaps that distance kept him from knowing of the Snow Rebellion and other misfortunes at Miami. He accepted the office on his return to America in September.

On arrival in Oxford in October, 1849, President Anderson found the campus "looking like a horse barracks"—broken doors and windows, weeds, bricks and cinders in the yard, brush and locust shoots springing up beside the paths. He became superintendent of grounds, without additional salary, turning over the work to his son John, Miami 1853. John Anderson repaired the college fence to keep hogs out of the yard and set out the first hedge that enclosed the campus. When President Anderson left in 1854, the college was neat, orderly and intact except for 485 empty window lights.

A tall, blond, handsome, courtly man with wide experience and easy bearing, President Anderson was the leader Miami needed. He came to a college with 68 students; he left it five years later with 266. He met students warmly, in chapel and classroom, in their lodgings and his own home. He and his faculty—Moffatt, Elliott, Stoddard, Swing, R. H. Bishop, Jr. —were both liked and respected. The sullen years were over.

From the start Miami had been a religious college, the principal training ground of Presbyterian ministers in Ohio. Morning prayers and Sunday worship were compulsory, with a voluntary college prayer meeting on Thursday night. One of Dr. Anderson's accomplishments was to make the chapel services as attractive as they had been in Bishop's time. To morning prayers he brought his own manly sincerity and instead of theology a friendly concern for the spiritual life of all his students. On Sunday afternoons the chapel hall filled up with students and townspeople, and the president's reflections on truth, beauty and holiness made the drab room a place of meditation while the winter dusk came on. In a revival of religious life at Miami he brought to Oxford a series of distinguished preachers—Rice, Beecher, Davidson, Steele, Chidlaw, Mills. But the most winning figure in the old chapel pulpit, the best witness to the inner grace, was President Anderson himself.

Conscience does not develop under authority but in freedom, and the Miami of the 1850's led students to seek their own philosophy in fire-lit rooms or under the stars on winter nights. But the chapel helped them to take their souls seriously and to make college a search for meaning. The old room was bare enough, whitewashed walls and undraped

windows letting in a sunless northward light. And the services were simple—a brief prayer, a singing of Psalms in
"Rouse's Version," a meditation by the president or one of the
faculty, a brief concluding prayer, and then the announce-
ments for the day. Nothing to cast a spell or leave a memory,
yet Miami men did not forget that morning session. From
the daily chapel they took a sense of the college unity, and
of something above and beyond the daily round. They came
out less self-occupied, less separate, than they went in. Something had drawn them subtly to a center.

On Saturday mornings the students read essays from the
chapel platform. After a twenty-one-year-old sophomore had
read an essay against religion Dr. Anderson called Henry
MacCracken, then in the preparatory department, into his
home and asked if he would read an essay in reply. Young
MacCracken copied the president's notes, ridiculing the
sophomoric atheism, and read the essay on the following
Saturday. "It carried the sympathies of the college," he recalled years later, "for I was a sub-freshman tackling a mature sophomore." A few days later, meeting the boy in the
college doorway, the president smiled broadly. "People are
saying, Mac, that it was not quite fair for you to answer
Bingham's serious essay with ridicule and nonsense."

President Anderson was religious but not dogmatic, and
his interests were as broad as life. In his classroom he kept a
cabinet of fossils, picked up from the crumbling bluestone
along the Tallawanda, an endless fascination to his students
in moral philosophy. He began a program of college sports,
the Miami Cricket Club playing in front of present Stoddard
Hall and students fencing, boxing, wrestling in a gymnasium
room under the roof of the main building. In squirrel season
a holiday was declared for hunting. The only student com-
plaint arose when the well rope broke. In November, 1854,
Abner Jones noted in his diary: "This week I wrote a petition
to the faculty, desiring that the old oaken bucket, the iron-
bound bucket, should hang in the well. William secretly laid

it on the chapel table. Thus the president saw, read, and announced it. Accordingly a bucket was the next day provided, much to the gratification of many students."

The fraternities, however intense their rivalries and friendships, did not divide the college. Under the same leaky roofs lived Greeks and non-Greeks; in the University Inn, the first campus dining room, they ate together. Men from all the fraternities mingled at the long table in the Girard House, opposite the town hall. The favorite eating-place of seniors was Mrs. Hughes' boarding house across the street from present Benton Hall. They climbed the five steps of the stile over the campus fence, dodged the cowpiles in the college common, and crossed the lane to the Hughes house on the corner. In the kitchen merry Ann Reagan baked the best rolls and pies in Oxford. From the head of the table Mrs. Hughes, widowed daughter-in-law of the man who had opened the Miami grammar school in 1818, asked the students to say grace. They ducked their heads and muttered "Bless this food and forgive our sins" and began eating. Among the men at the table in the early fifties sat Ben Harrison, Whitelaw Reid, David Swing, Gates Thruston. After graduation, in reunion times, Mrs. Hughes' boys gathered again at the long table. Swing was a professor then, teaching the preps and collecting money from villagers and alumni to give the college buildings a new coat of whitewash.

As superintendent of grounds President Anderson sold the hay from the commons for $30, "a larger sum than it has brought for some years." From a dense grove on the site of present McGuffey Hall, hundreds of locust posts were cut; in 1854 they yielded $84.25. Living costs were rising, and in this year the faculty appealed to the trustees for a reconsideration of their salaries. They got a reconsideration but no raise, to the trustees' regret. Miami never had a better faculty.

Benign Professor Elliott lecturing on Greek antiquities—it seemed he must have been there, in the cobbled marketplace of Athens where barefoot Socrates with his tattered cloak across his shoulders discoursed on the improvement of the soul, or in the courts of Sicily where Plato traced geometrical figures in the sand for the education of the young king Dionysius. He walked through the woods to Western College to teach a class of girls; in the lecture room, looking up vaguely from his text, he called them "Young gentlemen," and the girls replied "Yes, ma'am." Courtly, gentle, absent-minded, he was a favorite guest at Oxford gatherings. One evening, arising from the dinner table, he trod on the cat's tail. Quickly he bowed and murmured, "Excuse me, madam." Born in Scotland, he had come to the far West, but his mind went east to the classic past. He was modest and innocent, learned and forgetful. While serving as Miami librarian he could never keep the accounts; at each annual report he apologized for "seemingly having mislaid records of withdrawal." But he never was in doubt about the art and science of antiquity. He talked of the ancient Greeks as of old acquaintances.

Professor Thomas Matthews, mathematician, was also a lover of art and music, who made those devotions seem related to calculus. An uncle of President Grover Cleveland, he had held public office and could refer in the classroom to experience in the field. As Ohio state civil engineer he had surveyed through the woods and river bottoms, running the lines of the Ohio and Erie Canal. Thousands of farmers, tradesmen and travelers were in his debt, as well as the students in his mathematics room.

Presiding in the one-room laboratory building was Orange Nash Stoddard, for twenty-five years professor of natural sciences. A homely, long-nosed, slope-shouldered man, his photograph looks like Henry David Thoreau, and he had that Yankee's mixture of curiosity and transcendental faith. An expert ice-skater, he wore his own path through the snow to the Western College pond. He came home at dusk, crossing the college yard with skates over his shoulder and his mind on tomorrow's science lecture. One of his good friends was

genial and candid John Witherspoon Scott, former professor
of science at Miami, who returned to Oxford in 1849 with
two carryalls full of girls and began the Oxford Female Institute. Dr. Scott arranged to have his advanced class attend
Stoddard's demonstrations. Once a week, to the delight of
Miami students, a file of girls, Stoddy's daughters among
them, came down Walnut Street, crossed the campus stile
and gathered in the science room to watch experiments with
chemistry and magnetism. To the Miami boys Stoddard was
the "Little Magician." When the college could not afford an
electrical machine, he made one. During a crashing thunder-
storm a student taking refuge in the science hall doorway
was killed by lightning. It made the whole campus wonder.

But Stoddard's science was more than magic. It was the
scholarship of an ingenious experimenter who was also a
devout believer in God. See his notes for his opening lecture
on chemistry: "The Field of Chemistry as wide as nature's
self. Value of Chem. —1st, to train the mind, 2nd, its uses in
life. Education embraces relations to God, to life, to self.
We 'progress,' whither? Often to old discoveries, or old fol-
lies. This is a Gordian age, *cutting* not *solving* difficulties.
Dandies of body or of mind must go smoothly along, showy,
superficial. . . . In Chemistry the three topics, light, heat and
electricity, branch out boundless. How little we know! So in
all things, so here." There were wisdom and humility in that
dim science room.

Homely, awkward young David Swing soon forgot himself,
and hearers forgot his awkwardness, in the ardor of his teaching. He had a kindling mind, poetic insight, a natural elo-
quence. For a decade he was a gifted Miami teacher, modest,
simple, generous, before he went to Chicago and became the
preacher of his generation.

R. H. Bishop, Jr.—soon he was "Old Bobby" to Miami men
—wore a full beard, early grizzled, and looked with keen and
kindly eyes through steel-rimmed spectacles. As boy and man
in Oxford he saw every class graduate from Old Miami. He

had a shrewd understanding of undergraduates; he knew
when to be stern with them and when to relent. One winter day in his Livy class some of the boys put pepper on
the stove. When the sneezing began, Old Bobby opened the
door and stood in it. Without comment he conducted the
recitation from there while the students suffered their own
punishment. As years went by he kept trace of the alumni
and knew them all; Miami was his family. He alone stayed
on when Old Miami closed its doors, and he was there when
the New Miami opened, ready to receive new generations of
students. All his life he loved classical learning, but he loved
people better.

This was the faculty that asked for a raise in 1854. They
needed and deserved it, but the money was not there. Ten
years earlier, Joel Collins, superintendent of buildings, had
advanced $1000 for repairs, and he was still waiting for re-
payment. In 1855 he resigned from the Board of Trustees,
and in recognition of his long services the members voted to
give him a silver pitcher on Commencement Day. Meanwhile his note again fell due, and once more the treasurer
had no money to pay it. Collins then offered to renew the
loan, at 6 per cent instead of the current 8 per cent, and he
specified that the first $50 of interest should be used to buy
a silver pitcher. So with Collins' own funds the trustees
bought the pitcher and presented it to him at the graduation
under the campus trees. Still the $1000 note was unpaid. Two
years later it was sold to Elias Kumler, an Oxford banker.
When he demanded payment the trustees borrowed $500
from Collins to pay off the balance due the banker. And Joel
Collins loved Miami till the day he died. What money the
University had not already got, he left to establish a health
service for the college students.

Miami in the 1850's was ringed in women's colleges: "female education" came to Oxford all at once. In the west end
of town in 1849 John Witherspoon Scott established the
Oxford Female Institute, having brought the students and

faculty in two four-horse buses from College Hill beyond
the edge of Cincinnati. On rolling acres southeast of the
Miami woods the white gate of the Western Female Seminary swung wide in 1855; its first class of girls was welcomed
by a faculty just arrived from Mt. Holyoke. In 1856 on leafy
grounds northeast of the village, beyond the Botanical Gardens, the Oxford Female College opened its imposing building (now Fisher Hall for freshman men); after theological
trouble with his trustees Dr. Scott had left the Institute to
organize this new college. In 1867, deep in debt, the Institute joined with Oxford Female College. Its towered building was sold to the Oxford Retreat Company in 1882, and
the Institute became the home of Oxford Female College—
forty-six years before its final merger with Miami.

In the 1850's Miami men visited all the women's colleges
in the gala Commencement season. In turn they entertained
the college girls at their own senior party and took them to
the roof of the Main Building to enjoy the circling view of
woods and meadows—a scene which amiable, far-traveled
Bayard Taylor, on a lecture visit, described as equal in quiet
beauty to any vista in the world.

Before the Commencement gaiety came the examination
week, especially strenuous for seniors. In June of 1853 the
faculty protested that students were called out for road work
while examinations were in progress. The local ordinance
required young men to perform two days' work a year on the
public highways, and certain senior men had arranged their
summons at the end of term. Road work, the faculty induced
town officials to say, must be done between April and October, but not especially on examination days.

At the end of examinations and before the protracted
exercises of Commencement, the students held a celebration
of their own—the Burning of Logic. Gathering at midnight
at the college door, with the village band playing a dirge,
they marched by flickering torchlight to the college gate and
on up High Street to the market house in the public square.

It was a grotesque procession, featuring spectral pall bearers, the ghosts of three famous logicians, a pillow-stuffed Undistributed Middle, a Dilemma with horns like a Texas steer, and a ragged Beggar of the Question holding out his hat in both hands.

Each year the class had a formal printed program of the ceremony.

BURIAL OF LOGIC
Order of Procession
General Ization
WITCHES
GHOSTS (of Aristotle and others)
BAND
Major Premise—Major Term
Miss Anna Logy and Old Aunty (Ante) Cedent
Miss Kate Gory and Barbara Celerant
Old Whately and Rev. Dick Tum
UNDISTRIBUTED MIDDLE
DILEMMA
Beggar of the Question

The order of exercises indicated: March to the Grave, with marchers chanting, "Farewell, Old Logic is defunct—"; at the grave a poem by A. M. B. Guity and a sermon by the Reverend Dick Tum. While the mourners chanted

> The mighty Logic sleeps at last,
> The dews of death are on his brow—

a torch was touched to a heap of firewood. Finally the Logic text was cast into the flames, to the chorused groans and jeers of all the mourners. Back to the midnight campus the procession went, chanting together the witches' song:

> His greasy corpus we will burn
> And gather up his ashes vile.

Though they burned the book with malediction they had learned the rigors of Whately's *Logic*. Forty years later the

Ohio Society of New York gave a dinner for three men who had achieved eminence in public life: Henry M. MacCracken, chancellor of New York University; Whitelaw Reid, editor of the *New York Tribune;* and John Shaw Billings, director of the New York Public Library and the man who had persuaded Andrew Carnegie to build libraries across the nation. All three had marched in the great Burning of the Logic in 1856.

President Anderson resigned in 1854 and the trustees elected William Holmes McGuffey, then at the University of Virginia, as his successor. McGuffey declined. They then chose the Reverend John W. Hall of Huntsville, Alabama. Under President Hall came the first attempt at an organized athletic program. In 1857 the University bought some gymnastic apparatus and students promptly organized the Miami Gymnastic Association; they rented a barn at $60 a year and engaged a German tumbler from Cincinnati at $40 a month as their coach. At the end of the year in a "gymnastic festival" they won a match with several Turnverein gymnastic clubs from Cincinnati. This victory spurred the citizens of Oxford to raise $150 for more apparatus. But the students could not find enough money to retain their teacher, and interest dwindled. By 1859 the barn-gymnasium was closed and the mats and parallel bars were stacked in the basement of the Main Building.

In 1853 an "English-Normal" program had been organized —to "train up teachers for our common schools." It was kept going until the dwindling enrollment of the early 1860's. In 1856 came a step toward the elective system; French and German were allowed in the regular college course as a substitute for Greek. There were few takers, perhaps because the modern language teachers were ineffective. In 1858 the option was withdrawn and Greek was required of all students. For another twenty years the core of the Miami curriculum remained what the universities had had for centuries: Latin, Greek and mathematics. Said David Swing:

"We boys who struck the institution about 1850 enjoyed three lectures in botany and had a little taste of geology as far as it harmonized with *Genesis;* and in the last years there were moments of French and half-hours of English composition. English literature was never alluded to, and the general impression among us was that nothing good had been written since Homer and Virgil."

In 1856 came a new mathematics professor who introduced practical engineering. A big, hearty, ruddy-faced man, Robert White McFarland built a brick house just east of the present University Center and set out the hemlocks that still shade that corner. To Miami he gave the land where McFarland Observatory stands. His own astronomy class he met at night on the railed platform of his own roof. From that house Professor McFarland went off to the Civil War at the head of a company of Miami students. Years later the Beta chapter thought of renting the McFarland house but concluded it was too far out in the country.

In 1859 the old west wing of the Main Hall was abandoned. A builder had poked around the walls in 1845 and said they would not fall down for fifty years. But the west wing had a leaking roof, broken stairs, sagging doors and windows. President Hall asked the trustees to turn the boys out, adding, "It will then be possible to keep glass in the windows."

In that same year the railroad came to Oxford. All the villagers and students cheered the arrival of the first train on the Cincinnati, Hamilton and Dayton line. Now the mail, once brought by post-rider, later by stagecoach, came direct from Cincinnati, and Oxford was linked more closely with the world. In 1860 the railroad was extended to Indianapolis, and Oxford had a daily schedule of trains. Into the Greek and Latin rooms a new sound came, the locomotive wailing across the fields. Soon it would carry Miami men to war.

Chapter IX

A COLLEGE DIVIDED: 1861-65

U P ON THE PLATFORM ROOF of the Main Building the
chapel bell was ringing. Across campus paths streamed
the 150 boys of Old Miami, and with them, on this April
morning, some villagers of Oxford. It was Saturday, April
13, 1861, and already the news was spreading. "Charleston
Harbor . . . General Beauregard . . . Fort Sumter."

The five men of the faculty were in their places on the
platform bench. The bell rang again and the door was bolted
against late-comers, though the room was crowded to the
walls. President John W. Hall stood above the open Bible on
the lectern. He looked over the hushed room and began
reading the 46th Psalm: "God is our refuge and strength, a
very present help in trouble."

President Hall was a Southern man, born in North Carolina, educated in Tennessee, a preacher in Alabama before
he came, in 1854, to this Ohio college. He had not hidden
his belief in states' rights, and already his loyalty to the
Union had been questioned. He was a divided man, in a
Northern college that numbered students from five Southern
states. The war came close to him.

In its past half century Miami University had developed

113

strong ties with the South. A former president, George Junkin, was now president of Washington College in Lexington, Virginia, and the father-in-law of a young Virginia Military Institute professor whom the nation would soon know as "Stonewall" Jackson. In the Miami class of 1842 was Joseph R. Davis of Mississippi, a nephew of Jefferson Davis; he would become a general officer of the Confederate army. A former professor of mathematics, Albert T. Bledsoe, from Virginia and West Point, was to become assistant secretary of war in Jefferson Davis' cabinet and to represent the Confederacy as a commissioner to England. J. J. McRae, Miami '34, had been governor of Mississippi 1854-58; now, a withdrawn member of the United States Congress, he would soon begin a term in the Confederate House of Representatives.

President Hall was a short, sturdy man with a grizzled beard and coarse hair tinged with gray. His shaved upper lip showed strong lines bracketing a stern yet kindly mouth. From under heavy brows his eyes looked out of a brooding sadness. As he read the Psalm, "Come behold the works of Jehovah; what desolation he hath made in the earth," his voice broke with emotion. Outside a song sparrow trilled in a redbud tree, but there was a somberness in the soft spring morning.

President Hall closed the Bible and spoke briefly of the news from Fort Sumter. After years of tension the bonds of Union had severed. At this moment guns were shaking the Carolina coast; how far that thunder would roll no man could say. The day of reckoning had come.

Then he clasped his hands and bent his head in prayer. "Spare us, O God of Jacob, we beseech Thee, from the great calamity that threatens our Nation. Dispel these gathering clouds of civil strife. Let not the dire calamity of fratricidal war distract and divide our so long happy, prosperous and united people. Thy throne, O God, is for ever and ever."

This was a Saturday morning, with no classes to follow. He urged the students to go to their rooms and study for the

Monday recitations. The chapel was dismissed. Outside the students gathered in tight little groups, Southern boys apart from the others. No one was thinking of conic sections and Herodotus.

Shortly after noon the bell rang again, and again students crowded into the chapel. Voices called "Dodds—Dodds!" Ozro J. Dodds, a rangy senior from Indiana, editor of the *Miami Journal,* pushed through to the platform.

"I do not know how you feel," he said, "but as for myself, I have determined to offer my services to the governor of Ohio."

While shouts filled the room, Dodds began writing on a sheet of paper. Soon 160 names—students with some village youths among them—were signed on a roll of volunteers. Ozro Dodds had learned close-order drill under Lew Wallace in a Hoosier military company. He was chosen captain. Outside, the University Rifles fell into ragged ranks and began marching under the campus trees.

When Captain Dodds telegraphed Governor William Dennison, Miami 1835, word came back: "University Rifle Company accepted. Report at Camp Jackson, Columbus, Ohio, at the earliest practical moment." But many of the students were under age and had to withdraw. Thirty-one were left to sign the muster roll. Then, at a public meeting in the town hall, the ranks were opened to Oxford villagers.

For a week, with Captain Dodds counting cadence, they drilled under the budding April trees and marched up and down the unpaved High Street. Professor O. N. Stoddard sent to Cincinnati for rolls of silk, which the Oxford women made into a company banner. The girls of Oxford's three female seminaries, after some long sewing sessions, presented each man a shirt of bright red flannel. Meanwhile a squad of Southern students marched on the far side of the Main Building.

On Monday, April 22nd, in their red shirts, the University Rifles formed at the west end of the campus. The flag was presented and a committee of townswomen gave out pocket Testaments. President Hall made a farewell speech, asking the care of Providence on this company and all men caught in the mighty current of war.

The company marched to the homes of the faculty to hear their parting words. Professor David Swing, soon to begin his long and famous ministry in Chicago, stood in his doorway on East Street, a slight, grave, homely figure with the April sun lighting his pale and rumpled hair. They remembered what he said: "From what I have known of you in the classroom, I will expect to hear great things from you on the field. That flag you bear represents the principles for which your forefathers gave their lives. I hope you will all return, but if any of you fall on the field, you will die in a noble cause. While your ambition is only to save the Union intact and the flag from dishonor, yet history reveals that great times make great men."

Led by the Oxford brass band, cheered by the townspeople, the company marched up High Street on its way to the station. There a group of Confederate students was waiting; together the boys of the North and the South boarded the train. At the Hamilton junction, twelve miles away, the two groups parted. They shook hands, made their farewells, and climbed onto separate trains—bound for Columbus and Cincinnati.

Thirty-five students were in the University Rifle Company. Two of them would die in battle—Nathan P. Dunn at Chickamauga, Joseph H. Wiley at Stone River. A dozen would lie wounded in field hospitals and prison camps. Strapping Bob Adams would be breveted brigadier-general before the war was over. Ozro Dodds would wear a lieutenant colonel's maple leaves. Two would be majors, five captains, three adjutants. Two others, fifteen-year-old Calvin J. Brice and James T. Whittaker, would be sent back, crestfallen, to college. But the war would wait for them. Whittaker served as a naval surgeon three years later and Brice became a captain in the 180th Ohio Volunteer Infantry.

The train crawled through the spring-rife country—apple trees bursting white in the farmyards and dandelions spattering the pastures—with long stops at the junctions. It was after midnight when Captain Dodds marched his company through the dark Columbus streets to Goodale Park where sentries passed them into Camp Jackson. On a hillside under half-leafed trees they broke ranks and slept on the ground. They were in the army now.

Four days later, on April 27th, the University Rifles became Company B of the 20th Regiment, Ohio Volunteer Infantry. They went on an inglorious mission, guarding railroad bridges in West Virginia and fearing they would never smell gunpowder.

At the end of their three-months service the 20th Ohio returned to Columbus and was mustered out. Most of Company B re-enlisted for three years' duty. Four men from Oxford entered the long term as commissioned officers, many of them in the 81st Regiment, Ohio Volunteer Infantry.

After a winter in the field in northern Missouri the 81st Ohio was ordered to join General Grant's army for the spring campaign through the South—the capture of Fort Henry and Fort Donelson had brought Union control of the Cumberland and Tennessee rivers. At St. Louis the 81st, freshly armed with short Enfields, embarked on the big steamer *Meteor*. Three days later they were steaming up the Tennessee.

The *Meteor* was loaded to the rails. On the main deck horses and mules stamped and lunged amid a jumble of wagons, artillery pieces, tiers of supplies and ammunition. The regiment bivouacked on the upper deck. For eight days they subsisted on hard tack and river water; then they broke into some sutler's stores of crackers, cheese and bologna. Above them in cabins on the texas deck was Governor Richard Yates of Illinois with a party of officers. Dick Yates had been a Miami student thirty years before, but he did not recognize the Oxford boys of the 81st.

At midnight on March 16th the *Meteor* churned into Pittsburgh Landing and tied up to a leaning sycamore. By daybreak the restless men had their baggage off and were huddled around campfires in the dripping woods.

For two weeks they drilled and waited while Grant's army was assembling. The men of the 81st heard that Buell's army was to join them for a sweep to the South; they knew that a Confederate army under Johnston and Beauregard was camped at Corinth, Mississippi, twenty-five miles away. But the March rains kept their minds on mud and misery. They all had diarrhea—"Tennessee quickstep"—from drinking river water.

At last the rains stopped and Easter morning, April 6th, broke radiantly over the hills. There was the fragrance of bacon and coffee, the tang of cooking fires, vireos and cat-birds singing, the scent of peach blossoms on the wind. Whistling and humming, the men knocked the mud from their boots and cleaned their Enfields. They were standing inspection when the rumble came from over the hill—toward Shiloh Meetinghouse. Thunder grew in the cloudless sky.

The rest of Easter day was hellish. Cannon shells crashed through the tree-tops. Horses plunged and screamed. The roar of musketry rose like a wall. Back—back the regiments were forced. They had no stopping-place; Grant had not prepared for defense, holding the West Point theory that fieldworks make men timid. When gunboats on the river found the range, Union shells came screaming.

At noon the 81st was ordered to Snake Creek to hold the bridge to Crump's Landing. Through the littered woods the Federals fell back. At last, in the long smoky shadows of late afternoon, Buell's first division arrived and the lines stiffened. At dusk, over the road from Crump's Landing, Lew Wallace crept in with his tardy division.

All night the big guns pounded while the men huddled

under shattered trees. In the gray dawn Buell's fresh regiments attacked and the whole Union army got into motion. They pushed on doggedly, through cannonade and musketfire, around stubborn hillocks and through gashed ravines, past the scarred log Shiloh church and beyond it, retaking the field they had lost. Wrote one of the Oxford boys: "No one who was on that march can ever forget it. . . . The dead in all manner of mutilation were everywhere intermingled with the hundreds of wounded. . . . Friend and foe were intermingled and it seemed that every man in gray had a companion in blue."

In the last weary charge on that awesome afternoon the 81st Ohio Regiment overran the 20th Tennessee and captured its colonel. While prisoners were being taken to the rear someone spoke of Oxford, and the captured colonel cried, "Is this the Oxford company?" Yes, he was told, and there were other Miami men in the sector. In a broken voice the colonel said that his son Joel Battle, Miami '59, who was his adjutant, had fallen earlier in the day. He asked the Oxford men to look for his body.

High-spirited and magnetic, Joel Allen Battle of Lavergne, Tennessee, had been a favorite on the Miami campus and a leader in the Erodelphian Literary Society. After graduation he married an Ohio girl and began studying law in Cincinnati. He was there when the news came from Fort Sumter. With a northern wife and a northern college, he expected to have a career in Ohio. Now he was a man divided, and he planned to go abroad till the war was over—after arranging his business in Tennessee. But the fervor in the South claimed him. His father was the colonel of the 20th Tennessee Confederate Infantry; Joe Battle became his adjutant.

Silence had come back to the Shiloh woods on Tuesday morning, April 8th, when John Lewis of the 41st Illinois Regiment and Cliff Ross of the 31st Indiana walked over the strewn ground where the Tennessee brigade had met the shock of Hurlbut's 4th Division. They passed the huddled dead in blue and gray and were stopped by an upturned face. It was their Miami classmate, Joe Battle.

Through the broken woods they carried the body to the camp of the 31st Indiana. They made a flimsy coffin out of cracker boxes. With a third Miami man, John R. Chamberlain of the 81st Ohio, they dug a shallow grave on sloping ground in the rear of the regimental camp. When they had smoothed the earth again Chamberlain slashed a white blaze on a black oak tree facing the grave. The body of Joe Battle was never moved.

Back on the Oxford Campus the students had formed a "Home Guard," marching to the commands of Robert White McFarland, professor of mathematics. In May, 1862, when President Lincoln called for 300,000 three-months volunteers, the college company became a part of the 86th Ohio Regiment. Sixty-six Miami students from five states served with Captain McFarland in West Virginia, guarding federal stores on the Ohio and holding a rebel force from crossing Cheat Mountain. At the end of September the regiment was mustered out; the college company returned to calculus and Greek antiquities at Miami.

The next summer, 1863, at a new call for six-months men, the 86th Ohio formed again, and Professor McFarland reported with a company of Miami students and Oxford townsmen. McFarland was commissioned lieutenant colonel. While the regiment was gathering at Camp Cleveland, Morgan's cavalry came up through Kentucky and began the daring sweep through southern Indiana and Ohio. The reorganized 86th Regiment joined in the chase.

With stunning swiftness and surprise Morgan led his two thousand troopers past Cincinnati. While gunboats patroled the river and federal cavalry, artillery and infantry tried to cut him off, he raced northeastward. "If Morgan [had gone] one day longer," wrote one of his pursuers, "he could have watered his horses in Lake Erie." But he was not making for Lake Erie; he was headed for the upper fords of the Ohio.

Seven hundred of his men were captured at Buffington Island, and the rest raced on. Twenty miles upstream three hundred got across the river before the federal gunboats came. Morgan led his remnant toward the Muskingum River below Zanesville. Here the Miami men joined the pursuit.

With four companies of the 86th, Colonel McFarland boarded a steamboat at Zanesville and hurried down the midnight river. They were just too late. At daybreak, when they came in sight of Eaglesport, the last of Morgan's horsemen were crossing the Muskingum. Landing his men a mile above the village, McFarland cut across country. Lines of dust in the summer sky showed him Morgan's movements—bearing away to the northeast. The 86th struck the road in time to glimpse the raiders' rear files and to give them one volley at long range. At noon in another curtain of dust came the advance columns of Hobson's federal cavalry, and the 86th gave over. Morgan's men fled on. It was five days before they were overtaken at Salineville, where Morgan surrendered.

The dusty prisoners were crowded into a train for Columbus, with Colonel McFarland in charge. Like a mathematician he counted them—565. At Columbus they marched between two lines of Union troops to Camp Chase, and McFarland counted the same number. He had not lost a man.

Five months later, after a bleak campaign in the Kentucky mountains at Cumberland Gap, the 86th Ohio returned to Cleveland and was mustered out of service. Back in Oxford, Colonel McFarland, still in uniform, picked up his logarithm tables and began teaching. He talked freely of his war experience, mixing military memories with altitudes and azimuths.

In Miami University there were still some Southern students, from Union families, or families divided, in Kentucky and Tennessee. In the fall of 1863 a new boy came, a lean and sunburned youth of eighteen. Watchful and quiet, William M. Mayes of Pleasant Grove, Kentucky, took his place among the "Southern bunch."

One day Professor McFarland brought to his class in mensuration, surveying and navigation a perpetual calendar he had devised. It could be used for thousands of years back, adjusted for Old Style or New Style, and for thousands of years ahead; yet it was compact enough to carry in a pocket. To demonstrate it, McFarland offered to fix the day of Paul Revere's Ride or Perry's Victory on Lake Erie or the rout of Morgan's horse thieves at Buffington Island.

At the mention of Morgan, Billy Mayes' head came up. His knuckles clenched white and he shot a look at the open classroom door. McFarland was still wearing his uniform with its double row of Union buttons. His strong gray eyes swept the room and settled on the startled face of Billy Mayes. He held up the calendar device. What date would the boys like to verify?

Mayes was a good student, alert and curious, but now he closed up like a horse touched with a frosty bit. He stared at the floor, his hands twisting a pencil and a muscle flickering in his cheek. He did not watch the demonstration that fixed the day of Morgan's surrender.

Thoughts wander in a classroom, but no one else ever sat in the old mathematics room with the thoughts of Billy Mayes. He could see the hay wagons creaking into Burkesville on the Cumberland—a mound of hay on a bed of loaded rifles—and Morgan riding at the head of the columns four-abreast to the crossing at Turkey-Neck Bend. From the rail of the captured Louisville Packet *J. J. McCoombs*, with the horses stamping on the deck behind him, he could watch the Indiana shore come up, dense and green and hostile. At midnight a file of horsemen, lost on the edge of Cincinnati, lighted fires at a crossroad to see which way the dust was drifting, to find slaver dropped from the horses' mouths; while they halted men fell out of the saddle, dead with sleep. In long morning shadows the dusty file was singing

"I'll bet ten cents in specie
That Morgan wins the race"

while plundered shoes and bolts of calico swung from their pommels. On the bank of the big river he could see the water lapping, feel the lash of willow branches and then the coolness of the water and his aching arms pulling him toward the Kentucky Shore. . . . At home in Pleasant Grove his mother fed him, laid out clean clothes and burned his raider's uniform. In September his father, a Union man, brought him across the Ohio to college. Now Bill Mayes, an uncaptured, unparoled Confederate soldier, sat in the Northern room avoiding the eyes of a Union officer who had counted Morgan's men on the way to prison.

"There is small profit in classroom problems," Professor McFarland often stated. "That is not practical surveying." So he led the class, at his quick-cadence step, out the College Corner pike to correct some boundaries. With a tripod on his shoulder Billy Mayes fell in step with the big man in Union Blue. For them the war was over.

On April 10, 1865, came the news from Appomattox. Oxford's church bells rang through the twilight, candles glimmered in the windows on High Street, a bonfire blazed beside the market house. Next morning at the sound of the chapel bell students and townspeople streamed over the campus paths.

President Hall spoke briefly and gravely of the nation's suffering and closed with a troubled prayer of thanksgiving. Might the land never again be darkened and this college divided by fratricidal war.

The editor of the *Miami Monthly* had written: "While many students in other colleges have given up their books and gone off in some military company, yet we know of no college, either East or West, which has sent out in a body such a number to represent us in the wars."

Now some of the Miami boys would return with men's lines in their faces, taking up their Greek and logic while Shiloh and Chickamauga sank back into memory.

Chapter X

INDIAN SUMMER

THE *Miami Student* began publication on May 8, 1867. Years later, tracing its origin through a broken sequence of periodicals to the *Literary Focus* of 1827, it came to consider itself "the oldest college newspaper in the United States." Hardly a newspaper, the original *Student* appeared bi-weekly and was soon reduced to monthly publication. But it kept its readers informed of visiting lecturers, Literary Society programs, baseball rivalries ("Miamians 27, Olympians 64"), and the current building program.

The first item in the first number of the *Miami Student* was a rhymed "Lament from an Ancient Alumnus" on the demolition of the West Wing of the Main Building.

> Builder! spare that pile!
>   Touch not a single brick!
> In youth I spent a while
>   Within its walls—how thick!
>
> Builder! forbear thy blows!
>   E'en though its doorless halls
> Invite the rain and snow,
>   Oh, spare its tottering walls.

After fifty years of wear and tear the West Wing was coming down. Its upper rooms had stood empty for a decade.
Windows and doors were gone, the roof dripped after every
shower, the rickety stairway was a peril. Now a new president, Robert Livingston Stanton, had taken hold and the old
hall was going.

When President Stanton came for a preliminary look at
Miami in the summer of 1866, there were two public con-
veyances in Oxford. The elongated hack, "the Longfellow,"
carried people in Commencement season to Western College
and Scott House (Oxford Female College, now Fisher
Hall) and on special days it took picnic parties to the Tallawanda and Hueston Woods. The smaller omnibus met the
trains and delivered guests to the Girard House on High
Street. Doubtless President Stanton got his first impressions
of Oxford from the omnibus, to the lazy clip-clop of Wes
Logue's team of sorrels.

Climbing the hill from the station, he soon saw Dr. Bu-
chanan's college for young ladies—the Oxford Female Institute. High Street was drowsing in the summer afternoon, with
a couple of loafers in front of Joe Hayden's gun shop and a
dusty team of horses tied outside of Henry Styhr's saloon.
He passed Nagel's wagon shop, the three-story Mansion
House on the Main Street corner, Pap Ringgold's shop
(though the war was over Ringgold was still busy hating all
abolitionists) and the tobacco shop of cigar-maker Crawford,
a man who wore out his life in Oxford always homesick for
Baltimore.

Across the street, around the barn-like market house, the
town square lay baking in the sun. It was treeless, but supported a crisscross stubble of hitching racks; on Saturday
the township farmers drove in with loads of apples, pump-
kins, cabbages, potatoes, and home-cured hams and sides of
bacon. Around the square were the town opera house, Harry
Gath's furniture store, and Tom McCullough's grocery store
and livery stable. The north side of High Street, east of the

square, was lined with lofty elm trees, their dry leaves rusting on the roofed gallery that shaded the shop fronts. On the next corner stood the Girard House, a popular boarding place of Miami students. From there the campus looked like a woodlot, until you saw the peeling whitewashed walls of the West Wing with its empty window frames. Even the Trustees' records described it as "the main dingy and dilapidated edifice."

A weedy slanting path led through the campus. Oxford as yet had no sidewalks, but paths which changed by season—muddy, grassy, dusty, frozen. At night the streets were dark as a forest, though Richard Butler, editor of the *Oxford Citizen*, had hung up a new kerosene street lamp in front of his house on Church Street. On Sunday evenings he lit the lamp and sat on the fence to hear the exclamations of people coming home from church.

The university to which President Stanton came had 166 students and was running into debt. To attract more students the new president proposed repair of the two dormitories and rebuilding of the wing of the Main Building. While the old West Wing was hauled down, he had workmen busy erecting a new president's mansion across from the south gate of the college yard; the house that Stanton built later became "Bonham House." In its friendly drawing room the Stantons entertained new students with receptions and served an annual oyster supper for the seniors. With the clatter and debris of repair and rebuilding, the Center Building could not be used for recitations. Ground floor rooms in the two dorms, enlarged by knocking out partitions, served as temporary classrooms.

At the same time some improvements were coming to the village. Dr. Keely, a tree-loving dentist, got the town officials to move the hitching racks to the borders of the public square. He then filled in holes and set out rows of shade trees. The village council passed an ordinance establishing the grade of Oxford streets and requiring householders to lay down sidewalks. Still, stray horses, mules, cattle, swine and geese roamed the streets, and the college enrollment went on shrinking.

President Stanton did not lack energy or ideas. He was a brother of the abolitionist leader Henry Brewster Stanton, whose wife, Elizabeth Cady Stanton, was the foremost feminist of America; aggressiveness ran in the family. President Stanton applied to the Ohio Legislature for an appropriation to support a law school. When the Legislature declined, he successfully organized a series of law lectures by Miami alumni. He sought direct aid from the Presbyterian Church (he had served as moderator of the recent national Presbyterian assembly) but found the church unwilling to endow a university controlled by the state. It was proposed that control of Miami University be transferred to the church, but the state constitution prevented that. Somewhat earlier, in 1865, the synods of Ohio and of Cincinnati had offered to endow four chairs at Miami University, provided they could name the incumbents. This proposal was finally accepted by the trustees, but already a movement had developed to establish Wooster College as a Presbyterian institution in Ohio. Church support then turned to Wooster, and Miami was forgotten.

In 1862 the Congress had passed the Morrill Act, granting public lands to the various states for the support of agricultural and mechanical colleges. For eight years—until The Ohio State University was founded—Miami officials sought a share of the $340,000 which Ohio realized from the land grant. All their efforts yielded nothing. When the Ohio Legislature in 1867 voted a substantial sum to create a state agricultural college, hopes leaped up in Oxford. Miami with its spacious campus and Botanical Gardens seemed an attractive site for such a college. University officials invited a delegation from Columbus. They met them at the depot, showed them all the rural advantages of Oxford, and gave them a formal reception at Professor Stoddard's house—Mrs. Stanton being

ill that day. When they escorted the visitors to the train the
Miami future looked brighter. That night the students were
busy. When the faculty filed into chapel next morning they
found a haystack in the middle of the floor and beside it a
plow, a harrow and a farm wagon. Nibbling at the hay were
a cow, two horses, pigs, ducks and chickens. Across the platform hung a sign Agricultural College. There was no chapel
service that morning, and soon came the bad news. The
Ohio Agricultural College was to be located not in Oxford
but in Columbus, as the beginning of The Ohio State University.

The cow was the hardest animal to get out of the cluttered
hall and the worst to clean up after. In those years Miami
had a famous Irish janitor, Fardy Devine, who alternately
befriended and berated the students. While prodding the
cow wedged in the chapel chairs, Fardy turned to the grin-
ning boys in the doorway. "It's not the first time a full-grown
calf has gone through the Greek room."

The new west wing of the Main Building was completed
in 1870, at a cost of $20,000 raised by alumni subscription.
The president and the secretary moved into offices on the
first floor and the college convened each morning in a commodious chapel above. The students contributed twenty-five
cents each to buy twelve kerosene wall lamps so that the
room could be used for evening lectures. A new furnace
failed to heat the chapel, and in winter months the morning
prayers were conducted in the dim and cheerless Greek
room. Want of heat was given as a reason for abandoning
the Sunday afternoon religious service, which had been a
fixture at Miami since 1824. A better reason was the reluctance of students and the indifference of the townspeople.
President Stanton was as devout a churchman as any of his
predecessors, but he could not resist the slow tide of secular-
ism that followed the war.

Even in a dwindling college there were new activities to
contend with the traditional Bible study and student prayer

meetings. In 1869 the first Miami annual, the *Recencio,* listed ten baseball clubs, a University Velocipede Club, a Miami Chess Club, and a Serenade Band.

The final improvement to the Main Building was the raising of a tower (its twin would be added thirty years later), and the walls were painted red. The old whitewashed college became a memory.

Despite the Germanic tower and the new red walls Miami was in a fading season. Enrollment went on shrinking; there were empty chairs in all the classrooms and when the college assembled the new chapel was half empty. Yet America was in the midst of a spectacular expansion. In 1869 the last spike was driven in the Union Pacific Railroad and the new telegraph flashed the word to the world. The huge resources of the interior were released—oil and coal in Pennsylvania, iron and copper in Michigan, the vast pine forests of the upper Mississippi, the sleeping fertility of the prairies, the mineral wealth of the Rockies and Sierras. American wealth and power were bursting on the world like a sunrise. With these energies surging through the nation old colleges expanded and scores of new colleges were springing up. But Miami seemed a backwater cut off from the strong currents of the national life. The village cattle passed through the broken fence and children gathered walnuts around the college buildings while the long autumnal shadows crept across the leaf-shrewn yard.

To liven the curriculum President Stanton proposed a new department of military science. In May, 1869, as an official visitor to West Point, he was assured by President Grant that an officer of the regular army would be assigned to Miami. He arrived in September—Colonel Caleb H. Carlton, a West Point graduate and veteran of Chicamauga, Missionary Ridge and Sherman's march through Georgia. For a few months the students studied military law and engineering and dragged a cannon across the college yard. They were to use the old chapel as a winter drill room. But in December Colonel Carl-

ton was called to Omaha to answer charges that as commander of a post in Wyoming Territory he had irregularly
disposed of commissary stores—bacon, mackerel and beans—
to the amount of $7,000. In Oxford the military program col-
lapsed, until a restless night in April when the artillery squad
dragged the cannon through the moonlight to Western College and fired a blank charge at Peabody Hall. Next day the
Western girls pushed it into the pond, a maneuver which
attracted newspaper notice as far away as Boston. Colonel
Carlton returned that spring and the military classes were
resumed. He stayed another year, with small success. The
students in tranquil Oxford had lost their interest in field
fortifications and military law.

In 1870 Professor Stoddard went to join the new faculty
of Wooster College; he was offered $500 more than his
Miami salary and he could not afford to stay. Then only
"Bobby" Bishop was left of the old faculty. Professor Elliott
had already gone to the McCormick Theological Seminary
in Chicago and David Swing had become minister of Chicago's Westminster Church. One notable newcomer to the
faculty was Andrew Dousa Hepburn, who in 1868 inaugurated a department of English language and literature. Dr.
Hepburn understood the things that young men feel and
wonder about; he knew the end of education, which is the
acquiring of a sense of values. He was everyone's choice for
president when Stanton resigned in 1871.

To replace Professor Stoddard a far-traveled scientist came
to the Miami faculty. Professor Henry S. Osborn, from Lafayette College, had studied in England, France and Germany;
he had memories of travels in Arabia and voyaging up the
Nile; his house and laboratory were strewn with relics from
distant lands. He made the old chapel into a new science
hall, filling cabinets with three thousand mineral specimens.
At the long raised table he introduced new ideas of teaching
science, including the dissection of freshly asphyxiated rats
and rabbits and the demonstration of internal organs.

To the students the little vine-covered science building was no longer a classroom; it became "Old Egypt," a place of dusty and exotic learning where Dr. Osborn drew maps of the Arabian desert and the Valley of the Nile. In a litter of test tubes, beakers, flasks, scales, old books, boxes of minerals and catalogues bulging with pressed plants, he worked happily while the boys played baseball outside. At night he was still there, sorting notes for his lectures on "Buried Cities of the Old World," "The Arabs and Their Homes," "Afoot in the Holy Land." Bending in the lamplight in Old Egypt, tracing the journeys of Saint Paul through harsh and haunted lands, he was a reminder to Miami students that college has a far reach.

In November, 1870, Elizabeth Cady Stanton, an assured and handsome woman with strong blue eyes and snowy hair, lectured in the chapel on "The Coming Woman." By that time President Stanton was a going man. He resigned at the end of the year, grimly presiding over his last Commencement. He had not seen the increased enrollment that he foretold, nor did his wife inherit the fortune he expected. He left the college deep in debt and his own house unpaid for; it went to his creditors, one of whom was Professor McFarland. Stanton moved to New York, where he became an editorial writer for the *New York Independent*. Fourteen years later on the steamship *Nevada* en route to Europe, he died at sea.

It must have seemed on that Commencement day in 1871 that he had accomplished nothing in Oxford. But his son, Robert Brewster Stanton, was in the graduating class, and he soon became the most famous civil engineer in America. Just ten years after his Miami graduation he was building the famed "Georgetown Loop" on a narrow-gauge railroad high in the Colorado Rockies. A few years later he surveyed the Grand Canyon, making the first descent of the Colorado from Utah to the Gulf of California, and wrote a monograph on possible railroad routes along the Colorado River. After his death the United States Geographic Board named a dramatic spire of rock in the Grand Canyon "Stanton Point." As a mining engineer he directed projects in Canada, Mexico, Cuba and the Dutch East Indies.

Robert B. Stanton learned science, he said, from bruising climbs in the Rocky Mountains and studies around the campfire; but the foundation went back to the classical curriculum at Miami—the training to think clearly, to analyze correctly, and to relate facts to each other. "That training," he wrote years later when a bleak specialization had invaded the colleges, "was the glory of Old Miami."

But scholarly President Hepburn was not satisfied with the past; he wanted changes. The traditional senior vacation, a month of freedom before the Commencement, was canceled; now the seniors were kept at their studies until graduation day. Written examinations replaced the oral examinations of years past. Afternoon classes were scheduled, despite the students' protests that they interrupted a long afternoon of study. To bolster enrollment free electives were allowed for any student not seeking a degree. And new degrees were offered, Bachelor of Science and Bachelor of Literature, for those who did not choose the traditional curriculum.

"Heppy" was a favorite of all Miami students, who revered him as earlier generations had revered President Bishop. A man of handsome presence and distinguished bearing, he balanced wisdom with a quiet humor. He was devout without solemnity. Janitor Fardy Devine had a permanent quarrel with students who stole his firewood for their own stoves. At last he complained to the president. At morning prayers Dr. Hepburn gravely repeated the janitor's grievance and warned against stealing Fardy's fuel. Then he opened the Bible to the 20th chapter of Proverbs and read the text for the morning: "When there is no wood, the fire goeth out."

In 1873, with enrollment dwindled to eighty-seven students, the fire went out in Old Miami. The last week of June brought a final flurry of activity. On Sunday the chapel was filled for a Baccalaureate service. On Monday a committee of the Board of Trustees reported: ". . . that your Board has tried everything expedient for increasing the endowment; by appealing to the Churches, the Alumni, the State and to the liberality of individuals:—but in vain.

"Therefore, Resolved that instruction in the Collegiate Department be suspended, and R. H. Bishop and R. W. Mc-Farland or Osborn be appointed a faculty to conduct a Grammar School . . . to prepare young men for admission to college . . . and that the remaining income of the University be applied as rapidly as possible for the extinction of our [$8,000] indebtedness; and when that is done be safely and productively invested, with a view to a full reorganization at the earliest practicable period."

In a nostalgia for years past when Miami was the foremost college in the West, the fraternities held their annual suppers, and on Class Day the seniors went through the burlesque ceremony of the Peace Pipe, the senior sachem solemnly handing the pipe to the junior spokesman—who would have no successor to receive it. On Wednesday the alumni gathered for their supper under the huge walnut tree in the Bishop lawn. After a reading of one of Bret Harte's poems, Ozro Dodds, now a member of the Ohio Legislature, told Mark Twain's "Jumping Frog" story. Finally all joined hands and voices in *Auld Lang Syne*. That night the literary societies held "Exhibitions." On Thursday came the Commencement, under the trees where now the Beta Bell Tower stands. A recent faculty ruling limited each senior to a five-minute oration; even so it was a lengthy program. On Friday trains carried the students and alumni away, the last carriages rattled off toward Hamilton and Cincinnati, and the dust settled in deserted High Street. The years of Old Miami were ended.

"Colleges rise up like mushrooms in our luxurious soil," wrote one observer in the 1860's. "They are duly lauded and puffed for a day, and then they sink to be heard no more." At the end of the Civil War there were 104 living colleges in the United States and 412 dead ones. Surveying the dead colleges, Theron Baldwin said: "If a headstone were put up for each [defunct college] . . . the traveler after lengthened journeys by lake and forest and prairie might find himself still within the enclosure of this apparently limitless burial ground."

Now Miami had joined the list of colleges where the light had failed. The reasons were several. Since the war Miami had lost its substantial number of students from the Southern states. A postwar inflation had shrunk the real income from the university land rents, and in a period when private benefaction was flowing into American colleges, Miami had no benefactors; Calvin Brice, the first substantial benefactor of the college, did not begin his gifts until the new Miami opened in 1885. The conservative administration of President Stanton ignored the demand for a "progressive" curriculum with a more modern and scientific course of study. The democratic West had turned away from the aristocratic curriculum of the classics, but Miami persisted in the old tradition. The only relaxing of the classical rigor was the surrender of Latin in the Commencement program; Elam Fisher, graduating in 1870, delivered the first salutatory oration in English. Finally, the growing movement of coeducation was resisted by the Miami faculty and trustees. The Civil War had replaced the American schoolmaster with the "schoolmarm," and there was widespread need for the academic training of women. But Miami held back. Dr. Hepburn, who modernized the course of study, would not give ground in his opposition to women students. Though Oxford had an important role in the education of women, Miami remained a men's college until the end of the century.

With the closing of Miami in 1873, President Hepburn went to Davidson College in North Carolina, where he became president. McFarland soon went to the new Ohio State University as professor of mathematics and civil engineering.

Professor Osborn worked on in the clutter of Old Egypt, writing books on metallurgy and Biblical history and carefully tracing his maps of the Judean wilderness. Professor Bishop, who had seen every class graduate in Old Miami, took a look backward and felt reassured. "I have seen her [Miami] in 1849 when as deeply in debt and with fewer students, she was involved in difficulty and trouble. She did not perish then and she need not perish now."

Bishop ran a small Latin school for a couple of years, and in the winter of 1876 Osborn offered a "Private Science Course," with but a few takers. Meanwhile grass grew in the campus paths and barbed wire, a new invention from the prairies of Illinois, was strung on locust posts to keep the cattle out. The Botanical Garden, including the old Student Burying Ground, was rented for pasturage.

In 1877 the University grounds and buildings were leased to two educational entrepreneurs, Messrs. Trufant and Marsh, who opened the Miami Classical and Scientific Training School. They renamed the two old dorms Washington Hall and Franklin Hall, and lived there with their students. They used only the classrooms on the first floor of the main building.

Isaiah F. Trufant was a short, stout, bearded man, called "Potty" by the schoolboys. Byron F. Marsh was a younger man, still in his thirties, with a boyish face hidden by a full beard. An expert marksman, he astonished the boys by shattering targets in the air with a .22 caliber rifle.

Trufant and Marsh offered a thorough college preparatory course, including music lessons by a member of the Oxford College faculty and a "Telegraphic department" taught by Sam Allen, the Oxford station agent. The school attracted a gratifying enrollment of boys from Ohio and from a distance. Among them were "Kid" Tweed, son of the notorious political boss of New York City, and three Wilder brothers from Honolulu; their father was a leading sugar planter in the Sandwich Islands.

In 1885 the trustees reclaimed the campus and advertised the reopening of the university. The Main Building, empty for a dozen years, was renovated—rotting sills replaced, glass fitted into scarred window frames, walls and ceilings plastered, floors repaired, slate blackboards hung in classrooms, and verandahs added at the three doorways. Then Miami was ready for a new beginning. "The university was reopened in 1885," wrote historian Henry Howe a few years later, "and whether it will regain the position it once held among Ohio's colleges is not yet easily answered."

Meanwhile Isaiah Trufant went West to buy up Kansas land, taking some Oxford money to invest for his friends in the village. He lost it all.

PART TWO

NEW MIAMI

1885-1969

Chapter XI

AGE AND YOUTH

O<small>N SEPTEMBER</small> 17, 1885, every carriage, trap and buggy in Oxford was at the village depot to meet the morning train, and some hundreds of visitors had a free ride through a festive town. Flags and banners lined High Street, shop fronts were bright with autumn flowers, Chinese lanterns swayed in the autumn breeze. At the slant-walk corner of the campus, above a new cattle-guard, hung a sign of welcome. After twelve years the doors of Miami University were open.

That evening, after a picnic supper on the new-mown grounds, the college bell rang from the roof of the Main Building and the clangor of church bells came across the town. With a din of horns, tin pans and fire-crackers, a procession of visitors, villagers, alumni and new students moved across the campus and up High Street. In the public square, by a bonfire's leaping light, they heard speeches from the trustees and the new president, Robert White McFarland.

That evening the future of Miami looked as bright as the bonfire. The college debts were paid and $50,000 had been accumulated as a permanent endowment; railroad-builder Calvin Brice of the class of 1863 had underwritten two professorships; and the State of Ohio had appropriated $26,000

for current expenses and the repair of the university buildings. Except for the previous payment of a few tuition fees
for Civil War veterans—the first G.I. bill—this was the first
state support for Miami. It was the beginning of an annual
appropriation that would grow from $2,250 in 1886 to more
than ten and a half millions eighty-two years later for the
fiscal year 1968–69.

The last speaker in the ruddy light was Professor Bishop,
who had stood by during the darkened years now ending.
He had been back in the classroom since September, 1884,
when he organized a freshman class in preparation for the
reopening of Miami. To the twelve freshmen of that year,
reciting their lessons in a room of North Hall—Trufant and
Marsh were using the Main Building—Old Bobby was the
entire faculty. His beard was a bit longer and more grizzled,
his tall frame was more stooped, but his eyes still looked up,
shrewd and stern and kindly, from the text, and his voice still
rumbled: "Parse it, young gentlemen, parse it." Now, at the
full reopening of the college, he had some hopeful things to
say of the future.

When the speeches were over and the bonfire sank, the
crowd roamed the streets, singing, shouting and blowing
horns, and again the village bells rang out. For a while, at
least, there was a happy harmony of town and gown, trustees
and faculty, alumni and new students.

In that crowd were just forty students, half of them from
the preparatory department. New Miami was a new beginning and a small one. But when the town fell silent and the
students crossed the dreaming campus, with leaves rustling
underfoot and the college tower lifting in the starlight, Miami
was something venerable and exalted. The autumn darkness
held a sense of all the generations of young men who had
reveled and aspired there before them.

For these forty students the trustees had assembled a small
strong faculty. President McFarland had returned to Miami
from Ohio State, where he was professor of mathematics,

astronomy and civil engineering. Dr. Hepburn had come back, from the presidency of Davidson College, to resume his teaching of English language and literature. Professor Oliver Holben had come from Paris where he had been director of an international academic association. Professor Joseph Francis James had left the curatorship of the Cincinnati Society of Natural History to open a new department of botany and geology. Professor Henry Snyder had come from Ohio State to teach physics and chemistry. Professor Bishop handled the Latin and President McFarland the mathematics. These men had a small student load—three or four boys to a recitation—but an extended schedule of classes. They staffed a curriculum including both the classical and scientific departments of study.

It would have been a problem, that first year, to conduct any larger classes. As McFarland said: "There was the $20,000 [the State's grant for the repair of buildings] and that meant dust, lime, mortar, sticks, chips, mud, bats, bricks, beams, boards, teams, oils, paints, glass, gravel, picks, shovels, iron, slate, men, boys, animals, all at once. . . . Every room in the [Main] building was torn up, and we were driven out and kept out four months." But it was a happy confusion, promising comfort and convenience to come, and spirit was high. Classes met in the old dorms, and even there they recited against the clatter of hammers and saws. A chemistry laboratory was being formed out of two rooms of the North Hall. President McFarland stressed the importance of the burgeoning sciences.

To Oxford when the college was newly opened came Henry Howe, tireless traveler and historian, then revising his *Historical Collections of Ohio*. McFarland took him up to the roof of the Main Building and pointed out the landmarks. In his new edition Howe described "a magnificent panoramic view of a rich country undulating in all directions with cultivated and grassy fields interspersed with woodlands." He also referred to the financial struggles of Miami: "Its starving treasury receives occasional pittances from the state. The university was opened in 1885 after a lapse of twelve years, and whether it will once again regain the position it once held among Ohio colleges is a question not easily answered."

To bridge the gap between the Old and New Miami, the editors of the monthly *Miami Journal* proposed "to make our paper a medium of communication between the past generations of students and the present generation," and it welcomed echoes from the past. For several years the *Journal* sought contributions from alumni, who recalled the loyalties, rivalries and aspirations of the pre-war college. Sketches of eminent graduates were featured in the magazine, along with the biographies of early faculty members. So the struggling New Miami recalled the luster of the University which had been "foremost in the West."

After the noisy first year came an academic quiet, and a growing academic struggle. President McFarland was a vigorous, weathered man with coarse gray hair, shaved cheeks, and heavy mustache and chin whiskers. He had strong beliefs, strong feelings and no diplomacy whatever. Blunt, positive, often impersonal, he had years earlier barred his own brother from his mathematics classes, refusing him a hearing by the faculty. Shrewd business sense had led to his owning property in Oxford, including the president's mansion which Stanton had not been able to pay for.

To the conservative college with its deference to its own traditions, McFarland brought an awareness that the classical curriculum was no longer adequate, that higher education was inevitably growing secular and scientific, and that coeducation was coming. He was the first lay president of Miami and the first non-Presbyterian. Reared a Methodist, he had become something of a free-thinker, and so he drew doctrinal suspicion and disapproval from his neighbors and colleagues. When he ended compulsory attendance at chapel, he was accused of abandoning the religious foundations of Miami. It was rumored around Oxford that he made infidels of his students: "Boys, you know that we don't take stock in Moses like our fathers did." He gave up any thought of finding church support for the college and directed all his efforts toward increased support from the State.

With President McFarland on the side of science and a progressive curriculum were Professor Snyder and Professor James. Snyder was a busy little man working up demonstrations of lenses, prisms and induction coils in his laboratory and always ready to give popular lectures, illustrated with lantern views, on "Science in the Kitchen" and "Science on the Farm." He lived with his wife, Minnie, in South Hall, where the boys harassed them by throwing pokers, stove lids, and occasionally an entire stove, down the stairs. Professor James lived quietly in the present Simpson Guest House, preparing his lectures and writing monographs on plant science and mineral formations.

On the side of the classical studies were Hepburn, Bishop and Holben. Dr. Hepburn became the leader of McFarland's opposition. Between these two men there was a whole set of differences: McFarland had served in the Union army, Hepburn had Southern leanings; McFarland stressed the sciences, while Hepburn lauded literature; McFarland favored the admission of women students, Hepburn hated coeducation; McFarland minimized the place of religion, Hepburn became the college chaplain, conducting voluntary morning prayers and preaching on Sunday afternoon.

They were two strong men, sharply divided, and their difference soon entered into their personal relationship. McFarland scoffed at Hepburn's services on the chapel platform —"Miami is the most religious place in the world, to hear them tell it. Every week they publish the name of the saint who conducted chapel or spoke to the Y.M.C.A." He regarded Hepburn as hypocritical and referred to him in private as "the Hyp." Meanwhile Hepburn charged that the sciences were unduly favored, optional chapel attendance had led to laxness in class preparation and attendance, and the college was suffering generally under a dogmatic president.

Despite these differences, McFarland was never less than fair to his colleague. Hepburn was a poor manager financially, and McFarland approved an addition of $200 to his salary for conducting the chapel services which he viewed so dimly. As superintendent of buildings, he set aside four rooms in North Hall, rent-free, as living quarters for the Hepburn family.

Dr. Hepburn had influence with the trustees, who were predominantly conservative. When a Greek professor was elected in 1885 the appointment went to one of Hepburn's former students at the University of Virginia. A distinguished classicist and more of an aristocrat than Miami had ever seen, John Robert Sitlington Sterrett arrived in Oxford in 1886, with his man-servant, and moved into rooms in North Hall. Sterrett was in Greece at the time of his appointment, preparing for an archaeological expedition in Asia Minor; hence his delay in joining the Miami faculty. He had been abroad for twelve years, taking a Ph.D. degree in Germany, continuing classical studies in Rome and Athens, and leading parties of archaeologists into Assyria and Babylonia. Miami was his first teaching assignment. In North Hall he unpacked his books and papers, including notes of nine hundred inscriptions collected on his last tour to Assos and Tralleis. Now he was a neighbor of Dr. Hepburn, who worked in a cluttered study on the ground floor.

While these two scholars bent over their texts, the students lugged potatoes, corn meal, cabbages and firewood up the stairs. They chopped kindling and sawed logs in the hallways —despite the unrepealed rule of 1836: "If any student shall cut, split or saw wood in any of the rooms, halls or passages . . . he shall pay a fine of two dollars." They cooked their meals on iron stoves and studied by the glimmer of oil lamps. The old dorms had not changed from earlier years. Outside in the woods stood the college latrine, a low stone crypt with four cold cells. Traditionally called the "gin," it had replaced the perishable wooden backhouse of the 1830's. There was no college bathroom, but in the upper halls, beside bins for wood and potatoes, stood a galvanized tub and a battered pail. There was plenty of cold water in the three college wells. Once a year, in June, pugnacious little Fardy Devine, with his reeking pipe and dented derby, swept the dormitory halls. There was an accumulation of twigs, bark and sawdust, ham bones, potato peel and apple cores, by then.

To students in this primitive setting Professor Sterrett brought a sense of the international world of scholarship. He had attended four German universities and had held offices in the American School of Classical Studies at Athens, the American Philological Association, and the American Archaeological Institute. From his Miami study he corresponded with scholars in Germany, Italy and Greece, and wrote his account of *An Epigraphical Journey in Asia Minor* including translations of 397 inscriptions he had found on ancient city walls and crumbling temples.

In 1887, after half a century in the classroom, old Bobby Bishop was retiring. To fill the chair of Latin came another young cosmopolitan scholar, Alfred Emerson. Emerson and Sterrett had been graduate students together in Munich; now they were colleagues, exchanging memories of Germany, Italy and Greece in their battered rooms in North Hall. With Dr. Emerson came his brother Edwin, who enrolled as a sophomore. Edwin Emerson had grown up in Germany where his father was in the consular service. To the *Miami Monthly* he contributed sketches on European travel and education and he promptly won a reputation as the most persistent caller at the women's colleges. The Emerson brothers introduced tennis to the rustic Miami campus, despite the dubious views of President McFarland.

With discord in his faculty, with enrollment dragging and division growing among the trustees, McFarland was re-elected for one year in 1887. It was a stormy year and the

opposition grew. Solidly the classical bloc voted against Mc-
Farland, Snyder and James. Hepburn was secure, but Sterrett
was perhaps vulnerable. Though the students praised his
teaching and took pride in his international reputation, Mc-
Farland reported to the trustees that he was "a dead weight
on the college."

That winter came an exchange of letters unique in the
records of Miami. From McFarland to Sterrett: "Messrs.
Boyer and Pann [undergraduates] desire to occupy the room
now used by your servant. Of course you know that the
buildings are all under my care and charge.

"You put your servant in that room without asking me: the
room is an excellent one, and the young men have first choice.

"If you desire a room for your servant, there is but one in
the building which can be used, viz.: the NE, third story
room. Of course, also the cost per session is the same charged
the students, $5.00 per term, according to the order of the
Trustees.

"The young men wish to take possession today."

From Sterrett to McFarland, the same day: "I have received your note and in reply have simply to say that I do
not understand that the buildings and rooms are wholly under your control. I do understand that you are wholly subject
to the control of the Executive Committee. When the Committee, through its proper officers, give directions, I shall
comply."

Six days later the Executive Committee wrestled with this
problem, asking Professor Hepburn's counsel. They also had
a letter from Sterrett: "The room they [the two students] are
reported as wishing to secure, is in all respects the most
undesirable for their purposes. They, as most of the other
occupants, do their own cooking, and keep large piles of
wood brought from the farms of their parents. There are no
wood boxes or coal bins connected with the room I am using,
—wood of necessity would have to be piled up in the hall. . . .
These young men have been in the habit of splitting and

sawing the wood in their rooms and in the halls, until Dr. Hepburn, after repeated attempts, succeeded in checking the evil in part. Dr. Hepburn tells me that one of the applicants is one of the rudest, most unmanageable boys he has ever had to deal with at college. . . ."

The Committee also had a letter from McFarland: ". . . Dr. Sterrett, as you see, cares nothing for the accommodation of the students,—he cares only for himself. He is a *dead weight* on the college. Should there be one or two more such, the University could not stand it."

Perhaps McFarland sensed that the ruling would go against him. He asked to be relieved of the custody of the buildings, and the trustees appointed Hepburn to that duty. So Sterrett's man-servant remained in the disputed room.

That spring Sterrett and Emerson resigned. Both went on to notable careers: Sterrett at Amherst and Cornell, and Emerson at Cornell, the American School in Athens, and the University of California. With them departed the dashing Edwin "Birdie" Emerson. He finished his college course at Cornell and Harvard and began an adventurous career as newspaper reporter, Rough Rider with Roosevelt in Cuba, and foreign correspondent.

The first Commencement of New Miami was held in 1888 with a graduating class of three. In silk hats and Prince Alberts they planted their class oak beside the newly-bricked Slant Walk, tying their colors, old gold and blue, to its slender trunk. In this festive week the trustees declared all the chairs of the faculty vacant (there was no tenure to trouble them), though immediately re-electing Hepburn and Snyder.

McFarland was out. He had worked hard if not happily at his office. He had been president, librarian, superintendent of grounds and buildings, adviser and admonisher of students, appealer for funds to the State Legislature and the alumni— all in addition to teaching thirty-five hours a week. Now he retired to his brick house on Exterior Street (Patterson Avenue), where he grumbled about the extravagance and folly of his successor.

The alumni had great ambitions for Miami and exalted ideas about its presidency. Someone, somehow, thought it an appropriate office for the English philosopher Herbert Spencer. Though he was not formally chosen, it appears that the offer was made, perhaps by a sanguine alumnus or trustee with the understanding that Calvin Brice would provide an exceptional salary for him. However, Herbert Spencer, at work in London on his synthetic philosophy between attacks of dyspepsia, was not persuaded to come to a struggling college in Ohio. In June the trustees proceeded to elect E. D. Warfield, a young lawyer from Louisville.

Ethelburt Dudley Warfield was a new-sounding name in the list of Miami presidents, and he was a new kind of man. Tall, distinguished, athletic, young—a dark beard made him look older than his twenty-seven years—he was a graduate of Princeton, had studied at Wadham College, Oxford, and had taken a law degree at Columbia University. Unmarried, he kept a butler and a cook in his house on Church Street; he entertained frequently and well. During visits to Cincinnati he enjoyed the society of the Tafts, Longworths and Herrons.

Warfield promptly brought to Miami a fashionable young faculty from Princeton and Yale. Bridgman in Greek, Johnson in philosophy, Cameron in German and French, Hargitt in botany and geology, Merrill in Latin, Parrott in the preparatory department—all were at the start of their careers, with their names to make. They were a bachelor faculty, sophisticated and cosmopolitan, a wholly different cut from "Old Bobby" Bishop sitting in his dooryard with the yellow leaves drifting down. Dr. Faye (Lafayette) Walker, pompous head of Oxford College, called them the "dude faculty," while the women of Oxford murmured that they had danced in every capital of Europe. McFarland muttered about their "juveninity." Certainly they brought a wave of youth, ardor and glamor into the battered old college.

Warfield had the good luck of the young and confident. At the time of his appointment, June 21, 1888, the Republican Convention was in session in the huge Exposition Building in Chicago. Four days later, on the eighth ballot of the convention, a Miami man was nominated for the presidency. When word reached Oxford the Alpha chapter of Phi Delta Theta hung a huge flag from their third-story hall in the Mansion House. Attached to it was a placard: "Gen. Benjamin Harrison, a graduate of Miami, Class of '52, member of Phi Delta Theta." At the same time another Miami man, Calvin S. Brice, was named chairman of the Democratic presidential campaign. The struggling little college was represented in the national arena.

When students arrived in September they found a log cabin—reminiscent of the campaign of Ben Harrison's grandfather, Old Tippecanoe—in the middle of High Street; beside it rose a lofty Harrison and Morton pole. Miami was in the midst of the political ferment. For a week before the election students paraded by torchlight and serenaded the Republican professors with campaign songs. On election night President Warfield and most of the college stayed at the telegraph office till three A.M. Then Warfield sent a message of congratulation to the President-elect. The next day Hoosier wagons rattled into town with bells ringing for Harrison. The village band played in the public square. Students paraded till midnight, carrying Harrison banners and singing Harrison songs.

Weathered old Miami was young again. There were just twenty-seven students in the college proper, but the future was before them. Professor Hargitt fitted out two upper rooms in North Hall as a biological laboratory. The department of chemistry received a shipment of "technological diagrams from Vienna." On Sunday afternoons Dr. Hepburn gave religious lectures on "The Life of Jesus" to a chapel full of students and townspeople. Mrs. Snyder, wife of the science professor, organized a University Quartette which gave concerts in Oxford and communities nearby. The young faculty men rearranged the library books according to the new Dewey system and made a card catalogue; now the library was open for eight hours every day, with current periodicals strewing the old eight-sided McGuffey desk. Both President Warfield and Professor Snyder addressed the Cincinnati Electrical Convention.

In this yeasty year a new sport, sparked by President Warfield and Professor Bridgman, came to the Miami campus. Bridgman, a broad-shouldered dark-mustached young scholar, had played football for Yale. Now he kept a football on the top shelf of his bookcase in North Hall, beneath pictures of classic temples and Athenian sculpture. In the mornings he taught Greek to seven boys—one of them, "the best student," was R. M. Hughes who would become a later president of Miami. In the afternoon he joined his colleagues on the football field, and he expected his students there as regularly as in the Greek room.

That fall there came to college a tall, thin fifteen-year-old, without the slightest interest in athletics. Years later, when he was organist of the Brick Presbyterian Church in New York, Clarence Dickinson recalled: "President Warfield started athletics that year, and we all *had* to play." The new boy was assigned to the scrub team and so he was on the side against the faculty. One chill afternoon he remembered especially, with players swarming on the field and the first lamplight showing in the college windows. "President Warfield, who was six feet four inches tall, broke through the line, knocking men right and left—till I was the only one between him and the goal! I can still hear the spares yelling 'Hold him, Dickie! Hold him!'—but he knocked me sprawling."

On the 6th of December, reported the *Miami Journal,* "President Warfield sustained a painful injury to his knee while playing football." Perhaps that kept him from appearing in a historic game two days later. On December 8, 1888, the University of Cincinnati played Miami on the trampled campus. Professor Marc Parrott, a veteran of Princeton football who would become a famed Shakespeare scholar, captained the Miami team. The average weight for Cincinnati was given as 162 pounds; Miami was lighter, 142 pounds, and supposedly faster. But speed was of little use on that wet day. The game, played in a pouring rain, ended in a scoreless tie. The next season the Miami team played a schedule of four games without a loss, with a total score of 100 to 4. That year the college colors were chosen—red and white—and an athletic association was organized. The era of athletics had begun.

At Miami as elsewhere the old college pranks diminished with the growth of organized sport. No more sheep were carried into the classroom, no cattle turned into the chapel, no raccoon fights staged in the dorms. A few hours on the athletic field worked off a student's restlessness.

Still Dr. Hepburn had small use for football—a young man's years in college were all too short for the urgent business of learning. Possibly he felt that Warfield's impressive salary, $3500, was not being earned at football. In any case Hepburn kept at the business of scholarship while the thud and rush went on outside his windows. In the small chaos of his study he wrote his lecture notes and turned the graceful phrases of his chapel meditations. At midnight, with the college soundly sleeping, his window was a lonely glimmer in the darkness. But he had company in the lamplight—Captain Lemuel Gulliver and Corporal Trim, good Vicar Primrose and raffish Moll Flanders, wandering Prince Rasselas and aspiring Paracelsus, Alton Locke and Henry Esmond, and rumpled Herr Teufelsdröckh in his lofty littered study, a place far from old North Hall and yet not unlike Heppy's own strewn lair.

Neither did Hepburn approve coeducation, which began that year. The Reverend W. J. McSurely, a University trustee, pleased with the new president and his faculty, entered his

daughter as a special student. The boys soon stopped grum-
bling; Ella McSurely was just one person and she came and
went quietly. But Dr. Hepburn never accepted the change.
For a year she attended his class without a sign of recognition. With his colleagues and the trustees Hepburn argued
against coeducation, but it was a losing struggle. Soon all
Miami classes were open to women, and a traditional integrity was gone from the college.

For sixty years Miami had been masculine, except for the
weekly procession of Oxford College girls crossing the campus stile and crowding into Old Egypt for a science lecture,
with the boys watching from a distance. At receptions in the
women's colleges relationships were mannered and formal;
man and girl had little ground for conversation and no opportunity for anything more. From these brief encounters
the Miami men went back to the male world of their books
and batching, their Literary Halls and classrooms. So that
for a few years a young man with intellectual pursuits could
evade Nature, or postpone it, while his mind reached out. It
meant a singleness of life, a concentration of interests, and
the asceticism that encourages learning.

Now, with Miss McSurely who would be a life-long
spinster, the walls were breached and a new kind of college
life was beginning. It would lead in the twentieth century to
a too-easy and diverting companionship of the sexes; eventually even to undergraduate marriages and to students who
came unprepared because they had been up all night with
a colicky baby. If Dr. Hepburn did not foresee all this, he
knew that the intellectual ends of college are a jealous pursuit. Yet he lived to see his name given to the first women's
residence hall at Miami.

A liberal and gracious new president, Leila McKee, had
come to Western College and the old barriers between Miami
and Western were down. To the traditional "walk around"
—the Miami boys noisily circling Peabody Hall while Miss
Peabody warned her girls away from the windows—the two

faculties added picnics on the Tallawanda, bob-sled rides on winter nights, receptions and collations at the College. Soon three of the Miami faculty, Warfield among them, had married young teachers from Western College.

President Warfield was a versatile man, at home in the drawing room, the football field, the classroom and the lecture hall. In addition to teaching history and political science, he managed to give lectures around the region on "Scientific Cattle Feeding" as well as "The Education of Farmers' Sons." He restored compulsory chapel and also liberalized the curriculum. He won small but regular appropriations from the state and raised funds for a science building. A proposed name for the new building was Warfield Hall, but it could not have been built without the benefactions of Senator Brice and so it was named for him.

In 1890 Calvin Brice offered to match the State's grant for a science building. That winter the Legislature voted $10,000, later adding $5,000 for equipment. Brice gave $15,500; he had previously contributed to the salary of the president and the faculty. These benefactions, along with his wife's gifts to her own Western College, did not strain the resources of the railroad, steamship and banking fortune which Brice had amassed in the Gilded Age. A poor boy, sharp-faced and undersized, he had lived as a Miami student on nine cents a day, cooking oatmeal on a cranky stove and wearing one suit of clothes year after year. But even then he had a prophetic shrewdness. As a Miami freshman on an autumn night he was taken snipe-hunting, an errand he agreed to after insisting that his mentors buy him a lantern. Leaving their victim in a wild and lonely thicket across the Tallawanda, the upperclassmen started back to town. Still laughing, they went into an Oxford tavern, where they found young Brice setting up drinks for his friends on proceeds from the bartered lantern.

The college enrollment was still small in 1890—it hadn't touched seventy since the reopening—and enthusiasm for

President Warfield was waning. He was criticized for his youth, his extravagance, his lax discipline, even for spending his summers in Europe. The criticism of laxness came from Dr. Walker of Oxford College. He suggested that Miami get a new president, the kind of man who could cross a field and persuade a farmer's son to attend the university—where, he added, all students should live under the supervision of married professors with an 8 P.M. curfew. Walker referred scornfully to the dude faculty and said it would take a good man to build up Old Miami.

When this screed appeared in the *Butler County Democrat*, Warfield was out of town. The students met his train, and with red flares and a brass band they escorted him to his home on Church Street. There they cheered the president, his new wife, his faculty, and jeered Dr. Walker.

There was genuine regret, at least among the students, when Warfield resigned to accept the presidency of Lafayette College. With his going, the young faculty dispersed. A more aggressive administration and a more seasoned faculty would take over in the fall of 1891. They found an old college invigorated by a tenure of youth.

Chapter XII

WIND FROM THE WEST

ON A JANUARY DAY IN 1890, a big, strong, weathered man stood over a raw new grave at Longmont, Colorado. Nine miles away rose the front range of the Rockies, white with snow; beyond, dominating the skyline above Estes Park, the square tower of Long's Peak stood up timeless and enduring. The wind came cold from the mountains, but the big man did not feel it. A minister, he had many times read the ritual: "Earth to earth, ashes to ashes, dust to dust, looking to the resurrection in the last day—" Now he had himself to console.

He had come to Colorado in 1885 as minister of the Presbyterian Church in Longmont and president of the newly-founded Longmont College. Since then he had stood above three graves of his own. His first wife had died of tuberculosis in 1886, and an infant daughter had died four months later. Now a second wife had died, following the birth of her second son. When he walked back through the straggling streets of Longmont, William Oxley Thompson must have felt that his life was ended. He was thirty-five years old.

Back in Ohio, young Will Thompson had been called the best farm hand in Muskingum County. During harvest or haying, said a neighbor, he would take one side of the wagon and two men would take the other. At Muskingum College he was janitor, kindling fires before daylight, as well as scholar. In Illinois he husked corn in the fields while word went around that the new teacher had arrived and the Long Ridge school would open on a certain Monday morning. In northwest Iowa he preached to Sac County farmers and then drove across the prairie to repeat his sermon at the crossroads school. There his wife fell ill and the young minister asked for an assignment in the mountains of Colorado. After a summer of camping in Estes Park, Rebecca Allison Thompson seemed improved. But she died the next summer, in her twenty-fourth year. After a year he married a gifted young graduate of his college. Now, three and a half years later, Starr Brown Thompson was buried at the age of twenty-four.

Years later, in an address in the depression-dark February of 1932, William Oxley Thompson said: "If I am not mistaken, the human race was intended to be a race of hope." A native vigor and hope soon revived the young minister at Longmont. While his sister cared for his three small children, he drove across the plains to Greeley where his brother was publishing a paper; he traveled to Denver, Cheyenne and Laramie for church and college meetings; he preached in his own pulpit on Sunday mornings and then rattled up the road to Berthaud to preach in the afternoon. In the spring he broke this busy round to attend the Presbyterian general assembly at Detroit, and there he met some Miami trustees and alumni. Back in Longmont he announced his acceptance of the presidency of Miami University.

When he arrived in Oxford, an imposing, windburned man in rumpled clothing, college was out for the summer. But the villagers recognized an educator wholly unlike President Warfield and his Eastern faculty. Robust, confident, hearty, Thompson came like a wind from the West, stirring up the drowsy village and filling the empty campus with expectation. He moved his sister and the three children into a house on Church Street. Then he was on the road, looking for students. The college roll listed sixty undergraduates and sixty-two preparatory and special students, including seventeen women. President Thompson wanted more.

Nominally professor of political science and history, Thompson did little teaching during his eight years' tenure. His colleagues met the classes while he made the rounds of churches, county fairs, farmers' and teachers' institutes. Given a pass from the C. H. and D. Railroad, he tirelessly traveled that territory. Ready to speak on many subjects, he always found room to stress the purpose and opportunity of Miami University. In 1892 with the Republican nomination of Benjamin Harrison and Whitelaw Reid, the only political ticket in history with both candidates from the same college, and with Calvin Brice proposed as a Democratic nominee for the presidency, Thompson could point to the eminence of Miami alumni. With his vigor and the luster of the college in years past, it is strange that he did not fill the halls and classrooms. He did attract some students; a lecture at the Preble County Teachers' Institute in 1893 brought Alfred H. Upham to Miami. But during eight years of tireless effort he never saw the enrollment reach one hundred fifty. In those years most Miami students came from nearby counties; Ohio had forty colleges and Miami's appeal was limited. Professor Roger Bruce Cash Johnson, the Princeton philosopher who had remained from Warfield's faculty, said that his students were "an intelligent and enthusiastic body of young men." But President Thompson confessed that while two thirds were average or above, another third was "helpless."

Before the end of the century the old classical curriculum, unworldly and aristocratic, had lost its appeal. The majority of Miami students did not take a degree—through the 1890's the senior class averaged ten—but chose subjects that would prepare them for the study of law or medicine or for the practice of business, and they departed short of graduation. President Warfield had tried to develop a more modern curriculum, but the conservative trustees were not persuaded. When he resigned he had a parting word: Miami should be stable, sturdy, and not over-hasty to rush into new paths, yet he believed that "once past the half-mile stone, the junior year should open up the whole sphere of modern progress." He urged upon the trustees and his successor the offering of a science curriculum along with the traditional course of study. President Thompson succeeded in establishing a B.S. degree in 1893. He had the industrious support of Professor Snyder, the busy lecturer and experimenter, whose annual reports always cited a popular demand for scientific studies and a growing opportunity for young men with scientific training. A further step toward curricular freedom was the offering of alternative courses, with a choice of Greek or modern languages, leading to the A.B. degree. To stimulate scholarly effort honors work was introduced: a student could win departmental honors by maintaining a superior standing in his courses, passing a comprehensive examination based on collateral reading, and writing a thesis.

For its small, provincial student body the college was providing new facilities. At the Commencement of 1892 Brice Hall was dedicated. Equipped with steam heat, a gas machine and an Edison three-kilowatt dynamo, it was as different from Old Egypt as electricity is from candle light. Chemistry and physics occupied the main floor, biology and geology the floor above. After sessions in a lecture room fitted with charts, models, demonstration apparatus, display cabinets and a human skeleton, students could work at dissecting and experimental desks. Science had taken a giant stride since O. N. Stoddard gave his charming lectures in Old Egypt. Now Miami could begin the training of the men who would work in the laboratories, research institutes and experiment stations of the twentieth century.

Though he had never seen a football before he came to Miami, President Thompson saw that the new sport was intrenched with town and gown alike. At the State Fair in

Columbus in 1894 a featured "Football Tournament" promised competition between Ohio State, Akron, Denison, Wittenberg and Miami, with a grand prize for the highest-scoring
team. At Miami Thompson appointed an athletic board of
control and in Ohio at large he supported an intercollegiate
athletic association, a movement which attracted enough notice to be reported on October 21, 1896, in *Harper's Weekly:*
"Last winter the Ohio Inter-Collegiate Association, composed
of Denison, Miami, Cincinnati, Ohio State, Kenyon, Marietta,
Oberlin, Otterbein and Wittenberg, drew up eligibility rules—

1. Each player must attend at least eight hours of recitations per week.
2. No student holding a degree is eligible.
3. No student may receive any form of compensation for
   engaging in athletics.
4. Managers, at least ten days before a game, must exchange lists of players certified . . . by the president
   of the college."

The account added: "Cincinnati and Miami had a football
game scheduled for this month. In accordance with the rules,
Miami submitted a certified list of players. Cincinnati's manager declined to do so, and on the day of the game, when
appealed to by Miami . . . Cincinnati disclaimed membership
in the association. The game was played with four ineligible
men on the Cincinnati team, but they were outclassed, never-
theless, and beaten by Miami."

In 1895 Miami sports were moved from the upper campus
to the present athletic field. For twenty dollars the trustees
sub-leased four acres at the southeast corner of the Botanical
Garden from a Mr. Griner who had rented the entire tract
for pasturage. The field was cleared and drained; a couple of
carpenters built an eight-foot fence with a High Street gate
guarded by a shed-like ticket office. Professor Edward P.
Thompson's surveying class laid off a half-mile track, a baseball diamond and a football playing field. Down dusty High

Street trooped students, faculty and villagers to watch the contests on Miami Field. The old playground west of Stoddard Hall was planted to grass and shrubbery.

When Brice Hall was completed (it comprised the eastern third of the present building) the trustees decided to convert Old Egypt into a gymnasium. A new floor was laid, some mats and apparatus were lugged in, but the students still regarded that dim old relic as belonging to the campus squirrels. Then in 1896, with increased revenues from the state, the trustees appropriated $25,000 for a new gymnasium building. While it was going up, President Thompson had a new talking point in advertising the college.

The gymnasium, built on the site of the present Ogden Hall, had a bicycle room in the basement; a reading room, assembly room, locker room and shower baths on the main floor, and a gymnasium floor above. Around the playing floor hung a running track—twenty-one laps to the mile. Officially named for John W. Herron, a trustee since 1860, it was generally called the Miami Gymnasium as Herron discouraged the use of his name. It was electric-lighted, the wiring again supplied by Professor Snyder and his students. Snyder complained of a lack of laboratory materials, saying that had it not been for the work on Brice and Herron halls he could not have kept his students busy.

If President Thompson could not fill the classrooms, he kept the college treasury flourishing. A man of practical force and political shrewdness, he could talk about farming as readily as philosophy and he met the predominantly rural Legislature on common ground. Aided by Brice, a United States Senator during the early '90s, and Herron who was a member of the State Senate, he secured annual appropriations of some $15,000. The attitude of the state, he reported, was kind and cordial, and he believed the time was right for seeking firm and lasting support. It came in 1896, with passage of the Sleeper Bill which provided for a tax levy to support Ohio and Miami universities. On his return from

Columbus with this accomplishment, he was met by the entire student body. In a carriage decked with flags and bunting they drew him through the village streets.

The Sleeper Bill, which in its first year produced $22,000 for Miami, remained in force for ten years, and by 1906 the state's obligation to Miami University was fully established. The bill required the abolishing of tuition for residents of Ohio, but Thompson had already persuaded the trustees to reduce the former $45 tuition to a $10 matriculation fee.

Along with his Miami labors President Thompson took a warm interest in the fortunes of Western College. He became a member of its board of trustees and in 1896 served as its presiding officer. He was also a warm friend of Oxford College, but it was more than educational interest that led him there. In June of 1894 he was married to an Oxford College dramatics teacher, Estelle Godfrey Clark. Then the three small Thompson children had a mother's comfort and concern.

Somehow this busy president found time to write a weekly newspaper column for his brother's *Greeley* (Colorado) *Sun* —a wide-ranging comment on politics, labor, woman suffrage, the silver question, the Chicago World's Fair, and the evils of college hazing. At home he put an end to the perilous ritual of painting the Old Main tower; no more freshmen would hang aloft at midnight with a dripping pot and paint brush.

In these years the West came to Oxford on the lecture platform. Alumnus Robert B. Stanton spoke from his own strenuous experience on "The Canyons of the Colorado." Elizabeth Bacon Custer talked of her life on the plains with her dashing husband before the fateful Battle of the Little Big Horn. Joaquin Miller in fringed pants and a beaded jacket read and lectured from the chapel platform, declaring "There is more poetry in the rush of a single railroad train across this continent than in all the gory story of burning Troy." The "Poet of the Sierras" had a special interest for the

Miami audience; he was born just a few miles from Oxford
in a covered wagon headed west, and some twenty-five years
later in Idaho he was married to a girl who had grown up
in Oxford.

Even in quiet Oxford entertainment was growing. James
Whitcomb Riley, William Dean Howells, James Lane Allen,
George Washington Cable all came to the village in the nineties. A Wild West show with Texas steers and bucking horses
raised dust in the public square on the Fourth of July in
1896. On another day a crowd of Miami students went to
the Hamilton fair grounds to see Buffalo Bill's great spectacle
of the vanishing West. College dramatics began with *The
Doctor of Alcantara* staged in the Oxford Opera House and
As You Like It on the banks of the Tallawanda. In the latter
appeared Elizabeth Hamilton and Sarah Norris of Oxford
College, who would be dean and assistant dean of Miami
women in the years ahead. In a winter week of 1897, with
the "Cinematascope" showing at the town hall, Oxford was
introduced to motion pictures.

As the end of the century approached, Dr. Thompson proposed a celebration. In 1899 it would be seventy-five years
since the opening of the college. As part of a Diamond Anniversary observance, Thompson urged construction of the
long-proposed east wing of the Main Building and the
modernization of the entire building. Plans called for a new
heating plant, a system of electric lighting, a second tower
to match the one erected in 1869 and the lengthening by
thirty feet of the west wing. This extension permitted enlargement of classrooms and the administrative offices on
the main floor and the adding of a balcony to the chapel on
the floor above.

In this anniversary year the old dorms were provided with
steam heat, electric light and modern bathrooms. Out came
the old lamps and lanterns, the battered stoves and rusty
stove-pipe. The last crumbs of sawdust were swept up in
the dented hallways and all at once a student's cooking pot,

his hatchet, ax and cross-cut saw were obsolete. After three-quarters of a century the old rugged dormitory life was over.

Now there was a faculty of fifteen, twice the size of Bishop's faculty; there were two janitors and a librarian, W. J. McSurely, and a campus of five buildings—for a college considerably smaller than Miami in its peak years half a century before. But the world had changed, and in education as elsewhere the luxuries of one generation became necessities in the next. At the end of the century a college required laboratories, reading rooms, assembly rooms, gymnasium and athletic grounds—as in another half-century it would need social centers, an auditorium, a natatorium, a theater, projecting rooms, listening rooms, galleries and museums.

The anniversary year, with workmen swarming over the Main Building and President Thompson advertising the celebration to be held in June, was a year to remember. That summer Old Egypt stood dark and lifeless amid the waving bluegrass with a mossy water trough beside it for the use of birds, squirrels and the stray summer cattle. A broken window admitted jays, squirrels and chipmunks; nuts and acorns were hidden in the old laboratory shelves. Somehow on a summer night in 1898 the old ruin burned. The walls crumbled and fell, the charred bricks were hauled away, and there was nothing left of Old Miami's science building except the weathered pier stone where Professor Scott had set up his telescope in years long past.

Early in September workmen began excavation for the new wing of the Main Building. A new professor of French appeared, young Dr. Edgar Ewing Brandon, ready to teach students to think in French as well as English; soon he would have them reading French newspapers and magazines in the library. Students arrived for the term, moving into modernized lodgings in the old halls. Then in the middle of the month, on the opening day of college, Professor Snyder was found dead in his Brice Hall laboratory, with a vial of fresh-mixed poison beside him.

A nondescript small man with a bushy, dark mustache and his wife fluttering like a bedraggled, exotic moth beside him, Henry Snyder had been a campus character for fourteen years. His wife, Minnie, affected gypsy clothes and sang soprano. They lived vexatiously in South Hall, where the rowdies once interrupted Minnie's singing by throwing a stove down the stairs. Professor Snyder was patient, friendly, industrious, always ready to speak on the wonders of science or his summer travels, and every student in the college either derided or admired him. Scores of lectures he had given, wearing a Prince Albert and striped waistcoat above his baggy "teaching" trousers. As his assistant, running the stereoptican or holding the apparatus for demonstrations of electrical phenomena, he had the help of an Oxford townsman, William Pugh. Pugh also played the guitar, providing musical accompaniment for Minnie's solos. The South Hall rowdies had a rhyme about those programs:

> Henry's goin' to lecture,
> Minnie's goin' to sing,
> Willie's goin' to play
> On the hi-lo-ding!

Some time after the town stopped buzzing over the melancholy end of humorless, busy, uncomplaining Professor Snyder, his wife was married to William Pugh. They went to live in Columbus.

To fill the vacancy in science President Thompson quickly brought to the campus Raymond M. Hughes, an honor graduate of 1893, who had done further study at the University of Chicago and the Massachusetts Institute of Technology. At this time Professor Langsdorf, with his silky side-whiskers, Prince Albert and top hat, returned from a year abroad. During Langsdorf's leave the Latin and Greek had been taught by A. H. Upham, valedictorian of the class of '97. Now "Billie" Upham was appointed principal of the preparatory department. President Thompson took pride in his selection of young teachers. With Hughes, Upham and Brandon, he now had two future Miami presidents and a vice-president in his small faculty.

In November the president and faculty of Western College entertained for Mrs. Calvin S. Brice, an alumna and benefactor; a month later came word of the sudden death of Senator Brice. His death cut off the career of an empire builder—he was projecting a railroad system in China when he succumbed to pneumonia—and a flow of benefaction to his college. He had been chosen to preside at the Diamond Anniversary alumni reunion in the following June.

On a winter night four students, returning from a trip to College Corner and, guilty of singing after ten o'clock, landed in the village jail. President Thompson paid out fifty-three dollars for their fines—later repaid by the Board of Trustees—and sent them quietly to their rooms.

On the first Saturday of May the Athletic Association held a field day. Professor Langsdorf, in silk hat and whiskers, leaned his Columbia bicycle against the fence and umpired a baseball game. Other members of the faculty kept time and score for the track and field events. The cheers of the spectators were answered by the screams of peacocks sunning themselves around the fountain of the Oxford Retreat —in happier years the Oxford Female College. Professor Johnson took on a series of students at tennis and then sat with them under a tree, telling of his student years in Germany and his visit to tranquil Königsberg where Immanuel Kant took his daily constitutional, eight times up and down the Philosopher's Walk, with his old servant, umbrella under arm, trudging along behind him. Fardy Devine, passing with a scythe on his shoulder, observed that tennis was a waste of time and the college might better give him the ground to raise cabbage and potatoes.

In June the scaffolding came down and a twin-towered Old Main was ready for the anniversary. Fifteen hundred flags decorated High Street and the campus was freshly

mowed and trimmed. For five days, beginning with a Baccalaureate service in the enlarged Bishop Chapel (newly
named for Professor Bishop) and ending with Commencement
under the trees, crowds filled the campus. The Buckeye State
Band played a medley of airs between the scheduled events
—class day exercises, oratorical contests, reunions of the Literary Halls with the veterans recounting memories of fierce
debates and glowing declamations, fraternity banquets and
receptions. The program included the Golden Jubilee of Phi
Delta Theta which had grown "from six at first" to ten thousand members of sixty-four chapters from Maine to California; its founders were memorialized on a granite tablet set
into the wall of North Hall. At the gala alumni meeting
General Ben Runkle read a formidable Miami poem, calling
the roll of the Old Miami faculty and paying rhymed tribute
to a long list of noted alumni. At the anniversary Commencement, John R. Simpson, president of the graduating class and
a later benefactor of the college, delivered "A Plea for Diplomacy," and two other seniors orated on American democracy.
The Honorable Whitelaw Reid, recently a member of the
commission to negotiate peace with Spain, spoke of "Our
New Duties"—measuring America's new stature and responsibility in world affairs. After a reception in the new library
room of Old Main, visitors streamed up High Street to the
public square. A band concert, a display of fireworks, and
the celebration was over. In the fervor of the anniversary,
some talked about a Miami enrollment of two hundred in the
twentieth century.

Two weeks later with Oxford settling into its summer
somnolence, President Thompson resigned. He had accepted
the presidency of The Ohio State University.

That fall the Reverend David Stanton Tappan, honor graduate of the class of 1864, moved into the president's office
and settled his wife and eight children in a house on High
Street across from the "slanting path." A short, square man
with level eyes and a determined mouth, Dr. Tappan had

no innovations to propose. During his first year he advertised the college in forty-four neighboring newspapers; in the following term the enrollment was increased by four. One of the added students was his daughter Julia, who met her future in Dr. Langsdorf's Latin class. She was married to Professor Langsdorf in the summer of 1900. A year and a half later they went to Hiroshima, a Japanese city that would come to the world's attention forty-four years later, where Langsdorf served as missionary and religious editor.

During the quiet and brief regime of President Tappan the fraternities flourished despite his indifference and the Literary Halls declined despite his encouragement. The football seasons brought a long string of defeats—which may have been the cause, or the effect, of Coach Greenleaf's habits. According to the record Greenleaf "was intoxicated so often that his duty was not satisfactorily performed." Though he had no enthusiasm for coeducation, President Tappan handed diplomas to the first women graduates—three members of the class of 1900.

That summer a water closet was installed in the west wing of the Main Building, not a hundred feet from the college well. A few months later came an epidemic, forty cases of typhoid fever in the college and a hundred cases among the townspeople who had prized the cold sweet water of the college well. The well was closed, and the South Hall became a hospital. Two students died and there were other deaths in the village. The youngest victim was Lucy Tappan, the president's favorite daughter. In April, 1902, Dr. Tappan resigned, to return to the Presbyterian ministry.

In Columbus, close to the State legislature, President Thompson directed the growth of The Ohio State University with its burgeoning graduate and professional schools. In the late winter of 1906, to assure that university's claim upon the state, he argued for the Lybarger Bill, which called for full development of Ohio State while supporting only the Normal Colleges at Miami and Ohio universities; the act would have reduced the two century-old colleges to teacher-training schools. There were immediate protests in both Oxford and Athens, and both universities rallied their supporters in Columbus. For two long weeks President Benton and his trustees fought for Miami's future.

The bill was defeated, and in its place the Legislature passed the Eagleson Bill, which defined the scope of the three institutions and provided for their support. It fixed "for all time" a policy directing Ohio State to develop fields of technical and professional training, while Miami and Ohio would remain essentially colleges without technical or graduate instruction beyond the work for the Master's degree. This act assured Miami of a future consistent with its past. On a glowing October day twenty-two years later, when the long procession filed into Benton Hall for the Upham inauguration, William Oxley Thompson was there, big, bald, and beaming as though he had never questioned Miami's future.

Chapter XIII

"THE SPIRIT OF THE INSTITUTION"

IN THE COOL SEPTEMBER MIDNIGHT voices carried across town and all the villagers knew that another college year was beginning. It was the nightshirt "walkaround," a noisy procession circling through the Western College campus and then heading up High Street. "Hail, hail, the gang's all here" —the chorus swelled as they crowded onto the lawn at Lewis Place. A light flickered in an upper window. Then President Benton stepped out on the railed porch roof, wearing a nightshirt and holding a candle. He made a short and comprehensive speech, commending the unity of the students, the traditions of Oxford, and "the spirit of the institution." With a cheer the parade moved on toward Oxford College.

The spirit of the institution had never been so high. President Guy Potter Benton had come in the summer of 1902, a short, stocky man with a big head, a ringing voice and vibrant energy. A native of Ohio, he had come to Miami by way of the West; for fifteen years he had been in school and college administration in Kansas and Iowa. From the day of his arrival in Oxford he believed in Miami's future and he made others believe in it. During nine years at Miami he never grew tired, doubtful or disheartened.

Dr. Benton liked ceremony; to the rural campus with hay-cocks under the trees he brought academic regalia and the formal academic procession. His inaugural, on September 18, 1902, also inaugurated the use of academic robes. Unfortunately it was a threatening day, with a fitful sky and gusts of leaves blowing across the speakers' platform. When the gowned and hooded faculty began the march from the campus gate, the band was silenced by a crash of thunder. A sudden downpour turned the procession into a rout. Visitors, alumni, faculty and students broke for the shelter of Old Main.

In the crowded chapel the ceremony went on—Dr. Hep-burn speaking for the faculty, President Thompson of Ohio State representing the Ohio colleges, and Governor Nash, his rheumatism aggravated by the weather, speaking with grace and feeling for the State of Ohio. Outside the rain diminished but the sky was darkening to evening. In a solemn twilight, Dr. Benton gave his address, earnest, confident, idealistic, on "Education for Manhood." He ended on a familiar note: "Miami University has a glorious history because it has insisted on quality rather than quantity. It must so continue."

But for many years Miami had needed more students than had come, and no president could resist the desire for numbers. In the previous June the college had closed with one hundred seventy-five students. When the September roll was counted, a few days after Benton's inaugural, there were two hundred seven, the largest enrollment since the Civil War. In chapel the jubilant new president promised the students a half holiday when the figure reached two hundred fifty, and a full holiday if it ever touched three hundred.

When the freshmen hung their flag from the tower and rang the college bell, the sophomores came storming. All afternoon the battle raged through the towers of Old Main. At 6:30 President Benton called the leaders out. He organized a final five-minute rush on the campus, and the ragged classes went to supper. That was the last year of the bruising, dangerous struggle on the steep stairways and disputed landings. The next fall a stocky frock-coated figure in the midst of a tattered melee refereed a pole-rush in the college yard. Benton considered himself the students' best friend. "The president knows his students. Professors may address them as Mr. or Miss, but the president knows and calls them by their given names." He wanted his home to be the refuge of every tired, homesick, or restless student; he would rise at any hour of the night to give counsel or sympathy to a student in need. "My boys" was his phrase for the student body.

One of Benton's innovations was a horse-drawn mower, which put an end to the campus haycocks. It was symbolical of the modernizing of the old college. Standard furniture was supplied for all the dormitory rooms. The *Miami Student* was assigned an office in Old Main, and the monthly paper was enlarged. A full-time music instructor organized the first musical ensembles and with the gifted Professor Loren Gates came the first organization of college players.

On a gray February day in 1905 the villagers voted saloons out of Oxford, ending a problem that had plagued every Miami president. That fall the first Junior Prom was held at the Oxford Retreat, the couples strolling past a flock of stately peacocks on the autumn grounds. In 1906 came the first full-time football coach, and in that year President Benton proposed developing a fraternity row on High Street, University lots to be leased to fraternities that would build stone or brick houses costing not less than $6,000. To Miami, as to other colleges, these years brought a proliferation of "activities," and President Woodrow Wilson of Princeton found it pertinent to declare: "The real purpose of a college is its academic program and not its sideshows." Academically Miami was broader and freer, if not more rigorous, than in years past. By 1910 more than half of the studies were elective.

With his sense of ceremony Dr. Benton began a tradition

at the Commencement of 1903. The academic procession, students leading, marched across the campus to the tent-covered speakers' stand. There it formed a double rank through which President Benton and the speaker, Bishop MacDowell of the Methodist Church, led the way to the platform, the entire procession reversing. One of the graduating seniors in that line of march was Robert Hamilton Bishop IV, great-great-grandson of the man who had presided at Miami's first Commencement.

Since the red cottage on the site of Brice Hall in President Bishop's early years, Miami had not had an official president's home. On their arrival in Oxford Dr. Benton, his wife and two daughters moved into the Deke house on Walnut Street, and there Benton was concerned about "the right social standards being established and maintained by your president." While the trustees considered building a president's mansion on the campus, an alumnus offered the use of Lewis Place.

The handsome spacious house on High Street had been built in 1838 by Romeo Lewis of Connecticut. Here his wife, Jane North Lewis, reared her nephew, Philip Moore, who was graduated from Miami in 1870. In 1903 Philip Moore, after a prosperous career as a mining engineer in Kentucky, Colorado and Montana, offered the use of Lewis Place as a president's residence. That fall the Bentons moved into the many-chimneyed house; there was a fireplace in each of its sixteen rooms. In 1929 the state bought Lewis Place as a permanent president's mansion.

During his first year Benton enlarged the faculty and the course of study. Departments of history and of economics and sociology were added. Physics and chemistry were made into separate departments, and plans were begun for enlarging Brice Hall. To the ranks of Hepburn, Brandon, Johnson, Williams, Hughes and Upham, President Benton added Professors Hayes, Hadsel, Culler, Powell, Handschin, Bradford, Gates, Fink, Burke, Davis, Todd, Young, Clark, and a name known abroad—Frederick William Stone. If not the most important member, "Cap" Stone was easily the most famous. For ten years, 1874-84, he had been "champion athlete of America." Holder of world's records in the high jump and the 100-yard dash, he had won contests all the way from England to Australia. A lean, bald, free-striding man with up-turned mustache, he ran a lively physical education department in Herron Hall. Every time he stepped outside, a string of village boys fell in behind him.

Benton had arrived at Miami at a propitious time: in the spring of 1902 the State Legislature passed the Sesse Bill, establishing normal colleges at Miami and Ohio universities. "The girls are coming," Dr. Benton announced in September. He was sanguine enough to expect fifty of them, and all at once seventy-eight girls were lugging their baggage from door to door in the village, begging for rooms. It was worse the next June, when Miami's first summer session opened. Two hundred and fifty summer students were expected; four hundred sixty-nine came, and Oxford's homes were overflowing. Benton tried to rent Oxford College as a dormitory but the Oxford College officials would not agree; that arrangement, however, was made two years later. Now the long drowsy Oxford summer, with grass going to seed on the campus and an occasional farm wagon stirring up the dust of High Street, was only a memory.

With a third of the students women, Miami needed a new residence hall. Dr. Benton proposed using one of the men's dormitories, but the trustees preferred to wait for state funds for a new building. Hepburn Hall was built in 1905 and Elizabeth Hamilton, a graduate of Oxford College and a teacher there, was appointed dean of women. Generations later, looking back to the first years in Hepburn Hall, Miss Hamilton recalled: "I didn't really know what a dean of women was supposed to be, or know, or do." But she filled the office with humor, dignity and distinction for forty years, while the women's enrollment grew to two thousand.

Hepburn Hall could not have been less appropriately named. Andrew Dousa Hepburn, staunch foe of coeducation, was nearing retirement, and the trustees, apparently with no sense of irony, chose his name, over Hepburn's "vehement protest," for the first women's building. He was still opposed to women in Miami, though he had grudgingly acknowledged them in his chapel prayer: ". . . Guide, direct and bless all these young men—and bless too these young women. Thou knowest, Lord, that thirty-five per cent of them are women." In ignorance or charity the girls hung a large crayon portrait of him in their main parlor. A handsome likeness of the robed and snowy-bearded patriarch, it dominated the reception room. But it is not recorded that Dr. Hepburn ever stepped inside the hall.

In June of 1905 the Commencement procession marched past Brice Hall, which was being enlarged to three times its former size, and paused at Hepburn Hall to dedicate the building. Then it moved on to the broad Commencement tent, on the site of Irvin Hall, where Secretary of War William Howard Taft gave an address on "The Duties of Citizenship." Among the straight-backed chairs on the platform a sturdy new settee from the Hepburn Hall parlor was provided for the speaker. Taft was the son-in-law of John W. Herron, president of the Board of Trustees.

Two years later when enrollment had passed seven hundred, a library and an auditorium were under construction. And that winter came the only serious fire in Miami's history. On a bright cold January afternoon in 1908 workmen on the new auditorium saw smoke pouring from the attic of Hepburn Hall, three hundred feet away. When the volunteer fire department arrived, the upper part of the building was aflame. There were no casualties, but that night a hundred homeless girls were on the town. Professor O. B. Finch and his wife took nine of them for the remainder of the year. By the next fall Hepburn Hall was rebuilt and reopened.

When Harvey C. Minnich, superintendent of schools at

Middletown, became dean of the Normal School in 1903, President Benton had an able and congenial administrative colleague. Together they gathered a strong Normal College faculty, including Anna E. Logan, Frances Gibson Richard, Professors Whitcomb, Davis and Heckert, and Alice Robinson. Dr. B. M. Davis, a pioneer teacher of agriculture, started a forestry nursery on the site of Withrow Court. Miss Robinson, gifted, charming and twenty-two, made art so exciting that no room was large enough for her classes. Together Benton and Minnich sought an integration of the Normal School and the College, with only the "methods" courses being offered separately.

With men and women together in most classrooms, some resentment and rivalry developed. There were the Old Miami traditions to remember and the new courses to jeer. A snide letter in the *Miami Student* stated that a certain Miami man was about to change his course and "take up music, nature study and basket weaving in the normals." Though a unified institution was desired, it was clear that the Normal School would lack identity and independence until it had a building of its own and some measure of separation from the College.

In 1902 a landscape architect had been asked to choose a site for a future Normal School building. Benton's own suggestion was that it be "across the road"—a location that later became the Fraternity Row on High Street. But when in 1908 the Legislature voted $45,000 for a building, it was placed on the main campus, in the dense locust grove at the southwest corner of the original "University Square." The locust thicket was cleared, the land drained, and the south wing of McGuffey Hall went up along Spring Street. It was opened in 1910.

For seven years the Normal School had made unsatisfactory use of the Oxford public school for practice teaching, with some added use of the Miami preparatory department. The preparatory department was closed in 1910; by then high schools were preparing students for college. In that year the "William McGuffey School" was opened in McGuffey Hall as a University practice school.

At the beginning of the twentieth century, thanks to the offices of a Miami man, the name Andrew Carnegie meant libraries. Prompted by John Shaw Billings, director of the New York Public Library, Carnegie offered to build a public library for any English-speaking community in the world that would contribute, for its maintenance, ten per cent of the building's cost. In twenty years this offer produced 2811 libraries, for which Carnegie paid a total of $60,000,000. In 1906 Andrew Carnegie offered $40,000 to build a Miami University library, provided that sum was matched from other sources. The amount was raised, after some strenuous alumni efforts and a pressuring of the faculty, and the building was completed in time for the Centennial celebration of 1909. An imposing if not very practical building, it contained stacks, reading rooms, reference rooms, and on the heavy balcony under the great dome six useful seminar rooms—one of them became a McGuffey Museum. It was named Alumni Library, though a more interesting and appropriate name would have been that of John Shaw Billings. A member of the Class of 1857, Billings remembered that "the Miami library was open for the drawing of books every Saturday, and as the allowance of two books would by no means last a week, I used to get other boys to let me draw books in their name, so that I usually took out as many as I could carry." Forty years after the dedication of the Alumni Library, the name of John Shaw Billings, who had been a distinguished surgeon before he turned librarian, was given to Miami's natatorium. In 1923 the Carnegie Corporation gave $50,000 to enlarge the library building.

First occupied in the winter of 1908 was the auditorium and administration building. The president, dean, and business manager climbed to offices on the second floor; the main floor provided a registrar's office, a Y.M.C.A. room and an office for the *Miami Student*. The *Recensio* staff was given the old president's office in the Main Building. The auditorium had a spacious stage where Professor Gates was soon producing fine performances of Shakespeare. Here the Miami Glee Club, organized in 1907, gave regular concerts. The room seated 1200 and was large enough, it was supposed, for all Miami's future.

Into the new building moved new officers. Hepburn, retired in 1908, had held three titles: head of the English department, dean of the College of Liberal Arts, and vice-president of the University. Now Professor Brandon became vice-president, Hughes became dean, and Upham headed the department of English.

As early as 1906 President Benton anticipated the approach of Miami's hundredth anniversary in 1909. As a reminder of the past the college published in 1907 a facsimile reproduction of the first University catalogue of 1826. Professor Upham, chairman of the Centennial, made plans for a gathering of educators and alumni for the Commencement week of 1909. Meanwhile the rotund Bert S. Bartlow of the Class of 1893, perennial bachelor and Deke, gathered data for an *Alumni Catalogue* with biographical sketches of every trustee, teacher, graduate and student of Miami during its first hundred years.

In planning the program Professor Upham wanted his classmate Ridgely Torrence to contribute a Centennial Poem, but Torrence begged off.

New York City
July 18th, 1908

My dear Upham:

You are wise and you are kindly of heart and I love and cherish your personality but for once your goodness has overstepped your wisdom. I am not the man. To you and you only the laurels belong. I am remote, melancholy, slow. With all my real affection and admiration for Miami I could not for the life of me utter one strophe on this subject. I have no faculty for occasional verse. I never wrote such things in my life and I shouldn't know how to go about it. I could never get a sufficient head of steam. Then too I have gotten so far away from lyrical writing during the past year or two that I hardly know what it looks like. I have been so steadily devoted to playwriting. No I cannot do it although I am deeply grateful to you for the honor and the kindness of the offer.

But thou art the man, and if alma mater can't rise up in you in song then the poetry of earth has ceased. I wrote to Bartlow [Secretary of the Centennial], the silver-toothed orator of the Tallawanda, that my hand and my heart were for you in the cause, and from where he sitteth on the brazen floor of Olympus I know he will stretch forth his hand bearing the bays for your poll. Then sing and may the Nine play their splendors about your skull and lips until Aeolus himself enters The Retreat. And I expect to be present to listen.

It was good to hear from you but I should like to have a long talk. We will have much to tell each other the next time we meet. I want to hear your experience at the helm there with Heppy taking his grog in the cabin.

Please present my best wishes to the lady—

And believe me
Faithfully yours,
Torrence

So there was no Centennial Poem, but its absence could not have been missed in that third week of June, 1909.

The celebration began with a "Students' Night," the undergraduates parading with humorous and historic floats through the town and campus. The following days were filled with receptions, exercises, concerts and reunions; the senior class play, *Twelfth Night*, was a grateful respite from the rounds of speech-making. On Centennial Day twenty speakers filled the platform under the trees—including Governor Harmon of Ohio, five past presidents of Miami, and a dozen eminent educators. On the hot and cloudless Commencement morning Professor Brander Matthews of Columbia and the Reverend Lyman Abbott, editor of *The Outlook*, addressed the crowd, and incidentally the fifty-five members of the Class of 1909, the largest in Miami history.

In that graduating class were six future members of the Miami staff: W. S. Guiler, H. H. Beneke, C. S. Bunger, Vernon Lantis, and the Misses Florence Kerr and Nellie Finch, as well as a future bibliophile and benefactor of the Miami library, O. O. Fisher.

After the speeches were forgotten and the reunions but a memory, there remained three lasting souvenirs of the Centennial. The three thousand biographical sketches in Bartlow's Alumni Catalogue showed how Miami men and women had entered into the life of their times, Professor Upham's book on *Old Miami* looked back at the fading past, and President Benton's *The Real College* discussed the responsibilities of the small college in the twentieth century. The Upham book, happily illustrated by Alice Robinson, preserved for New Miami the lore and luster of the Miami that was gone. Better than a Centennial Poem, it was a wise, warm and charming narrative of the famous old college.

President Benton had established a plan for sabbatical leave for his faculty, and the first leave of absence was granted to him in 1909-10. With his family he spent the year in Europe. He returned to Miami for another year and then, in 1911, became president of the University of Vermont. His later career took him to Europe as head of the war-time Y.M.C.A. and educational director of the American Army of Occupation, and to the presidency of the University of the Philippines. In Manila his endless energy began to fail and he fell victim to an obscure Oriental disease. After a prolonged illness in the Minneapolis home of Professor and Mrs. Dwight Minnich (his older daughter had married the son of Dean Minnich of the Miami Normal College), he died in 1927. His funeral was held in the Miami auditorium, newly named Benton Hall, and he was buried in the University lot in the Oxford cemetery.

In the crowd at the graveside on that warm June day were many who remembered the vigorous young president of 1902 and the new vitality he brought to an old college. A few of them recalled his fortieth birthday. When the chapel bell rang, on the 26th of May, 1905, President Benton was detained by visitors in his office. Several minutes late, he rushed up the stairs and into the doorway. "Cap" Stone gave the signal. A burst of cheers greeted the president who strode, pleased and puzzled, to the platform. There a spokesman for the students presented him with an oil painting. Dr. Benton responded with a becoming speech and announced the chapel hymn. But Miss Logan asked him to sit down, and Professor Culler presented a cut-glass pitcher as a gift of the faculty. The president made a second response and again announced the hymn. But a procession of students came marching down the aisle carrying the old pulpit which had disappeared from the chapel, to the president's distress, a week before. Again Benton made an acceptance speech, after which he succeeded in announcing his favorite hymn, "A Charge to Keep I Have." There was no time left for the regular chapel sermon, but President Benton commended the spirit of the institution and declared a holiday.

Chapter XIV

A FULL-GROWN COLLEGE

COMMENCEMENT is always the same and always different. On the 15th of June, 1912, to the strains of band music under the trees the procession formed in front of the Auditorium (Benton Hall) and marched to the new women's residence. It paused there while the building was named Bishop Hall and dedicated with a brief address by the Honorable David Lewis Gaskill of Greenville. The march moved on to the Old Dorms which, once again remodeled, were formally rededicated and new names given to their separate sections. Old North Hall with two entrances became Johnson and Elliott, and the three entrances to South Hall were named McFarland, Stoddard, and Swing. The procession then swung back past Main Hall where the Bishop Chapel had been renamed the College Commons and was serving as a dining room for men; the balcony was furnished with pool tables for after-meal enjoyment. In the auditorium President R. M. Hughes presided at his first Commencement exercise. Among the graduates were Joseph Clokey, who later became a dean of the School of Fine Arts and a ranking composer, and Harold E. Neave who would have a business career with the Scripps-Howard Newspapers and long service as a Miami Trustee.

In the fall of 1911 Professor Hughes, just returned from a sabbatical which he had spent observing college administration in the United States and England, had declined to be made president but took the title "acting president" of the University. On assuming office he made two appointments that were to outlast his own tenure by many years: Wallace Pattison Roudebush was named secretary to the president and Marie Marshall was made executive clerk. New faculty appointments included H. C. Brill in chemistry and A. W. Craver in English.

It was two years before Hughes agreed to become Miami's thirteenth president. Then, at the Commencement of 1913, with characteristic candor and diffidence, he accepted the office "realizing my lack of wide experience, the small range of my learning, and my limited ability." Even as he spoke, a slender, smiling, straight-standing man with kindling eyes and a reassuring Ohio drawl, his ability shone through. He added, "I know that the successful work of this college does not depend on the president." But no one else hesitated to relate the success of Miami in the next fifteen years to the honesty, vigor and foresight of Raymond Mollyneaux Hughes. He once described a successful college president as a man of sufficient learning to direct a company of scholars and of enough worldliness to deal with legislative committees and boards of trustees and the lay public; he added, "If he can have innate dignity and a sense of justice, along with a personal vigor and warmth, he is ideal." Though he did not intend it as self-appraisal, he was describing himself.

When he was teaching chemistry, Professor Hughes had complained that he did not have ideas. The president's office changed that; for fifteen years he had a constant flow of ideas about the campus, the classrooms, the curriculum, about the university of the past, the present and the future. He introduced a system of intramural sports, an artist-in-residence, a rotating appointment of officer-of-the-day among the faculty. He increased scholarship aid and student employment.

"The poor boys at college are usually the most valuable members of the college community, and we want as many at Miami as we can get." The first land-conscious president of Miami, he foresaw new buildings and with the help of W. P. Roudebush he doubled the lands, adding Cook Field, the Oxford Retreat, and the new South Campus for women. On his first tour of alumni clubs in 1911 he spoke on "Miami: A Full-Grown College," but he foresaw an expanding future.

In September President Hughes came into Benton Hall trumpeting with hay fever and a new college term began. Each year brought changes and developments. In 1911 the *Alumni News Letter* began publication as a quarterly in the Miami Bulletin Series. In 1912 the Women's Student Government Association was established and the Library was enriched by the Samuel Fulton Covington Collection of Ohio Valley History. In 1913, $8,000 was allotted for a temporary chemistry building, a one-floor laboratory and classroom building just west of the present Hughes Hall. In 1914 came the first Alumni Homecoming, with a soccer game and a cross-country race preceding the football match with Denison; five hundred alumni watched the afternoon sports and gathered for a smoker in the evening. That year began a series of conferences on business administration, with John R. Simpson, '99, vice-president of William Filene's Sons in Boston, discussing the responsibilities of business enterprise. In 1915 McGuffey Hall was enlarged and the University Orchestra gave its first concert. In 1916 there was talk of paving High Street, but before any bricks were laid a dusty Commencement crowd filled the athletic stands to watch a Miami pageant, written by Professor Upham, depicting episodes from the life of Old Miami: the Bishop Bust, the Cremation of Logic, Chemistry in Old Egypt, the Snow Rebellion, Lottie Moon's Capture, the Burial of Joe Battle, the Story of Oxford College, the Advent of the Miami Girl. Then, even to remote and dreaming Oxford, came the war.

In the fall of 1917 a University battalion marched and

maneuvered over the campus and the faculty offered a series of war talks to public audiences, having tried them out in the college chapel. The football team compiled a season score of Miami 202, opponents 0. At the Homecoming an exhibition drill replaced the snake dance between halves of the game.

By the beginning of 1918 a Miami service flag showed men in virtually every training camp in the country and a number "Somewhere in France." Coach George Little, after his championship football season, had become a captain at Camp Sherman. Henry Beckett, '11, was editor of a service magazine at Camp Sheridan, and Ben Lucien Burman, ex-'17, was beginning a long writing career with contributions to a paper of the 24th Engineers. Guy Potter Benton was directing the Army Y.M.C.A. in Paris, and Colonel John R. Simpson, '99, was procuring French equipment for the Ordnance Department.

During the summer of 1918 the War Department established the Students' Army Training Corps in colleges enrolling more than a hundred men above eighteen years of age, and in September Miami was a different place. President Hughes had become a district director of the S.A.T.C., with offices in Columbus. Vice-president Brandon was in France as an officer in the *Foyer du Soldat*. In Oxford four hundred Miami men were roused by reveille at 6:15, marched to meals, classes, drill and study. With taps at 9:30 the campus was left to the owls, hooting in the autumn dark.

Four companies made up the Miami Corps. Company A was quartered in North Dorm, Company B in South, Company C in the houses on Fraternity Row, Company D in the other scattered fraternity houses. A. H. Upham, as acting vice-president, was in charge at Miami. He had a strenuous introduction to college administration.

Early in October the nation-wide epidemic of influenza struck the village. Within a few days half the students and a third of the faculty were ill. The Miami girls were sent home, except for a score who stayed as nurses' and kitchen aides, and Bishop Hall became a hospital. Four students died there, and three others died at home. In a few golden October weeks Miami passed through the most sudden, widespread and fatal epidemic of her history.

Meanwhile from the Schelde to the Moselle the allied armies were moving in the last great offensive of the war. When word of the Armistice reached Oxford on November 11th, the church and college bells rang and the Corps marched to a special chapel service. Three days before Christmas the four companies, lined up before the auditorium, were paid off and discharged. The next summer High Street was paved and a Memorial Gateway was built for the athletic field.

In 1915 had come word of the largest bequest in Miami's history. As a memorial to her brother, Dr. George C. Ogden of the Class of 1863, Laura Ogden Whaling of Cincinnati willed the University something over $400,000, of which sum $250,000 was to be used for construction of a men's residence hall and $10,000 to assist needy and deserving students. After eight years of litigation the bequest was reduced to $260,000, and in 1923 work on Ogden Hall began. It required the moving of Herron Gymnasium. The will had stipulated that the new building should stand west of Herron Hall, along High Street on the upper campus. A tentative location was fixed on the site of the men's tennis courts, directly across from Lewis Place. But it was decided that that part of the campus should be left in its natural state and Ogden Hall was then located on the site of Herron with that building being moved four hundred feet to the east.

To move Herron Hall cost $30,000, more than it had cost to build; it also cost a score of huge old forest trees. There were in Oxford many lovers of the wooded campus and the most determined of them was Jennie Brooks, the daughter of a retired headmaster of a Cincinnati school. High-spirited, outspoken, imperious in her somewhat fragile way, Miss

Brooks wrote stories and sketches for the leading magazines; some of them were collected in a volume *Under Oxford Trees*. She wandered through the woods in all seasons and knew every woodpecker's nest in the college trees. When workmen began devastation behind Herron Hall, Jennie Brooks protested. She took her stand at an oak trunk, defying the ax-men, until she was carried bodily away. She never forgave that violation, but happily her later years were lived in the old McFarland house at the end of Spring Street, across from the primeval woods of the lower campus.

When the land was cleared Herron Hall, jacked up and put on rollers, inched its huge way eastward. On its new location, somewhat remodeled, it served for ten more years as the University gymnasium before it was turned over to the Miami women.

The year 1923 saw Ogden Hall rising on the vacated site. It was a near neighbor to the old North Dorm but a far cry from that original Miami lodging. With lounges, assembly rooms, reading and recreation rooms it was a student center as well as a residence hall. The spacious main lounge, named for Charles H. Fisk, classmate of George Ogden in 1863 and legal adviser to Mrs. Whaling, became a gathering place for students, a meeting place for alumni, a friendly, dignified and comfortable room for conferences, recitals and chamber music.

Meanwhile Wells Hall, built partly by a bequest from William B. Wells of St. Louis, was rising on Spring Street. An addition doubling the size of the Library was provided by state funds plus $50,000 from the Carnegie Corporation. Its enlargement freed a former reading room for the quarters of the Scripps Foundation, where Professors Thompson and Whelpton were beginning their far-reaching work in population research. The University Hospital, built by alumni subscription to the Centennial Fund, was taking shape in a former cow-pasture east of the old McGuffey house. Beyond High Street a clatter of building came from a new residence for freshman men, the first unit of the present Swing Hall. Before these buildings were done, work began on the final section of McGuffey Hall, the first wing of the Industrial Arts Building (Gaskill Hall), and a new classroom building (Irvin Hall) on the site of the old women's tennis courts just east of the Library. And beside the slant walk Thobe's fountain, "designed, donated and built" by Harry S. Thobe, Oxford stone-mason and Miami's most rabid football fan, bubbled in the shade of the ancient elms.

Into Irvin Hall, named for a long-time trustee from Dayton who had headed the building committee, moved six departments of the college. Soon the new walls were softening with ivy and the rooms were gathering associations: the English classes of Professors Rea, Craver, Ross, Bachelor and their colleagues; the mathematics of W. E. Anderson and his staff; the political science of Howard White and ex-Congressman French of Idaho; the English history of Professors Robinson and McNiff and the American history of Smith and Joyner. In sunny laboratories in the south wing Professors Evans and Stanfield unfolded the green world of botany, Professor Stark developed a department of bacteriology, and R. L. Edwards began turning out his long line of able physicists.

Across the quadrangle the old Main Building had become a hall of languages, with Professor Clark humorously and learnedly expounding Greek and Hadsel Latin, Handschin and Breitenbucher conducting German classes, Brandon and Irvin teaching French, Jones, Barr and Russell Spanish. The English tongue held on in the lower floor where D. S. Robinson, Patten and Van Tassell were teaching philosophy and psychology; Bain and Cottrell stirred up moot questions in sociology; Wickenden attracted students to religion; and Professor Gates with Adelia Cone, soon to be aided by their young colleagues Abegglen and Williams, directed speech and dramatics. Up on the third floor in the old Literary Halls Professors Hodgin and Carter presided over classes sketching plaster casts of the Discus Thrower and Lorenzo de Medici.

With the purchase of the Oxford Retreat and its sixty-nine acres of dense and open woodland, the Miami campus was extended to the Tallawanda. First suggestions for the new use of the old towered building were a school of fine arts, a school of business, a music department, a residence for women. But when it was reopened in 1927, named for Judge Elam Fisher of the Class of 1870, the old hall, once Oxford Female College, rang with the voices of freshman men. Its first faculty proctors were Bergen Evans and J. M. Bachelor.

In 1923, opening the 100th year of college instruction, President Hughes spoke of Miami's growth as its hardest handicap. He had just returned from a visit to the English universities and he made a comparison: "Merton College at Oxford enrolled one hundred twenty students in 1880 and now enrolls one hundred thirty-two, a growth of twelve students in forty years. When we contrast our growth from thirty-eight in 1885 to 1474 now, we can realize how much of our energy has gone toward problems of expansion." Miami was growing beyond closeness and unity. The auditorium would not seat the student body, and for 1923 President Hughes announced a rotating chapel requirement instead of the daily gathering of all. But he assured the continuance of small classes, he urged personal acquaintance of the faculty with students, and he proposed dividing the colleges into smaller units which could develop their own identity.

Finally he outlined a program for the year, for the decade, and for the century. Enrollment for 1923 was 1500; by the end of the decade he foresaw 2500 and by the year 2023 he envisioned 5000 students at Miami. (The enrollment passed 5000 in less than thirty years.) His aims for the decade included an increase in the proportion of men, an increase in the percentage of men preparing to teach, the developing of a housing plan for the faculty, and the increase of college land to at least three hundred acres. His program for the cen-

tury called for a retaining, at all costs, of personal relationship between students and faculty, ample provision for very
able students, and the developing of the Tallawanda for
water sports. The first objective on his list was unchanged
for the year, the decade, and the century. "Emphasize spiritual values over material things."

That Centennial year was full of activity—new buildings,
new student organizations, an enlarged faculty. But a year
later President Hughes, bugling with his September hay
fever, was still thinking of the real objective. He observed
that in the fourteen years since 1911 Miami had tripled in
size, but he asked a question: "Has the institution grown
nobler and finer and more influential for good?" Looking
back to his own memory of the Miami of 1890, which was
little changed from the college fifty years before, he saw
that colleges in the twentieth century are much more plastic
than in the past; their spirit and character can change very
quickly. For Miami he was concerned that the character of
the older college should be preserved in the new.

Chapter XV

ARTIST-IN-RESIDENCE

"By the gracious conditions of this fellowship, the first of its kind in America, it was decided that I should simply continue my own work as a poet and dramatist, informally in touch with the life of the university, where a studio has been built for me in a quiet grove of the campus."

—Percy MacKaye

O NE OF THE NEWEST FASHIONS in American colleges is to have a working artist on location. Poets, novelists, painters, sculptors, composers—they are a new kind of academic man. The colleagues of chemists, anthropologists, historians and teachers of freshman English, they have no textbook and no classroom. Yet they belong to the academic program, not the sideshows, of the campus. If it is worthwhile for a university to study artistic work it must also be worthwhile to support the artists who create it. There are now scores of artists-in-residence in American universities. The idea began in Oxford almost fifty years ago.

In November 1920, at the annual meeting of the National Association of State Universities in Washington, President R. M. Hughes of Miami University was assigned an indefinite topic: "The Most Important University Problem." Always a brief man, he spoke for four minutes on a problem which had plagued none of his presidential colleagues. "It may not be the most urgent problem from the university standpoint," he granted, "but tremendously urgent from the point of view of the country." He proposed that the universities become the patrons of creative artists.

The reasons were ready: At the close of World War I the United States had entered an age of prosperity and power; now, if ever, should come a golden age of art. Writers, painters, composers were not wanting, but patronage was. "There is no one that is in the main more poorly paid than the creative artist." In the past the great artists have been under the patronage of the nobility, or of the rich, or occasionally of the state. In America there is no institution so fitted to be the patron of art as the colleges and universities. And—the gift is to the giver—"nothing would do more to leaven the increasing materialism of the American university than to have a great creative artist working on the campus."

A definite man—he had originally been a chemist—President Hughes then listed some artists who would grace any college in the land. Among the poets: Witter Bynner, Bliss Carman, Robert Frost, Vachel Lindsay, Edwin Arlington Robinson, Percy MacKaye, Sara Teasdale. Among the painters: Frank Benson, Cecelia Beaux, Paul Daugherty, Robert Henri, Joseph Pennell, Abbot Thayer. Among the musicians: Arthur Farwell, Ruben Goldmark, Edgar Stillman-Kelley, Charles Martin Loeffler. Among the sculptors: George Grey Bernard, Frederic MacMonnies, Paul Manship, Lorado Taft. Two of these artists, he said—Edgar Stillman-Kelley and Percy MacKaye—already held fellowships at the Western College and Miami University respectively. He might have added that the two fellows were neighbors in the village of Oxford, Ohio.

There was a final word, in those four minutes, about the duties attaching to the fellowship. It was not a professorship;

it involved no academic assignment. The artist's sole obligation was to work in his own way in his chosen field. President
Hughes thought there were between fifty and a hundred colleges in America that could support a working artist.

The first response was in the press—not only in educational
journals but in mass magazines and daily newspapers. "A
most enlightened business," Walter Lippman called it. *Col-
lier's* editorialized "A New Hope for Artists." Said the New
York *Globe:* "Our material wealth and material aims have
brought us to a climax of indecision ard moral futility. It
would be no more than fair if we should endow a few chairs
of creative writing with a little of the wealth which burdens
us, in the hope of finding leaders to deliver us from the sun-
baked wilderness of pure commercialism." And the *Christian
Science Monitor:* "For a bold step forward of the progressive
ideal . . . keep an eye on the little town of Oxford, Ohio."

In that little town, across a meadow from each other, lived
the first two artists-in-residence. They were close friends
in Oxford, and before. In fact young Stillman-Kelley's first
New York commission, in 1887, had come from Steele Mac-
Kaye, Percy's father—the composing of an overture and in-
terludes for *Paul Kauvar,* MacKaye's drama of the French
Revolution which contained pointed parallels with the recent
Haymarket riots in Chicago. The Percy MacKayes and the
Stillman-Kelleys met later in London, at the first European
performance of MacKaye's *Jeanne D'Arc,* and still later in
Berlin where Stillman-Kelley was composing and teaching.

In 1910 President Guy Potter Benton, in Berlin on sabbatical leave from Miami University, became acquainted
with the Stillman-Kelleys. After eight years abroad Edgar
Stillman-Kelley had thought of returning to America; Berlin
was too gay and too expensive for a composer with his big
work yet to do. President Benton wanted to invite him to
Miami where he could work in quiet and security, but before
his arrangements were made a cable came to Jessie Stillman-
Kelley saying that Western College, in the same Ohio village,

needed a piano teacher. Six months later she was teaching at Western College, and in an empty farmhouse on the edge of Oxford her husband was beginning work on his *New England Symphony*. She soon won him an artist's fellowship, and President Boyd of Western College built them a cottage in the wooded campus. There in his roomy studio Edgar Stillman-Kelley composed his pre-eminent work, the musical miracle play *Pilgrim's Progress*.

In 1919 in the intermission of a New York performance of *Pilgrim's Progress*, Percy MacKaye appeared at the Stillman-Kelley's box. "This is a stupendous work," said MacKaye, "Where did you find time and quiet to think it all out?" When Stillman-Kelley explained his connections with Western College, MacKaye asked, "Would there be a place for me?"

Among visitors to the Stillman-Kelley studio in Oxford was Guy Potter Benton's successor, and it was natural that President Hughes should think of establishing an artist's fellowship at Miami. When he asked where he might find the right artist, the Stillman-Kelleys had the answer. Soon Percy MacKaye and his family arrived in Oxford.

A house was ready for them, on the site of present Hamilton Hall, but MacKaye looked doubtfully at an airless work room on the balcony of the Library, with a row of windows just under the high ceiling. What he wanted was a low roof and a fireplace. Three months later he moved into a studio cabin—the students called it "the poet's shack"—in the deep woods of the lower campus. That winter at a plank table beside the broad fireplace he began writing a long narrative poem.

> Inland among the lonely cedar dells
> Of old Cape Ann, near Gloucester by the sea,
> Still live the dead in homes that used to be.

When *Dogtown Common* was finished in March 1921, MacKaye read it to a group in the Stillman-Kelley studio.

He had a cold that evening. Coming in out of the raw night
he looked both drawn and swollen. When he took off his coat
there was a hot water bottle, slung around his neck. But in
the swing of his reading—

> There lie the lonely commons of the dead—
> The houseless homes of Dogtown. Still their souls
> Tenant the black doorsteps and the cellar holes. . . .

he forgot his distress. Warmed by his own voice he threw off
the hot water bottle and gave himself to the spectral tale of
witchcraft in colonial New England. A few nights later he
read the poem to an audience of students and faculty in
Benton Hall. He was a slender, intense and lonely figure on
the wide platform, a hand darting up to push back his loose
shock of hair, his voice rising and falling like the sea-surge
on Cape Ann.

That spring MacKaye wrote an article on "University Fellowships in Creative Art," published in *The Forum*. "Secluded in the quiet of a great grove, my studio . . . has
already afforded opportunity for a kind of uninterrupted
thought and creative experiment. . . . And it has also provided
occasion for a kind of informal interchange of ideas and
friendship with both faculty and students."

Here Percy MacKaye gave himself the benefit of a doubt.
A producing poet he was—three books during his three years
at Miami—but he was not a magnet to whom students and
faculty were drawn. A shy and aloof man, not easily ap-
proachable, he kept his colleagues at a distance. His first
studio open house brought on a headache, his wife pressing
cold cloths to his brow while the students sat stiff and still
in the firelight. Once a week an English class came through
the woods, guided by the yellow lamplight in his window.
They found the poet distantly friendly, with a basket of red
apples on the table. While they munched apples and watched
the fire, he read some stanzas from "The Rime of the Ancient
Mariner." Some nights his daughter Arvia helped to bridge

the gap, passing hot roasted chestnuts between the students' halting questions on contemporary poetry.

No doubt MacKaye sighed when the weekly visit ended. He poked up the fire, laid out his books and papers, and happily lost himself in *This Fine Pretty World,* a folk play of the mountain people in the remote hollows of Kentucky. Long after midnight his lantern groped out of the forest path, his shadow scissoring across the college yard. Beyond the fields he saw a light burning in Stillman-Kelley's studio.

If not a lively exchange with the community, there was the example of a man at work in his own way, in the urgency of his imagination. For the academy the artist has a touch of mystery and power. Crossing the quiet campus, passing to the library or the faculty club, he is not bounded there. He belongs also to the arena—the symphony halls, the galleries, the literary supplements. He knows a world beyond the ivy walls.

Occasionally MacKaye left the campus for a lecture trip or a visit to his publishers. During his first Ohio winter he met Robert Frost in New York. Frost: "Percy, where are you living now?" MacKaye: "I'm at a college. In Ohio." Frost: "What are you doing there?" MacKaye: "Just living, writing. Robert, you ought to get a college to support you." Frost: "How can I get one?" MacKaye: "I'll talk to President Hughes. He'll have an idea." A few months later Robert Frost became poet-in-residence at the University of Michigan.

Meanwhile Frost had written to MacKaye in Oxford: "The arts seem to have to depend on favor more or less. In the old days it was the favor of kings and courts. In our day far better your solution, that it should be on the colleges, if the colleges could be brought to see their responsibility in the matter. We are sure to be great in the world for power and wealth. . . . But someone who has time will have to take thought that we shall be remembered five thousand years from now for more than success in war and trade. Someone will have to feel that it would be the ultimate shame if we

were to pass like Carthage (great in war and trade) and leave
no trace in the spirit."

In Oxford Percy MacKaye found one friend from past
years in New York. Ridgely Torrence had been persuaded
to leave the staff of *Cosmopolitan* magazine for a stint of
teaching at Miami; in New York he had lived in William
Vaughan Moody's apartment, near Washington Square,
which had once, also, been the home of the MacKayes. Now
in the Torrences' second-floor rooms on Campus Avenue the
two families met again. One winter afternoon Torrence read
the poem he had written years earlier for wide-eyed Arvia
MacKaye, now a Miami student.

> Arvia, east of the morning,
> Before the daylight grayed,
> I heard a night-song's warning:
> "This bubble-world shall fade." . . .

In his classroom up the creaking third-floor stairs in the old
main building Ridgely Torrence was miles away from his
students. But they remembered something grave and ardent
in his presence, and the long hair lightly trained across his
fine bald brow.

In 1921 Torrence went back to New York, becoming poetry
editor of the *New Republic*. Two years later the MacKayes
returned to New Hampshire, and the abandoned "poet's
shack" in the Miami woods was claimed by squirrels and field
mice. It was pulled down before 1941 when Ridgely Torrence came again to Miami, as fellow in creative literature.
In the University guest house, next door to his old friend
President Upham—alphabetical seating had placed them together in the college chapel forty-five years before—Torrence
worked on his biography of the Negro educator John Hope
and occasionally met groups of students. He had previously,
in 1938, been poet-in-residence at Antioch College. It was a
familiar appointment then.

Now the artist-in-residence has a definite place in American colleges, a place so definite that a faculty may seem incomplete without him. He contributes something precious to the college, as President Hughes saw fifty years ago, and in turn the college sustains him. It gives him a measure of security; it also gives him a community to belong to. Too many claims may be bondage for an artist, but a few claims are vital. Robert Frost has made one poet say to another:

> Don't join too many gangs . Join few if any,
> Join the United States and join the family—
> But not much in between unless a college.

Chapter XVI

DEATH OF THE ELMS

WHEN PRESIDENT HUGHES RESIGNED in 1927 to become president of Iowa State College, it was almost inevitable that his successor would be Alfred H. Upham. President Upham had spent eighteen years at Miami, as undergraduate, principal of the Academy, professor of Greek and Latin, professor of English, director of the Centennial, secretary of the Alumni Association, university editor, and acting vice-president. He had written the *Alma Mater* and the nostalgic story of *Old Miami*. He knew the university, past and present, as though it were his own life. Apart from graduate study at Harvard and Columbia he had acquired experience in the East and West, as a professor of English at the Utah Agricultural College and at Bryn Mawr. He returned to Miami after seven years of accomplishment as president of the University of Idaho.

"Upham weather" was a phrase coined at Idaho for the charmed weather that came with public exercises during his years there. It was Upham weather in Oxford when he was inaugurated on Homecoming Day 1928, a blue and golden day with the long procession moving across the leaf-strewn campus. His inaugural address was not about college administration or the complex world of modern man; it was an essay on "The Art of Teaching." President Upham was at heart a teacher and a scholar. A naturally literary man, reserved and reflective, he had developed other capacities, political and administrative; he could deal with alumni, trustees and law-makers. But he never forgot that the real business of college was in the study and the classroom. He was a graceful writer, a composed and charming speaker, with personal warmth partly hidden by his formality.

The Miami he presided over was a very different institution from the little college he was half-homesick for, and he tried in many ways to make the two the same. He had a conception of Miami as a growing, vigorous, expanding university enriched and integrated by its memories of a simple, mellow college in an unworldly setting. Throughout his tenure he saw the institution grow more diverse and worldly, but he still held up before it the values of the small college that he cherished.

In 1929 he established the Adviser System, bringing all students into a personal relationship with the faculty. Especially valuable for freshmen, this plan placed resident advisers in all the men's and women's halls. The advisers were also teachers, with a modified classroom schedule. They could offer both personal and academic counsel, and could hope that it would be heeded. Here was an endeavor to meet the need, each year more pressing, that had led both Presidents Hughes and Benton to wish for a Professor of Individual Attention.

Through years of growth and increasing diversification President Upham tried to keep the college unified, homogeneous, and personal. He retained a semblance of the traditional chapel exercise, requiring a rotating attendance at weekly assemblies where the university was drawn together. He held out for the small, informal classes of the past. Meanwhile he developed the new schools of Business Administration and Fine Arts. The School of Business Administration was a natural outgrowth of the business courses that had been introduced into the Liberal Arts College in 1923. The School was formally established in 1928 under Dean Harrison C. Dale, newly-arrived from the University of Idaho. To its original faculty, including Professors Todd, Shearman, Beneke, Dennison, and Glos, would soon be added a sequence of vigorous young instructors; this faculty has tended to be younger than the other divisional staffs. The School of Fine Arts was established in 1929 under Dean Theodore Kratt, another Upham colleague from his years at Idaho. Its first faculty, including Professors Hiestand, Hodgin, Carter, Mead, Foster and Miss Lyon, was soon augmented by other accomplished musicians, painters and architects. In the growing School of Education E. J. Ashbaugh was appointed to the dean's office in 1929.

In President Upham's first year the historic Oxford College for Women was merged with Miami, and the old college hall became a residence for freshman women. This was a merger already familiar in Miami families; President Upham himself had married Mary Collins McClintock, an Oxford College graduate. In honor of Caroline Scott, the daughter of the founder of Oxford College and the wife of Benjamin Harrison, the Daughters of the American Revolution gave $70,000 toward the remodeling of the building, which was officially called the Caroline Scott Harrison Memorial. But the official name did not take. For nearly a century the long-verandahed hall on College Avenue had been Oxford College, and when the Miami girls moved in, it was "Ox College" still.

In 1931 the University Gardens were laid out beyond the chain of ponds of the Fisher Hall campus, and a nature path led from the formal terraces through primeval woods along the Tallawanda. After half a mile of rustling shade and rustic bridges the path climbed into sunlight near the mounded old Lane tomb behind The Pines. It soon became a favorite walk for Sunday afternoon, but its full mystery and charm were reserved for a winter morning after a long snowfall when the virgin path and the heaped white bridges waited for the first soundless footprints. The college bell, ringing from the upper campus, came from another country.

In this same year, as a gift of John R. Simpson, '99, Miami acquired the Rogers cottage, next door to Lewis Place. A hundred years old, the house was full of local tradition. It had been the home of Professor Clement Moffatt, poet and classicist, and of Professor Joseph Francis James, collector of lichens, geodes and trilobites. For years after he returned from missionary labors in India it was the home of the Reverend William Rogers, one of whose granddaughters became the wife of President Hughes. In 1937, remodeled and entirely rebuilt within its seasoned walls, it became the Simpson Guest House, its doors open to artists, lecturers, and other official visitors to Miami.

In 1929 President Upham announced the development of a new fraternity square on Tallawanda Road across from the dense pine grove that bordered the Botanical Gardens. Soon four fraternities selected sites and began their building plans. Along Tallawanda Road, amid some ragged rows of shrubs and saplings that comprised the old "Forestry Experiment Station," builders staked out the lines of a new gymnasium. Construction began the next year, and in 1932, to the strains of *Pomp and Circumstance*, the first Commencement procession filed into Withrow Court. At the same time the new chemistry building, to be named Hughes Hall, was rising southeast of Stoddard Hall.

The new gymnasium had been long awaited, and by no one more impatiently than Harry S. Thobe. A brick-layer by trade and exhibitionist by nature, Thobe boasted that he had laid the first brick and the last in Herron Gym; he meant to do the same in Withrow Court. An aging, agile, irrepressible man, Thobe was conspicuous at all athletic events in his red-and-white pants, coat and shoes, with his red-and-white megaphone and umbrella, his hula dance and his string of fire-crackers. "I had a dream last night!"—he always dreamed Miami victories and was ready to predict the score. Freshmen found him the perfect theme subject, sophomores tolerated him, seniors jeered. Dean Brandon abominated him and even tried to chase him off the football field. Ralph McGinnis, alumni editor in the '30s, wrote some Thobe copy which deserves to be remembered: "Misled, misunderstood, goofy, or loyal, whatever he might be, Thobe loves Miami in his own peculiar way and has given a great deal of energy, some money, and the best years of his life unselfishly to her. His methods may have lacked dignity but never sincerity. . . . A half dozen times a year Thobe and Dean Brandon have put on an act which alone was worth the price of admission at football games. This act was a remarkable exhibition of dignified pursuit on the part of the good Dean and of naïve innocence on the part of Thobe. Mr. Brandon, fully conscious of the dignity his position demanded, and Thobe with no dignity at all but an unlimited zeal for the home team, curving around the track in front of the east stands was a sight few can forget. Both alike, Dean Brandon with his cigarette getting shorter and shorter and his neck getting redder and redder, and Thobe with his feet getting more and more out of control were oblivious to the wide variety of advice, encouragement and just plain abuse emanating from the delighted crowd."

President Upham was generally on the side of "Thob"—for some reason he gave the name one syllable instead of the customary two—and thought Oxford would be poorer and plainer without him. The president was pleased to greet all the distinctive villagers—"Whispering" Logan Peake, booming a greeting above the clop-clop and rattle-rattle of his horse cart; Old Forbes, thick as an oak trunk and Scotch as a briar, always ready to set down his wheelbarrow and philosophize about God, gardens and the virtue of boiled greens; lean, limping, tobacco-chewing Dad Wolfe, the campus watchman, eager to advise president, faculty or students on any subject; benign old Peter Bruner, once a slave, who in a silk hat and a former president's long-tailed coat, opened the door for every official reception. Dr. Upham valued all the old town characters and regretted their passing from the changing scene.

In the year of Miami's 125th anniversary, 1934, with the encouragement of President Upham and the combined efforts of the dramatics, musical and literary organizations, the Pageant of Miami was presented on Miami Field. Under a full moon, with floodlights playing across the field, hundreds of students acted out scenes in the University's past, and at the end all joined in singing *Old Miami, New Miami*.

President Upham prized all the University's traditions, but there was an emerging tradition in the 1930's which he deplored. For years the Miami women had held a May Day ceremony at twilight in front of Hepburn Hall—at which officers of the Women's Student Government Association were presented. At the climax of the affair they crowned the May Queen and twined their colors around the May Pole. In burlesque of this ritual the Miami men, on the last night of April, held their Crowning of the April King. It was a wholly native and spontaneous tradition, which expressed the restlessness in the spring night and recalled the years when Miami was a man's abode. Their travesty of the May Day began robustly, and within a few years it grew bawdy. It ended in a raucous parade up High Street, with rolls of toilet paper arching into the trees; some of those streamers defied the reach of the grounds department for days afterward. President Upham had the help of the elements in putting an end to this burlesque. For several successive springs, April ended in sodden weather, and both the men's and women's ceremonies were rained out. Then the Women's May Day was permanently moved indoors, and the men had nothing to travesty. So ended the ribald Crowning of the April King.

In 1931, amid the gathering economic depression, came a troubling occurrence which the courts and newspapers la-

beled the Jean West Case. Early in April Jean West, 19,
through her father in Portsmouth, filed suit in the Common
Pleas Court of Butler County to enjoin Miami University
from dropping her for scholastic failure. Miss West, a freshman in the School of Education, was dropped at the close
of the first semester. However, because she had shown some
ability in art, she was allowed to enroll for the second term
in a changed curriculum. Again, in April, she failed to make
the required grades and was again dropped from the college
rolls. Through her father she petitioned the University Senate
to set aside the action of the Academic Council. The Senate
upheld the action and Miss West was permanently dropped
at mid-term of the second semester. It was then that the suit
was filed in the Court of Common Pleas.

Hearing was held in Hamilton on April 20th. The judge
allowed attorneys for both sides eight days in which to file
briefs. Meanwhile Miss West was permitted to attend classes
as a spectator—an agreement reached in private conference
by the attorneys. On May 12th the judge ruled that according to the statute authorizing Miami University—"the benefits and advantages of the State University shall be open to all
the citizens within the State"—the institution had no right to
drop Jean West from its rolls. Attorneys for the University
filed an appeal.

By this time newspapers throughout the state and region
had the story. Editorials were divided, some asserting that
an orderly and aspiring student should be allowed to pursue
her studies although she could not pass them, others arguing
that college attendance was not a right but a privilege reserved for those who could meet required standards. At issue
was the principle of mass education in public institutions.

The court had declared that schools supported by the state
have a right to expel students for immorality, insubordina-
tion, or infractions of rules and regulations of conduct, but
not for failure to meet scholastic requirements. "Why should
not people who are mentally slow have the right to go to

school?" Until the Legislature makes legal provision for dropping students for scholastic failure, the decision concluded, the University cannot deprive a student of the right of attendance.

On December 1, 1931, the Circuit Court of Appeal in Cincinnati reversed the previous decision and affirmed the right of Miami University to drop a student for scholastic failure. President Upham, with a long-drawn sigh, summed up the position of the University: "Public education is not a privilege everyone may enjoy, but a special privilege for those who show an aptitude for intellectual pursuits." Miss West's father stated that he would carry the case to the Supreme Court.

Meanwhile in September, 1931, Miss West had entered Ohio University at Athens. That was the end of the Jean West Case, but some hard questions about higher education and lower intellectual abilities remained. Those questions would grow more urgent as the tide of students swelled in years to come.

Oxford was out-of-the-way but not out of reach of the depression. By 1932, with millions of Americans unemployed, prospects for college graduates grew dim, and it was believed that the "mature economy" of the nation could not make use of the current flow of college-trained youth. At the same time crowded conditions were reported in the state mental hospitals. In Columbus the House Finance Committee recommended abandoning one of the four Ohio normal schools (at Kent, Bowling Green, Ohio and Miami universities) and using its facilities for more important purposes. "With the saturation point in the teaching profession reached six years ago," stated an editorial in the Cincinnati *Times-Star*, "the committee says that one of the schools can well be converted to a hospital for the insane."

This blow never fell, but depression was a state of mind as well as a state of business and for five years its shadow lay across the colleges. What should trouble them was not the

flight of the dollar but, as Archibald MacLeish said, the flight
of the American idea. In those years college had its greatest
chance to shape the minds and aims of a new generation, to
press a search for the way to use nature's wealth and man's
science to make a just and enlightened society. Nothing less
than that was the task of the colleges in the twilit thirties.
Miami, always conservative, did not raise new banners of
political and economic change. But it introduced into old
courses some new search for an understanding of America's
problems, capacities and prospects.

Enrollment held steady in the early thirties, around 2200,
ten per cent of whom were subsidized by the federal government. The Federal Emergency Relief Act made funds available to two hundred twenty students for work at thirty cents
an hour, with a maximum payment of $15 a week. Thus the
faculty got some research and clerical assistance and the
depleted grounds force got student help in raking leaves,
shoveling snow, and mowing the new season's grass. This
work was assigned to students who could not otherwise meet
the minimum college expense of $400 a year. Miami had
always been an inexpensive college with many opportunities
for student employment. The program of FERA, later conducted by the National Youth Administration, fitted easily
into the Miami tradition. In 1934 with a state appropriation
of $450,000 Miami was educating one third more students on
one third less money than in 1928.

In the fall of 1934 a new federal policy ruled that subsidized students must not replace workers normally employed
at the college and that they must perform tasks not normally
performed. This rule took student help away from the
grounds force and the clerical staff, though it left a number
of faculty members with student research assistants. Other
socially useful tasks were found in welfare, health and recreational agencies in Oxford, Hamilton and Middletown. In
this year six hundred students applied for financial relief,
with assignments going to a quota of two hundred sixty-six,

twelve per cent of the University enrollment. During the year the federal government spent $4000 a month to keep these students in college.

In 1936 under a grant of federal funds from the Public Works Administration—the University paying fifty-five per cent of the cost—the historic South Hall was rebuilt. The century-old brick structure stood, but all the interior was new. Down came the old walls with bricked-up fireplaces and stove-pipe openings, out came the battered old stairs and hallways. The new building, still redolent of the past, was ready for use in the fall of 1937, and in that year a similar reconstruction began on North Hall. Newly built and joined by a terrace court, the halls were given new names— Stoddard and Elliott—from old associations. Both buildings had two fronts, one facing the library quadrangle and the other looking into the woods where a new quadrangle would develop.

By 1936, while federal construction was improving the campus, there were signs of a general economic recovery. Enrollment that fall jumped to 2600. Fourteen new members were added to the University staff; one of them, George F. Barron, would become a future dean of Fine Arts; another, F. Alton Wade, had just returned from exploring the Antarctic with Admiral Byrd. In this year The Pines was leased by the University, with purchase to follow, as a girl's dormitory. So ended the Oxford Retreat, a hospital for mental and emotional disorders, whose patients had been led on daily walks through the lower campus. Now The Pines, like Fisher Hall its predecessor, was filled with college songs and voices, and the Oxford Retreat sank back into memory.

At Commencement in 1936 the Alumni Association awarded the first Bishop Medals. They went to a country doctor, a Y.M.C.A. secretary, and a woman teacher of the deaf. So began a new tradition of University recognition for graduates who fulfilled in life the Miami motto *Prodesse Quam Conspice.*

Meanwhile Dean Howard Robinson of the College of
Liberal Arts had resigned, and William E. Alderman came
from Beloit College as his successor. Under the foresighted
direction of Dean Alderman the college would expand into
the College of Arts and Science, keeping pace with a changing culture while it retained its position as the academic core
of the University. In 1937, called to the presidency of the
University of Idaho, Dean Dale resigned from the School of
Business Administration, and Dean R. E. Glos took charge of
the most rapidly growing of Miami's divisions. Two years
later Joseph W. Clokey, Miami 1912, replaced Dean Kratt as
head of the School of Fine Arts. Already a noted composer,
Dean Clokey managed to carry on creative work along with
his administrative office.

On a mild moonlit evening in April, 1938, a spontaneous
gathering of students and faculty at Lewis Place welcomed
the Upham family home from a sabbatical trip around the
world. The next evening a faculty reception in Ogden Hall
repeated the welcome and a few nights later President Upham gave an informal report of his travels to a faculty club
meeting in the Ogden Assembly Room. He surprised and
delighted his colleagues by reading a series of rhymed impressions of Japan, India, Egypt, Italy and Spain, all mingling humor and shrewd observation. Along with a traveler's
impressions of storied lands—

"The pageant that is India is passing by today,
    With bullock-carts and camel-trains along the dusty way"

there were some somber notes of the approaching war—

"Here's an old road wending
        Over meadow and hill and glen;
        Whenever you listen you hear the sound,
        The tramp of marching men."

Published a year later, *Rhyming Round the World* was a
unique account of an educator's holiday.

In January, 1939, in a climate of growing rivalry and clashing interests between the six state-supported universities of Ohio, President Upham proposed the creation of an Inter-University Council to coordinate undertakings and avoid unwise duplication of effort and resources. The plan met immediate response. In this association the six universities soon found means of effective cooperation which strengthened them all. A few years later President Howard L. Bevis of Ohio State declared: "In the capacity of founder, of chairman, of counselor and guide, Dr. Upham left his mark upon the council. By the same token he left an enduring mark upon the development of higher education in Ohio."

Despite years of depression and then years of war, the Upham administration brought to Miami a balanced growth. In 1940 Symmes Hall for men and Hamilton Hall for women enlarged residence capacities and increased a need for new academic buildings, a need that would not be met until the construction of Upham Hall after the war was over. In 1940 the enrollment stood at 3500, and the effort toward military preparation brought the first aviation courses. Flight training was provided by the Queen City Flying Service in Middletown until the opening of the Miami airfield in 1943.

As war approached a somberness came to the campus—the death of the elms. It was slow at first, a few great trees dying majestically in the summer air. By 1943 it was an epidemic—*phloem necrosis*—against which all the efforts of Grounds Superintendent Conrad were helpless. That September returning students missed the leafy canopy over High Street and found fires flickering up the long hill in the dusk—oil drip fires burning the great stumps out. The snarl of the bandsaw was a daily campus sound; with crumple and crash the withered elms came down. In three years 1500 were removed. The largest, eighty-six inches across with one hundred forty-five rings, had been a sturdy tree when the first bricks were laid in the first college building.

When President Upham walked the campus at evening

with his black Scotty "Tammas," he had problems to ponder. The central one he had stated for himself and his faculty: "How may Miami University render the full measure of service in this emergency and still keep effective the values which have made it what Miami is?" By 1944 the University was conducting four wholly different programs: a V-5 program in Flight Training, a V-12 college for Naval cadets, a civilian university, a radio training school for enlisted Navy men and women—with a total of 3700 on the campus. To all of them, in uniform and out, he shared, in his quiet-spoken way, his ideals for the University.

Under new burdens and tensions the president did not lose his patience, humor and tolerance. But he did lose strength and health. At midnight on the 16th of February, 1945, he suffered a heart attack and was taken to the University Hospital. There, early in the morning of February 17th, Miami University's Charter Day, he died.

On that day he was scheduled to speak at the graduation exercise of the final class of WAVES who had been in radio training at Miami. His notes "Farewell to the Waves" were found on his desk. They were read at the graduation, and though the voice was not President Upham's, the kindliness, the glint of humor, the love of Miami, and the personal idealism were unmistakably his.

Less than two years ago the Navy band ushered you in— 100 of you.

You were curiosities to us then. All our fingers—and yours— were crossed. But we soon came to know you and appreciate you.

There is no "type" Wave: bounding main and tiny ripple, silent eddies and "loud sounding sea."

A cross-section of the better sort of American girl—what we like to think our civilian girls are.

I don't know what Miami has taught you. Maybe I'd better not inquire.

You have taught us—
> *Neatness and precision*
> *Courtesy—The man nobody knows*
> *Good spirits—"40 singing seamen"*
> *Loyalty to a great purpose.*

Miami is your Alma Mater now and she bids you "God speed."

Oxford is an old town, Miami an old college. But for nearly a century and a half they have cherished youth in their bosom and have bidden it venture forth to respond to a high calling.

Three weeks later in the McGuffey Auditorium the University Senate heard a memorial statement of the life and character of President Upham. It was a black winter night with the world at war and the room gray because of a power shortage. The memorial saw the change that one life had spanned. "He first came to the college in a horse and buggy; he lived to dedicate the Miami airport." But his colleagues remembered how he had thought of the unchanging things: the long search for wisdom, the old paths under the college trees, the old streets echoing with the footfalls of an endless procession of youth.

Chapter XVII

"ANCHORS AWEIGH!"

O N DECEMBER 5, 1941, the *Miami Student* ran a lead story
with a three-column headline: "Don Bestor's Orchestra
to Play for Hop Tonight." College life was in full swing, a successful football season had just ended, and a name band was
coming to play for the first class dance of the year. A pleasant
week end was beginning.

But the week end brought a somber day. On Sunday afternoon a startling word passed from person to person, from
house to house, from hall to hall. There was a touch of winter
in the air. Faculty members in their homes, students in their
halls stared out at the thin snow while radio voices described
the disaster that had struck Pearl Harbor.

On Monday December 8th, an extra edition of the *Student*
carried a black headline: "War Declared." There were no
references to the Sophomore Hop, to the football season just
ended or the basketball season beginning. The front page
was all war—President Roosevelt's address to the joint session
of Congress; a message to Miami students from Professor
French, former congressman from Idaho; and a word of
counsel from President Upham. A student poll predicted the
length of the war with Japan, estimates ranging from three

weeks to ten years. There was also a cartoon of a campus-dressed student—checked jacket, pegged trousers, saddle shoes—seeing himself in a mirror. The reflection showed a man in battle-dress—steel helmet, khaki field clothes, a rifle riding on his shoulder. Humorously, realistically, Miami saw what was coming.

The University administration and faculties went into action. A week later the *Student* announced a list of war emergency courses to be offered in the second semester. The offerings, including production management, personnel management, meteorology, navigation, map-making and reading, and signalling and communications, were designed to prepare students for service in war industries and the armed forces. President Upham declared: "College is not an escape from the responsibilities of patriotic citizens. . . . College is not an alternative to service; it is actually a preparation for better service."

With the swiftness of military events in Europe, Africa and Asia, and the many currents of speculation and opinion in the United States, there appeared in this quiet college town a need for discussion of the problems of a nation at war on two continents. Student forum groups met locally and went to neighboring communities to discuss means of defense, the conduct of the war, the changed role of America in the world.

Before the semester was over students began to enlist in the armed forces, the first of five thousand Miami men and women in uniform. At the end of the term two faculty members left the classroom for military service and one to enter war industry. They were the first of seventy staff members who eventually served in Europe, Africa and Asia, and of fifteen who assumed duties in government and industry. Meanwhile in Oxford the Student-Faculty Council sponsored an immediate financial drive for the Red Cross and a drive for the sale of War Savings Stamps and Bonds; the senior class voted to invest the proceeds of the Senior Ball in War

Savings Bonds to be added to the fund for a Memorial Union Building.

The first winter of the war, maps of the Pacific Islands were posted on bulletin boards and people became familiar with names like Tulagi and Guadalcanal. Fireside groups in residence halls and houses discussed: What and Who Shall Be Drafted? What Contribution Can a College Student Make to the War Program? Should Students Marry in the Face of War Conditions? How Can the Nations Solve the Problem of Economic Relations in the Post-War World? How Can Permanent Peace Be Organized in the Post-War World?

The War Emergency Courses were well supported by the student body. Faculty members teaching new courses on short notice were heartened by the enrollment of hundreds of students. Meanwhile a committee studied the entire University program in the light of the war effort of the nation. In the first week of May all students registered for war ration books, and Lt. G. L. Dosland arrived in Oxford to organize the Naval Training School (Radio) which Miami University had contracted to operate for the U.S. Navy

The first class of the Naval Training School marched to barracks in Fisher Hall on the last day of May. They were one hundred fifty-one men from forty-one states, having received their boot training at San Diego and Great Lakes. Soon the old Oxford Retreat laundry was fitted up as a code room for radio instruction, a mess hall was built on the west side of Fisher Hall, and sentry boxes guarded entrances to the Naval Reservation. That summer new classes of trainees moved in. They had a monotonous, concentrated course, going from code to typing and back to code again. On Wednesday nights they marched uptown to see a motion picture, and they roamed High Street "at liberty" after their Saturday noon parade on Cook Field. Oxford had become a Navy town.

In September, 1942, a second class seaman stationed at The Pines grinned and said: "The fleet has landed and the situation is well in hand." Returning college students found six hundred uniformed men quartered at The Pines and Fisher Hall. University officials waited uneasily for clashes between civilian students and Navy trainees, but the two groups decided to tolerate each other.

That fall a group of faculty men organized a Miami Volunteer Training Corps. Within two weeks four hundred fifty students were enrolled. They paid their own fees for equipment and materials and began a series of night-time meetings which included close-order drill, demonstrations of small arms, lectures on chemical warfare and military organization. At the same time University women were enlisted in first aid classes, in hospital training, drafting courses, and as hostesses at the local USO clubroom.

Students carried on War Bond drives, with weekly goals to meet. A War Stamp desk in the rotunda of the Library was a daily reminder of this effort. In a new war style at the Junior Prom women wore corsages of War Savings Stamps. In the women's halls physical fitness committees emphasized rounded diet, regular sleep, vigorous exercise.

In April of 1943 Oxford saw its first women in uniform when a company of WAVES alighted from a special train. Bystanders noticed that under their cocked Navy hats all the girls had red hair. Later came an explanation: the Navy command office had meant to send to Miami WAVES who already had a knowledge of stenography; but, according to the story, someone mistakenly pressed the IBM button for red hair instead of for typing. On arrival the red-haired company marched down Spring Street, past McGuffey Hall, and took up quarters in East Hall. There they found that the displaced college girls had left messages in the rooms: "Washed out by the WAVES." In June a second detachment of WAVES, with various-colored hair, took over West Hall.

The WAVES were a part of the Radio Training School, with their own equipment set up in the Reserve Book Room of the University library. Bare plank tables were wired with

transmitters and the da-dit sounded from eight in the morning till ten at night. The girls came in shifts, marching to
cadence, with classes alternating all day long. Sometimes
girls fainted at the long table, but they learned faster than
the men. They were all volunteers, averaging two years older
than the men, and they had had more previous education.
Later in the year a company of Navy nurses and a company
of women Marines were added to the women's enlisted corps
at Miami.

With weekly Naval reviews on Cook Field and Navy blue
swarming up High Street when liberty began, Navy slang
became a new language in this college town. "Scuttlebutt"
was as familiar in college halls as in Navy quarters; the washroom became the "head"; a lonesome person had the
"mokes"; and instead of "Hey, Joe. Time to get up. Calis-
thenics in fifteen minutes,"—the word was "Hey, Mac. The
windjammer's blowing his head off. Roll out and hit the
deck. Monkey drill in fifteen minutes."

In 1943 with two thousand Naval trainees and a large civilian Summer Session enrollment, Miami saw a busier summer than any in its history. Navy shows were produced in
Benton Hall, a Shore Patrol policed High Street, busses shut-
tled Navy classes to and from the swimming pool, platoons
marched on all the campus paths.

That summer there were weekly discussions of "Freedoms
We Are Fighting For." On humid nights faculty members sat
late over new manuals and textbooks: most of them had
undertaken new courses in the war-time curriculum. Classics
men were teaching mathematics, foreign language men were
teaching radio code, fine arts men were teaching meteorology.

By September, 1943, the civilian student body was largely
women, and the *Miami Student* began the year with a
woman business manager and a women's business staff as
well as a women's editorial staff. A new feature of the paper
was a column "Our Men in Service." Within two weeks it

took the brisker form "G.I. Flashes," a lively, readable column reporting activities of former students in training camps across the country and in theaters of war on three continents.

The Student War Activities Council (SWAC) undertook the organizing of social events for the men in uniform, the recruiting of USO hostesses, the leading of drives for Red Cross classes, blood donors, and war bond sales. One of its tedious and significant tasks was the mailing every week of the *Miami Student* to three thousand men and women in the armed forces. There were times when a letter might come back after being forwarded vainly from station to station, camp to camp, at home and abroad. It was a formidable task merely to keep service addresses up-to-date.

In an attempt to include the transient trainees in the college life, University affairs were kept open to all. On a crisp autumn evening in Benton Hall, Robert Frost lectured to ten solid rows of blue uniforms, with civilian students jamming the rest of the hall; the WAVES had marched in early. Throughout the summer "tennis court" dances on Saturday nights attracted both students and trainees. SWAC organized women's serenades for the sailors at Fisher Hall, an attention wryly appreciated by the men who had to be in quarters while the girls were at large. At the conclusion of each four-months training term the Radio classes were given a "Commencement." In dress blues they marched into Benton Hall, facing their officers and petty officers on the stage. Before receiving their ratings they were addressed by President Upham who wanted them to regard themselves Miami men, "to have the high traditions of Miami walking beside those of the Navy." After graduation the class marched to Fisher Hall. They packed their sea bags and said farewells. While the band played "Anchors Aweigh!" they marched past the familiar campus to the train. Soon they were at battle stations with the scattered fleets.

Autumn of 1943 saw the students dressed in checked shirts

(tails out) and blue jeans rolled to the knees. When some women members of the faculty questioned the decorum of that dress, the women students conducted a poll which supported the garb as an expression of the rough-and-ready spirit of a nation at war. Blue jeans, the girls insisted, were appropriate wear for classroom, campus, and dining hall.

By January, 1944, forty-five Miami men were dead from military action, and many more were wounded. In Oxford bandage-making groups worked at long tables, hearing radio news of war while their hands were busy rolling, trimming, packing pads of gauze for shipment to battle areas thousands of miles away. At the same time the College of Liberal Arts adopted a three-year pre-professional curriculum for nurses.

In the snowy winter of 1944 groups of Miami teachers set out for classrooms in Dayton. At midnight they returned, talking in low voices in the cold. They were the staff of a program of Engineering, Science and Management War Training Courses. Their teaching was being put into practice in the offices, laboratories and conference rooms of Dayton's wide-spreading war plants.

A tradition in the *Miami Student* had particular point in the spring of 1944. In recognition of the University Charter Day the paper had repeatedly published features of the life of the college in bygone years. The issue of March 24, 1944, given entirely to the theme "Old Miami—New Miami," found quaint practices in the University's past, and a photograph of the five *Student* editors of 1872-73 (three of them mustached) was in pointed contrast to the all-woman staff of 1944.

On the hot Sunday of May 28, 1944, was held the first combined Baccalaureate and Commencement ceremony, and the first Sunday Commencement, in Miami history. Scripture was read by Naval Chaplain Merlin Ditmer, Miami '40, on leave from the fleet. President Upham read a tribute to Miami men who had lost their lives in military service. The Commencement address was given by Carl J. Hambro, president of the Norwegian parliament, who was living in the United States and conducting a government in exile since his country's occupation by the German army.

The final contingent of WAVES had arrived in Oxford in the fall of 1944, and it was announced that the final class would be graduated from the Radio Training School in the coming February. This was the first sign of the turning tide, when college facilities would be turned back to civilian students. Meanwhile Miami girls came back from summer employment in factory, farm and camp. Immediately one hundred fourteen of them enrolled in bandage-making groups organized by the Student War Activities Council.

In September, 1944, the college year began with twenty-five medically discharged veterans enrolled in academic courses. They came to college, the first of a great number, from experience in Africa, Europe, and the islands of the Pacific. Most of them had spent months in military hospitals before being discharged to civilian life. In a guest editorial in the *Miami Student* one of them spoke for all: "It is a long way from bullets to books . . . a long way. The soldier in combat has seen how cheap human life can be. He knows how precious it is. . . . The returned student veteran believes in the future of America. He has had a part in shaping that future. He knows that his new role of student is not only the greatest of all privileges but is also an obligation born of the blood of the men he has known who have perished in battle."

During the winter of 1944-45, in an effort to understand the problems of adjustment to a peaceful economy at the war's end, a series of panel discussions was held in Benton Hall. Visiting specialists and local student and faculty representatives, sitting at a table together, grappled with some of the hard questions of the time—censorship, the rehabilitation of returned veterans, the problems of organizing the nations for world peace. By this time nearly ten thousand Navy men had been trained in Oxford, including six thousand radio technicians, and the Navy Department ranked the Miami training school as one of the top radio schools in the country. With this program on the campus civilian students were constantly aware of the war and of the fast-changing world. Oxford was less isolated in the 1940's than at any other time in its history.

In the spring of 1945 war-time travel restrictions led to the selection of Oxford as the "southern" training camp for two professional baseball clubs. In mid-March the Columbus Red Birds, under Manager Charlie Root, and the Rochester Red Wings, under Burleigh Grimes, arrived for a month of spring training. The two clubs were quartered on separate floors at The Pines. Every day they worked out on Miami Field, to the delight of all the village. On the twelfth of April at four o'clock, while they were in the midst of their final practice game, word came of a press report from Warm Springs, Georgia. President Roosevelt had died. The game was called. The players walked slowly to their locker rooms and the fans went home in silence.

That month the news from abroad brought a prospect of war's end in Europe. In high spirits the Miami students planned a Spring Day which would be enjoyed by its participants and beneficial to the college grounds. On a sunny April morning the college bell rang at seven-thirty. Hundreds of students, armed with rakes, spades and shovels, launched upon an all-campus clean-up, to make up for the lack of care in a time of shortage of man-power in the University's maintenance staff. All day students and faculty members worked, played baseball, tennis and tug-of-war, and ate picnic meals in the open air. The day ended with a carnival and dance in Withrow Court.

As the end of the war drew near and a United Nations Organization was under way in San Francisco, *Les Politiques* sponsored a mock conference on international organization. It was a colorful affair with costumes of many nations, an idealistic keynote address, and a crowded session of committee reports and proposals. The post-war world began to take shape and color in people's minds.

On May 8th Benton Hall was jammed with a convocation giving thanks for the end of the war in Europe, and it seemed that a few more months might bring the end of the war with Japan. That convocation was a brief and quiet service. From it students filed out under the big service flag symbolizing five thousand Miami men and women in uniform and one hundred fifty dead on the fields and seas of battle.

Chapter XVIII

ON THE G.I. BILL

O<small>N</small> J<small>UNE</small> 22, 1944, the federal Congress enacted Public Law No. 346, and on that day the Miami president's office mailed the monthly *Service Bulletin* to three thousand men and women scattered from Italy to Australia. Public Law 346 would bring some of them back to Miami, along with hundreds of other veterans who had never heard of the old slant walk, Thobe's Fountain or the Tallawanda. "The Serviceman's Readjustment Act of 1944" made available a college education to any person under twenty-six who had served in the military or naval forces after September 16, 1940, and whose education had been interrupted by that service. It was popularly called the "G.I. Bill of Rights." The law provided tuition, fees, books, and subsistence of $50 a month for a single student, $75 for one with dependents.

Not till the fall of 1946 did the full tide of G.I. students reach Miami. But during the summer of 1945 the awesome atomic devastation obliterated Hiroshima and Nagasaki, and the Japanese government surrendered. In September, with the numbed world at peace, 2200 civilian students enrolled at Miami, 1700 of them women. The 500 civilian men students were outnumbered by 750 men in uniform in the Navy programs.

The year 1945 brought many changes as a college geared to war training shifted its aims and energies to the more traditional pursuits. The first faculty men returned from leave for military and governmental service, while some of their colleagues set off for foreign assignments. Professors L. P. Irvin and H. C. Christofferson assumed responsible posts in the Allied Military Government in Germany. Professors McNiff and Jones were sent to Europe as educational specialists in the U.S. Army educational program. Soon Professor Breitenbucher would become director of the American university program in the storied old halls of Heidelberg.

With the lifting of gasoline rationing and travel restrictions, an enthusiastic crowd of alumni came to Oxford on a crisp week-end in October. They followed the Miami marching band (reorganized after a two-year interval) to a crackling bonfire on Cook Field. They saw a Homecoming parade and a Miami-Ohio football game. At Withrow Court they gathered for a football dance with music by the traditional Campus Owls.

Late in 1945 millions of men were being separated from the armed forces, and the colleges got ready for the veterans. On an eight-acre plot south of the McGuffey playground appeared the first house-trailers and prefabricated dwellings of "Veterans' Village." The first thirty couples moved into the village on the first of April. A special group of courses was arranged for these and other veterans just discharged from military service; one hundred fifty men earned six hours' credit between April and the end of the term in June.

Along with the veteran students at the beginning of April, 1946, a new president arrived at Miami. On April 4th at a Benton Hall assembly Vice-President Morris introduced to the student body Miami's fifteenth president, Ernest H. Hahne. With a warm smile and a brisk, engaging manner, President Hahne took charge of the changing college. At the June Commencement Vice-President Morris was surprised with an honorary degree, to the delight of all his colleagues.

Then, after forty years of varied service to Miami, he retired and went on a fishing trip.

President Hahne, who had been a popular and prominent member of the faculty at Northwestern University, was an economist with an additional law degree, an authority on public finance. He foresaw growth for Miami and had no misgivings about it. He knew and upheld the methods of the large universities—big lecture classes, a strong alumni organization, and efficient university administration. He soon enlarged the library budget, strengthened the department of architecture, and encouraged the growth of the Graduate School. To the faculty he emphasized the importance of research and publication. He helped to plan a more vigorous alumni organization and he sought alumni counsel as to the kind of institution the changing Miami University should become. For change was more evident than tradition in the post-war college.

In September 1946 the full tide of G.I. enrollment came. The campus was thronged with young men just forgetting the routine of camp and base and shipboard. On the library steps under the thinning persimmon tree they lounged in the autumn sun, talking about Midway Island and Saipan, Pearl Harbor and Sorrento, Omaha Beach and the Rhine bridgeheads, Port Moresby and Okinawa. In the college enrollment of forty-one hundred there were two thousand veterans.

Hundreds of them were bivouacked in rows of double-deck bunks in Withrow Court—like the Army all over again —until Thanksgiving when they moved into a veterans' community on the south campus. Rows of barracks from Camp Knox and Camp Breckinridge were quickly named "Miami Lodges" before some more derisive name developed. The lodges housed single men, who took their meals at a central cafeteria. Across Oak Street were the longer rows of Veterans' Village, one hundred ninety-six prefabricated duplex dwellings brought from the big Willow Run aircraft plant outside Detroit. All spring and summer W. P. Roudebush and

Old Miami was a college of three buildings, which in the twentieth century were named Harrison, Elliott and Stoddard halls. On the open field beyond Main Building snowballs were rolled in the Snow Rebellion, companies of northern and southern students marched to cadence in 1861, and the first football matches were played in 1888. The first president's house, inside the fence, was enlarged from a one-room schoolhouse built in 1811.

In the old Literary Halls great issues were debated, rivalries were remembered, and the authority of the college faculty was defied.

The three
Erodelphian
graves were
inscribed
"Vale,
mi frater."

[Eclectic School Series.]

THE
ECLECTIC FIRST READER

FOR

YOUNG CHILDREN.

WITH PICTURES.

BY W. H. M'GUFFEY,

PROFESSOR IN MIAMI UNIVERSITY, OXFORD.

CINCINNATI:
PUBLISHED BY TRUMAN AND SMITH,
150 MAIN-STREET.

First published in 1836, the McGuffey Readers rode the wave of western expansion. After the Civil War they were standard schoolbooks in thirty-seven states. In the twentieth century the Reader pictured became a collector's item.

In 1937
this century-old
cottage
opened its doors
to guests of
the University
as
Simpson
Guest House.

Lewis Place,
with its spacious
rear gardens,
became the
president's home
in 1903.

At each Commencement season
the alumni of Old Miami gathered
on the lawn at Bishop House.

Oxford's first sidewalks were laid
just after the Civil War.

In 1909,
the
Centennial Year,
brick gates
replaced
the cattle-guard
at High Street.

A bicycle club flourished in the nineties.

Bearded, silk-hatted Professor Langsdorf never missed
a track meet.

In 1895 ten acres were claimed for an Athletic Park, even though Janitor Devine thought sports a waste of time and pasture.

In 1903 President Benton — with bow tie — organized the Pole Rush to replace the perilous Tower Rush of years past.

*In 1927
the former
Oxford
Female College
became
Fisher Hall
for
Miami men.*

*The original
Thobe's Fountain
bubbled
under the elms.*

*Oxford
Female College,
at its opening
in 1856,
was called the
"finest
college edifice
in the West."*

OXFORD FEMALE COLLEGE,

OXFORD, OHIO.

Rev. Robert D. Morris, A. M., President,

AIDED BY A FULL CORPS OF EXPERIENCED TEACHERS,

This Institution is under the care and control of the Synod of Cincinnati. Its accommodations are seldom surpassed. The buildings and grounds are spacious and beautiful, and have cost nearly $100,000. The establishment is supplied with water, heated by steam, and lighted with gas. The course of study is full and thorough. Students have the benefit of the lectures on Botany, Chemistry, and Natural Philosophy in Miami University.

Oxford is 28 miles north-west of Cincinnati, on the Junction Railroad from Hamilton, and is famed for its healthfulness, and for its rare educational, social, and religious advantages.

Constant attention is paid to the health, manners, and habits, and above all, to the moral and religious improvement of the pupils.

*Elliott Hall,
"plain
and strong" by
trustees' wish,
was opened
in the autumn of
1828;
in 1937
it was rebuilt.*

TERMS.

For Boarding, Tuition, Washing, Lighting, and Heating-Room, and all charges in the Regular Course, $87,50 per session, of five months, beginning Sept. 1, and Feb. 1. Music, Painting, and Modern Languages, extra.

VACATION IN JULY AND AUGUST.

For circulars, with full and specific information, apply to the President or Rev. W. S Rogers, Secretary.

In the twentieth century the Alumni Library with stack room for a half-million volumes replaced the "library chamber" in Old Main where McGuffey's octagonal table was in daily use.

In Bishop Chapel, on the second floor of the Main Building, the college convened daily.

Amid a learned clutter in Old North Hall lived "Heppy," foe of coeducation.

Said the South Hall boys: "Henry's goin' to lecture, Minnie's goin' to sing."

Born, February 3, 1809.   Died, November 4, 1847.

MENDELSSOHN MUSICAL,

COMMEMORATIVE OF

FELIX MENDELSSOHN-BARTHOLDY.

GIVEN FOR THE

MIAMI UNIVERSITY FACULTY,

BY

Mrs. Henry Snyder,

AT THE

TOWN HALL, OXFORD, O.,

THURSDAY, FEBRUARY 3, 1887.

FIRST NUMBER AT | EIGHT O'CLOCK P. M.

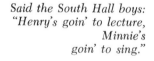

BROWN & OSBORN, PRS., OXFORD.

For a century and a half the Slant Walk has been the main artery of the campus.
Once a dusty path through a pasture, it was graveled in the eighties. For many
years it was illuminated with Chinese lanterns for the Commencement season.
In the early days Slant Walk ended at the two old dorms where students fed
their stoves with wood from the forest.

Commencement, 1905, was held on the present Beta Bell Tower site.

In the program of 1852 the name of Benjamin Harrison was misspelled.

Here Percy MacKaye wrote "This Fine Pretty World."

MIAMI UNIVERSITY.

PROGRAMME OF THE
Exercises on Commencement Day.

JUNE 24, 1852.

MUSIC.
PRAYER.
MUSIC.

Latin Salutatory,	DAVID SWING,	Williamsburgh.
Poetry of Religion,	HARMER DENNY,	Pittsburgh, Pa.
Poor of England,	BENJAMIN HARRIS,	North-Bend,

MUSIC.

JAMES A. HUGHES, . . . Somerville.
Public Opinion, . . . JOHN P. CRAIGHEAD, . . . Dayton.

MUSIC.

Free Thought and Free } Action, { ISAAC S. LANE, . . . Middletown.
The Federal Constitution, LEWIS W. ROSS, . . . Butler County.

MUSIC.

Harmony of Contrasts, . SAMUEL LOWRIE, . . . Pittsburgh, Pa.
He is the Freeman whom } the Truth makes Free, { JAMES H. CHILDS, Pittsburgh, Pa

MUSIC.

Science and Art as Aids } of Christianity, { WM. H. PRESTLEY, . . Pittsburgh, Pa
The Useful, ... A. C. JUNKIN, ... Xenia.

MUSIC.

Mystery, ... DAVID MOOROW, . . . Cambridge. (Excused.)
Oration, ... JOHN KNOX BOUDE, . . . Oxford. (Excused.)
Oration, ... JOHN S. BAKER, ... Cincinnati. (Excused.)
Death of Socrates, . . . JOSEPH WALKER, . . . New Concord.

MUSIC.

Valedictory, ... MILTON SAYLOR, . . . Lewisburgh
BENEDICTION.

Intelligencer Print, Hamilton.

We the undersigned students of Miami University, hereby agree to form ourselves into a military company (Rifle) to be governed by the rules and regulations of the regular service and State militia —

Names

Geo J Dodds.
Henry M. Williams.
J A. Whiteside
J C Wakefield
J. Corwin
John H. Shepherd
James Y. Hall
Cha J Powell
Samuel Ruston
W. Nelson Dunn
A G Dyer
J A Kumler Jr
A H Rowan
W R Hollingsworth
David Shaw
A Addison Duff
George V Halliday
Lewis B Wright
Chas A McDaniel
B M Powell
J R Orr
D C Kyle
H M Cooper

Names

Jno W Hyman
C A Murray Jr
Wm Jessup Jr
W C Lewis
L S Bennett
R A Leonard
Bros M Morris
Samuel Lewis
Jno E Hill Jr
M V H Talbert Jr
R S Brown
J C Snodgrass
J W Owens
Frank V Evans
J H Wiley
W H Evans
Jas M Lough
J G Aten
C S Brice
William L Porter
Jos M Wilson
A Britton Jr
R N Adams
A D Kimball
James Heazeltine

On the roster of the University Rifles, signed in April, 1861, appear the names of students who fought in crucial battles of the Civil War.

World War II:
the weekly
Naval Review
on Cook Field.

Joel Battle
of Tennessee,
buried at Shiloh
by classmates
at Miami.

Ozro Dodds,
commander
of the
University
Rifles.

In World War I the Students Army Training
Corps drilled on the football field.

Every quarter hour from the time when they serve as a campus-wide alarm clock until they say "Goodnight" at ten, the Beta Bells ring over Oxford. The Beta Theta Pi campanile was presented to Miami in 1939, a hundred years after the fraternity was founded in the original West Wing of Old Main.

Miami University Art Museum, created by famed architect Walter A. Netsch, is art itself as well as a "Home of the Muses".

Kumler Chapel, inspired by a venerable village church in Normandy, was dedicated Thanksgiving Day 1918 when the allied nations were giving thanks for the end of World War I.

On the Western campus ten field-stone bridges span wide ravines and winding waterways.

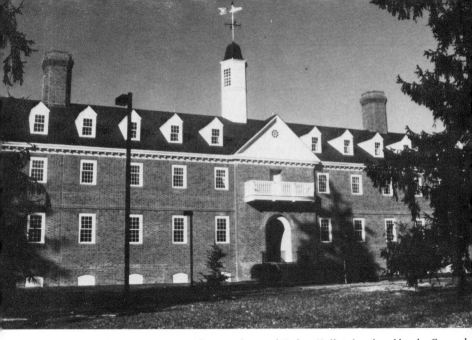

Marcum Conference Center, on the site of storied Fisher Hall, is bordered by the Conrad Formal Gardens and primeval woods of the Tallawanda valley.

During final construction of Yager Stadium, Weeb Ewbank of football fame and Redskin fan Phil Shriver look from fifty-yard line to the lofty press box.

A 50th anniversary gift of ΔΔΔ sorority the Armillary Sun Dial facing MacCracken Hall is an enduring time-piece — waterproof, shock-resistant, antimagnetic, and self-winding.

Ron Stevens Photo

Kingpin of the Miami University Library system, the Edgar Weld King Library acquisitioned its one millionth volume in 1982.

Dedicated in 1949 the Upham archway looks westward to the old halls where Miamians studied Latin, Greek and Logic by candlelight and eastward to the arc of science halls that frame the original campus forest.

A later Patterson Avenue landmark, across from the Art Museum, is the Murstein Center, a hearthstone for the far-flung Miami alumni.

In 1914 the Patterson homestead became the home of Western College presidents. Sixty years later it was made the seat of the Western College Alumnae Association.

Foster Cole of the business office and Professors Albaugh, Albert and Erickson had been at work creating Miami's first facilities for married students. On July 22, 1946, the 195th family moved in, and "Vetville" was fully occupied. (An office used the 196th unit.)

The married veterans took up Operation Textbook with cheerful industry, working their math problems and writing themes while their wives washed dishes and put the baby to bed. The dwelling units were cramped and crowded, drafty in cold weather and stifling when the summer sun beat down. But it was a happy, orderly, self-governed community. Some G.I. wives went to classes with their husbands. Others enrolled in non-credit courses in sewing, cooking, home nursing, interior decoration, first aid and consumer guidance.

Fifty years earlier, most Miami students came from the southwestern counties of Ohio and had never been away from their native region. Now Miami freshmen were writing themes about North Africa and the Solomon Islands, about villages in New Guinea, hill towns in Italy and jungle camps in the Philippines. The Bookwalter prize in composition was given for an eye-witness account of the bomb-test at Bikini atoll. Greer-Hepburn prizes were awarded for stories of American airmen over Italy and soldiers in Japan. Experience from the far side of the world came to college on the G.I. Bill.

In the summer of 1947, among military veterans returning to the faculty and the student body, came John E. Dolibois, '42, home from an army assignment as interpreter at the Nuremberg trials. In Ogden Hall he moved into the newly-created office of executive secretary of the Alumni Association. At the same time Mrs. H. J. S. Mann was expanding the quarterly *Alumni Newsletter* into a handsome, lively, six-times-a-year publication, *The Miami Alumnus*. At the end of the summer Mrs. Mann and Secretary Dolibois met with two alumni, Paul McNamara, '29, and Charles Ray Wilson, '26, to discuss an alumni study of a Long-Range Program for

Miami. They believed that the alumni generally were more concerned with the future of the college than with its past.

What followed was a careful, thorough, deliberate discussion of Miami policies. Sub-committees under the direction of Edward M. Brown, '31, Richard J. Young, '28, Dwight E. Minnich, '10, Thomas McNeil, '30, and J. Oliver Amos, '31, considered five areas of policy—Admission and Scholarships, Student Life, Faculty and Curricula, Intercollegiate Athletics, and Public Relations.

The general report of this committee was published in 1949. It recognized the facts of change (there were five thousands students on a once-rustic campus), but it noted that "the size and relative isolation of Oxford, its dignity, charm and lack of distracting interests have helped Miami preserve its character." It placed the greatest value on the quality of instruction in the University and the close personal relationships between faculty and students. Miami, thought the committee, should not grow beyond five thousand and it hoped that with this formidable number the college could retain its past friendliness, simplicity and commonly shared spirit. The report quoted the words of former President Hughes at the inauguration of President Hahne: "I am arguing that Miami's greatest future will grow from high distinction in superior teaching and in care for the individual student." Here were the old deep memories of Miami, going back to President Bishop who addressed the first student body as "My young friends." But there were five thousand students to cope with in 1947.

The pressure had shifted from military training to the colleges, and makeshift buildings were moved from camps to campuses. To Miami, on recommendation from the United States Office of Education, the Federal Works Agency assigned nine buildings from Wright Field and Camp Perry. They were moved to Oxford late in 1946, and fortunately the Miami grounds were spacious enough to absorb them without conspicuous clutter. One became the Redskin Reservation, a temporary Student Union shouldered against Herron Hall; it was a dim but popular resort with a constant stream of students taking coffee breaks at all hours of the day. Two of the structures were thrown together, with a connecting wing, for a temporary architecture building. Another building on lower Spring Street housed the Audio-Visual Service. One was set up east of Gaskill Hall for aeronautics and radio laboratories. One, settled in the woods near Fisher Hall, was used for a Naval rifle range. A quonset hut behind Withrow Court became an arena for wrestling, tumbling and remedial physical education. "Number Nine" on Maple Avenue became a temporary Fine Arts building. The most conspicuous was a faculty office building beside Irvin Hall; it was made conspicuous so that it would the sooner be disposed of.

But it is hard to give up any building in a growing college, and the "temporary" barracks-type F.O.B. now enters its second decade as an academic building. The structure which housed the Audio-Visual Service was really temporary, because it occupied the site chosen for the University Center. The building was pulled down in 1954 so that construction of the Center could begin, and the busy Audio-Visual Service moved to further temporary quarters in two of the abandoned lodges near the spreading women's campus.

On winter mornings in 1948 freshmen from the east campus tramped past a chaos in the frosty woods. On the site of the vanished MacKaye studio a crane was lifting structural steel and men unloaded brick and stone beside glowing salamanders. There was a thin snow in the air when some two hundred students and faculty gathered for the laying of the cornerstone of Upham Hall, Dean Alderman presiding. President Hahne recalled that since the first Miami cornerstone was laid in the forest, the Ohio wilderness had been transformed into the fourth most populous state in the Union. C. Vivian Anderson, president of the Board of Trustees, compared the men of Old Miami with the G.I. students of the present; both were heirs and defenders of a free society.

Architect Charles F. Cellarius, looking from the unfinished Upham archway to the old halls above and the snowy woods below noted that the new building would stand between the past and the future. West was the past, the old original college campus; East would be the campus to come, with buildings bordering the ancient uncut forest. Under the arch of Upham Hall the past of Miami would look through to the future.

A year later the departments of English, philosophy, mathematics, and air science moved in, while construction began on the building's north wing which would provide classrooms and offices, laboratories and museums for the biological sciences. An attractive feature of Upham Hall was the Alfred H. Upham Memorial Room, directly above the central archway. A comfortable and dignified meeting room, the gift of alumni, it was warmed with many shelves of books and with a portrait of A. H. Upham presented by Mrs. Upham and her daughter. The portrait showed the president reserved and reflective in academic dress, but with a gleam of humor lighting the eyes under their curiously folded lids. Among the books was a shelf of Oxford titles, including Miss Olive Flower's *History of Oxford College* and a copy of a new edition of President Upham's *Old Miami*. There were reminders of the past in this room where faculty, trustee, and alumni committees planned for the future.

Meanwhile another building ceremony had taken place on the east campus. On November 17, 1948, John B. Whitlock of the Board of Trustees presented to President Hahne the newly-completed Whitelaw Reid Hall. The speaker was Whitelaw Reid, editor of the *New York Herald Tribune* and grandson of the alumnus for whom the hall was named. Two days later the building was the subject of an editorial in the *Herald Tribune*.

An alumnus who was devoted to the past and ambitious for the University's future was Joseph M. Bachelor, '11, who had returned to his college to teach English after twenty years of editorial work in New York. A bachelor who made Miami the center of his affections, he spent seven years as head-resident at Fisher Hall, and from that tumult he moved to the quiet of a farm cottage two miles across the Talla-wanda. From his garden terrace on summer evenings he watched the sun set over the wide wooded valley and the spires of Oxford. There he spent the last years of his life, studying, editing, entertaining his friends at formidable sup-per parties around the fireplace on winter nights or on the terrace in the summer dusk. Illness forced his resignation from teaching in 1946. A year later, on a gray December morning, alone in his reading chair, with unfinished work on his lapboard and a fire glowing on the hearth, he was stricken with a heart attack. He died the following day in a Hamilton hospital.

With a love of the Oxford countryside and with royalties from anthologies and textbooks, he had bought successive tracts of land, much of it in woods and pasture, along Hark-er's Run. He left that valley land, four hundred acres, to Miami University as a Wild Life Preserve. The gift was dedi-cated on Alumni Day in 1951, as a part of the 40th anniver-sary of J. M. Bachelor's class. It was an overcast mild day, with birdsong from the fence rows and a summer wind rip-pling the meadow grass. Professor Hefner of the zoology department and Edward M. Brown, '31, spoke of this spacious gift of land and of the man who had left it.

President Hahne had taken office with zest and enthusiasm, but illness shadowed his Miami years. He grew drawn and worn, but he kept up with the work in his office, and at public events his old smile flashed out. By 1949 there were three annual Commencements, in February, June and Au-gust, and the president was always busy. He established a fully organized Graduate School—replacing the division which had been in operation since 1928—offering work for the Master's degree in science, education, business adminis-tration and fine arts, as well as in the social sciences and humanities. He helped to plan a celebration for the twenty-fifth year of the School of Business Administration. An economist himself, he was concerned about the standard of teaching in that division and he took pride in the record of its twenty-five classes of graduates—a record freshly reviewed in a directory edited by two of that number, Professors C. R. Niswonger, '29, and J. S. Seibert, '32. At the same time the School of Education was observing its fiftieth anniversary, and Homecoming visitors had three new buildings to visit: the John Shaw Billings Natatorium, Frances Gibson Richard Hall on the women's campus, and the new west wing of the Alumni Library. Illness kept President Hahne from presiding at these dedications. Late in November, 1952, while the campus was quiet with the Thanksgiving holiday, he died.

Miami has been both lucky and unlucky in its executives. It was the University's good fortune that a good vice-president was on hand at President Hahne's death. After thirty years as a Miami undergraduate, member of the chemistry department, assistant dean of Liberal Arts, and vice-president, C. W. Kreger knew the strength and the weakness, the capacities and resources of Miami. As a freshman on a September midnight in 1915, running across the dark campus from sophomore pursuers, he collided with a man who introduced himself: "I'm R. M. Hughes. Who are you?" Thirty-eight years later he was acting-president of a restless, growing university.

In 1952 the 5000th student to enroll, just before Registrar W. C. Smyser made his October report, was Bundid Chuangsuvanich from Thailand. Students from fifteen foreign countries were on the campus. For eight weeks Miami was host to a group of foreign teachers observing American institutions. The post-war nations were curious about each other and eager for exchange of ideas and practices. The college horizons had never been so broad. In the following summer Professor George Grosscup took a party of fifty travelers on the first European tour of "Miami University Abroad," a season of travel and study which could be used for college credit. After that trial run, Miami University Abroad became a regular part of the University's summer program. University lecturers and counsellors on the tour have been Professors Snider, Altstetter, McNiff and Montgomery.

In 1953 the exodus from the lodges began and nearly four hundred freshmen streamed into two new residence halls on the east campus. Collins and McBride halls recalled two doughty men who had defended Miami when its opponents called it a college "in the gloom of the Beechwoods" which could never fulfill the hopes of its founders. Now their names were part of a university that had surpassed their boldest expectations.

Chapter XIX

THE LIBERATING ARTS

O N VARIOUS OCCASIONS President Upham had said: "Miami has everything that money cannot buy." In November 1952 appeared a volume entitled *Financing Higher Education in the United States,* by John D. Millett, professor of public administration at Columbia University and executive director of the Commission on Financing Higher Education. The book was concerned with what money can buy for colleges and universities.

In the winter of 1952-53 a committee of Miami trustees and faculty met repeatedly at the Queen City Club in Cincinnati. Around the table sat C. Vivian Anderson, John B. Whitlock, Hugh C. Nichols, J. Paul McNamara, Wayne L. Listerman, Larz R. Hammel, and Professors Robert F. Almy and Howard White. In consultation with them were Reuben Robertson, Jr., president of the Champion Paper and Fibre Company, and Marvin Pierce, Miami '16, president of the McCall Corporation. That spring they made their recommendation, and the Board of Trustees elected as the sixteenth president of Miami University John D. Millett. In September Lewis Place was alive with three Millett boys, a stream of callers, and a restless young president and his wife. Catherine

Millett soon had the affection of both town and gown. Between the tasks of furnishing Lewis Place and getting her family settled, she studied the University directory. At the president's reception a few weeks later she seemed to know the entire staff. With her effortless warmth and charm she instantly won them all.

President Millett was a native of Indiana and an honor graduate of DePauw University, and he voiced a satisfaction on his return to the Midwest. He was just forty-one, but he had been away for twenty wide-ranging and eventful years. Upon graduation from DePauw in 1933, he had gone with his honors professor, Harold Zink, on a year-long trip around the world. "Travel," wrote Francis Bacon, "in the younger sort, is a part of education; in the elder, a part of experience." For tall young John Millett it was a part of education, permanently stretching his mind and enlarging his perspective. The *Wanderjahr,* a capstone to his undergraduate studies in political science, was followed by graduate study at Columbia University and an appointment to its faculty. But his training, interests and capacities led beyond the classroom. Along with some specialized teaching he served on government and educational commissions. Early in the war he was commissioned a major in the United States Army and he rose to the rank of colonel in the Army Service Forces. After the war he was assigned to the headquarters of the European Command in Germany. Returning to the Columbia faculty in 1947, he also served on the Hoover Commission on Organization of the Executive Branch of the Government, and in 1949 he was made executive director of the Commission on Financing Higher Education.

At a time when Miami was facing new problems and opportunities it was the institution's good fortune to have the leadership of a vigorous young administrator widely acquainted with the men and movements of American higher education. The simple provincialism of the Old Miami had faded into tradition. President Millett, without personal memories of the dreaming old college, could direct its development into new avenues and dimensions. Bold, impatient, always looking ahead, he respected the Miami past but he did not confuse that with its future. With the widest-ranging mind of all Miami presidents, he was equally at home in scholarship and in administration. He loved travel; his favorite cities were Peking and Rome. He liked bright red motor cars. To the president's office he brought a national point of view and an idea of a big, busy, varied university unified by a community academic life.

At his inauguration in Withrow Court on a cloudless October day in 1953 President Millett stressed the importance of broad and thorough college education. As a foundation for professional skills he wanted every student to gain a comprehension of the vast range of man's intellectual effort. A few months later he proposed a major change in the Miami curriculum. Under his chairmanship a faculty committee planned the content of a Common Curriculum, which was adopted in 1954. It laid down general requirements for students in all divisions, designed to acquaint them with "the magnificent boundaries of human knowledge and to emphasize the attributes of the humane man, whether his special interest be in the arts, in philosophy, in social organization, or in science." Though there were choices and options within the program which made the curriculum something less than common, this was a means of restoring, in an increasingly disparate university, a basic comprehension of the realm of knowledge.

In the twentieth century America had developed a belief that all must be educated and yet there was nothing in particular that an educated person must know. Now Miami was joining the movement toward a general education, a common body of knowledge and discipline which could become a basis for shared purposes and aspirations. It had been observed that the old disciplines of Rhetoric, Logic, Classical Literature, Natural and Moral Philosophy, were all but lost in the proliferating new curricula, and their absence left a vacuum quickly filled with opportunistic and vocational studies—studies designed to aid the individual as a competitor rather than as a citizen and a human being. Yet it was the discarded disciplines that had produced the modern democratic state, and without them new generations could not understand the creative principles of their own society. The Common Curriculum aimed to bring all Miami students to an awareness of the nature of the universe and of man's place in it and of his destiny.

To the enlarging Miami came an increased awareness of the role of the university in scholarly research. It was recognized that Miami's largest task is the teaching of undergraduates, and that resources did not permit the acquiring of extensive research facilities and the freeing of the faculty from a demanding classroom schedule. Yet encouragement was given to scholarly production, and certain new facilities were provided. The Pickrel Fund, the President's Fund, and funds of the Miami University Foundation and of the Alumni Association provided assistance for research programs. Grants from national institutions and foundations and from government and industry supported specific projects. In place of the older sabbatical leave—inaugurated by President Benton in order to send his faculty to Europe—there was announced a system of Service Leave, which would provide time to be devoted to fruitful scholarly projects. The post of "Research Professor" allowed a partial release from academic routine for the furthering of professional and scholarly production.

The growth of the graduate division and plans for its further development were evidenced by the creating of the Graduate School. In 1957 Professor W. E. Smith relinquished the chairmanship of the history department to become full-time dean of the Graduate School, and graduate programs, already extensive in the School of Education, were strengthened in other divisions and departments. Fifty years ago it had been agreed among the state universities of Ohio that

specialized and professional training would be centered at
The Ohio State University. By the 1950's it was evident that
this arrangement must be changed. Ohio, in terms of its
wealth and population, was lagging in production of fully-
trained scholars. At Miami the Graduate Council undertook
to strengthen the advanced study at the level of the master's
degree and to consider extension to the Ph.D. degree level
at a later date. Plans for a Miami University publication im-
print, in cooperation with the Columbia University Press,
were being made as the Sesquicentennial year, 1959, approached.

The growth of the University demanded a new Administration Building. Its location as a part of the new east
quadrangle moved the center of the campus into a region
that had been deep forest until the twentieth century. During
its construction in 1955 workmen felled a massive white oak
whose rings showed it to be two hundred forty-three years
old; it was a sturdy sapling when Céloron de Bienville jour-
neyed down the Ohio River claiming the valley for Louis
XV of France. Sawed into railing it became some thousands
of feet of green campus fence to protect the grass from
students in a hurry. Not without controversy the chimneyed
and colonnaded building went up. A university with an architecture department must embrace some architectural con-
victions which depart from the eighteenth century designs
chosen for the Miami campus. An effect of controversy was
to modify certain elements in the design of new buildings,
yet the Miami architecture, generally, remained conservative, as the college has been in other ways.

The Miami of the 1950's was in a constant state of construction. On the women's campus the war-time Lodges came
down and new residence halls went up. Scott and Porter halls
were named for two young women of old Oxford, Caroline
Scott, the wife of Benjamin Harrison, and Elizabeth Porter,
the wife of David Swing. The new East Dining Hall, seating
five hundred fifty, was built in the woods beyond The Pines,

and near it went up the newest hall of the freshman campus. William Dennison Hall recalled a gifted man and a notable career. Graduated from Miami in 1835 and admitted to the bar in 1840, William Dennison married the daughter of William Neil of Columbus, founder of a historic stage line and a famous hotel. Elected governor of Ohio in 1860, Dennison asserted strong Union leadership. He sent Ohio troops to the western counties of Virginia, which were generally opposed to secession, with the result that thirty-four counties withdrew from the Old Dominion and entered the Union as the State of West Virginia. He served as president of the Republican National Convention that re-nominated Lincoln and he became Postmaster-General in Lincoln's cabinet. In this office he was retained by President Johnson but he resigned when Johnson began to assail the Union party. Governor Dennison then returned to his railroad and business interests in Columbus. He died in 1882, but in 1956 his name came back to the Miami campus.

That winter a centennial was celebrated at Fisher Hall. Now sharing its grounds with five other freshman residence halls housing nearly a thousand men, the old towered building had long stood alone on its spacious campus. In its past was a sequence of men and women, old and young, burdened and carefree. First were the Oxford College girls, singing their songs on the verandah and strolling the campus paths. Then for forty years the patients of the Oxford Retreat looked out barred windows at bubbling fountains on the terrace and peacocks sunning in the grass. During the years of World War II the building furnished quarters for hundreds of Naval trainees who learned radio code at rows of transmitters on plank tables in the former laundry. And now, a century old, the hall resounded with the life of Miami freshmen.

To round out the residence hall system, construction began in 1957 on spacious grounds south of the Veterans' Village of a group of buildings to provide small apartments for married students. And all the way across the town, on Tallawanda

Road, where once the University had a forestry experimental planting, ground was broken for two new residence halls for upperclassmen.

Planning for the University's physical development had been for forty-five years the sustained interest and responsibility of Wallace P. Roudebush. As a boy he had walked, through rain and snow and sunshine, from a farm on the Brown Road to classes in the preparatory department. As a Miami undergraduate he was a leader in almost everything, and upon his graduation in 1911 President Hughes selected him as "secretary to the president." His first undertakings were to refurnish the two men's halls, which had but recently been equipped with electricity and running water, and to pay off the debts of the Athletic Association. Living in the house that McGuffey had built across from the old south gate of the college yard, he had a warm feeling for Miami's past, but in his mind was a constantly enlarging picture of its future. The quadrangles, the buildings, the gardens, the playing fields were all developed from the master plan in his mind. He directed the University's physical growth from ten buildings in 1911 to sixty at the time of his death. He managed the University financing that extended the residence halls from four to twenty-six. At Columbus he represented Miami with the State Legislature—a big, virile, quiet-spoken man mingling with the committee members. In that smoky atmosphere men saw his shining integrity and they gave him their unreserved esteem and respect.

His sudden death in April, 1956, came at the time of the completion of the Administration Building. At the building's dedication in June Governor Frank J. Lausche paid warm tribute to Wallace Roudebush as an embodiment of the best character and aspirations of Miami University. Into his dual office of business and financial management went Foster J. Cole, business manager, and Lloyd Goggin, treasurer. And in the marble foyer of the new building was placed a memorial plaque to Wallace P. Roudebush.

A final detail of the Administration Building was a flagpole to be erected in front of the colonnade and to replace the weathered old flagstaff on the west tower of Harrison Hall. The new pole, a gift of alumni, was delivered on a bright April day in 1957. A tapered, tubular steel shaft, to be topped by a spread-winged gold eagle, it lay on the ground beside the cement base and was given two coats of paint. When a derrick arrived to raise it, on the morning of April 25th, the lawn was empty. The pole weighed 2965 pounds and was 77 feet long, but it had disappeared. President Millett, already ruffled by the fact that Northwestern University, after having lured away Miami's football coaching staff had just that week hired Miami's successful basketball coach, asked, "Northwestern get the flagpole, too?" But it was not that far away. It was found in the woods below Upham Hall, where some scores of grunting students had carried it at midnight. The pole was erected and the flag fluttered in the April sky.

In the summer of 1956 in the newly-enlarged library Professor E. W. King turned over his office to L. S. Dutton. When Mr. King came to Miami in the fall of 1922 the tree at the Library doorway was plopping ripe persimmons on the steps and the Library contained 55,000 volumes. When he left, the persimmons were still falling but the library had grown to 305,000 volumes and each of its two new wings was larger than the original building. In these years Mr. King added greatly to the Ohio Valley Historical Collection, he built up a famous McGuffey Collection, and he personally made a distinguished collection of children's literature which the University acquired at his retirement. The library is the heart of a university. Nowhere had Miami developed more significantly in the twentieth century than in its library.

On Alumni Day, in June 1957, while the biggest of all alumni reunions was gathering on the green below Reid Hall, another tie with the past was broken. Word passed through the crowd that Dean Brandon had died. He had come to

Miami in 1898 as a young professor of Romanic languages. Since then, he had served as vice-president, dean, and acting president. He had seen Miami grow from sixty college students to nearly six thousand. His gifts to Miami, in addition to a lifetime of teaching and administration, included Brandon Field, in the new fraternity square on Tallawanda Road, and a language laboratory for more effective teaching of foreign languages.

In this year, to the recent retirement of Professors Edwards, Brill, McConnell, Beneke and Craver, was added that of Professors William E. Shideler of geology and Joseph Mayer of economics. The emeritus list was growing.

In the summer of 1957 workmen put the finishing touches on the University Center. The spacious building had required removal of the old McFarland house across from the entrance to Western College, though the dark Canadian hemlocks which Professor McFarland had planted were left to murmur in the winds. The building was opened in September, 1957, being first used for the president's reception at the beginning of the year. In the following days students and their parents streamed through the building, student organizations moved into new quarters in the west wing, and the entire academic community found new facilities for social and recreational activity. The old alumni gathering place was the big walnut tree beside the Bishop house, where "Old Bobby" called by name every visitor from years gone by. The Center would become the meeting place of Miami alumni and visitors for generations to come.

With its lighted portico inviting through the wooded campus, the University Center offered many new facilities. It had a book store, ball room, music listening room, reading room, game rooms, dining rooms and lounges—comforts that were not thought of when the students of Old Miami lounged around the college well. It contained a University Club, an idea that would have puzzled Professor McFarland lighting his way home with a lantern on moonless nights. Half a century ago the McFarland house, with its orchard, garden, and a tag of hayfield, had seemed remote from the college yard. But now it was a "Center" location, between the east campus, site of seven of the men's halls, and the spacious women's quadrangles, with residence buildings and Harvey Hiestand Hall, the new Fine Arts building, growing up beyond it. All those acres had once been cattle pasture.

Yet the aim of the college and its essential effort remained the same as in the generations past. In 1957 President Millett wrote a small book with wide horizons. Distributed to freshmen and to seniors, *The Liberating Arts* was both an introduction to the higher learning and an over-view of the fields of scholarship. In five brief and luminous essays it described the realm of knowledge, beginning with the Humanities, surveying the Social Sciences and the Natural Sciences, discussing Philosophy as a capstone of knowledge, and concluding with the place of Religion in the higher education.

The book was wholly in the Miami spirit and tradition. It described the endeavor of the colleges "to give their students some sense of the scope of man's knowledge, some understanding of the exciting history of its development, some awareness of how knowledge accumulates, some appreciation for the worth of intellectual achievement, some discriminating judgment amid the conflicting claims of truth, sensitivity to the limitations of knowledge, and an intellectual devotion to the values of a good life." It viewed knowledge as a necessary technique in vocation or profession, and also as a source of personal satisfaction and of enlightenment in daily life. It saw the liberal arts as liberating arts— which first made the individual free as a person and then helped to broaden the freedom of the individual in society. It suggested that knowledge as technique and knowledge as satisfaction are not antithetical but complementary; both, indeed, are essential in our society. So it called upon the student to take up the endless quest for knowledge. One could not expect to finish that journey, to arrive at the end of the mind's seeking. But an old Spanish proverb says "The Road is always better than the Inn," and it is the nature of the scholar to travel hopefully.

Chapter XX

THE AVENUES OF LEARNING

THE EIGHTH OF FEBRUARY, 1956, was a dull gray day with some dirty snow patching the campus and workmen hammering in the nearly completed Administration Building. Students were shuffling into the Library for the final day of pay-line. Notices in faculty boxes announced an Arts and Science staff meeting to discuss the bringing of more *good* students to Miami—a project which Dean Alderman pressed with all his resources.

It was another day in mid-winter, at the beginning of a term. But one thing was different. On the third floor of Upham Hall students filed into five classrooms where there were no instructors. The shades were drawn. Chairs were banked to face two tall-stilted television screens in the corners of the room. As the bell rang a proctor closed the door. The dead screen came to life. Into Room 317 came the voice and features of Professor David Lewis, and a course in Introductory Sociology was under way—though Professor Lewis was standing before three cameras in a studio in the temporary Communications Building behind the power plant. In other classrooms down the hall students watched Professors Mitchell, McNelly and Bergstrom on the screen and took

243

notes on Educational Psychology, Human Physiology and Human Biology.

On the following Friday the *Miami Student* ran a front-page cartoon: "New Addition to the Faculty." It showed a wise-looking TV screen wearing a mortar board, carrying a cane in one hand and a textbook in the other. Instruction by television had come to old Miami.

Three months earlier to the University Senate President Millett had announced a grant of $135,000 from the Fund for the Advancement of Education to conduct an experimental study in teaching procedures. With prospects of a huge increase in university enrollments within a decade, there was need to determine whether and how college faculties could instruct more and more students. In 1956 Miami, like most other American colleges, had sufficient staff to teach by the traditional procedures. But by 1966 the pressure of increased numbers would require new methods. The study at Miami, one of several related experiments across the country, was an attempt to prepare for the future.

Teaching by closed-circuit television was a part of the experimental program at Miami. While students took notes from TV lectures and at the close of the hour dropped their questions into a box on the proctor's desk, two other innovations were being tested. In the freshman course in Principles of Modern Business and in General Biology, sections were taught by graduate assistants under the supervision of a regular staff member. The departments of government, English, geography, mathematics and psychology conducted large lecture sections, ranging from fifty-five to one hundred forty, and the results of the instruction were carefully compared with those in small control sections, ranging from twenty-seven to thirty-seven, where Miami's traditional teaching method, personal, informal and discursive, was used.

The purpose of the Miami University Experimental Study in Instructional Procedures was to determine the relative effectiveness of large and small group instruction. Along with this major purpose the study aimed to improve large group teaching procedures and to develop audio and visual aids for use in the improvement of college teaching generally. Evaluation was emphasized from the start, with an evaluation analyst using the data from the experiment to judge whether or not class size could be increased without a loss in student learning.

In the second year of the study the number of experimental courses was increased. During 1956-57 there were still four multiple-section courses taught by television, each balanced by a control section of traditional procedure, and there were again two courses taught by graduate assistants under supervision of veteran instructors. But the large lecture courses were increased to seventeen, and they represented all divisions of the University except that of Fine Arts.

The experimental study was to continue for three years and the final report would be made at a symposium for educators during Miami's Sesquicentennial year, 1959. Meanwhile, progress reports showed that comparable achievement resulted from experimental and control sections. While students generally preferred the traditional small classes, their acquisition of subject matter was not diminished by assignment to a television or lecture section. And while they would choose the traditional small class, most students indicated that they would voluntarily enroll in a television or lecture section if it assured them of an instructor of known excellence. The study in teaching procedures, still in progress as the Sesquicentennial anniversary approached, was casting long shadows over Miami's classrooms in the future.

Not only would teaching resources need to be stretched in the years ahead, but there would be need for an increased number of qualified college teachers. In anticipation of this need Provost Kreger in 1956 devised a Graduate-Undergraduate Fellowship program to give prospective college teachers an opportunity for special preparation. The plan called for the finding of undergraduates whose interests and abilities promised successful careers in college teaching and the nominating of these students as Undergraduate Fellows, each one assigned to a faculty sponsor. The Fellow was introduced to some of the intellectual and social life of his major department. He assisted the sponsoring professor, as circumstances allowed, in class work, research and paper grading. With him were shared some of the professor's intellectual pursuits and some of his leisure. So he obtained understanding of the tasks and the satisfactions of the academic life. A Graduate Fellow in this program gave fifteen hours a week in assistance to the sponsoring professor, in addition to his own graduate study, and received a $1600 stipend along with the waiving of fees. The Undergraduate Fellow was considered "in training" for the Graduate Fellowship program.

In the first year of this plan for recruitment of potential college teachers there were thirty-one seniors assigned to professors in fourteen departments and three Graduate Fellows in two departments. Appointments for 1957-58 were twenty-nine Undergraduate and five Graduate Fellows. By that time the program had attracted nation-wide interest as a means of enlisting and preparing college teachers for the years ahead. This program was concerned with the future— the endless future, if one recalls Henry Adams' statement. "A teacher," he said, "affects eternity."

In the bright month of May, 1957, State building inspectors roamed through Harrison Hall, from the dim basement with its old furnaces rusting in the walls to the trap doors that open onto the windy platform roof. When they made their report, the days of Harrison Hall were numbered. They found the floors and stairways of the old building below the required standard of strength. So began its evacuation. A building crane, moved in from the construction job at William Dennison Hall, raised its gaunt arms to the third floor windows. Out from the old Erodelphian Hall, which had become an art studio, came the sculpture casts of Moses, David and Lorenzo d'Medici. These heroic figures reclined in the grass of the quadrangle while the crane dangled desks and cabinets from the top-floor classrooms. From second-floor faculty offices came tons of books. Classes in the building were restricted in size, and the Towers Theater, the original bare, square chapel room of Old Miami, was limited to classroom use. Life was ebbing from the old building.

For a century the Main Building had been the heart of Miami University. There McGuffey lodged when he first came to Oxford, there Beta Theta Pi, Delta Zeta and Phi Kappa Tau were founded, there the Literary Halls flourished and dwindled. The building contained Miami's first gymnasium room, its first hall of science, its first library chamber. It was barricaded in the Snow Rebellion of 1847 and decorated for the college's re-opening in 1885. For nearly a century it had housed the University's administration. When faculty books were removed from the sociology offices in 1957, a wall, enclosed years before, was opened into the vault that had contained the university archives. In hundreds of musty pigeonholes were thousands of papers—some William H. McGuffey signatures on academic records, many annual professor's reports, hundreds of pieces of correspondence pertaining to past anniversaries, and bundles of receipts for land rents paid to the University in years gone by.

Harrison Hall, re-named in the 1930's when the old "edifice" had ceased to be the main building, was judged to be beyond renovation. Architects began drawing plans for a new Harrison Hall that would rise in its place, with lines reminiscent of the structure that had been Alma Mater to many generations of Miami men.

Herron Hall, too, had served its time. The Miami gymnasium, replaced in the 1930's by Withrow Court, had been converted into a women's gymnasium. As the Sesquicentennial year approached, plans called for a new women's physical education building across from Hamilton and Richard halls on the South Campus. And fronting High Street just below the site of Herron Hall excavation began in 1957 for Laws Hall, the new building of the School of Business Administration. Its name was another link between the new Miami and the old.

The name of Samuel Spahr Laws seemed new on the Miami campus, though students and faculty for nearly forty years had walked daily past it. In the rotunda of the Library stands the Houdon statue of George Washington, "presented to Miami University in 1920 by S. S. Laws." The statue is arresting enough to keep the passing throngs from studying the inscription at its base. Originally commissioned by the State of Virginia, bronze copies of the marble statue now stand in the Treasury Building in New York City and at the entrance to the Chicago Art Museum, as well as in the Miami Library. There is an appropriateness in that figure in the Library rotunda, for George Washington had signed the Act of Congress granting the township of land which was the original support of Miami University.

Samuel Spahr Laws, valedictorian of the class of 1848, was a far-ranging man. Inventor, educator, physician, theologian, financier, he fitted a series of careers into his ninety-seven years of life and left a record of achievement in diverse fields.

His first career was in the church. Graduated from Princeton Theological Seminary in 1851, he served for three years as a Presbyterian minister in St. Louis and then as a professor of physical science in Westminster College at Fulton, Missouri. A year later he was elected president of the college. At the outbreak of the Civil War he was president of the Presbyterian synodical colleges in the South. Laws was a Virginian and a believer in states' rights. When he refused to take an oath of allegiance to the federal government he was committed to the Illinois State Prison; for nine months there he worked on a translation of Aristotle. Paroled, he went to Europe, spending two years in London and Paris. On his return to America in 1863 he joined the Gold Exchange on Wall Street in New York. During the war the "Gold Room" in the Stock Exchange was the center of financial activity; its quotations governed the nation's commerce. Elected vice-president of the Exchange, Laws devised a mechanical indicator, the origin of the stock market printing telegraph, which issued a steady stream of figures. Laws had worked in a tool factory in his youth, before coming to Miami, and at Princeton along with the study of theology he had studied electricity under the famous Joseph Henry. In 1866 he patented his machine and had had it installed in the offices of fifty subscribers. Soon the subscribers increased to three hundred, and the improved stock market "ticker" was the national vehicle of financial news.

In 1869 an unknown young mechanic named Thomas A. Edison arrived in New York. While waiting for a job he slept in the battery room of Laws' Gold Indicator Company. He studied the ticker machine with an inventor's interest, and he was in the room when it broke down. He replaced a spring, adjusted the contact wheels and soon had the machine stuttering out its stream of figures. Then—as Edison recalled years afterward—"Dr. Laws came in to ask my name and what I was doing. I told him, and he asked me to come to his office the following day. His office was filled with stacks of books, all relating to metaphysics and kindred matters. He asked me a great many questions about the instruments and his system, and I showed him how he could simplify things generally. He then requested that I should call next day. On arrival, he stated at once that he had decided to put me in charge of the whole plant, and that my salary would be $300 a month! This was such a violent jump from anything I had seen before that it rather paralyzed me for a while. I thought it was too much to be lasting, but I determined to try and live up to that salary if twenty hours a day of hard work would do it. I kept this position, made many improvements, devised several stock tickers, until the Gold &

Stock Telegraph Company consolidated with the Gold Indicator Company."

Meanwhile S. S. Laws had decided to study law, and while studying law he became interested in medicine. He was admitted to the New York bar in 1869, awarded a law degree from Columbia College in 1870 and an M.D. from Bellevue Hospital Medical College in 1875. In 1876 he was elected president of the University of Missouri, where he served for thirteen years. In 1893 he became professor of apologetics at the Presbyterian Theological Seminary in Columbia, South Carolina. He kept up his scientific and medical pursuits, writing pioneering works on neuro-psychology. This amazing man, citizen of the world of knowledge, wrote for the Miami University Diamond Anniversary in 1899 a recollection of his student years at Miami. Sixty years later his name on a Business Administration building could remind young Miami men of the stature of their forebears.

With a prospective bulge in applications Miami officials in 1956 considered a new admissions policy. President Millett said: "A state university by its very nature cannot expect to establish admission standards comparable to those imposed by our highest quality private colleges and universities. There is room for a wide variety of talent and energy in our system of higher education. It is a function of a state university to help promote that wide variety." Yet he went on to discuss selective admission. For several years it had been the practice to require that students in the lower half of their high school graduating class take pre-college tests. On the basis of these tests, plus recommendation of the high school principal and the applicant's high school standing, students might be admitted on warning. In 1958 the Board of Trustees adopted a policy providing that the University might give preference in housing to students other than those who have been admitted on warning.

In 1957 under a new practice of granting Admission with Honors, appropriate certificates were awarded to two hundred thirty-five high school graduates who by academic record, recommendation of their school principal, and ranking in the Ohio General Scholarship Test showed promise of superior intellectual achievement.

With all signs pointing to increasing enrollment in the nation's universities, Miami prepared for growth, within practicable limits. As a residence college, it could not accept more students than housing facilities allowed. The residence halls under construction or projected for completion in 1959 fixed a limit of some six thousand two hundred students. For this quota the aim was to attract capable students and give them a demanding and rewarding course of study.

A part of the celebration of Miami's Sesquicentennial was the building from contributions of alumni and friends, of a University Chapel. Non-sectarian, it would provide a place of meditation and worship for individuals and groups. Rising at the end of a broad walk leading west from the University Center, it would represent the values and aspirations of a college that had been fostered by the churches and served by men who believed in a religious foundation for higher education.

The Miami of 1959, with hundreds of acres of grounds, scores of buildings and thousands of students, was greatly changed from the college that Robert Hamilton Bishop presided over in the 1820's. Yet in certain ways it was the same institution. The income from its never-revalued land grant remained at $7,000 a year, hardly enough to pay for its bookkeeping. Though highways and motor traffic brought crowds of people on special occasions, the college was still removed from the strident world. It remained an inexpensive college, offering an opportunity for education at a minimum cost, and the prohibition of student automobiles kept its social life simple and self-contained. It continued to be a college of liberal interests and conservative practices, regarding intellectual breadth and liberation as the best things it could give its students. The relationship of faculty and students was still informal, with frequent meetings outside the classroom and a ready exchange of interests and ideas. And, as the daily chapel service was the heart of Old Miami, the new University Chapel symbolized its sustained concern for spiritual values.

The quest for understanding ticks like an everlasting clock on a college campus. In 1891 when the first section of Brice Hall was built, President Warfield said it would contain the science of Miami for the next hundred years. Now, three times its original size, that hall contains a single department of science—a department that had no separate existence when President Warfield dedicated the building. The course of study changes, but the pursuit of knowledge goes on from generation to generation. And despite all the bread and circuses that have been added to American universities, the meaning of college is still the burning of a study lamp at midnight.

"The sweetest path of life," wrote David Hume, "leads through the avenues of learning, and whoever can open up the way for another, ought, so far, to be esteemed as a benefactor of mankind." It was for this purpose that the founders of Miami, a century and a half ago, lit the old lamps of learning and piety in a new country.

Chapter XXI

THE SESQUICENTENNIAL YEAR

O N A SERENE September day in 1958 a grappling bucket
on a swinging crane bit off the roof of the east tower
of Harrison Hall. After a century and a third the old Main
Building was coming down. At various times it had included
lodging rooms, recitation rooms, the Literary Halls, a chapel,
a library chamber, the president's office, the secretary's office,
a printing room, a scientific laboratory, a gymnasium room,
a dining commons, an art studio and a theater. Early in 1959
foundations were laid for the second Harrison Hall, with
twin towers and a portico reminiscent of the first, that
eventually would house one department rather than a college. The old was giving way to new as the sesquicentennial
year began.

To observe the university's 150th anniversary, plans had
been developing under the direction of Professor John Ball
in a Sesquicentennial Office that looked across the new
quadrangle to the old dorms and Hughes and Upham halls.
A committee of alumni, headed by J. Oliver Amos and Paul
S. Hinkle, both of the class of 1931, a committee of the
faculty under Professor Joseph S. Seibert, '32, and numerous
other groups of students, alumni, faculty and staff had

arranged a year-long series of special events and observ-
ances. Already the original edition of *The Miami Years,
1809–1959,* had appeared, and after a national competition
a Sesquicentennial medallion was issued. On one side the
medal showed a Miami figure holding the lamp of learning
and on the other a crisp design of buckeye leaves and an
outline map of Ohio framing "150 Years of Growth and
Service." Though the jurors did not know it, this prizewinner
was the work of Robert B. Butler of Miami's Art Department. While pondering his design Professor Butler had been
chiseling the bas-reliefs on the recently finished Hiestand
Fine Arts Hall.

The anniversary year echoed with sounds of growth. There
were nearly 7,000 students on the Oxford campus, with another 3,000 enrolled at the off-campus centers in Norwood,
Hamilton, Middletown, Dayton and Piqua. And more were
coming. As the spring days lengthened, construction grew
on Laws Hall for the School of Business Administration,
the Radio-TV building to house the Miami University Broadcasting Service, Dennison Hall for freshmen men on the east
campus, and Brandon and McFarland halls for upperclassmen on the onetime golfing fairway along Tallawanda
Avenue. Rising on Spring Street were the Sesquicentennial
Chapel, the Physics-Mathematics building to be named
Culler Hall and a new wing of Gaskell Hall to accommodate
the growing Audio-Visual Service.

The year-long celebration brought to the campus a sequence of distinguished visitors and events. It began on Charter Day, February 17, with officials of the State of Ohio,
members of the Board of Trustees, the presidents of the other
state universities in Ohio, officers of the Alumni Association, a
representative group of students, and officials of the town
of Oxford gathered at a gala luncheon in the University
Center. Dessert was a seventy-pound birthday cake topped
with a model of the new Harrison Hall and decorated with
symbols of Miami's growth and service. That afternoon an

all-university convocation in Withrow Court heard the University Orchestra and the A Cappella Singers perform Professor Otto Frohlich's composition "Homage to Miami." After the reading of greetings from President Dwight D. Eisenhower of the United States and Governor Michael DiSalle of Ohio and a congratulatory resolution from the Ohio General Assembly, President James L. Morrill of the University of Minnesota discussed "The State University: Its Opportunity and Obligation in American Higher Education." To all attending the convocation went a copy of the Sesquicentennial souvenir book; among its many photographs were the architects' drawings of six new buildings and a center spread in color of Professor Marston Hodgin's painting of "Old Main" in its last winter.

Charter Day festivity was still in the air on February 18 when the Philadelphia Orchestra in crowded Withrow Court began a program with the Brahms "Academic Festival" Overture, written in tribute to the University of Breslau in 1881. During the intermission conductor Eugene Ormandy was awarded an honorary degree. On March 22 members of the Metropolitan Opera Company in concert with the Cincinnati Symphony, under Max Rudolf, offered an evening of operatic arias, ensembles and overtures. At year's end, on December 15, the Cincinnati Symphony and combined Miami choruses gave the final musical event of the Sesquicentennial.

On March 22 came the first of several symposia. Discussing "The Artist in American Society Today" were Philip R. Adams, John Ciardi, Norris Houghton, Clifton Fadiman, Richard Neutra, Millard Sheets and Halsey Stevens. Early in May a two-day discussion of "Energy and the Social Implications" brought to the campus scientists from this country and abroad. October 9 brought the dedication of Laws Hall and a day-long program on "Education and the Economy." Speakers at the dedication were Dean Courtney C. Brown of the Columbia University Graduate School of Business

and Ohio Governor DiSalle. Later in the day "New Directions in the Management of Business Enterprise" were explored by J. Kenneth Galbraith of Harvard, Mark W. Cresap,
Jr., president of the Westinghouse Corporation, Dexter M.
Keezer, vice-president of the McGraw-Hill Publishing Company and Howard J. Morgens, president of Procter and
Gamble; this panel was moderated by Dean Paul M. Green,
Miami '26, of the College of Commerce and Business Administration, University of Illinois.

On April 10, making his seventh visit to Miami, Robert
Frost delighted a standing-room-only audience in Benton
Hall. Before reading his poems he commented on education
and self-discovery, observing that students must find out
what they are before they can decide what they want to be.
He paid tribute to Miami president Raymond M. Hughes,
who in 1920 proposed that universities support creative
writing by having "artists-in-residence." "I've spent a good
deal of my life at universities as a result of President Hughes'
plea for imposing poets upon the colleges," said Robert
Frost, who became a resident poet at the University of
Michigan in 1921. After his reading came an honorary degree,
with the white hood of Humanities looped over the snowy
head of the poet. President Millett's citation designated the
"beloved and much honored poet laureate of America, whose
writings, lectures and conversations have deepened the understanding of the poetic expression of man's experience
for many generations of students." During the next three
days Robert Frost was greeted on campus paths by countless students, and he held memorable conversations with
groups of students and faculty. From a previous visit, he
remembered walking before his evening lecture through the
Fisher Hall gardens where workmen were setting out smoke
pots against a threatened October freeze. When they said
they were "getting ready for frost tonight," the ruminating
poet said, "I'm doing that too," and went on with his walk.

Two 1959 visitors were members of President Eisenhower's

Cabinet. On February 26 Fred A. Seaton, Secretary of the Interior, spoke at an assembly and was honored with a degree. On June 6, Alumni Day, visitors streamed in to Oxford, thousands of them driving with Miami red-and-white license plates; 8,400,000 Ohio plates in the university colors had been issued in April. That Alumni Day was also the first day of sale for a 12-cent Benjamin Harrison stamp, in deep Miami red, with Oxford as the place of issue. Post-master-General Arthur E. Summerfield spoke at a luncheon in the University Center, and the Oxford Post Office, with special canceling machines and a special crew, sold 325,000 of the new stamps. Various first-day covers showed, along-side the canceled stamp, the old Harrison Hall, the new Harrison Hall, and several pictures of Benjamin Harrison.

On that eventful Alumni Day, Representative Paul F. Schenck of the Third Ohio District presented a framed copy of a resolution of the 86th Congress congratulating Miami University on its Sesquicentennial. The resolution, approved on May 25, had been read into the Congressional Record with an accompanying sketch of Miami's history.

Miami University was the second state university in the old Northwest Territory, provided for under the provisions of the Northwest Ordinance of 1787. . . . By act of May 5, 1792, the President of the United States was authorized to grant letters patent to John Cleves Symmes and his associates . . . provided that the land grant should include one complete township . . . for the purpose of establishing an academy and other public schools and seminaries of learning.

After Ohio became a state in 1803, the State legislature assumed responsibility for making sure that John Cleves Symmes would set aside a township of land for the support of an academy. Such a law was passed by the State legislature April 15, 1803. . . . Finally, on February 17, 1809, the State legislature created Miami University and provided that one complete township in the State of Ohio in the

district of Cincinnati was to be vested in Miami University
for its use, benefit, and support. A commission of three
men was set up to locate the university. In 1810 the legislature provided that Miami University should be located in
Butler County within a township of land to be known as
Oxford Township, and empowering the trustees to lay out
a town of Oxford.

Miami University, Mr. Speaker, is located in beautiful
Oxford, Ohio, and is a very important center of education
and culture. Its achievements are legion because its graduates are known throughout the world for their accomplishments in many professional fields. Some 6,000 resident
students are currently enrolled in the several schools which
make up Miami University. Several additional thousands of
students are enrolled in off-campus centers which are located
in areas throughout the great Miami Valley. . . .

In the fulsome language of a congratulatory resolution the
Congressman declared that "it would be impossible to do
justice to all the famous graduates of this great school"—
though he went on to name ten of them. Several of those
named were featured on Alumni Day at an alumni convocation on Miami Field. In the afternoon shadows they spoke
briefly on "The Alumnus and His University"—Ernest H.
Volwiler, '14, chairman of the Abbott Laboratories; Katherine
J. Densford, '14, director of the world's first university school
of nursing at the University of Minnesota; John Edwin Hull,
'17, former Supreme Commander of United States and United
Nations forces in the Far East; Earl H. Blaik, '18, longtime
West Point football coach and currently vice-president of
the Avco Manufacturing Company; and Bergen Evans, '24,
author, professor and TV personality.

On Sunday morning, June 7, no traffic passed through
Spring Street. In ranks of chairs on the pavement and the
shaded campus beyond, under the tapering white spire of
the Sesquicentennial Chapel, a Baccalaureate assembly heard
the Reverend Julian Price Love, '15, describe this interfaith

chapel as "a house of prayer for all nations and for all kinds of people." President Millett closed the dedication with lines from Robert Frost:

What if it should turn out eternity
Was but the steeple on our house of life
That made our house of life a house of worship.

On the next day a new Miami tradition began with the first wedding in the chapel, the marriage of Sally Gross, '58, and Herbert Fairfield, '59.

At the June Commencement 819 degrees were conferred. With two other graduations, in February and August, the class of 1959 numbered 1,248. It was only natural in an anniversary year to relate that to the past. The whole number of Old Miami graduates, from 1826 to 1873, was 1,085.

The Oxford summer, somnolent in years past, was eventful during 1959. An art exhibit on the theme "The American Scene in 150 Years of American Art," borrowed from museums, galleries and private collections, drew many visitors to the gallery in Hiestand Hall. Late in June came a two-day conference on "Schools for the Future." Addresses by President Novice G. Fawcett of Ohio State University, Fred M. Heckinger of the *New York Times*, Paul R. Hanna of Stanford, H. Bentley Glass of Johns Hopkins, W. Lloyd Warner of the University of Chicago and Henry Steele Commager of Columbia University were followed by discussion sessions with Miami faculty and guests. The conference ended with a platform discussion by journalists, educators, editors and scientists; the panel included W. A. Hammond of the Miami class of 1914 and James H. Rodabaugh, '32.

The year of Miami University's founding became a famous year—famous for the birth of a number of men who achieved eminence in the history of America and Europe. As a part of the Sesquicentennial observance the university presented a series of lectures on four of those men. On Lincoln Day,

February 12, Charles Feinberg of Detroit, a collector of Whitman manuscripts, spoke on Abraham Lincoln as seen in the writings of Walt Whitman. In April Paul B. Sears, chairman of Yale University's conservation program, lectured on the career of Charles Darwin. A week later Harry R. Warfel of the University of Florida reviewed the poetry of Edgar Allan Poe. In the final 1809 lecture Howard Mumford Jones of Harvard discussed Oliver Wendell Holmes.

On April 17 and 18, in Oxford radiant with spring, four eminent visitors gave answers to a question posed by Woodrow Wilson in 1909—"What Is a College For?" The conference was opened by August Heckscher of the Twentieth Century Fund and Mark Van Doren of Columbia University. On the next day Robert M. Hutchins of the Fund for the Republic and Max Lerner of the *New York Post* outlined "The Shape of a College for the Future." In another session undergraduates from Miami, DePauw, Kenyon College and the University of Wisconsin—two of them Rhodes scholars elect—discussed "Student Needs in a Changing World." Other viewpoints in this conference, cosponsored by the Humanities Center for Liberal Education in an Industrial Society, the General Motors Corporation and the Woodrow Wilson Foundation, were expressed by visiting industrialists, editors and educators. The principal papers of the conference were published, with a foreword by President Millett, under the title *What's a College For?*

While educational aims, hopes and dreams were in the spring air, several new appointments were made on the Miami University staff. Four deans were named: H. Bunker Wright took charge of the growing Graduate School; C. Neale Bogner became acting dean of the School of Education; F. Glenn Macomber filled a new post as Dean of Educational Services; and Karl F. Limper succeeded retiring W. E. Alderman as dean of the College of Arts and Science. The Reverend Hardigg Sexton, Miami '18, was made director of the Chapel. Former graduate dean William E. Smith became director of the newly enlarged McGuffey Museum.

One event of 1959 was not planned but would be remembered by all of Oxford and the university. When it was learned that Senator John F. Kennedy would visit Butler County, he was invited to Oxford and a platform was set up on Miami Field. On the morning of September 17, with the largest convocation in Miami history filling the west stands, a motorcade drove in from High Street. Out of the lead car stepped President Millett and the young Senator from Massachusetts. In 1959 John F. Kennedy had a long road ahead to the Presidential nomination and election, but he was confidently running. Tall, slender, debonair, with his quick smile and a hand jabbing the air, he soon had 6,000 Miamians applauding. He spoke for twenty minutes on "The College Graduate's Responsibility in Politics." After singing the Alma Mater, students swarmed around him. No one knew that he would be President and that recent Miami visitor Robert Frost would read a poem at his inaugural under the sunlit dome of the Capitol and that in four years both would belong to history. But there was something electric in the September air. After that convocation a reporter in the *Miami Student* concluded: "Though not committing himself as a candidate for the presidential nomination, Kennedy gave indication that he is likely to be on the ticket in the Ohio Democratic primary." More prophetic was the *Student* columnist who saw in the young Senator "the patrician in politics" and sensed in him "the coiled springs of ambition and an air of mission." For both campus political clubs the Kennedy visit was vitalizing. A year later, in the fall of 1960, the Miami Young Democrats were manning a campaign post across from the Post Office on High Street, handing out ribbons, buttons and literature.

Three years later, Friday, November 22, was a sunless day in Oxford. On that chill gray afternoon the startling word "assassination" went over the campus and people crowded around radio and television screens for news from Dallas. At four thirty, two students walking past the Bell Tower crossed the grass to the university flagpole. They put down their books and lowered the flag to half-staff. At that moment other students were filing into the chapel and the village churches for silent meditation. There was no Thank God It's Friday crowd in High Street.

On Monday morning, November 25, 1963, while the funeral procession moved through the streets of Washington, thousands of students and faculty filled Withrow Court. In a memorial service opened by the Miami Symphony with the solemn second movement of Beethoven's "Eroica" and the Men's Chorus singing Allegri's "Misere Mei, Deus," President Millett quoted Pericles' funeral oration in Athens 2,400 years earlier, spoke briefly of President Kennedy and concluded with words from Lincoln's Gettysburg Address. At the close of the service the convocation sang the hymn "Lest We Forget," then stood in silence while a bugler played taps and from the steps outside the Air Force and Naval Reserve units fired a 21-gun salute. All that week letters and columns poured into the office of the *Miami Student*, which had space to print only a sampling of them.

During the Sesquicentennial year the remains of the first president of Miami University, buried for over a century in a mounded grave in Cincinnati, were brought to the campus that he loved. Before his death at Farmers' College in Cincinnati in 1855, Robert Hamilton Bishop had directed in his will: "I give my body to the Directors of the Farmers' College, to be placed in a coffin and enclosed in a strong box and placed in a mound . . . without any artificial monument unless it be an evergreen planted upon it." He was so buried, at the edge of a deeply wooded valley; his wife, surviving him just two weeks, was buried in the mound beside him. Many of his former Miami students visited that grave. When Farmers' College closed in the 1870's its buildings were

occupied by the Ohio Military Institute. In 1957 that preparatory school was closed and the sylvan property was
acquired by the Cincinnati Board of Education. Planning to
build a new Aiken Senior High School on the site, the Board
informed President Millett of the possibility of moving the
Bishop graves to Oxford.

On June 19, 1959, when morning shadows were deep on
the old burial mound, President Millett, Foster Cole, Arthur
Conrad and the present writer arrived just ahead of three
maintenance men and a truck from Oxford. Digging began,
with as many superintendents as workmen. Legends had
grown around the old mound. Staff members of the former
Military school joined the circle. One said that Dr. Bishop's
favorite horse was reported buried along with the coffins;
another had heard that the Bishop cow was buried there.
Spades cut through brush roots and into sand; work went on
while the sun climbed overhead. No bones appeared, no
horns or hooves or horseshoes, but at noon a spade struck
something solid. Soon two boxes were uncovered, lying side
by side in an east-west direction. With all men present using
crowbars and shovels, one box, somewhat the larger, was
levered onto the other. Then the party took off for lunch.

Returning to the excavation, the men pried off the lid of
the upper box, which was found to be lined with sheet zinc.
Inside was a coffin that measured 74 inches; President Bishop
had been described as a tall, lean man. Though damp, the
wood was firm after 104 years underground. Inside were
some shreds of fabric and an intact skeleton. A cameraman
from the *Cincinnati Enquirer* arrived in time to focus on Dr.
Millett standing above the open box—the striking photograph, said an observer, might be called "The First and
Sixteenth Presidents of Miami University." The second box,
somewhat shorter, contained a skeleton of lighter structure
than the first, with bits of disintegrated cloth and a few
rusted buttons.

The two coffins were closed and loaded onto the university

truck. A sack of earth from the mound was added, and the workmen drove back to Oxford. There each coffin was placed in a new outer box of oak sawed from a tree that had grown on the site of Culler Hall. Growth rings showed that the oak had been on the campus when President Bishop took charge of the pioneer college. The new grave was an unmarked grassy mound at the edge of the flowering gardens beyond Fisher Hall.

One year later, on June 4, 1960, a memorial service for the first president and his wife was held in the formal gardens. In the presence of a hundred alumni and faculty and twelve members of the Bishop family, President Millett recalled the place of Robert Hamilton Bishop in Miami history. He concluded: "Once again President Bishop lies beside his beloved wife in a mound unmarked by any artificial monument and with evergreens nearby. . . . And here we have placed a marker in a boulder from the nearby creek bed which records the simple facts of birth and death and their connection with Miami University, for Robert Hamilton Bishop and Ann Ireland Bishop."

That warm June afternoon another ceremony under the campus trees marked the dedication of the Bishop Memorial Gates. They were a Sesquicentennial gift to the university from Constance Mather Bishop as a memorial to her husband, Dr. Robert Hamilton Bishop, '03, and trustee 1918–55, the fourth bearer of that name. The gates before the looped drive through the old campus forest provided a new front entrance to the university. Through them would come an endless stream of youth to the university that President Bishop had served at its beginning.

Chapter XXII

MIAMI MURAL

IN THE SUMMER of 1962 on a vacation trip to the Seattle Exposition, President and Mrs. Millett and their young son, Stephen, stopped at the cottage of Professor and Mrs. Edwin Fulwider on the rim of Lake Couer d'Alene in northern Idaho. The mountain cottage was bright with western paintings, but there was another painting in President Millett's mind. After supper, while twilight colored the waters of the lake, he talked about a panorama, covering an entire wall, that would depict Miami history.

In Oxford a new wing of the University Center, to provide added dining space, was extending eastward toward Patterson Avenue. The ground floor would become an addition to the Redskin Reservation snack bar. The second floor would provide an enlarged 1809 Room and a cafeteria with windows looking toward Western College. The third floor would become a banquet room; for the 900 square feet of its inner wall President Millett proposed a Fulwider painting that would narrate 150 years of university tradition.

Next morning, with the Milletts on the road again, Edwin Fulwider was left to think about the problems of a painting that would dwarf the painter. Big subjects were natural to him—he had done western mining towns and windy mountain passes—but he had never worked from stepladders and staging. He began there in his summer studio, sketching figures and episodes of a pictorial narrative. In September he brought to Oxford a panel 36 inches long; it would be enlarged 24 times for the finished work.

That fall with the new wing of the Center under construction, work on the mural began in the roomy studio of WMUB-TV behind Bonham House. On a plywood panel 68 by 13 feet the original 36-inch sketch was enlarged to a half-size drawing in pastels. Consulting university histories, photograph albums and books of architecture, costume and local history, the artist delineated the changing college. On the wall of that silent studio went students declaiming in the old Literary Halls, marching off to war, cheering their first football team, crowding lecture rooms and concert halls.

The half-size drawing, 34 feet long and 6 feet high, was photographed in six segments by the Audio-Visual staff. Overhead film positives were then projected and enlarged on a Belgian canvas 70 by 18½ feet. In three long working days Professor and Mrs. Fulwider traced the entire mural. Then came the coloring—clean, fresh colors dominated by Miami red and white—from more than two hundred jars of oil paint. The last brushstroke went on in June, and the Fulwiders headed west for the summer in Idaho.

In September, 1963, the new wing of the Center was complete. In the WMUB studio eleven men rolled the huge canvas on a 15-foot tube and lowered it into a sling. Trucked to the Center, it was carried up to the new banquet room. There the west wall was coated with an adhesive of white lead and Venice turpentine, a formula from fifteenth-century Italy. Unrolling the canvas and pressing it to the wall was a day's work. It fitted there like a glove. That fall a student competition for the naming of the banquet hall produced a happy designation; it became the Heritage Room.

In June of 1962 the president of the graduating class had

presented the class gift—a check to provide the Miami Mural. On Homecoming Day in October of 1963 the handsome Heritage Room was dedicated. Visitors found a light, spacious, colorful banquet hall with red carpet, red chairs and white tables and with the heritage unfolded on the wide west wall. There in lively colors and lilting design were hundreds of life-size figures, a score of campus scenes and a skyline of the seasons with the roofs and towers of twenty-five college buildings. The story began with a surveyor sighting the campus boundaries in the forest; it ended with students before a classroom TV screen. On that Homecoming Day delighted visitors pointed out McGuffey at his eight-sided desk, students rolling snow into the Old Main Building, the arrival of the girls of Oxford College, Professor Stoddard's science lecture, young Ben Harrison beside bonneted Carolina Scott on a college bench, the bicyclists of the 1890's, the Centennial Commencement, the MacKaye studio in the woods, the G.I. students of Vetville after World War II, the Hiestand Gallery, the chapel spire, the timeless Tallawanda picnic twosome, the new Harrison towers against the sky. Already the class gift of 1962 was enhancing the heritage.

To explore that panoramic painting a program of narrative, music and moving spotlight was created by Professor Paul Yeazell of the Miami broadcasting service. For scores of groups and organizations a Heritage Room dinner was followed by the narration of "The Biography of a University." One picture is worth ten thousand words. That winter after an all-day snowfall a group of students on the midnight campus reenacted the 1848 rebellion, blocking a doorway of the new Harrison Hall with a barricade of snow.

Meanwhile the university was expanding. On the south campus on a bright September morning in 1961 Chairman E. W. Nippert of the Board of Trustees presented five buildings—McCracken, Dodds, Anderson and Stanton halls and the Harris Dining Center. They were accepted by Dean of

Students R. F. Etheridge. It was the biggest dedication in Miami history.

The old was not lost in the new. In the same month the McGuffey Museum acquired the McGuffey Collection of Miss Maude Blair of Detroit. With the addition of those three hundred volumes, including proofsheets of two editions, rare McGuffey Primers, and German and Spanish editions of the Readers, the Miami collection surpassed those of both the Ford Museum and the Library of Congress. Acquired by the university in 1960 as a gift from the Emma Gould Blocher Foundation, the historic McGuffey House, now in the midst of the expanding campus, provided a natural setting for the McGuffey Collection. In a Charter Day ceremony on February 17, 1966, the McGuffey House was designated by the National Park Service as a national historic landmark.

During the 1961 Commencement weekend Miami athletic history was recalled at a retirement dinner for George L. Rider, who had completed forty-four years of coaching. In 1917 his first Miami football team had compiled a season score of 202 to 0. Since then George Rider had made his own name and Miami track teams known throughout the country.

On the south campus, near the women's residence halls, a new Herron Hall for women's physical education was opened in October 1962. Speakers at the dedication were Larz Hammel and John B. Whitlock of the Board of Trustees; Cincinnati Councilman Charles P. Taft, grandson of John W. Herron, for whom the building was named; and Professor Margaret Phillips, head of Miami women's physical and health education for more than forty years.

When Withrow Court was opened in 1930 its 3,000-seat capacity looked large enough for any Miami crowd in the next hundred years. It was outgrown long before 1966, when the gymnasium space was doubled though the central arena could not be enlarged. Visitors to the New Withrow Court dedication lingered along the trophy cases and the tradition-laden halls. There were pictures of the athletic squads of sixty-two years, of coaches and athletic directors, of individual record holders in track and field. To the Olympic games Miami had sent sprinter James Gordon, finalist at Los Angeles in 1952; Bill Mulliken, who led the world's swimmers in the 200-meter breaststroke at Rome in 1960; and Bob Schul, winner of the 5,000-meter race at Tokyo in 1964. Jay Colville, a veteran of the Miami athletic staff, went to Australia in 1956 as trainer for the United States boxing team.

Miami's football story became national news in 1959. In that season the coaches of three of the top four teams in the country, according to the Associated Press ratings, were graduates of "little Miami." Number one was Louisiana State, coached by Paul Dietzel, '48. Number three was Army, under its veteran coach Red Blaik, '18. Next came Northwestern, coached by Ara Parseghian, '49. In professional football the leading teams of both Western and Eastern divisions were coached by Miami graduates—Paul Brown, '30, with his Cleveland Browns and Weeb Ewbank, '28, with the Baltimore Colts.

In January, 1959, Paul Dietzel spoke at a Miami assembly in Benton Hall; that night at a New York dinner he was named Coach of the Year. In the same month Ewbank, whose team had defeated the New York Giants for the world title, was named Professional Coach of the Year. As reported in the *Miami Alumnus*, Ewbank's clinching victory showed "the kind of precision and determination typical of Cleveland Browns teams which had won six straight professional world championships under guidance of Paul Brown, Miami, '30, 1950 through 1955, and of the 1955 Brooklyn Dodgers who won the World Series under Walter (Smokey) Alston, Miami, '36, as manager."

How does Miami do it? sportswriters were asking—how does little Miami of Ohio, where the stadium is a joke and the low-key recruiting is controlled by the rules of a small conference, consistently field fine teams and produce brilliant coaches? At the Miami All-Sports banquet of 1958 Ara Parseghian gave a wholehearted answer. "Because of its tradition, environment, athletic ability and academic standing, I am proud to be associated with Miami University," he said. "I hope you members of Miami's squad will come to realize what those things can mean."

On October 25, 1959, the *New York Sunday News* ran a two-page feature on "Miami of Ohio, Whose Sons Shine," pointing out that without overemphasizing sports Miami had produced a number of outstanding coaches. "No college," it declared, "has even remotely approached the record of Miami grads in the massive assault on the top-rung of the coaching profession."

After the Purdue game in 1961 Athletic Director John L. Brickels had a letter from the manager of the Purdue Memorial Union noting that "your football squad was complimented by our foods staff as the most exemplary football players in their experience of feeding football teams." On an autumn visit to Oxford strapping Governor Frank Lausche, coming out of a convocation at Withrow Court with students swarming around him, asked, "Where is the football team?" They were not ganged up in their red and white sweaters but were scattered among the student body. At about that time Economics Professor R. E. Berry remarked in print on "the excellent impression that our athletes make here and away, the absence of strutting, arrogant campus athletes . . . and the very evident fact that athletes neither receive nor expect special consideration in academic affairs." He credited it to the general university atmosphere and the caliber of the student body. But, he added, "much of the credit must go to the coaches."

An odd part of Miami's football tradition is that its most reverberating victories have come away from home. After a quiet Saturday afternoon in Oxford, cheers have filled the town when the final whistle sounded in some Big Ten stadium. One of those times was October 13, 1962. Chanting

"Miami 10, Purdue 7," students swarmed down to empty Miami Field and tore up both the north and the south goalposts. Back up High Street they marched, raising the goalposts in the middle of High Street in front of Snyder's and the Purity. Traffic used the side streets while the October dusk came on. At ten o'clock that night 5,000 cheering students closed in on the busload of returning players. They carried Coach John Pont and his team on their shoulders to Withrow Court. Next morning a sign in front of the Deke House announced "Rose Bowl Tickets for Sale Here." Five years later Coach Pont took a team to Pasadena. After a winning season at Yale, where he was succeeded by Carmen Cozza, his Miami classmate of 1952, he led the Indiana Hoosiers to a Big Ten title and a Rose Bowl game on New Year's Day, 1968.

Commenting on the term "little Miami," an editorial in the Akron *Beacon-Journal* observed that "a more descriptive term for Purdue's conquerors would be 'Old Miami.' Founded in 1809 the school was sixty years old when Purdue was founded. Among the ranking twenty [in national football] only the University of Maryland (1807) has a longer history than Miami's." The mellow history of Miami was not overlooked by sports reporters. A New York writer summed it up: "Far from being a football factory, Miami of Ohio is an idyll of the healthiest traditions of American campus life, where a lack of over-emphasis produces a more well-rounded man."

By 1960 the university had outgrown Withrow Court, and a new 9,000-seat assembly hall was planned for convocations, commencements, all-university concerts and basketball games. It was to occupy Cook Field at the eastern end of the central campus. On second thought the Trustees reconsidered: the huge arena would dwarf the academic buildings and would deprive Miami of the open green, alive at all seasons with athletic practice and intra-mural sports, that made so inviting a prospect. In the summer of 1966 construction began on the former fairway at the bend of North Tallawanda Avenue.

The final basketball game was played in Withrow Court on March 2, 1968, with 3,914 spectators crowded in. The game was lost to a nationally ranked team from Dayton, but it was a night charged with history. While the record crowd gave ovations to both teams and coaches, to the graduating seniors, to President Shriver and the women sponsors of Tribe Miami, there was an awareness of thirty-seven years of tradition—athletics, concerts, commencements, lectures, dances, carnivals and convocations—that haunted Withrow Court. When the crowd streamed out, with a quarter-moon gleaming through the bare March trees, some of them looked down Tallawanda where the dark bulk of the new assembly hall stood against the stars. On December 2 Miami would face the University of Kentucky in that arena, and new traditions would begin to gather there.

With growing enrollment and mounting pressure for admission the university needed to make the fullest use of its facilities. After a year of study and discussion a trimester calendar was adopted; it became effective in September 1965. With fifteen-week terms between Labor Day and mid-December and between early January and late April, the third, divided term could be scheduled in late spring and summer, with a month's break before the next academic year. By shortening the final examination period a semester's work could be encompassed in a trimester. Students enrolled for three terms could complete a college program in three years; others could use the four-month interval for travel and employment. Freshmen could begin their studies with any term.

A three-year "experiment" with the trimester plan proved both successful and disappointing. It was good to complete a term before the Christmas holidays, and the Easter recess was gladly traded for an earlier Commencement. Many of the faculty found added time for research and writing. Conferences and workshops increased in number and variety. In the summer of 1968 thirty workshops ranging from Aerospace Education to Problems of Inner-City Schools brought groups, large and small, to the campus for varying periods. Yet no marked increase in use of university facilities was realized, as a booming enrollment for fall and winter shrank to less than half capacity in the third trimester. With war enlarging in Vietnam, draft-deferred men students did not choose to accelerate their college course, and the girls had no reason to hurry through. In the new terms there was an unbroken pace of academic assignment, with no breaks for reading and term papers; one result was a lessening of student course load to fourteen or fifteen hours instead of the traditional sixteen or seventeen. With an April Commencement the spring athletic program was crippled and a new generation of students went through Miami without experiencing the magic "spring in Oxford."

In the late 1960's calendar became a stubborn question with students, faculty and the university administration. The question was intensified when the expanded state university system was urged to adopt a common quarter calendar. Miami, jealous of its historic autonomy and dubious of the eleven-week quarter term, was not persuaded. A 1967 survey showed preponderant support, by both students and faculty, for the trimester plan. But the urging for statewide uniformity increased, and in December 1967, the Miami Trustees voted to adopt the quarter calendar beginning September 1969. In every department of the university, course offerings were reviewed and revised for conversion to a quarter system.

Though the trimester plan had seemed a progressive innovation, it was far from new at Miami. In December 1867, the Board of Trustees "resolved that the college year should be divided into three sessions," beginning in September, January and April. That three-term schedule was in force for four years from 1868 until 1872 while enrollment dwindled; after a final two-semester year the old college closed its doors in 1873. On this "experiment," almost a century later, the trimester plan again lasted just four years.

During the winter of 1964 President Millett served as a consultant at the U.S. Office of Education, commuting between Oxford and Washington, where he directed preparations for the operation of the Higher Education Facilities Act of 1963; he was also on call at Columbus, where the newly created Board of Regents was shaping a master plan for higher education in Ohio. For thirty years the Council of State Universities had made common cause before the Ohio General Assembly. But more cooperation and far-range planning were needed. To meet those needs the Board of Regents was created, its purview to be the entire state-supported system of higher education in Ohio. The Regents would be headed by a chancellor-director.

On February 24, 1964, Chairman Larz Hammel of the Miami Board of Trustees received from President Millett a letter that began: "It is with great regret and a genuine touch of sadness that I must hereby tender my resignation as President of Miami University." To the University Senate on March 3 he announced his departure as of June 30. On July 1 he would become Director and Chancellor of the Ohio Board of Regents.

That spring both town and gown bade a reluctant farewell to the Milletts. A stag reception for the retiring president at the Oxford Country Club was followed by a dinner in the Heritage Room. Two weeks later President and Mrs. Millett were honored at a faculty dinner under a June moon on the University Center patio, where a John D. Millett Scholarship was announced as a faculty presentation. At the final Millett Commencement in a golden sunset on Miami Field, honorary degrees were awarded to three eminent Miami graduates—novelist Fletcher Knebel, '34, publisher Kenneth M. Grubb, '31, and business management professor John F. Mee, '30.

President Millett's eleven-year tenure had brought a steady

march of development to the university. Enrollment grew
from 7,500 (on and off campus) to nearly 15,000. Six classroom, laboratory and administration buildings and extensive
new residence facilities were added to the plant. The faculty
was strengthened and enlarged. The operating budget increased from five million to fifteen million dollars.

It was President Millett's suggestion that the new assembly building be named George Washington Hall, commemo-
rating George Washington's signing of the Act of 1792
(amended 1794) that provided for a township to support the
university, and that its main entrance might be dignified by
the bronze figure of George Washington given to Miami by
Samuel Spahr Laws in 1920. But upon President Millett's
resignation the trustees unanimously voted that the proposed
building should become the John D. Millett Assembly Hall.
It would soon begin to rise at the end of Tallawanda Avenue,
the site of all-university events of years to come.

Chapter XXIII

A SENSE OF MISSION

SINCE ITS CREATION in 1903 the Miami University Senate
had outgrown a succession of meeting rooms—in the old
Main Building, McGuffey Hall, Hughes Hall and Laws Hall.
As the staff grew and committees multiplied it was clear
that university business required the attention of a frequently
convened representative body. In December 1963 the Senate
passed an enabling act creating the Faculty Council, to
which it delegated legislative authority. Under chairmanship of the University president the Council roll comprised
sixteen elected members from the faculty and seven members
appointed by the president. The Council's actions were subject to review by the Senate, which continued to meet four
times a year.

Under Acting President C. Ray Wilson the Faculty Council began its bi-weekly meetings in September 1964. The
Trustees Room in Roudebush Hall proved too small for the
Council members and others who brought reports, requests
and information. After a few crowded sessions the Council
moved to the Student Senate Chamber in Warfield Hall,
which also proved inadequate. In the fall of 1967 it convened
in a lecture room in Laws Hall. To its meetings flowed a

broad current of business pertaining to academic programs, standards and requirements, faculty rights and responsibilities, and faculty-student relationships. Its debates ranged from probation penalties to honorary degrees, from the improvement of undergraduate teaching to the approval of Ph.D. programs.

Meanwhile a committee of trustees, under the successive chairmanship of John B. Whitlock and Lloyd O'Hara, aided by faculty and alumni advisory committees, had compiled more than a hundred names from which to choose a new president of the University. Interviews with a number of candidates away from the campus led to campus visits by a final list of eight. On February 6, 1965, members of the faculty met Dean and Mrs. Phillip R. Shriver of Kent State University at a reception in the Heritage Room. That evening the Shrivers were guests of the selection committee at dinner in the Benjamin Harrison Room. Next day, after a special meeting of the Board, Chairman Larz Hammel announced the election of Phillip R. Shriver as Miami's seventeenth president. He would take office on July 1.

During the spring Dr. Shriver paid several visits to Oxford. Miami students first saw their sturdy, smiling president-elect on Charter Day, when he was introduced along with Ohio Governor James A. Rhodes and Chancellor Millett of the Board of Regents at a Withrow Court convocation. In his Charter Day address Governor Rhodes described a 290-million-dollar bond issue to provide capital improvements in Ohio's public universities; as he spoke one could sense new prospects for higher education in the state. A few weeks later Dr. Shriver was presented to the faculty by Acting President Wilson at a gathering in the Towers Room. In answer to a broad range of questions the president-elect evinced a knowledge of Miami's past and a conception of its sound development in the years ahead.

A native of Cleveland, an honor graduate of Yale with advanced degrees from Harvard and Columbia, Phillip

Shriver had taught American history at Kent since 1947. He became dean of its College of Arts and Science in 1964. A man of scholarly mind, tireless energy, and buoyant purpose and personal warmth, he proposed to teach while being president; he asked to be scheduled for a course in American history.

In July 1965, Phillip and Martha Shriver and their five children moved into Grey Gables, across from the broad green of Western College. This native stone residence, built in 1930 by a retired president of Western College, had been purchased by Miami and used as a guest house. Now it became the president's home—on summer evenings President Shriver played softball with his children on the lawn—while Lewis Place was being renovated. The Shrivers moved into Lewis Place in the fall of 1966.

On October 14, 1965, a gold-and-yellow campus filled with visitors for the Shriver inauguration. The academic procession, representing more than two hundred colleges, universities and learned societies, formed in Harrison Hall and marched through leaf-strewn streets to Withrow Court. President Shriver's inaugural address evoked the sense of mission that permeated Miami history, a mission to advance and impart knowledge and to foster personal values in the education of all its students.

The new president quickly showed a concern for relationships within a multifarious university. He met with faculty groups and organizations. He spoke to alumni gatherings. He talked with student leaders at breakfasts, brunches, coffee hours and receptions. He urged faculty-student exchanges in dormitories, fraternities and faculty homes. On two evenings a week he taught history in a crowded classroom—the first president in fifty-three years to conduct a course of study. The 1966 *Recensio* described him as "this truly personalized president." He soon knew scores of students by name and hundreds by face. To a university forty times larger than that of Guy Potter Benton he brought some of the Benton personal concern and manner.

In administrative reorganization President Shriver named a cabinet of four vice-presidents: C. Ray Wilson for academic affairs, R. F. Etheridge for student affairs, Lloyd Goggin for finance and business affairs, and John E. Dolibois for alumni affairs and development. Through these men the president had direct approach to four vital areas of the academic community.

In 1961 Miami had entered upon a plan of cooperation with Ohio State University and Indiana University in the training of doctoral candidates. By this arrangement Miami graduate students took a year's work beyond the Master's degree and then went to the other university for a final year of residence; the Miami faculty shared in the general examinations and the directing of dissertation research. In 1964-65 nineteen students in twelve departments were enrolled in cooperative doctoral programs. By 1967 eleven Ph.D.'s "from the Ohio State University in cooperation with Miami University" had been awarded in the fields of chemistry, English and education.

In 1967 independent doctoral programs were begun in botany, English and geology, with others soon to follow. Advanced graduate instruction required the adding of specialists to the faculty and increased research activity by many others. A general concern was that undergraduate standards should be maintained and improved along with the growth of advanced offerings. Believing that teaching and research are complementary, the university enlarged its undergraduate honors program while it expanded research grants in many fields. To bring Miami scholars into closer communication with supporting agencies in government and business, an Office of Research was created in 1967, under direction of Dean Donald E. Cunningham. At the same time Director George Bowers of the School of Applied Science was named dean of that division. One of its rapidly growing fields was systems analysis. In 1967 the university trustees renewed, after a long interval, the policy of sabbatical leaves for qualified members of the faculty and staff. That year five faculty members had leaves that took them on research to other universities in this country and to Paraguay and England.

In the fall of 1966 the Deke house came down. Sixty years earlier President Benton had proposed a fraternity row on lower High Street, and university lots were leased to Phi Delta Theta, Delta Kappa Epsilon and Sigma Chi. The Phi Delt house was the first to come—in 1909—and the first to go; it was leveled in 1950. Now the Deke house was demolished, and in its place rose a Behavioral Science building that dwarfed the remaining Sigma Chi house. The new building was named Benton Hall, while Benton Auditorium was renamed for John W. Hall, the fifth president of the University.

So High Street lost the friendly look that for half a century had made an inviting approach to the town and the college. Ball games on the lawn, students on the porches and music pouring from the open windows were replaced by another classroom building, and the great old trees were gone. Another loss was the Dekes' wry humor; for years they had amused the campus with sardonic signs and banners on their iron balcony and grotesque objects on their terrace. The Dekes moved to Church Street, where new chapter houses were replacing old residences. Meanwhile on Campus Avenue some historic houses were renovated and enlarged for chapter residence, and a solid fraternity row bordered the campus on North Tallawanda.

In the fall of 1967 power saws felled a hundred trees on the lower campus where once the Indians had kindled campfires, and soon a giant crane was lifting steel beams to the skeleton of a new Chemistry building. Named Hughes Laboratories, the 6-million-dollar structure would house the

Chemistry Department, the Computer Center and an Instrumentation Laboratory to be shared by the several science divisions. The former Hughes Hall was renamed for Clarence W. Kreger, University President pro tempore, 1952–53. Beyond the shady grove that remained in the U of the Bishop Drive, Shideler Hall had been dedicated a few months earlier. Inside its glass portals a revolving geophysical globe, the gift of explorer Andrew Iddings, marked it, even to passing motorists; as an earth science building.

Now the lower campus, long the domain of owls and squirrels and a poet-in-residence, was a science cluster, while on the upper campus, where "Old Egypt" and Brice Hall had housed the first Miami sciences, rose the Edgar Weld King Library. Its first wing, with Emeritus Librarian King cutting the ribbon at its doorway, was dedicated on a mellow autumn morning in 1966. Jammed in between Clokey, Brice and Benton halls, soon to be gone, the dedication gathering was asked to visualize the eventual building that would dominate the upper campus. During a strenuous weekend sixty volunteer fraternity men transferred 40,000 volumes, pushing book trucks up and down ramps and across the quadrangle from the old library. In its open shelves the first wing of the new library housed only recent periodicals and books most useful to undergraduates; the Alumni Library was used increasingly for research.

Comfortably fitted, fully carpeted, bright, friendly and flexible, the King Library quickly filled with students. During the first week it was easier to get into the building than to get out. At the loan desk volumes were magnetized to allow passage through a turnstile with an electric eye. The gate locked at the approach of an uncharged book; it also sensed keys, a penknife or even a metal zipper and would not let them pass. When voltage was reduced it became more selective.

During meetings with students in their residence halls, President Shriver found a surprising interest in a building that looked forgotten. In a romantic setting, on the far edge of the east campus overlooking the university gardens and the deep woods of the Tallawanda, Fisher Hall had become a haunted place. The upper floors were empty, while a part of the main floor had been converted to a temporary university theater. Now the new Performing Arts Center was rising on the south campus, and Fisher Hall seemed doomed to demolition. But on a campus mushrooming with new buildings the old towered structure in its murmuring grove of pine, spruce and hemlock was a reminder of the storied past. In new dormitories and fraternity houses students exchanged legends, and added to them, of the handsome old hall that had been a women's college, a health resort and sanitarium, a Freshman dormitory, a Naval school during World War II and finally a theater.

Fisher Hall had authentic legends. Before it was added to the Miami campus, fraternity men carried a coffin through the midnight grounds and tied their initiates to the iron-grilled door of the Lane tomb in the Tallawanda woods. Voices sometimes called from barred windows in the sanitarium; one winter morning an inmate was found hanging by his own belt from an orchard tree beyond the greenhouse. That was clearly suicide, but a lasting mystery shrouded a student disappearance in the spring of 1953.

On Sunday, April 19, the campus was green, though a chill wind came with darkness and snow flurries whitened the old spired spruce trees in front of Fisher Hall. At midnight an upper-class counselor came in from a trip home to Dayton and climbed to his second-floor room. The lights were on, the radio was going, and on his roommate's desk a textbook lay open with a wallet and pocket articles beside it. The roommate was Ronald Tammen, a sophomore counselor in the Freshman hall. When an hour passed without Tammen's return, his roommate supposed he had gone to his fraternity, though it was odd he would not take a coat on that chilly night. When he didn't appear next day, university officials were informed.

Ronald Tammen was twenty years old, a Dean's List student and a member of the varsity wrestling squad. He played with the Campus Owls, a small dance band, and he had a car permit for transportation of that group. The car was found in its proper place, doors locked, with his bass fiddle on the back seat. There was no reason to suspect violence, but it was thought he might have injured himself in a night walk. At mid-week search parties, first the members of his fraternity and then four hundred cadets of the Air Force ROTC, scoured the Tallawanda woods for three miles above and below Fisher Hall. Workmen at Hueston Woods searched the shores of Acton Lake, five miles away. An old cistern behind Fisher Hall was drained. The Butler County sheriff and the State Highway Patrol widened the search, and the FBI checked bus, rail and air terminals in five adjoining states.

When Tammen's photograph appeared in a newspaper story a woman at Seven Mile, near Hamilton, reported that on that Sunday night she had been called to the door. In the porch light stood a bareheaded youth, asking where he could get a bus. He was dark-haired, polite, and a little confused, she thought. It might have been Tammen, suffering from amnesia, said the sheriff. No other clue was ever found.

That fall students in Fisher Hall heard a voice singing in the formal gardens and from the woods beyond the greenhouse. It was first heard on a Sunday night in mid-November, a voice that ranged from bass notes to something like falsetto. On the next two nights the voice was heard, approaching Fisher from the gardens and then fading in the woods beyond. On the second night two freshmen said they saw a long-haired, long-striding figure. On the third night six counselors, hearing the voice, caught sight of someone and chased him past the chain of ponds and across the golf course. On Wednesday night, November 18, a hundred students managed only to scare each other as they roamed the grounds. On Thursday night a tall figure in a long black coat was chased by twenty-five freshmen, who lost it in the wooded ravine. The leading pursuer confessed, "I was scared I'd catch up with him."

By that time the phantom was a thrilling, chilling rumor over the whole campus, and the nightly traffic through their domain was resented by the men of Fisher Hall. They wrote a letter to the *Student*: "Fisher Hall does not have some of the luxuries enjoyed by the new halls on the campus, snack bars, TV rooms, pool tables. But we do have a phantom and we want to keep him to ourselves. We request that students from other parts of the campus leave our phantom alone." By then the ghost of Fisher Hall was becoming a Miami legend.

In 1957 the building was examined by the State Architect and found unsafe for use as a dormitory. But the ghost stayed on. The building was empty for a year and then was taken over by the Drama department in 1958. The stairways were closed, and the old dining room was converted to a half-round theater. From their studios and workshops, theater students heard muffled sounds overhead; they saw unaccounted shadows crossing the windows and found objects—even the portrait of Judge Fisher—mysteriously displaced.

In the winter of 1967 a professional medium was brought to the old building for a public communication with the spirit. The two hundred tiered seats were filled when a mild, elderly man, who might have been a retired music teacher, took the stage. The lights were dimmed; the audience waited. In a gentle voice the medium addressed the unknown. During his silence a window rattled and an owl hooted from the trees. But nothing came. The seance was a failure. Next morning a theater class was startled by muffled sounds from the empty corridors overhead.

With the new Miami all but obliterating the old, students

wanted to save Fisher Hall. As probable demolition drew near, the movement grew. In a course project Architecture students worked on plans for a reconstruction behind the old portico and within the old walls. During the spring of 1968 members of the Conservative Club secured 2,400 signatures to a petition to preserve Fisher Hall; it was presented to President Shriver on the old south portico. Newspaper stories appeared in Oxford, Hamilton, Dayton, Columbus and Cincinnati. Eight new buildings were rising on the Miami campus, but it was the old building that made news.

The pursuit of a phantom was perhaps symptomatic of the 1950's. Throughout America in that decade students were politically passive. "The silent generation," a newsmagazine called them. In 1951 a *Miami Student* editor found that a look at college newspapers across the country showed general apathy and indifference. There were few campus causes, little interest in student government, no excitement except for spring raids on women's dormitories. Students were more inclined to fit in than to break out. Security was the acknowledged goal, and conformity was the road that led there. The "organization man," molded by the increasing technology and corporate structure of American business, had come to college.

With the sixties the campus climate changed. At Miami, as elsewhere, students were suddenly restless, innovative, assertive. "Student rights" became a cause, student government a crusade. After three centuries of submission to institutional authority American students began a drive for participation in university policy and operation.

With some 10,000 students in the mid-1960's, Miami University had outgrown its steadily expanding campus. Privately built apartment blocks were spreading across the town. From Sycamore Street to the woods of Collins Run students began keeping bachelor hall as in the Old Miami. But these men had the help of laundromats and supermarkets, and they invited girls for dinner. Commercial builders did not have to spell out the lure of an apartment: it was off-campus housing, with freedom, independence and un-supervised social life. New university halls were rising, but enrollment rose faster. Freshmen were required to live in university residences, but for a multitude of upperclassmen "an apartment" was the thing. In 1967 some 6,500 students were housed in thirty halls; off-campus housing attracted 2,200 more. The Oxford apartments bore traditional Miami names—Towers, Block M, Arrowhead—but they were a radical departure.

"This generation of students," wrote a university president in 1964, "seems to be hurt, angry, and in revolt." At Miami, as elsewhere, there was an evident dichotomy of work and pleasure to which the faculty, the students and the outside world contributed. Academic requirements were increasing, and students added to their own malaise by four days of strenuous study followed by a weekend of strenuous pleas-ure-seeking. In both thought and pleasure they demanded independence; their most reviled expression was *in loco parentis*. It was the task of the faculty and the administration to define the limits of freedom, and its responsibilities, to restate that the aim of university people is to choose the things of greatest value, and to point out that the choice re-quires a trained mind to save one from being deluded, an alert conscience to resist reckless impulse, and a disciplined will to pursue rewarding goals.

Free speech became the rallying cry of activists on the Miami campus. Student organizations asserted their right to hear unorthodox views and to invite speakers to Miami plat-forms without university approval. (History was repeating itself, the same contest had allied the Literary Societies against the faculty in the 1840's.) Despite political rumblings and editorial opposition in regional newspapers, and with the help of faculty groups, the students won this issue. Be-ginning in 1964 an annual "Voices of Dissent" symposium

provided a forum on economic, political and social controversies. To the campus came speakers as disparate as Linus
Pauling, Barry Goldwater, Arthur Schlesinger, Victor Reuther
and Bayard Rustin. Not a resistance movement, this welcome
for diverse viewpoints and philosophies became a university
program. Wrote President Shriver in 1967, "We believe this
planned opportunity for a presentation of dissenting points
of view is in the tradition of great universities." When certain students asked for the designation of a "Hyde Park
Corner" on the campus, they were reminded that the entire
university is a free speech arena, with no responsible viewpoint stifled or excluded.

By 1967 the wave of student protest had become a demand
for involvement in the governing of the university. A leaflet
distributed by a self-styled "Civil Liberties Board" announced a manifesto. "We come . . . with an opinion, with
a warning, with a promise—both to that mentality which
imposes upon us its ways and that mentality which, in the
vanguard of change elsewhere, might now take upon itself
the responsibility and the promise of change here." In these
times students could not wait to be educated; they hastened
to educate their elders. This was not a local movement;
student attitudes moved in a groundswell from restless urban
campuses and from national student organizations. Across
the country it was clear that students wanted to be included,
to be heard and to participate in the decisions of the academic community. The phrase "student rights" was replaced
by "student power." At Miami, where a sometimes scorned
paternalism helped them, students gained voting membership in a number of faculty committees. But they wanted
more; they wanted course evaluation and a weighing of
individual instructors, and they questioned the "relevance"
of curricular requirements, the reality and justice of the
grading system, the legality of conduct regulations and disciplinary procedures. Unaware that a campus has always
offered students sanctuary, shielding them from ineluctable

operation of the law, students raised a cry of "due process." In faulty English the manifesto leaflet protested: "Let us ask them why we as students, of all things, in an academic community, of all places, must be subject to incursions on our rights and personalities which no other citizen of this nation would dare tolerate, and which the laws of even this state do not prescribe." These fervent students advanced some foolish ideas—as do some faculty members on standing committees. But a revolution was in process, and there was a growing demand for a student bill of rights. The undergraduate, asserting his status as a citizen, was colliding with the whole history of American universities and their authority to regulate student requirements and conduct. Now this traditional authority was contested by occasional demonstrations, picketing, sit-ins and the insistence on due process. In this ferment (to the chagrin of activists among both the students and the faculty, there was not enough commotion at Miami to make news) the administration patiently maintained a concern for the student as a person and for his reasonable participation in university government.

Involvement was the aim of the most aware and concerned students, an involvement in the troubled world as well as in the changing university. This college generation was both rebuked and extolled by various observers, and not wholly understood by any. Some found the activist student headstrong, refractory, contentious, demanding rights without responsibilities, asserting his own views and intolerant of all else. Others saw this generation as searching, sensitive and idealistic, rejecting the materialism and impersonalism of a technological society and seeking direct personal relationships. From Miami in the mid-sixties more than a hundred students enlisted in the Peace Corps and many hundreds became volunteer workers in civil rights and allied programs. This was an alienated generation, for whom the old faiths and restraints were exhausted and irrelevant. Their grandparents had read Tennyson and Browning, their parents Edgar Lee Masters and Thomas Wolfe; these students turned to Joyce, Camus and Kafka. They made new assumptions about the nature of Communism, the rights of the poor and the use of the nation's resources. They worried less about paying their steadily mounting tuition (or having it paid for them) than about what they were being taught. The ivory tower had become an arena of controversy. More clearly than in any previous generation they saw the hypocrisy and rapacity of their society, and, supported by its affluence, they disowned it. This was one of the ironies that troubled them and their professors.

In radiant spring weather a somber weekend began in Oxford with news of the assassination of Martin Luther King at a civil rights rally in Memphis. In December 1959, early in his public career, Dr. King had spoken in the Towers Room of the University Center. At noon on April 9, 1968, the hour of his funeral in Atlanta, more than a thousand students and faculty gathered in the south quadrangle for a memorial service conducted by President Shriver, Professor Stanley Lusby and three Negro students, after which they marched silently through the campus and up High Street to the village green.

These students felt involved not with inherited loyalties but with the peasant in Vietnam and the slum dweller in American cities. Social reform seemed crippled by the nation's expenditure of vital resources in a war-torn little country across the Pacific. The threat of World War III and a nuclear holocaust deepened the concern. This was the first college generation to seek education in a world that risked annihilation. It was also the first college generation to be exempted from military service in wartime. That privileged status created feelings of guilt. Opposition to the war gave some students a reason for avoiding military service, but it did not allay the guilt; much campus alienation and activism were motivated by an unconscious search for atonement. When every evening's TV news showed American youths toiling and dying in distant swamps and jungles, the war could not be distant. Many students were uncertain—as were their elders—about the aims and effects of the war. The protesters made futile antiwar demonstrations, while a much greater number tried to find a basis for personal conviction. That concern brought to the Miami campus a list of internationally known statesmen, scholars, generals and journalists in the "As We See It: Vietnam '68" symposium. During the month of March this program, conceived, planned and conducted by the Student Senate, drew a total of 20,000 persons to a series of addresses, debates and discussions of the central issue of the decade.

On June 6, 1968, the day after the assassination of Robert F. Kennedy in Los Angeles, the leading article in the *Cincinnati Enquirer* quoted Robert Sherwin of the Sociology department on the crumbling of traditions and the resulting sense of drift, rootlessness and want of control over the sweep of life. This feeling of helplessness, Sherwin said, generates an intense impatience. The cry is "Now, now, now"; there must be immediate action. Professor Sherwin found this importunity voiced in classroom discussions; in the world outside it impels men to mindless violence. What is civilization, he asked, but a complex of traditions? In times of turbulence it is the task of education to recover the traditions that hold the world together.

Chapter XXIV

HORIZON

"OUR HORIZON," wrote Henry David Thoreau, "is never quite at our elbows." What was evident from a hut on Walden Pond is more apparent from a college window. A university always has prospects, new problems, new opportunities, new glimpses of expanding knowledge and new perceptions of the role of higher learning in an always changing world. When the Ohio Board of Regents published in 1965 the *Provisional Master Plan for Public Higher Education in Ohio*, it might have been entitled *Our Horizon*.

The U.S. census of 1960 showed that Ohio was the 5th state in population and the 11th in per capita income. Yet in per capita support of higher education Ohio stood 39th. California spent $32 per capita on its institutions of higher learning, Texas $15.09, Illinois $14.60. Ohio spent $13.14, and its state universities charged the highest fees. "In Ohio," John D. Millett noted in 1962, "nearly half of our college students are in the state universities; our hope for excellence in higher education rests with our public institutions."

The Ohio Board of Regents, created in 1963, was charged with framing "a master plan for higher education in the state, considering the needs of the people, the needs of the state, and the role of individual public and private institutions within the state in fulfilling these needs." The plan began with the bold statement that the colleges and universities of Ohio should expand their enrollment from 242,000 in 1964 to 410,000 in 1970, to 560,000 in 1975, and to 650,000 in 1980. To accomplish this it was projected that the state-assisted colleges, with combined enrollment of 146,000 in 1964, would have to make room for 265,000 students in 1970, 395,000 in 1975, and 470,000 in 1980. Such growth would require the creating of new institutions, including a number of community colleges, and the rapid expansion of existing universities. The recommendation for Miami: "Miami University in Oxford should be primarily a residential campus, with particular attention given to upper division instructional programs in arts and sciences, teacher education, business administration, fine arts, and applied science; to graduate programs at the Master's level in these same fields, and to Doctor's programs in selected fields of excellence." It was recommended that on its Oxford campus Miami University should give increasing attention to upper division and graduate level instruction; enrollment was projected to a maximum, in the 1970's, of 15,000 students. After the two-year program at the branch campuses in Middletown and Hamilton, qualified students could transfer to the Oxford campus. The enrollment of resident graduate students was expected to reach a total of 1,500.

As it approached the 1970's historic Miami University was more a part of a system than ever in its past. The Board of Trustees was reduced from twenty-seven to nine members; a quarter calendar was instituted throughout the state universities; a statewide formula of subsidy was based on enrollment of underclassmen, upperclassmen and candidates for Masters' and Doctors' degrees. After a long history of self-government, Miami was being drawn closer to the other state universities and to administrative agencies in Columbus.

Bigness became a new concern in the old village of Oxford,

which now had parking problems, weekend traffic lines and a five o'clock rush following the closing of university offices. A serenity had gone from town and campus. The old slant walk streamed with students, and on Friday afternoon High Street overflowed. While the Millett Assembly Hall was under construction the spring Commencement was held in double sessions, morning and afternoon; Withrow Court could not hold the graduating class and its guests. With 10,000 students expected in residence halls by 1972 and another 3,000 in fraternities and apartments, more growth was on the horizon.

The *Master Plan for State Policy in Higher Education*, published in 1966, projected a limit of 3,000 freshman residential students on the Oxford campus, one-fifth of them from states other than Ohio. Freshman and sophomore enrollment would total about 5,000, upperclassmen 7,000, graduate students some 2,000. In 1967 Miami accepted its first candidates for the Ph.D. in English, geology and botany. In 1968 doctoral programs were begun in history, political science, microbiology and psychology, with prospective programs in economics, chemistry, and personnel and guidance.

With more students Miami also was attracting better students. President Shriver reported in 1967 that the quality of the freshman class was the highest among all state-assisted institutions in Ohio and very high among all public institutions in the United States. Competition for admission had never been so keen. Three-fourths of the entering women came from the top 15 percent of their high school classes, and three-fourths of the men came from the top third. Test scores showed 79 percent of Miami freshmen ranking above the national norm for all universities. These students, better prepared than any previous generation, proved themselves in the college classroom. In 1967 more than 5,000 undergraduates were named to the Dean's List. By 1968 nearly a thousand were enrolled in Honors courses, where students met in small informal groups or in tutorial conference on an independent project. The development of Honors work was a priority of the growing university.

While the trimester schedule was in effect, 1965 to 1969, many students and faculty used the mid-April to September interval for foreign travel, study and research. Charter flights took Miami parties to Europe at minimum rates; during the summer Miamians crossed paths in cities from London to Athens, from Stockholm to Madrid. On exchange or Fulbright professorships, members of the faculty taught in England, Scotland, Nigeria, India, Japan, Iraq and Iran. Meanwhile, foreign students brought a cosmopolitan aspect to the Miami campus. In 1968 foreign enrollment totaled 102 students from 44 countries; more than half were from Asia and Africa. Twenty-eight of the number were graduate students, most of them seeking degrees in some field of science. In 1966–67 a distinguished Chinese author, Mrs. Eileen Chang Reyher, spent the year on campus as a visiting foreign scholar. During that year five students from the School of Education were doing apprentice teaching in the American school at Las Palmas in the Canary Islands; another group taught in the English language school operated in the U.S. Embassy in Prague, Czechoslovakia. Still other student teachers were at schools in Rome, Athens, Frankfurt, Brussels, Paris and Vienna. Meanwhile, under a grant from the Division of Foreign Studies, Department of Health, Education and Welfare, Miami entered upon an exchange of both faculty and students with the University of Paraná, Brazil. To the Miami curriculum were added Slavic and European studies, Latin American studies and Asian-African studies. In 1968 a Center for International Studies was established under the direction of Charles B. Fahs, formerly of the U.S. State Department. International affairs were broadening Miami's horizon.

After a year of study and planning, Miami established a study center in the Grand Duchy of Luxembourg. First planned for inauguration in 1969, the program found such ready response that it opened a year earlier. Under direction of Professor Warren Mason of the Political Science department, 38 students began their studies in the bilingual old city on the Moselle River. Students lived as paying guests with Luxembourg families. Courses in German and French, humanities and history, and social sciences were conducted by Professors Marcy Powell, Delbert Snider and John Romano, with special lectures offered by European scholars. Except for the language instruction, classes were taught in English. Miami students at Luxembourg enjoyed an intensive European experience combined with normal progress toward a degree. An orientation tour and a ski holiday were added attractions.

Back in Oxford, on the south campus beyond the University Center, rose the new Center for Performing Arts, with stages, halls and studios for music and theater. When the cornerstone was laid, Professor Homer Abegglen recalled, for a reunion of theater students of the past four decades, the former Towers Theatre in the original chapel room of the old Main Building.

The Miami University theater had begun in 1903, under the direction of Professor Loren Gates; in 1911 he organized Ye Merrie Players. In 1928 Professor Abegglen arrived from the Yale Drama School, and Mr. Gates had a technical director. The fall and spring plays were presented in Benton Auditorium, with the rest of the program consigned to the makeshift Towers Theatre in old Main Hall. That theater, the chapel room of the old college, had no dressing rooms; the cast donned costumes in classrooms down the hall. It had a pair of spotlights trained on a slightly raised platform with hand-drawn curtains. For want of an exit right, players had to climb through a window and run around the building. Across the hall, in a onetime recitation room, was the workshop, cluttered with screens, old stage sets, piles of furniture and rows of paint and glue pots. The whole place, with the south sun slanting through dusty windows, was filmed with sawdust. When water was needed, a stage hand lugged it from the men's room at the far end of the hallway. All this lack of facility, Doc Abegglen recalled, sieved out the dilettantes and stimulated inventiveness. The vitality of the Towers Theatre came from within.

When the old Main Building came down in 1958, the University theater moved to Fisher Hall, then abandoned as a dormitory. With the former dining room converted to a half-round theater, and the former manager's suite used as the director's quarters and the Post Office wicket as a box office, the Fisher Hall theater soon developed a tradition of its own. Students cheerfully made the long walk for castings, rehearsals and stage chores; their reward was an experience of mutual discipline and enterprise, of working together, under direction, in an artistic endeavor. Though it included professional training, this theater was a part of education.

In 1966 the Miami University Summer Theater, under Professor Donald Rosenberg, offered its first season. People from Oxford and miles around parked their cars in the twilight, strolled through the gardens and gathered in the tiered seats of Fisher Hall for the curtain. For three seasons a repertoire of Brecht, Ibsen, Shaw, Thurber, and Rogers and Hammerstein enlivened the summer nights of Oxford.

A hundred years ago the Miami alumni gathered for an annual supper under the spreading walnut tree beside the vanished Bishop house across from present Ogden Hall. They had talks and storytelling by the light of paper lanterns, and at last they all joined hands in "Auld Lang Syne." In the 1960's Alumni Director John Dolibois began working for an Alumni House, a center for alumni records and organization, a library for alumni publications and memorabilia, a meeting place for alumni groups. A location was chosen, at the southwestern corner of the campus, on the hill overlooking Collins Run. On a bright June day in 1968 the Murstein Alumni Center and adjoining Climer Guest Lodge were dedicated. Now the university community, as well as the Alumni Association, had a handsome social center built entirely by gifts of alumni and friends. Its first formal use came with an English Department Centennial reception on April 6, 1968.

In 1966 the Alumni Loyalty Fund listed contributions of $502,000, more than one-third of the alumni participating; no other public university in the nation matched that proportion. For general excellence of its alumni program the American Alumni Council ranked Miami in the top one percent among all colleges and universities. At that time the traditional Loyalty Fund became the Miami University Fund, in recognition of increased support from nonalumni, corporations and foundations. Under Vice-President Dolibois the Office of Development anticipated growing support of university programs from sources other than the State of Ohio. Across Chestnut Street from the Alumni Center, Grey Gables had been moved to the campus corner, where it housed the Admissions Office. On the former grounds of Grey Gables rose new residence halls, named for A. K. Morris and Bertha M. Emerson, who were warmly remembered by Miamians of the second quarter of the twentieth century. These halls formed part of a projected residence quadrangle across from the broad green of Western College.

During the hard times of the 1860's the annual Miami catalogue included the statement: "Tuition and room rent must invariably be paid in advance, and no reduction or drawback is allowed; and if not paid by the student it is charged to the Faculty who are made responsible to the Board of Trustees for it." For several years the last thirteen words were italicized, though there is no record of attaching faculty salaries for unpaid student fees. In the 1960's a major project of the development program was to create scholarship funds for widespread student aid.

Half a century ago President Hughes announced annual university goals for the next year, the next decade and the next century. Some of the objectives were immediate, con-

cerning academic schedules, buildings and fees. Others were
perennial and timeless: "Encourage in every way friendliness throughout Miami. . . . Retain at all costs personal
relations between students and faculties. . . . Develop small
colleges within the university. . . . Work for closer understanding among state institutions." By 1924 he envisioned a
student body of 1,500, which would grow in a decade to
2,500, and in the twenty-first century would reach 5,000.
But change came faster than anyone could foresee. Compare
the artist-in-residence for whom President Hughes provided
a cabin in the campus forest with the artist-in-residence fifty
years later: Percy MacKaye walked between his home on
Maple Street and his rustic retreat, but pianist David Bean
divided his time between Oxford and a New York studio,
with annual concert tours abroad. Not only in size but in
problems and opportunities Miami became a university as
changed from that of the 1920's as it was then different from
the old college of a century ago.

Yet Miami has a certain permanence. It still shapes and
characterizes its community; it is still a little removed from
the swift currents of time. Though most of its buildings are
modern, some old landmarks stand, and the names of Bishop,
Scott, McBride, McGuffey, Elliott, Stoddard, Hepburn and
McFarland are still at home on the wide spreading campus.
Much of the old forest is gone, but green space remains, and
every spring the redbud blooms among white sycamore
trunks along the Tallawanda.

Returning to Oxford four years after graduation, a member
of the Class of 1960 wrote: "I walked today in a college
quadrangle, and the past came back to walk with me. As I
followed the familiar paths the years gone by said 'Walk
softly, walk quietly, for here are the quiet years, the learning
years, the noisy years, the cynical years, the idealistic years.' "
Time brings endless changes to a college campus, but youth
is always confused, ardent, troubled, hopeful. Three and a
half centuries ago, in times as turbulent as the 1960's, John

Donne declared: "The University is a paradise; rivers of knowledge are there, arts and sciences flow from thence." That paradise is a place of discovery, and its paths are trod by an endless procession of youth. In his woodland studio where now the campus traffic flows, Percy MacKaye wrote:

Trees of Miami, beautiful trees,
What do you dream in your reveries?
. . . Truth, remembrance, youth, of these
You brood in your ancient reveries.

PART THREE

OUR MIAMI

1968-1984

Chapter XXV

BRANCHING OUT

S INCE its dedication in 1953 McBride Hall on Miami's east campus has been the home of some 6,000 freshman students. Perhaps a few of them remember the bronze tablet set into the brick wall of the north porch entrance.

McBRIDE HALL
This Building Is Named For
The Ohio Pioneer Who Served
Miami For Forty-nine Years
1810 - 1859
A Man Of Many Interests

JAMES McBRIDE
Surveyor, Merchant, Architect,
Codifier of Laws, Map-Maker,
County Official and State
Legislator, Historian, and
Devoted Friend And Trustee
Of This University.

The name is fitting to the Miami campus for it was James McBride who in 1814 assured inhabitants of the college lands that "on the banks of the Four Mile has been planted the stake where the Miami University will stand till time shall be no longer." At that time Miami University was no more than a

surveyor's stake in a tract of untrod forest, and the resolute
confidence of James McBride is heartening to remember.

Born in southern Pennsylvania and taken to Kentucky where
his father was killed by Indians, McBride at 18 years came to
Hamilton, Ohio by flatboat and began a merchant trade on the
Miami River. Five years later, a robust and versatile young
man of 23 with little schooling but a wide-ranging mind, he
served as secretary of the Miami trustees at their first meetings
in Hamilton. The Miami valley was then a rich region —
"Tickle the earth with a hoe and it laughs into harvest" — but a
remote one. It could produce boundless crops of wheat, corn,
tobacco, pork and wool, but its one natural highway, the Ohio
River, flowed west, away from the American market. The Ohio
and the Mississippi carried the frontier harvest to New Orleans, where some of it was consumed and the rest was loaded
into ships for the long voyage to Baltimore, Philadelphia and
New York.

In the summer of 1812 James McBride and Joseph Hough of
Hamilton formed a partnership to take a cargo of flour, whis-
key and apples to New Orleans. After weeks of hauling planks
and pegging them together, they had a flatboat ready. It was a
floating box, 18 by 80 feet, deep enough to hold six tiers of barrels down the center under the peaked roof, five tiers elsewhere.
Six feet of low-roofed deck at the stern made up their cabin,
which soon reeked of apples, potatoes, frying pork and drying
clothes. With their load aboard the partners pushed off from
the Hamilton landing. Poled and paddled by hand-power the
clumsy craft crept past the shoals, bends and bars of the Miami. It moved between big cooper shops and packing sheds at
Cincinnati and swung into the Ohio's current. Weeks later the
partners peddled cargo, a few barrels at a time, at landings on
the Mississippi and sold the rest in New Orleans. It was a long
trip to market, and they had a long trip home, riding horseback
through the gloom of the Natchez Trace and over the hills of
Kentucky. Next year, if the autumn rains were enough, they
would float another flatboat and load another cargo of whis-
key, pork and apples. Prosperity in the west rose and fell with
the rivers.

In Hamilton resolute young McBride was elected sheriff,
"the best office then in the gift of the people." He explored

Indian mounds and recorded pioneer adventure. He gathered a remarkable library, 5,000 volumes, that was destroyed by fire, but his manuscripts were saved. His glowing account of Miami University in the wilderness of 1814 pictured "youth assembled from the various quarters of the world, to learn the arts and become acquainted with rhetoric and belles lettres. Astonishing change!"

Astonishing man, McBride. When the Hamilton Branch campus was established in 1968 its first structure might have been given the name already planted on the Oxford campus. It surely belongs there among the names of present civic leaders— Mosler, Rentschler, Parrish—whose support is memorialized by campus buildings. Another name gratefully inscribed there is that of Bernard Phelps, a Miami veteran who made history as the first director of this regional campus.

At Miami-Hamilton the average student age is 27, which provides motivation and clarifies objectives. "Partying" is rarely heard in campus conversation. About half the students are presently employed, with classes scheduled in the evening. They will complete their formal schooling with a two-year "Associate" degree in such fields as Business Technology. Engineering Technology, Computer Technology, and Nursing. The campus nickname Peck Tech comes from both the curriculum and the location on Peck Boulevard. Originally that outlying segment of Hamilton was called Peck's Addition; now with a ready pun students publish the weekly news sheet "Peck's Edition." Students who choose the more academic rather than technical courses are generally planning to transfer, as juniors, to the Oxford campus or another university for completion of a 4-year degree.

Serving the community at large, the Hamilton branch offers non-credit "continuing education" courses of cultural and recreational content. "Learning Ladders" does the same for children, with Saturday classes in gymnastics, art, literary appreciation and even computer games. Further community enrichment comes with an Artists Series that brings to Hamilton distinguished speakers, musicians and performers. If James McBride could now look in on the Hamilton branch he would repeat that "astonishing" exclamation.

Older than most Ohio community colleges, Miami University-Middletown dates back to the end of World War II and the "Serviceman's Readjustment Act of 1944," widely known as the GI Bill of Rights. While the tide of GI students poured onto the Oxford campus, Miami educators and concerned citizens of Middletown began a downtown center for military veterans who sought a college education. During the 1950s classes were held, under commuting faculty members from Oxford, in the Middletown High School on Girard Avenue. From that seed Miami University-Middletown grew into a truly community college that opened career doors to young men and women and contributed to the cultural life of Middletown. Along with vocational courses for part-time students MUM offered programs in household and fine arts and a series of lectures and recitals that appealed to the larger community. In the 1960s that community connection brought the gift of 141 of the most beautiful acres in all Ohio.

On the northeastern edge of Middletown, originally the George M. Verity estate, including a deer park and golf course, these grounds became the campus of Miami University-Middletown. Under the executive direction of C. Eugene Bennett, Miami 1948, and the guidance of Dean Earl V. Thesken, the institution flourished. To its first buildings—Logan Johnston Hall, Gardiner-Harvey Library, Verity Student Center (names from the paper and steel industries)—have been added the Finkelman Auditorium and the Thesken Hall of Science and Technology. Nature trails, gardens, terraces, and outdoor sculptures enhance the hill-and-dale setting. Secluded and serene, the atmosphere at MUM helps students to find their own identity and encourages personal relationships between students and faculty. It is perhaps the most friendly and certainly the most attractive community college in the land.

While MUM is out of sight and out of sound of Middletown's commerce and industry, the educational program is undeniably relevant. Most of the students are in 2-year programs that give training for the technological and service industries that promise to provide increasing employment in Ohio. The Nursing program at Middletown has enviable repute, along with technical courses ranging from computer technology and electrical engineering technology to Library media technique. Accounting and Business Management draw capacity registration there, as on the Oxford campus. Community enrichment comes from MUM lecture and artist appearances in the Dave Finkelman Auditorium that recently included a Chinese magic circus and a Nobel Prize physicist.

Verity is an enduring name in Middletown. It came there in 1900 when Middletown had 9,000 population, and it came to stay. George M. Verity, the son of an itinerant Methodist minister, attended High School in Georgetown, Ohio, and learned bookkeeping in a Cincinnati Business School, a Community College of its day. In the 1890s he worked for a company that made roofing from locally produced metal sheets. In 1900, at age 35, looking for a site for a steel mill, he chose Middletown with its canal and railroad connections. In a one-room slab building with a bicycle at the doorway and a horse and buggy at the hitching post he erected a sign: American Rolling Mill Company. The first furnace fires were lighted on a windy March day in 1901.

At this time the vast Carnegie, Morgan and Rockefeller interests were forging the giant United States Steel Corporation in Pittsburgh. Although he lacked the billion dollars of the Pittsburgh trust, George Verity had a revolutionary idea. He envisioned a technology that would bring together the whole process—from blast furnace and pig iron to sheet iron, galvanized iron, and electrical sheet steel in a single integrated plant. Having created the world's first continuous process steel mill, the company snugged up its name to Armco. In 1911 it filled its first overseas order in a business that would eventually reach around the world. Now, at closing hour in the MUM library an occasional student gets up from a reading desk and walks in the midnight dark with stars in his eyes—after reviewing the life and times of George M. Verity.

International business brings to Middletown some international character, evidenced by the unique festival that has become an annual celebration. The Middfest '81, marking the 10th anniversary of Armco's first overseas export, focused upon the relationship of Middletown to the city of Luxembourg, five thousand miles away. Iron and steel are the leading industry in both places, and an ethnic mix characterizes both populations. To Middletown in the first week of October, 1981 came 70,000 visitors, drawn by an industrial and cultural exposition with music, dancing, costumes and cuisine from the thousand-year-old city on the River Alzette.

Miami University-Middletown was a collaborator in Middfest '81. A feeling of friendship and alliance between the two cities is based on shared values of liberty and freedom — freedom of the press, of worship, of trade and industry. An institution common to both cities is Miami University. Miami vice president John Dolibois was a native of Luxembourg who throughout an eventful career in America retained close ties with that county. While Middfest '81 was taking shape international news services reported his appointment as United States Ambassador to Luxembourg. His influence brough to Middletown civic and industrial leaders including the mayor of Luxembourg City. Music from Luxembourg included the Moselle Valley Brass Band in folk costume and the appearance of the Hon. Adrian Meisch, Ambassador to the United States; as a concert pianist he performed with the Middletown Symphony Orchestra. A leading Middletown attorney, Barry Levey, during a term as president of the Miami University Board of Trustees, was named Honorary Consul of Luxembourg in the State of Ohio.

While branching out in Butler County, Miami University was reaching into other lands and cultures. With expanding enrollment and curriculum it had become a cosmopolitan universtiy. Faculty members held Fulbright professorships in countries from England and Scotland to Nigeria, Indonesia, Korea and Japan, while the Oxford campus listed students from nearly fifty nations. Under the trimester calendar hundreds of faculty and students spent mid-April to September in foreign travel, study and research. Miamians crossed paths in cities from London to Athens, from Copenhagen to Madrid. On the Oxford campus a broadened Anthropology program embraced studies of peoples and cultures in Latin America, sub-Saharan Africa, and the Middle East. In 1968 a Center of International Studies was created under direction of Charles B. Fahs, a veteran of the U. S. State Department. Summer language institutes were organized in France, Luxembourg, Italy and Taiwan. Meanwhile Miami faculty and staff families were developing a pioneering COSEP service. Founded in 1971 by

Mrs. Dwight Baldwin this Community Service Program for
Foreign Students builds bridges of friendship between people
of Oxford and Miami graduates in distant lands.

In that international atmosphere, it seemed Miami University should launch a foreign study program somewhere in Europe. By background and personal experience, John Dolibois
was uniquely fitted to direct its inception and development,
with ready collaboration of Miami colleagues. From the start, he
had counsel and support from Provost Charles B. Wilson. A
Miami graduate of 1926, Dr. Wilson had become head of the
History Department at Colgate University, where he directed
annual conferences on American Foreign Policy with invited
scholars and panelists from many countries. As Miami's provost, and acting president during the interim of the Millett and
Shriver tenures, he drew on that Colgate experience in the
shaping of an Inernational Studies program at Miami.

In considering the location of a European Study Center,
attention was first focused on Switzerland — possibly Geneva,
or Zurich, or Lucerne. Other locations were pondered and discussed: Copenhagen, Vienna, Brussels, Heidelberg, Lille, Aix-
en-Provence. If his thoughts kept reverting to Luxembourg,
John Dolibois hesitated to urge a setting where he had such
personal ties. But in 1965, on a brief visit with relatives in Luxembourg, he found practical concerns outweighing the emotional attraction there. The least expensive Atlantic crossing
was by Icelandic Air Line, which flew a regular schedule New
York-Reykjavik-Luxembourg. In its central location, Luxembourg was but an hour's flight to a dozen European capitols. Its
bi-lingual culture and its political-economic influence as seat of
the European Coal and Steel Community and of the European
Common Market were making it a crossroads. The six tall
spires of Radio Luxembourg broadcast in several languages to
much of Europe. Before his visit ended, Dolibois made overtures to certain officials and educators, finding a ready interest
in the prospect of a European Study Center there. On return to
the Oxford base, he conveyed that interest and his own increasing conviction to Provost Wilson, who wholeheartedly
concurred.

In these years, a number of American universities were announcing cooperative programs with foreign institutions; the

usual arrangement consisted of a group of American students enrolled for a summer course, or for one or two terms, primarily in foreign language study. The Miami proposal was independent and autonomous, with its own curriculum, academic facilities, and faculty. It would enable students to live, study and travel abroad while continuing to earn Miami credits under guidance of Miami faculty in courses enriched by the collaboration of European scholars. Indeed, it was an attractive program, but was it a luxury beyond Ohio's means?

With realistic and tactful strategy, Dolibois went directly to the governor, who already had given his blessing to a huge rubber and plastics complex built in Luxembourg by the Goodyear Company of Akron and had created an Ohio Economic Commission in Belgium. Governor Rhodes responded heartily to the Dolibois concept. Without delay, he appointed a commission to consider the establishing of a Luxembourg Center for Miami University. As its chairman he named John Dolibois.

In April of 1967, Dolibois led the members on a tour of observation. For a few busy days, they explored Luxembourg City and its spring-rife countryside. After conferences with Luxembourg officials and the Ministry of Education, they were received at the U.S. Embassy by the ambassador, Mrs. Patricia Harris; a few seasons later, Mrs. Harris was a Miami guest in the Murstein Alumni Center. Following that exploration, President Shriver named a Miami committee, comprising Professor Dwight Smith of History, Vice President Robert Etheridge for Student Affairs, and John Dolibois, to confer with the Luxembourg Ministry of Education. Immediate results were the locating of potential classroom space in Luxembourg City and planned individual student lodging with Luxembourg families — an important part of the "international experience." In these discussions, the Miami committee had invaluable counsel from Dr. Leslie S. Brady, a Miami graduate and former teacher who had become Cultural Attache of the U.S. Embassy in Paris. Back in Oxford, the committee of four was enlarged to a planning committee under direction of Professor J. R. Breitenbucher of the German Department. In frequent and lengthy meetings, this body worked out details of logistics, curriculum and staffing. It proposed Dr. Warren Mason as director of the center.

Inauguration had been aimed for September 1969, but, with the obstacles behind them, the committee moved the date to 1968. A building on Rue Goethe in the lower city was adapted to classroom use. A reference library was assembled, with plans for its expansion. Six Miami faculty were settling into Luxembourg lodgings when the first students arrived, wide-eyed, in the rugged spectacular city. On a bright September day in 1968, the Luxembourg Center opened with a simple cere-mony. It was honored by the presence of the Grand Duke of Luxembourg.

Throughout the planning and implementing of this distant branch, Miami alumni support had kept if from financial foun-dering and provided scholarship aid for deserving students. Whatever their personal circumstance, the students shared a common experience in and beyond the classrrom and library. All had time for travel, for mid-winter ski trips, spring tramp-ing, and educational jaunts to London, Brussels, Paris, Berlin, Amsterdam, Rome, Vienna. By the time of its tenth anniver-sary, in 1978, the Luxembourg Center had its own alumni as-sociation, approaching a thousand members. It included some foreign students, even a few from Luxembourg itself, and stu-dents from about one half of the United States.

Chapter XXVI

.

CAMPUS CRISIS

CAMPUS, as we use it in America, carries a sense of belonging to something old, honorable and beneficent. It is a far cry from the Roman field of war, the Campus Martius. Yet in very recent American memory *campus* was a combat zone, a smoldering place of confrontation. In 175 years of history Miami University has had many seasons of growth, progress and development, as well as a few episodes of threat and crisis. The direst experience came in April 1970 when winds of change were lashing this nation and its institutions. At that time an unprecedented turmoil brought disruption to hundreds of campuses. A contagion of violence rocked foremost universities — Berkeley, Cornell, Harvard, Columbia — as well as remote colleges. Miami suffered less than many and survived intact. But it was tried by flood and fire.

In 1969 there were more than nine million fulltime students in American universities, nearly twice the student population of 1960. This was an angry and assertive generation, fedup with the Vietnam War, with corruption in politics and injustice in race relations. In many colleges students defied authority and derided tradition. They disrupted scheduled speeches, invaded classrooms, seized administrative offices, and halted normal operation. Their spokesmen vowed to destroy the universities in order to build a better world.

The Miami crisis came in a context of problems and upheaval. As spring of 1970 spread its green miracle over the land, this nation hovered on the edge of precipice. Nearly eight hundred universities closed thier doors, or prepared to close, while massed and marching students cried for revolution. In Ohio three State-run universities rumbled and erupted like volcanoes — Ohio University at Athens in the southeastern region, Ohio State University in the capitol city, and Kent State in the northeastern sector. The violence at Kent was less destructive than that at Athens and Columbus, but it was most bitter and frightening. Ostensibly in protest to the bombing of Cambodia, 12,000 miles away, three nights of rioting resulted in the burning of Kent's ROTC building, the trashing of downtown streets and the arrival of the Ohio National Guard. The ensuing tragedy — four students killed and nine others wounded —dismayed the nation and startled the world.

At Miami University the confrontation began in mid-April. For a year student groups across the country had held monthly "Vietnam Moratoriums" in protest of America's continued escalation of the frustrating and sickening war. During the past winter Miami participation in that protest had been curbed by severe weather, examination periods, and vacation breaks. With pent-up purpose the Miami Student Mobilization Committee planned a day-long demonstration on Wednesday, 15 April. The plan embraced a student "strike" for that day with "Free University" lectures replacing morning classes, a People's Lunch at the campus hub just west of Upham Hall, and an afternoon peace rally on the north lawn of the Administration Building. The rally leaflet did not mention racial concern although handbills circulated that morning called for a student strike on April 20, in support of demands previously made by the Black Students Association.

Moratorium Day passed quietly, with no general boycott of routine classes, a mere 75 students (of the campus 14,000) gathering for People's Lunch, and the afternoon rally peaking with a turnout of five hundred. That affair began with a Philosophy professor's talk on "Morality and the War," followed by a higher-pitched speech by a black graduate student whose announced subject "Racism and Vietnam" was belied by his focus on racism in Miami. Finally the president of the Black Student Action Association stressed the proposed April 20 strike and called on a coalition of concerned whites to support

five points listed on a handbill. These points, he said, "were requests when we started discussing them with the Administration last January and now they are demands." The points
included extension of the Educational Opportunity Program
to increase Miami's black enrollment, a plan of tutorial help
for additional black students, the creation of graduate assistantships for black students, and the hiring of additional black
faculty. At the close of the rally a black senior siezed the microphone and announced a march on the ROTC building (Rowan
Hall) in protest of militarism.

Rowan Hall, a small building of quiet dignity erected in
1949, was named for a Miami man who became a Rear-Ad-
miral in the U.S. Navy. Stephen Clegg Rowan, born in Ireland
in 1809 and brought to America at age 10, came to Miami in
1825 when collegiate instruction began. After continued education at the Naval Academy he served as midshipman on the
first naval vessel to sail around the world. During the Mexican
War as executive officer of the sloop *Cayene* he led a platoon of
marines into San Diego; in the Old Town Plaza they raised the
first U.S. flag on soil that became California. No one then
could imagine an American war in Indo-China. Rowan Hall,
standing between the Miami Sesquicentennial Chapel and the
power plant, could not accommodate the full ROTC unit. It
contained offices and a simulated Destroyer navigation bridge
above a "main deck" housing a pair of anti-aircraft guns and a
single-barrel gunmount of the Destroyer class. The installation
was of limited use in naval officer training, and it could not
contain a mass student rally.

Student marchers on that April late afternoon found the
brick building closed and empty, but they broke in with racket
that drew a number of bystanders. Soon a hundred students
surged in. Laughing and jeering they swarmed around the
naval emplacements. A petty officer appeared, asking the
intruders to stay on the main "deck" away from the Corps command posts. About 5 p.m. a rock combo pushed in. Quickly a
party was under way — music and laughter, clapping and
dancing, and cheers for the arrival of food and drink. There
were no blacks among these early occupants.

In recent weeks, after upheavals on other campuses, the
Ohio State government had outlined a contingency plan for

crowd control. Accordingly Vice President Etheridge shouldered into the room and made his way up the stairs to the
"bridge" level. There through a bullhorn he read a statement
that students breaking into university buildings were trespassers, subject to arrest. That announcement added zest to the
demonstration. After a few minutes Etheridge again raised his
bullhorn. He stated that the students, having made their anti-
ROTC point, should now vacate this U.S. Navy building. He
added that they could regroup in Hall Auditorium at the west
end of the central campus, a more suitable place for discussion
and debate. While his words were hooted down, a student
leader, using his own amplifier, voiced three demands:
immediate canceling of academic credit for ROTC classes,
promise of abolishing ROTC from Miami University, and the
granting of Black Student Action Association terms.

In line with the state government's contingency plan the Miami Security chief notified the Hamilton office of the State
Highway Patrol. On arrival at Rowan Hall four of those officers were greeted with hoots, boos and jeers. Word went to
Hamilton that more men were needed. The Butler County officer notified Columbus, and in the April dusk the Commander
of the Ohio Highway Patrol, with sirens blaring, arrived in Oxford to take charge. Meanwhile student leaders vowed to sit-in
night and day until their demands were met. The most assertive
of the agitators was a young man no one seemed to know.
When asked if he was enrolled at Miami he said he was a former student who had been editor of the underground news
sheet *Mandella*. When Etheridge once more read the state
ruling, some of the students left. To those remaining he stated
"You are no longer students of Miami University, but trespassers subject to state authority and arrest." When a phalanx
of some forty uniformed partolmen moved in, certain other
students departed. The rest, about 160 in number, locked arms
in defiance.

By this time hundreds of students had gathered outside the
building, and troopers were showered with sticks, stones and
debris. For transport to the Oxford City Hall, apprehended
students were pressed into an old school bus, which broke
down after a single trip. When Hamilton was asked to send
more men and transportation, 160 police and sheriff's deputies

responded. While milling students immobilized their vehicles, the police sprayed mace and tossed cannisters of tear gas. Police dogs on half-leash scattered crowds, which soon massed again.

Inside Rowan Hall voice horns repeated that all students remaining there were liable to arrest. Highway patrol men, on standby in noisy Spring Street, then moved in to clear the building. About 160 arrests were made. Some proved to be non-students, former students and local high school pupils. They were later called the "Miami 176," though the number booked was 155. Over the midnight campus went rumors, threats, alarms and fulminations. Roudebush Hall was locked tight but a throng of students heard black and white spokesmen declare that the classroom boycott previously set for April 20 should begin that very morning, April 16. The strategy was to strike while the iron was hot. Silence came to the littered campus at 2:30 a.m., while sheriff's deputies patroled the uptown streets.

Before daybreak Governor Rhodes telephoned from Columbus. He was about to fly to Oxford while a convoy of trucks was bringing National Guard troops to the Nike base just west of town. Arrived at 7 a.m. the governor conferred with President Shriver and held an impromptu news conference. That morning fresh posters called for immediate student strike and a noon rally on Roudebush front lawn. At that gathering, under a lowering sky, speakers denounced Governor Rhodes, cursed the police, chanted *Strike! Strike! Strike!* and appealed for campus-wide support. Handbills from the Black Students Association and a "concerned" white coalition demanded: support of black action terms, reinstatement of suspended students, and creation of a committee to investigate *all* activities of the ROTC and determine whether it should be abolished from the university. While the coalition offered to dictate the makeup of this committee, thunder rolled and rumbled overhead.

A gust of rain drove the crowd into nearby Withrow Court, where Student Senate leaders asked President Shriver to speak. Before he could mount the platform a black leader seized the microphone. "The president wants to say something. . . . Shall we let him? . . . Okay let's let the dude speak." To a massed 4500 students President Shriver declared that the university was already committed to increase black enrollment and black faculty, that though he opposed admission of unqualified students he had already been approving trial admission of slightly sub-standard blacks who did not apply for financial aid. He added that qualified black students were assured of financial grants and loans, and that black assistantships could be provided in departments with certified graduate programs. He refused, however, to waive suspension of students who had refused to vacate the ROTC building; their way to reinstatement was through due process. Proposal of an ROTC evaluation had recently been rejected by both the Faculty Council and the University Senate. This short direct presidential speech was interrupted by boos, cheers, affirming shouts and heckling questions, and repeated chants of *Strike! Strike! Strike!*

When President Shriver left the hall a somewhat shrunken crowd heard a black leader declare that the strike was now in force. Actual attendance of scheduled classes was diminished by one-fourth. That afternoon a gathering of faculty members, vexed that they had not shared in official discussion of the student demands, sent word to the president's office asking him to call special meetings of the Faculty Council and the University Senate on Friday (the next day), adding their intention to call their own meeting of "concerned faculty" if he did not concur. Response from the president's office was that the scheduled Faculty Council session on Monday, April 20, would be sufficient. While gossip and rumor gusted over the cloudy campus a steadying voice came from the Political Science department. In a widely circulated open letter Professor Reo Christenson emphasized that civil disobedience entailed a responsibility to accept its consequences, and that demanding amnesty while denouncing University paternalism was contradictory. "Faculty and student wrath," he concluded, "should be focused on two groups: those who needlessly precipitated this wretched affair, and those police officers . . . who seemed to relish the opportunity to exercise their power in unbridled fashion."

The Student Senate issued a statement: "Justice requires that civil law be restored, that all National Guardsmen, State Patrolmen and Butler County Sheriff's Deputies be immediately withdrawn." It concluded: "We do not condone the illegal occupation of state property, but feel the temporary reinstatement of those students involved is necessary until the legal procedure of due process can take place."

On the following day, April 17, President Shriver announced that the Highway Patrol had departed at noon, and the National Guard began leaving the Nike base at 2 p.m. without having come onto the Miami campus. Pronouncing the situation stabilized, he added that while amnesty had not been granted, suspended students could continue to live in their residence halls while due process was observed. Trespass cases were heard in Butler County Court One, and admission to classrooms would be subject to ruling by individual professors. The Student Senate created a special committee on the Abuse of Rights (SCAR) to begin investigation, with legal counsel, on the alleged violation of civil rights. Three uptown fraternities formed their own coalition to achieve public censure of law enforcement agencies "which indiscriminately used dogs, tear gas and clubs, and overtly broke the law on the night of April 15 and early 16." Under cloudy April sky the campus was still teeming and steaming.

On April 18, Saturday, the usual weekend diversion was replaced by heated debate and disputation. An unofficial meeting of "concerned faculty" drew some 120 members — a bare one-sixth of the Senate roll — who after three hours of talk went on record as "supporting the demands of the student coalition." They postponed for a Sunday meeting the question of faculty participation in the student strike, and the forming of a teachers' union. At the Sunday meeting — another three-hour session — about one hundred members approved two motions: to go, themselves, on strike in abetting the student demands, and to resolve that no punitive measures be taken against striking faculty. These were open meetings, attended by a student audience a thousand on Saturday and some four hundred on Sunday.

On Monday morning hearings began in the Oxford City building for the Wednesday night trespassers in Rowan Hall. That evening over the University's radio and TV channels and in an open meeting of the Faculty Council President Shriver announced plans that he hoped would resolve the strike: 1) proposal of a "pilot project" to admit 100 students of no racial restriction who though academically substandard would not seek financial waivers, 2) increased recruiting efforts for black students and faculty, 3) continued encouragement of contributions to the Educational Opportunity Program. While the Faculty Council adjourned a black spokesman stood with clenched fist declaring "The strike is still on."

The next day's attention was focused on the process of appeal for the suspended students. To lighten their liability and soften their penalty a "concerned" faction of the Faculty Council moved to commit the suspension appeal collectively to the entire University Senate rather than to continue individual hearings. The effort was defeated. Established procedure, with the Disciplinary Appeals Board making judgments, was affirmed. Response to this action was a wave of threats and fulmination. There was talk of a "library run" removing hundreds of books on course reading lists, of a telephone tie-up that would fill the university lines with "busy" signals, of a power sabotage that would darken the whole campus, of picketing food services and fuel deliveries. These rumors emerged from a rally where strike leaders spoke of "renewed efforts in nonviolent ways." What followed was an act of absurd madness. At 6 p.m. hurrying through 14 campus buildings students lashed open water faucets in lavatories, shower rooms, and laundromats. In twenty minutes more than two million gallons were drained from Oxford's two water towers. Floors were flooded, sewers overflowed, water pressure vanished, and Oxford was helpless if a fire broke out. City officials closed all the university mains until pressure could be restored. This was vandalism to the point of sabotage. Damage exeeding $5,000 was done to the town and college water systems.

On Wednesday the campus was strewn with handbills from the "Student Faculty Coalition." Under a heavy MORATORIUM headline came: "A period of negotiation. Everyone should return to classes. The moratorium does not mean the demands have been met. It means a shift in tactics. The moratorium indicates on the behalf of the strikers a willingness to negoitate. The moratorium will give the strikers a chance to return to classes and encourage further discussion of the issues. It doesn't mean you should lose faith or that the Coalition demands won't be met, but it does mean a shift in tactics to

increase the effectiveness of our sincerity." The redundancy of
this missive poorly masked a mingled frustration and wit's end,
a feeling directly expressed by the withdrawal of pickets outside of classroom buildings.

That evening, in a fact-sheet called "What's Right," the University Administration tried to replace gossip, rumors and dis-
tortions with a plain statement. Yet another blitz of handbills
signed "The Coalition" stated that "the Coalition will not
sanction any continuation of the flush-in or such things as
taking books from the library to disrupt education, calling the
administration building for the purpose of disrupting communications, or shutting off the electricity." It added: "This
strike is against the administration. Turning off water turns off
students."

On Thursday a new page appeared from a new source —
concerned "Miami Students." Condemning violence and disruption it pledged "unqualified support to President Shriver in
his efforts to handle this critical situation," and urged all students to attend the Saturday morning University Senate meeting. A statement from the Student Senate deplored the flush-in
and urged that it be "the last thoughtless and disruptive activity
at our university." The statement was handed to President
Shriver with 1036 signatures while many leaflets were still in
circulation. The Saturday morning Senate meeting drew more
than six hundred faculty members, a thousand students, and
various reporters from the outside press. A standing ovation
responded to President Shriver's pledge to increase efforts in
attracting black students and faculty. Declaring full responsibility for his decisions in the past ten days and nights, he
adjourned the meeting with the suggestion that people talk
with each other "so that each may be heard."

During a few days of quiet the Faculty Council Disciplinary
Appeals Board continued hearings with men and women students. Some stated opposition to the appeals procedure. Others
offered reasons for their actions on the Rowan Hall scene and
asked to be reinstated. To normal curricular routine was added
a previously scheduled Orientation for Black Students from
Ohio high schools. No one reported their impressions.

Age-old weather-lore tells of "the lull before the storm." The
week of May 4 began with shocking news and riveting scenes

on television. At noon on the sunwashed campus of Kent State University four students were shot to death by the Ohio National Guard. On the stunned Miami campus small groups of students talked with professors in the hallways and with President Shriver between telephone calls at Lewis Place and in his Roudebush Hall office. The tragedy at Kent was brewing violence across the state and nation. Reports of turmoil on other campuses led Shriver to declare Tuesday a "Day of Reflection" with classes replaced by informal dialogue throughout the Miami community. He hoped that free and general communication might lead toward "rational solutions of our problems." He would speak in the open air next morning.

At ten o'clock, May 5, a crowd of 4,000 gathered on the south campus overlook, heard their president ask that concern over the Kent crisis be kept low-key and orderly. (No one could have more concern than Phillip Shriver himself; for eighteen years prior to his Miami connection he had served Kent State from History instructor to Dean of the College of Arts and Sciences.) He hoped that Miami students would talk together not as partisans but as fellow citizens; he would be on campus throughout the day, ready to talk and to listen. Soon he was the center of 200 students seated on the ground of the Hub quadrangle, where other groups were gathered around various professors. After the lunch hour 3,000 students quietly formed a mile-long "Solidarity March" which circled the campus and in growing numbers massed below the Sun Dial Overlook. There two leaders of the Student Mobilization Committee used bull horns to denounce the Rhodes-Nixon measures in Ohio and Vietnam. The day of reflection was turning into a time of turmoil.

In dusk and darkness a restive student traffic streamed up the Slant Walk and dotted the uptown streets. At twenty-eight minutes past midnight a fire-bomb shattered a ground-office window in Roudebush Hall. Interior damage was limited by action of a security patrolman who chanced to be nearby.

On May 6, Wednesday, afternoon broadcasts reported Governor Rhodes' proposal of immediate closing of any disorderly state university. In Columbus Ohio State students were out of control, looting and pillaging academic and commercial buildings and snarling traffic in the streets. At 6 p.m. word came that

Ohio State University was closed. During the next three hours in Oxford voices shrilled through town and campus: "Rally at the water tower!" From that uptown center an inchoate march began, gathering numbers and tension as it moved down the Slant Walk and through mid-campus guards to the Sun Dial Overlook. President Shriver joined six thousand students there. He proposed that the next days, Thursday and Friday, be "Days of National Peace" devoted to dialogue and rational discussion, classes to resume on Monday "with determination to keep going until the end of the spring quarter." He would return to the sun dial next morning at 10 o'clock for talk with any and all who sought him. As the crowd dispersed in the warm May midnight it seemed to many that Phillip Shriver "once more had cooled off an explosive situation by his presence and his willingness to listen."

The apparent cooling was deceptive. Between midnight and 1:30 a.m. three fires were set. Security patrols extinguished a blaze in Kreger Hall on the campus hub and another in a storage hut on the south campus. Students passing on the Slant Walk saw smoke from a ground floor window of Hall Auditorium. With the help of security men they checked the flames in a store room under the wooden stage. This seemed the arson target, with the other fires meant as a diversion. Once aflame the wood and plaster auditorium would burn like a barn. At daybreak of May 7 stacks of new Strike posters were by chance discovered in an alley across the street from Hall Auditorium. That morning the campus was strewn with new handbills demanding a Friday strike to begin with a rally at the Overlook, and urging a mass migration to Columbus.

Soon after 10 o'clock that Thursday morning President Shriver faced a crowd at the sun dial Overlook. He declared that as of that moment Miami University and its branches at Hamilton and Middletown were closed indefinitely. All students must be gone by 8 o'clock that evening.

At an afternoon press conference the president gave three reasons for his decision: a prospect of uncontrolled turmoil, the safety of students and security of buildings, and the recent recommendation of the Ohio governor. He added that the faculty would immediately make plans for completing the academic requirements of the spring term. By president's ruling the executive Board of the Student Senate could remain in Oxford during the shut-down to assist in efforts to reopen the university. In its first action this Student Board released a constructive statement: "The overwhelming majority of the Miami University student body are convinced that violence is neither a legitimate nor an effective method of settling differences." It concluded that students, faculty and administration were doing everything possible to accomplish the early reopening of Miami University.

During ten days of closed campus the University Senate had a busy agenda. For the harrowed spring quarter it made concessions on course work and grading. Course content could be curtailed proportionately to time lost in the closed period. Students would be given the option of letter grade or of credit — no credit record in any or all courses. For incomplete course work the instructor could use S —- meaning satisfactory progress. In the area of university governance decision was made on the long pondered question of student representation. The Faculty Council now voted to add 12 student members to its roster of 24 faculty and administration personnel. Many faculty felt, as did most of the students, that this reform was overdue. To all Miami students went letters from the president's office and a "Status Report" from the Student Senate explaining plans for reopening the university. As a precaution against fire or other destruction, a corps of faculty marshals was organized for night time surveillance of empty buildings.

On Sunday, May 17, the campus came to life with an influx of students and the resuming of schedules. On Monday evening a Forum for an Open University was held in Withrow Court. Its sponsors, the Student Mobilization Committee, declared their desire to keep Miami open as a base for their operation of protest and reform. Amid continuous noise and confusion they elected a ten-members steering committee to coordinate further activities. In that direction they proposed an all-campus referendum on an immediate reform — the replacing of scheduled classes by a curriculum of informal courses "more relevant" than the classes scheduled. By the time this "alternate university" was described the initial forum turnout of 3,000 had shrunk to about 800. As this meeting dispersed there were calls for a "Rally at the Water Tower." By 10:30 a thousand were milling on the red brick blocks of High Street.

For some time President Shriver had been talking with students on the front lawn of Lewis Place. Now he went uptown and offered to talk at Lewis Place "all night if you want." Some few followed him there. At midnight he returned uptown and persuaded a larger group to leave with him. To free the traffic-clogged High Street where angry and frustrated drivers imperiled the heedless crowd, they clustered around a lamp post on the Slant Walk. Talk with several hundred students and some sixty faculty members began as discussion but turned into harrangue. Unless something was done, here and now, to relieve tensions over course work and grading, the university would be violently disrupted. Under that threat President Shriver offered another option: in any class students could choose credit or no-credit on work completed to that point in order to concentrate on courses they considered more desirable or more important. This decision at 1:30 a.m. concluded for President Shriver five unbroken hours of confrontation.

The next day was quiet but at evening streams of students again usurped the uptown streets. About 9:30 a fire was reported in a storage shed behind Fisher Hall. The sirens of a fire truck brought a traffic jam at Town Hall corner. On its return the fire engine was halted by students playing volley ball over the traffic light and connecting cables. At 1:30 a.m. the streets emptied, but in the City Hall lights burned on through a lengthy meeting of town and gown officials.

Next day the president addressed a letter to all students telling them of grave apprehension in the community. He asked them to avoid crowding uptown and to refrain from seeming to challenge the traditional concepts of lawful assembly. "Above all," he concluded, "please do not let yourself get involved in questionable actions instigated by someone else." At the same time a young professor was distributing his own brisk memo: "Townspeople are up very, very tight — getting very, very impatient. Ditto the police chief. It will take, literally, one stone thrown through one window to have the Sheriff called in. Let us isolate the few radicals and trouble-makers. Let us not provide them with an audience. Do not give them a chance to affect the lives of literally thousands of people by closing down Miami."

From the municipal office the Oxford Council declared a 9

p.m. curfew. Campus marshals, volunteers from the faculty, took their stations. It was an eerie assignment, patroling dark hallways alert for sounds of intrusion or a taint of smoke and flame. For academic persons it was a duty unprecedented, almost incredible. Posted in the Sesquicentennial Chapel, just thirty paces from Rowan Hall, one saw again, in memory, the blinking lights and drifting gas, the seizure, sit-in, drag-out, arrest and incarceration. Turning away from the street the marshal saw moonlight slanting through torn clouds above the empty overlook. Night thoughts are natural to a campus: the upward reach of life, affirming of truth and beauty, a feeling of *Alma Mater,* of being possessed as well as of possessing. But these night hours were long and the thoughts were fearful. Thoughts of a clenched divided world, of torn and divided colleges in history's most favored nation. On the northern wall inside the chapel doorway carved words were dimly visible.

> Guide us to wisdom,
> Lead us to the light.

The night thoughts held more questions than answers. In this somber season students had come to the hushed chapel alone and in groups — the young who looked in college for learning and understanding, for capacities to shape a better world. But how could one protest a brutal warfare in jungles ten thousand miles away and the despairing poverty of black citizens in America the Beautiful? The angry student and the groping faculty marshal shared the same dilemma.

On Friday, May 22, Oxford officials lifted the curfew. In good spirits the six fraternities on North Tallawanda and Bishop street gave a block-party, inviting the Oxford police and the Sheriff's deputies to join them in celebration. At midnight the waning moon looked down upon a town and campus at peace.

Traditionally a mellow memory book, the Miami *Recensio* for 1970 broke the mold. Entitled A YEAR OF CONTRAST AND CONFLICT its double-page frontis photograph showed President Shriver facing a defiant student with a microphone. The next page was a clot of black students with raised fists. Instead of idyllic campus scenes its front section showed a protest march in Washington and students massed on Oxford's High Street, the Withrow entrance under a one-word banner STRIKE!, a group of disheveled students astride the ROTC gun mount, washroom graffiti affirming ALL POWER TO THE PEOPLE, a pair of half-clad students lying in the sun beside a Cincinnati newspaper with black headline 176 ARRESTED AT MIAMI. In the sorority section an upbeat page showed the Delta Gamma chapter all in white middy blouses perched on the stairs and bridge-deck of Rowan Hall.

The year of contrast and conflict ended with an unforgetable Commencement. On the platform facing 2039 graduates and 10,000 audience was Colonel James McDivitt, husband of a Miami alumna and veteran of two space flights; he gave commissions to 104 Air Force and Navy ROTC cadets. Beside a gravely smiling President Shriver sat the world-famous young American Neil Armstrong. In his brief address the pioneer astronaut did not mention space frontiers but spoke of frontiers in society where young people must make constructive change. Then President Shriver called to the platform the president of the graduating class, Paul Franks, a native Australian who had become a citizen of Troy, Ohio. Saying that this class had seen more change than any other class in Miami's long history he urged the importance of tradition in a changing society and challenged his classmates to regain and revitalize the tradition of respect. As they listened in the vast silence of the crowded hall his words touched their own scarred memories and their inheritance of all the storm and stress of human history.

Chapter XXVII

MIAMI WESTERN UNION

THE weekend of June 15-17, 1973, was festive on both sides of Patterson Avenue. Under a big striped tent in Miami's south quad two thousand alumni signed class registers, while a record number of Western College women donned badges under a big blue banner in Clawson Hall. These women found their spacious campus adorned with two new buildings — Thomson Hall and the new [Hoyt] library. Some scores of people crossed and recrossed the long border street, husbands and wives with affiliation on both sides.

An unplanned unofficial highlight of the Miami reunion was a nostalgic activity on the corner of High Street and Talla-wanda. A week earlier, on the Miami Commencement day, Tuffy Potter had served toasted rolls to the final customers in his corner sandwich shop. For 43 years that friendly place had capped the old High Street fraternity row. Now the fraternities were replaced by academic halls and in the lengthening shadows of June 15 alumni overflowed that corner. Under the old maple trees an auctioneer was raffling Tuffyana. *Going . . . going . . . gone*! were the coffee urns, the soda fountains, the toaster grills, the tableware, and 21 wooden booths hatched and cross-hatched with Greek letters, class numerals, and twined initials.

On Saturday, June 16, the Western women heard four professors present "mini-units" of classroom learning. At

Alumnae Chapel while doves cooed in the great old Kumler cottonwood they had "A Time to Remember" recalled by a 1943 graduate who was a niece of their honored professor emeritus Isabel St. John Bliss. At the alumnae banquet on Saturday evening Mary Lee Brandenburg, president of the Alumnae Association, presented silver charms to 24 members of the 50-year class of 1923. The euphoria of two new buildings and A Time to Remember was not stifled by a brief statement from President Spencer that Western College and Miami University were preparing terms of an affiliation.

In the deepening June dusk while Miami alumni were lugging off their trophies from Tuffy's auction, President Phillip R. Shriver and President William C. Spencer held a joint news conference in Roudebush Hall across the street. Earlier that day in separate meetings their two Boards had passed identical resolutions. Each president was empowered "to prepare an agreement . . . for affiliation of The Western College with Miami University prior to the 1973-74 academic year." The Western resolution sanctioned the sale of McKee Hall to Miami, and the Miami resolution authorized the purchase of McKee Hall for a sum not to exceed $300,000. To the press President Shriver at first merely reported the agreement, leaving explanation and comment to President Spencer. His statement reviewed recent relations between the institutions. Following the creation of a Miami-Western Committee on Cooperation in 1970, Western students enrolled in certain Miami classes while Miami faculty began teaching a few courses at Western. Miami hospital and computer facilities were made available to Western, and Western opened to Miami students library space, intramural fields and cross-country runways. In 1971 Western suggested that 100 Miami men be lodged and boarded in unused Western residence and dining space. This led to Miami's leasing of McKee Hall, the admitting of men to Western classrooms, and to the change of name from Western College for Women to The Western College. In 1972 Western enrolled 55 freshman men among its 350 students. On June 10, 1973 the last all-women class was graduated. Now, five days later, came this resolution of affiliation. Spencer's comment concluded: "During the coming academic year both institutions will cooperatively work out details of a more permanent affiliation, which can create a practical and distinctive bond to best serve both The Western College and Miami University."

The press conference continued for an hour or more. Behind the kindly word "affiliation" lay hard cold facts, but there was no specific reference to deepening debt and importunate creditors, and only glancing notice of laws and regulations of a state university. This was essentially an upbeat briefing. President Spencer said he had proposed affiliation " because of the financial needs of Western College . . . the real financial crisis that pervades all of private higher education. Of the various alternatives [not mentioning bankruptcy, receivership, and public auction] an affiliation with Miami University seemed most proper." The two presidents referred to past discussions about having Western operate with Miami as a unit like those of residential colleges at Yale, Michigan State, Claremont and the University of California at Santa Cruz. If that conception could materialize, assuming approval and support of Ohio legislators, The Western College would become, on July 1, 1974, a new division of Miami University.

It was generally believed that to survive financially a college needs 700 students. Current enrollment at Western was 400; a goal of 750 had been planned for 1975. To attract and accommodate that number new facilities were required. So, importunate bond-holders were fended off while new buildings went up. It was a cruel logic — go deeper into debt in hope of future solvency. This policy had preceded President Spencer's tenure. In the night air hung the auctioneer's words at Tuffy's corner. Going . . . going . . . gone!

On July 10 both Western and Miami released a Memorandum of Understanding for Affiliation and Union. Its ten points included Western's transfer of all physical properties and assets while Miami provided $3,300,000 to meet Western's liabilities. To his own faculty President Shriver explained that one-half of that amount would come from Miami's dormitory and dining hall funds; the remainder would be sought from the state legislature. In the second week of August the enactment of House Bill 985 included an appropriation of $1,800,000 for acquisition by Miami University of the Western College properties.

In mid-August, normally the most relaxed time of year, Shriver appointed a planning team on the best use of The Western College of Miami University. Under chair of Professor Warren L. Mason with Professor Robert J. Wittman as executive secretary, the 15 faculty and staff members were to submit within three months three proposals for the development of Miami's new division. To the team was added a panel of 12 consultants from the Miami faculty, and three, to be named by President Spencer, from Western College. Immediately the planning team began work. President Shriver attended its first meeting, which concluded with a walking tour of the 208-acre Western campus, from Patterson Place, the traditional home of Western presidents, to the remote beechwoods overlooking the Tallawanda valley. Most of the buildings and much of the grounds were new exciting territory to this committee. Exciting, and at the same time sobering. They saw sagging floors, leaky roofs, scaling plaster, footways cracked and crumbling on the lovely Western bridges. Inevitably the Western plant had eroded during years of increasing debt. Although this lay outside the committee's province it had a bearing upon their academic assignment.

Ahead of the planning team was a strenuous agenda with twice-a-week meetings throughout September and October. Proposals had poured in from both Western and Miami faculty and alumni (ae) and from the interested public. The range of 112 separate recommendations is suggested by a sampling:

—continue Western's program of liberal arts and international studies
—create a 3-year resident Law School
—establish a 2-year University College of General Studies
—recreate a Women's College, emphasizing women's studies
—set up an Institute of International Studies and Foreign Commerce
—develop an Environmental Education Center
—organize a 4-year School of Creative Writing
—divide Miami's College of Liberal Arts and Sciences, with science based on the Miami campus and humanities on Western campus
—create a program of Great Books and Critical Experiments

Other proposals were focused upon Languages, Music, Religion, Biblical Studies, Public Administration, Human and Natural Resources, Health and Welfare, Continuing Education, and "Real World" Problems.

No doubt this exercise in dreams, hopes and speculations gave an educational lift to the Oxford community. More people were giving more thought to the goals and opportunities of higher education than ever before in Miami's history. During the 1959 Sesquicentennial observance a panel of visiting educators had lectured on the question "What's A College For?" Now that question was italicized. An open meeting drew more than a hundred faculty and students from both Western and Miami. Members of the planning committee spoke to a general meeting of the Western faculty. Circulation of reading lists and working papers stimulated both formal and informal discussion beyond the huddle of the planning team. A realistic rationale came with a scheduled visit by John D. Millett, former Miami president and chancellor of the Ohio Board of Regents; he stressed the value of curricular coherence and a learning sequence rather than a choice of free electives. From visits to innovative colleges in Michigan, Iowa and California the committee gained increased awareness of the problems inherent in experimental programs.

With all this observation, deliberation and discussion, the planning team put together a report widely circulated in a special edition of the MIAMIAN. It recommended for adoption in the fall of 1974 one of four alternate models of undergraduate liberal arts concentration.

a. A program of interdisciplinary studies
b. An integrated program of learning styles and modes of inquiry
c. A program of intellectual heritage and human values
d. A 2-year interdisciplinary program of general education

Each model included a core curriculum of 12 credit hours per term in the first two years, with an elective course from the main campus to be added. The third and fourth years comprised free electives on the Miami campus except for one or two Western seminars and an individually designed Senior project.

The four models were recommended equally. All were in keeping with the traditional liberal arts emphasis at both Western and Miami. They stressed, alike, the residential unit, the college as a learning community. With an aimed enrollment of 250 the first year, growing in four years to some 750, the student could retain individuality while sharing interests with intimate tutorial groups and self-directed study. The faculty would live on or near the campus in dormitory suites and separate residences.

From the four recommended curricula the University Senate chose the program of interdisciplinary studies focused upon a concept of the Creative Self. Its freshman courses were Selfhood and Personal Identity, the American Society and its Critics, and Principles of Order and Disorder in the Natural Universe. The sophomore courses were The Measure of Man, Comparative Cultures, and The Artistic Expression of Man's Ideas.

The merging with Western brought Miami University into the midst of a widespread interest in the relationship of private colleges to the State. In 1972-73 there came 29 closings of private colleges, seven institutional mergers, and six assimilations by state institutions. The adopting of a program of interdisciplinary studies reflected a growing concern over the supplanting of liberal arts by vocational and career education. The New York University philosopher Sidney Hook, who in 1969 had lectured to an impatient audience in old Benton Hall, averred that student violence and political action threatened humane scholarship and academic freedom. Now, just four years later, it seemed to many educators that the enemy of liberal education was neglect. In the calm that has come over our campuses, said an official at Columbia University, it may seem melodramatic to still speak of the university crisis, but a creeping crisis finds liberal education taking second place to career training. The Western College was in part a protest and an attempt at rescue.

The chosen program of interdisciplinary studies called for an eventual—in four years—16 fulltime faculty headed by a Dean and an Associate Dean. So that the dean could choose his people there was an immediate search, nationwide, for that appointment. On March 21, 1974, President Shriver announced the selection from three hundred applicants of Myron J. Lunine, age 44, "a teacher and administrator of varied experience." Since 1972 he had been dean of Hampshire College, the fifth institution in a cluster of Smith College, Amherst College, the University of Massachusetts, and Mount Holyoke College. Hampshire itself was a new venture in education, an experimental college occupying an airy site on high ground above the Connecticut River valley. All its students lived in coed dorms; they determined social regulations on the campus and were represented on all faculty committees. They chose their courses without restrictions. The College stressed independent study and no grades were given. It enjoyed certain cooperative measures with its neighbors — library, laboratory, visiting lectures, inter-campus transportation. In that consortium the dean of newly created Hampshire must have coped and collaborated with a large state institution and three private colleges of moderate size and distinguished reputation.

Mike Lunine — a first-name man — never told why after just two years at innovative Hampshire he sought the post of dean at innovative Western College. He did say, more than once, that he hoped to see "some liberalizing" at Miami. His background indicated a bent for mobility and change; he had brief stays at Iowa, Colorado, the University of Delhi, India, and the University of Istanbul, Turkey, and Fisk University. At Kent State, 1968-72, he was dean of the Honors and Experimental College. Described as "a man who had worked in a remarkable way to wed living and learning in new modes of academic programing," he liked "verbal and self-defining students." At Western College the Lunine family moved into the historic Stillman-Kelley studio-cottage between Patterson Place and Presser Hall.

Dean Lunine immediately began recruiting faculty for the Western College program. An interim committee had advertised in educational media: the *Bulletin* of the American Studies Association, the *Chronicle of Higher Education, Science, The Black Scholar,* and *Spokeswoman.* The advertisement stated: "Miami University, Oxford, Ohio, will open a new division, the Western College, in the fall of 1974. Directly adjacent to the main campus of 14,000 students, the Western College will provide a revolving curriculum in interdisciplinary studies, with initial emphasis in American Studies and Environmental Studies. We seek faculty with completed degrees, multiple competencies, interdisciplinary orientation, and a willingness to collaborate in a variety of teaching-learning situations. The Western College will be a distinctive intellectual community, stressing high teacher-student contact and clustered living-learning facilities serving a four-year undergraduate experience." Within a few weeks this notice drew more than five hundred applications. From that number the interim committee selected sixty leading prospects for consideration by the new dean. Of those chosen one-third were women and all had specialties in either humanities, social science or physical science. It was generally a young and unmarried faculty, a majority with degrees from Eastern universities.

During the first years tentative evaluations of the program were inconclusive. After four years President Shriver appointed a Special Task Force on Evaluation of the Western College of Miami University. It was asked to make a firm recommendation as to whether the program should be continued, modified or discarded. The result, a 74-page report, for consideration by the Faculty Council, the University Senate, and the Board of Trustees, was distributed January 12, 1978, and published as a special edition of the MIAMIAN. Its most persuasive pages came from two visiting consultants who in November 1977 had approached the Western College without previous knowledge or attitudes, except that they were attached to experimental divisions of their own institutions.

The two referees were Howard R. Bowen of the Claremont Graduate School in California and Theodore N. Newcomb of the University of Michigan. What they had to say was bracing indeed to the Western College staff and arresting, at least, to the Miami faculty at large. Dr. Bowen immediately remarked upon the national importance of Western College and its resistance to large, impersonal and bureaucratic organization. He wrote: "The unique place of Miami University in American higher education is due largely to its unusual commitment to undergraduate education conducted in a human setting and with concern for personal development of its students as individuals. This is seen in the rural setting, the stunningly beautiful campus, the emphasis on undergraduate study, the deep commitment to liberal education, the rich extracurricular life, and the limitation on the overall size of the institution." Looking more closely at the Western College he declared it "an astonishing success despite the considerable constraints under which it has been working." He found the faculty fully qualified, dedicated and hard-working, the students somewhat superior to Miami students in their test scores and performance, and the program imaginative, rigorous and consistent with excellent liberal education. Western College, he concluded, is off to a good start though it needs more student enrollment. Students, he suggested, could be attracted by public information about the program and clarifying of its separateness and autonomy. He also stressed the value of the old tradition behind the new venture. To see in the new Western an evolutionary outgrowth of the old Western would involve alumnae and friends of the old Western in a forward-looking rather than nostalgic fashion.

Dr. Newcomb from Ann Arbor deliberately sought Miami faculty members who did not favor continuation of the Western College—members who believed that interdisciplinary studies lacked the depth and rigor of academic disciplines and who considered Western College a financial failure. At the same time he found other non-Western faculty who had been impressed by occasional Western students in their classrooms and by Western colleagues with whom they had genuine acquaintance. Those who knew most about Western were more sanguine about its success. This observer found the Western faculty knowledgable, broadly informed, and critical-minded; he judged them to be devoted and effective teachers. Overall he thought them a more competent faculty than their counterparts in the Residential College of his own (Ann Arbor) university. The best indication of success would be found in the post-graduate experience of Western's students, but only time could provide that judgment. Dr. Newcomb concluded with an affirmation. "If it turns out that Western can be continued I would have considerable optimism about its future. . . . I believe it could become one of the few outstanding ones of its kind in the United States."

The result of the Task Force Evaluation was recommendation from the University Senate that the Western College program be continued and its divisional status be maintained. When Dean Lunine resigned in 1980, moving on to San Francisco State, Professor Curtis Jellison, a veteran of Miami's American Studies department, became Dean of the Western College, in 1981.

Meanwhile there had come some physical changes of the Western campus. When built in 1907 the Miami steam and power plant on Spring Street was comfortably distant from the Slant Walk campus dominated by Old Main Hall. Seventy years later its tall smokestack marked the very heart of the Miami campus. Now the needs of the Western College and of the greatly expanded Miami were met by a modern, efficient and economical plant on the edge of Bull Run valley beyond Peabody Hall. It was out of sight and out of mind, with miles of underground tunnels linking more than a hundred university buildings.

Western's decrepit Alumnae Hall was graced by an attractive bell tower where the Heath Chimes rang in all seasons. When it proved to be impractical to preserve the bell tower, Alumnae Hall was razed, while a free-standing Carillon Tower, built by gifts of Western alumnae and friends, rose on the Peabody Green. In the circling foundation wall are two cornerstones preserved from the original tower. On twin stone lamp posts bronze tablets memorialize alumnae leaders and faculty members who touched the lives of many generations of Western students. The chime is played from a console in Kumler Chapel. Its fourteen bells rang out on Sunday morning June 17, 1979. In the midst of change they echo the spirit and traditions of Western College.

The first Miami academic building erected on the Western grounds was Bachelor Hall, dedicated on a bright fall afternoon in 1979. It memorializes a Miami teacher who, despite his name and gender, befits the Western scene. Like the faculty of the old Western he lived with his students. For thirteen years he was head resident of storied Fisher Hall, where residential learning was a fact of life. An honor graduate of Miami in 1911, Joseph M. Bachelor went to Harvard for advanced linguistic study. His work on English vocabulary made him known to the Century Company, a leading publisher. For ten years he was a New York editor, contributing to the big new Century Dictionary. During that time Miami President Hughes repeatedly asked Bachelor to set a date for his return to Miami as a member of the English Department. In 1927 the Century Dictionary was published, and Fisher Hall, newly acquired by Miami University, was opened as a Freshman residence hall. Its faculty head was young Bergen Evans, class of 1924, who needed an associate proctor. So Bachelor settled there.

The next year Evans went to an older Oxford, as Rhodes Scholar, and Bachelor became head of Fisher Hall; his assistant was a newcomer named Havighurst. During the 1930s Bachelor acquired various tracts of marginal farm land northwest of Oxford. In 1940, after thirteen years with Fisher Hall freshmen, he moved to the solitude of a weathered farmhouse on those country acres. There, on a gray December morning in 1947 he was found slumped over a lapboard of books and papers on his rocking chair beside the cold stone fireplace.

Unlike most college teachers Bachelor was only half-academic. The other half was man-of-the-world. Sitting on the west porch of Fisher in the autumn sunset or beside his fireplace on winter nights, he brought to the weathered old hall a sense of the vibrant, restless, kaleidoscopic world beyond the campus horizons. Fifth Avenue, Washington Square, Madison Square, Greenwich Village, the Broadway theater and ferry boats criss-crossing the harbor were in his talk — along with memories of his Miami student years a generation past. From his faculty colleagues in Fisher Hall as well as from the stream of freshmen there he won a special respect as a man of Manhattan as well as of the ivy halls.

On the first day of term the freshmen trooped in. They came to Oxford by train, lugging their bags down High Street, past upper and lower campus, to remote Fisher Hall. All the lower campus was deep woods; Fisher was the only college building beyond Elliott and Stoddard halls. Below Miami Field lay the 30-acre grounds of Fisher Hall with the old towered building rising through the trees. It was off by itself, a separate and special place in its own serene setting. Bachelor never tired of reminding his freshmen that they had a campus of their own, which should draw and hold them together.

That reminder became a part of the Bachelor tradition. After the first dinner in the high-ceiled room, with 170 boys still at table, he addressed them. "This," he declared, "is a time you will never forget. All your life, in distant years and distant places, you will remember this September evening." Already the restless boys were quiet; they listened closely to the stocky man in rumpled clothing. "In a few minutes," he said, "you will leave this old building — some of you in groups, some in pairs, some walking alone in silence. You will go through these memory-haunted grounds, past the campus woods and on up to the old Slant Walk where students have dreamed and reveled for a hundred years. You will begin life-long friendships and loyalties. You will discover Miami University. In the moonlight you will feel the old college brooding on the endless questions of truth and error, right and wrong, ignorance and knowledge. With the discovery of Miami each of you will begin to discover himself. When you return to this hall at midnight you will be enlarged and uplifted. You will be more of a person than ever before. This is the beginning. Good luck to every Fisher Hall man."

That was Joe Bachelor — paternal, avuncular, trailing cigar smoke and sentiment, tritely nostalgic and emotional — and unforgettable. He was just forty years old but he seemed a wise and venerable professor. On those first evenings he worked a kind of magic. For all those youths he changed what would have been a noisy parade uptown into a personal pilgrimage. He told them it was a time they would never forget, and saying that made it memorable. In a word, he took Freshmen seriously. Believing in those boys, he made them believe in themselves.

Bachelor liked a glowing fire on the hearth of his front room. At night he met students there, alone or in groups. But he did his work in his bedroom, at a battered desk beside the window. On the window sill he kept a hot-plate, a teapot, and a box of cigars. He didn't seem to need much sleep. Always up for breakfast, he habitually worked past midnight — drinking strong tea, eating strong cheese, smoking strong cigars. He blew smoke rings — three, four, five rings drifting up through the lamplight. After a cigar he packed his pipe, and more smoke rings ascended. On his desk was the Shakespeare text, its margins filled with his neat square handwriting, and a pile of small squares of yellow paper. The yellow papers were his daily

Shakespeare quiz — a two-minute answer to a single question. His students dared not come to class with the assignment unread. In the classroom he read Shakespeare like an actor; his voice could command, intone or murmur as he became Macbeth, Falstaff, Mercutio. In that northwest room of Irvin Hall sixty students held their breath, while others, outside the door, listened in the hallway.

In 1930 Professor Bachelor began his unique course in "Words." A rigorous course it was always over-enrolled, with students waiting to get in. Now, when many college students seem deaf to their own language it is good to remember what Bachelor could do with English vocabulary. He began with the simplest things: how it happened that a hand-hold became a handle while a foot-hold became a pedal; how lamb in the meadow was still lamb on the table while a sheep in the field became mutton on the platter, and the "cold shoulder" was an unwarmed joint for an unwelcome dinner guest. This word-lore Bachelor worked into his textbooks, even into anthologies of readings where he opened the doorway of word derivations. An indelible impression, for example, is older than an indelible pencil, and older still is the Latin *in* (un) plus *delire* (destroy), hence indestructible. From the statement "Those plans were canceled," he recalled that a cancel was an Old French lattice, and canceling came to mean eliminating by drawing crossbars through something written; in time a cathedral chancel was so named for its latticed crossbar windows. One word led the word-man to another: indelible meant lasting, cancel meant eliminate, and eliminate was at first a purely physical verb — *ex* (out) plus *limen* (door); an offender kicked out of the door was truly eliminated. For the culprit that was uncomfortable, but *comfort* originally denoted things that were combatic rather than easy: *con* plus *fortis* made up a word of strength. Perhaps, the professor added, the softened meaning in our use of *comfort* has some bearing on the progress (or retrogression) of our society. Words, he insisted, should arouse enthusiasm, and saying that he was off again — on a great word from the Greek *en* (in) and *theos* (God), meaning inspired by God, acting as if God were in you. From such words, Bachelor wrote in the textbook, we may remember the great statement of Archbishop Trench: "For a young man, making his first discovery that words are living powers is like the dropping of scales from his eyes, like the acquiring of another sense, or the introduction into a new world."

Bachelor's inexhaustible word-lore sometimes made conversation among his colleagues in the faculty corridor of Fisher Hall. One night there was talk about surveying a farm tract Bachelor hoped to buy, and that led to "boxing the compass," a phrase that began when the compass card was floated in a bowl of glycerine, the word *compass* itself coming from the Old French *compasser,* to go around. Somehow that led to the odd combinations in the names of English pubs and inns: the Devil and St. Dunstans, the Elephant and Castle, the Goat and Compass — names pictured on the swinging sign over a tavern doorway. The Goat and Compass was most puzzling, until Bachelor recalled 17th century writers who reiterated "God Encompasses Us" — a profound and reverant concept. But carelessly and ignorantly repeated *God Encompasses* became Goat and Compass, bizarrely pictured by innkeepers and publicans in many shires.

There was ripe cheese, red apples and encompassing conversation around the Bachelor fireplace on winter nights. Often it began with the Broadway stage and ended with words, a moveable feast of the many-colored English language. Joe Bachelor had shared with Bergen Evans his long-range project of a dictionary of English idioms, a dream that Bachelor left unfinished but Evans carried it on in his prime-time television show "The Last Word" and in his *Dictionary of American Usage* and his vastly eclectic *Dictionary of Quotations.*

To his students a teacher like Bachelor brings the ardor and texture of the life he has lived — life warmed and fused by fires of thought and learning. Thirty years after his death a Miami woman graduate of 1938 remembered, from six hundred miles away, "Tuffy's rolls and coffee, the Campus Owls, broken romances, pop tunes of the '30s . . . Mr. Bachelor and his Shakespeare class which opened doors that have never closed and his WORDS that began an endless interest in the history of language."

This man with far-ranging mind loved the Four Mile valley, even its snakes and barn owls. *Bachelor,* he glossed through the smoke rings: from Latin *bacca,* a cow, and *baccalaris,* a vassal farmer. Through the Fisher Hall years he kept buying parcels of woodland, field and pasture. At his death he left to Miami University 400 acres of Wildlife Refuge. More than that, he left in thousands of students a bequest of indelible memories.

In early years Western College and Miami University were separated by the country road that became Patterson Avenue. It was frozen in winter, mired in spring, dusty in summer—until the first brick pavement was laid in 1916. The pavement extending through the village High Street was a collaboration of President Boyd of Western and President Hughes of Miami. Older than paved highway was the bond of families. Tappan Hall, now looking across a wide green fairway to the gray stone tower of Kumler Chapel, holds mingled memories. David S. Tappan, a Miami graduate of 1864 and president in 1900, was the father of eight children. His oldest daughter married a Miami professor who in 1902 moved to Hiroshima, Japan, as a religious editor. Forty-four years later Hiroshima made history as the tragic target of the world's first atomic bomb. The youngest Tappan daughter, Anna Helen, was graduated from Western College in 1909. She became a Mathematics instructor, then a professor, eventually a beloved Dean of Western College. Now preserved in beautiful Tappan Hall are ties with both Western and Miami.

Similar family ties, many of them, including the Covingtons and Williams, the Brices, Brills, Berrys, Fittons, Molyneaux, Becketts, Whitcombs, Liggetts, Listermans, Weidners, and Wallaces—link the two colleges. Patterson Place, the traditional residence of Western presidents and now the home of the College Alumnae Assoication, was built by James H. Patterson, a Miami graduate of 1857. Romantic relations of Western women and Miami men began in the early years. In 1857 Miami sophomore Abner Jones reported in his diary: "This evening at a Western parlor party I met the finest, and prettiest, and most intelligent girls I ever saw. . . . I think this is the place to choose a perfect wife." Since then Abner's thought has been embraced by a long list of grateful Miami men.

Finally one may recall a Western-Miami collaboration that has made educational history. A striking innovation in American colleges is to have a working artist on the campus. The rationale is simple: if it is important to study artistic work, it is imperative to support creative artists. There are now scores of artists-in-residence in American universities. The practice originated here in Oxford seventy years ago, when Edgar Stillman-Kelley was composing oratorios and symphonies while Percy MacKaye was writing lyric narratives and poetic dramas. In London in 1908, during a long residence abroad, the Kelleys attended the first European performance of MacKaye's poetic drama *Jeanne D'Arc,* and so began a lifelong friendship. In 1910 Jessica Stillman-Kelley took charge of the Western College Music Department, accompanied by her distinguished composer husband. They lived in Peabody Hall, where Jessie taught piano in a "music parlor." Her husband worked beside a kitchen stove in a Western College farmhouse near the Oxford Cemetery. In 1916 President Boyd built them a studio-residence across a tiny stream from Patterson Place. That studio is now a registered Historic Landmark.

When President Hughes planned to bring a creative artist to the Miami campus, the Kelleys urged him to invite MacKaye. For his "studio" Miami built a one-room cabin with broad fireplace in the wooded lower campus. Students dubbed it "the Poet's Shack." The MacKaye family, from Cornish, New Hampshire, settled in a frame house on Maple Street, the site of present Hamilton Hall, just across a pasture-meadow from the Kelley home. So the two pioneer artists-in-residence were neighbors, until 1924 when the illness of MacKaye's mother compelled their return to Cornish, New Hampshire.

In Oxford in 1934, Stillman-Kelley's 77th birthday was celebrated by a festive production of his famous PILGRIM'S PROGRESS oratorio. It was performed by a Miami-Western chorus and the Miami University orchestra. That year the Spring Number of the OXFORD CRITERION was dedicated to Edgar Stillman-Kelley.

A quarterly magazine of the 1930s, the OXFORD CRITERION was a unique bonding of Miami and Western. With no official connection to either institution, it was created and sustained by a group of students and faculty from both colleges. Copies are now collectors' items. Along with essays by a blind student, Mitchell Darling, and of "Prince Ned" Suhksavasti, a newphew of the King of Thailand, it contained portraits by

Philip Ronfor, Arvia MacKaye and Marston Hodgin, poems from E.C. Ross, Marion Boyd, Lucile Hodgin, Eleanora Handschin, and Margaret Hay, criticism by Dorothy Duerr and Dee Roth, the fiction of Louise Whipple, John Rood, Edward Sill, Walter Havighurst, and of Fletcher Knebel whose novels would be read forty years later in twenty languages around the world. This ambitious, exciting little magazine brought together the talent and aspirations of both campuses — a union that is still at work today.

Chapter XXVIII

THE ROAD AHEAD

IN writing his OLD MIAMI anthem for the 1909 Centennial, Professor A.H. Upham looked back at the decades past and then ahead — "Days of old and days to be." A decade later, supported by President Hughes, he proposed a development fund to augment the income from the State. In the anthem's third stanza the words "Larger usefulness awaits" voiced the hopes listed in the crusade: a college hospital, a new library wing, men's and women's gymnasiums, playing fields, loan and scholarship funds, increased faculty support — all to be provided by the one million dollar campaign. In 1920 Miami had a student enrollment of 900 and an alumni body of about 4,000.

On October 1, 1920 alumni dinners were scheduled in 25 centers in Ohio and beyond. The *Alumni News Letter* reminded: "October first! Keep your eye on it. That's when the drive begins, the big Miami drive for that million." Some of the 25 dinners had scant attendance and only a few of them generated much enthusiasm. Two months later Dr. Upham was called to the presidency of the University of Idaho, and the big Miami drive fell in the lap of 30-year-old Wallace Roudebush whose business office was already overworked. It looked like a long, uncertain road to a million dollars. The largest gift, $50,000 from the Carnegie Foundation, was conditioned by an equal amount from the alumni. That matching sum was raised, gymnasium funds were started, and some contributions helped along the $7500 purchase of Cook Field for intramural sports. An unlooked-for gift came from S.S. Laws, the oldest living alumnus; from the Corcoran Gallery in Washington he sent the Houdon bronze statue of George Washington, appraised at $15,000. For want of donors the college hospital, a scholarship fund, a lecture fund, and the two gymnasiums had to wait.

Sixty years later Miami University was a greatly expanded institution but the anthem was still timely. Days of old had lengthened and days to be were bright with promise. Again it was apparent that "larger usefulness awaits." Under leadership of Vice President John Dolibois and President Shriver a campaign committee launched a drive for $14 million.

The Million Dollar Fund of 1920—the fund that failed— lacked detailed planning, persuasive promotion, and the support of a strong organization. The Alumni Association of 1978 was a resourceful, versatile and confident body. Thanks to thirty years of John Dolibois leadership it had achieved wide recognition and national awards. To this 1978 crusade a campaign cabinet of 22 distinguished alumni brought influence in many fields and a deep commitment to the cause. These alumni leaders were also leaders in life; their names and faces bespoke the wide range of Miami talent and accomplishment: Wayne J. Albers, Robert L. Cottrell, William J. Liggett, Malcolm W. Owings, C. Roger Stegmaier, J. Oliver Amos, Ralph N. Fey, Herbert E. Markley, Ara Parseghian, Robert F. Tenhover, John D. Backe, Richard E. Heckert, C. Rollin Niswonger, John G. Smale, G. Sheldon Veil, Joyce Eldridge Brown, Robert E. Levinson, Lloyd H. O'Hara, Paul H. Smucker, Frank A. Vite, Ronald L. Wiley — it was a reassuring roster. Now the Alumni Association itself was not a mere list of names which could contain prospective donors; it was a highly motivated and well organized body of thousands of Miami men and women.

On the winter evening of February 1, 1978, two hundred Miami officers, faculty and alumni sat down to dinner in the banquet room of the Queen City Club in Cincinnati. At their places they found a colorful brochure with a wrap-around reproduction of the Heritage mural framing the words "Larger Usefulness Awaits." The title GOALS FOR ENRICHMENT was figuratively portrayed by an arresting MU logo. Created by

Carol Walker, '78, at the start of her career in graphic art, the logotype exemplified the sound planning and presentation of the Goals project. The design, a sturdy M in an upward-reaching U. gave an immediate impression of purpose and progress. Of countless people who would see this logo — on envelopes, stationery, brochures, workers' manual, even on pledge cards — very few would analyze its symbolism but none could miss its affirmation. In its fifteen pages of print and pictures the brochure asked a repeated question — Why is private support important to this State university? — and gave some ready answers.

The brochure, however, had to wait for close attention. First came a four-course dinner and the introduction, by John Dolibois, of three spokesmen for the twenty-two member Campaign Cabinet. Goals for Enrichment was the first major gifts campaign in Miami history. It aimed to provide $14 million for the furthering of excellence throughout the university. Its general chairman, Charles S. Mechem, Jr. '52, emphasized that Miami University is state-assisted rather than state-supported. Two-thirds of its operating budget is met by non-state income. Appropriations from the state, he explained, are limited to prescribed needs and purposes. Other projects, however, valuable, must depend on private support. Certain goals for enrichment had emerged from many deliberations by Miami administrative, faculty and alumni bodies and the Board of Trustees. The goals, both specific and comprehensive, ranged from a university art museum and a modern sports complex and stadium to the augmenting of resources for study, teaching and research in the science disciplines.

To the dinner guests, Ara Parseghian '49, gave something like a pre-game psyche-up, stressing team play, pride and motivation — all in the long Miami tradition. President Shriver emphasized the "community" character of a residential university and the dtermination to maintain and enhance the high academic standing of Miami University.

John Dolibois, chef artchitect of this large project, was mindful of the Miami past while looking with confident purpose at the road ahead. He recalled the explorer James McBride, first secretary of the Board of Trustees, when, in 1809, the university was established by law but had no actual existence. "On the banks of the Four Mile Creek," McBride said, "has been planted the stake where the Miami University will stand till time shall be no longer." Now, he declared, is the time to extend the fostering hand to cherish and protect this institution of learning which is to give a character and feature to future generations. Here, Dolibois observed, is our generation ready in our time to give the university "a larger usefulness." He stressed the goal of augmented academic resources essential to the exploring of new frontiers of knowledge. With a $5 million endowment for academic enrichment he foresaw faculty development by means of stipends for continuing study and creative research while merit scholarships and loans would attract and retain superior students. Both study and research would be stimulated by increased laboratory apparatus and equipment and by enlarged library resources. When he was a college freshman in 1938, half of the natural and social science taught in the classrooms of 1977 had not come to light. The "knowledge explosion" had yet to bring profound revelations. Listed in the "Goals" brochure was new language — photosensors, atomic absorption spectophotometry, questar telescope, paramagnetic analyzer, multidiscipline chromatograph, electron microscope, electron beam energy pump — a language of new questions, search and understanding.

To balance library aresources and laboratory instruments, John Dolibois saw the humane enlightenment of an art museum, designed for the preservation, display and study of works acquired by the university over many years. Such a facility would attract further gifts and acquisitions so that, like the library, it would bring increasing enrichment in the years to come. Already, Dolibois' stated, museum construction was progressing on an airy site across the highway from Murstein Alumni Center.

That sounded casual, almost matter-of-fact, as though it was a campus consensus that a boldly modern Art Museum merited a major effort and outlay at Miami. But behind the simple statement of *fait accompli* were years of dreaming, hoping, planning, striving — against indifference, inertia and some outright obstruction and hostility. Thwarted and circumvented time and again, Dolibois with a few abettors never gave

in. Thanks to trhe stubborn streak in his character, each
setback spurred new determination and sparked new strategy.
The final outcome vindicated his conviction that the stature of
Miami University would be heightened by a professionally developed museum with an affirmed educational program. Why
give priority to a Miami fine arts center? The answer became
clear. In the 1980's, Miami should include educational aims
and teaching programs that hitherto had been unknown or beyond available resources. But in vital institutions, time brings
new perspectives and opportunities. Art spans decades, generations, centuries. Great art outlasts cultural fads and curricular
fashions. Its study illumines all the areas of social and humane
learning.

Having worked closely with donors and architects, Dolibois
could announce that the interest of the largest donor to the
Goals campaign embraced both an art museum and a sports
stadium. Just inside the museum entrance is Yager lecture hall,
a gracious room seating one hundred and fifteen persons for
film showings, music recitals and art lectures; its arc of northern
windows overlooks a wooded glen with the gray stone tower of
Kumler Chapel against the northern sky. On the far side of the
campus in the Four Mile valley, will rise a sophisticated sports
complex including a new stadium. In a demonstration of surprising academic breadth, the estate of the late Fred C. Yager
'14, supports both the fine arts and intercollegiate athletics. In
a parallel instance, the McKie gallery in the museum bears a
name already fixed on the McKie Field, the baseball ground on
the north campus. Stanley McKie '19, a prominent figure in
Ohio business and politics, had been a varsity baseball captain.
His widow executed a neat double play in endowing both an art
gallery and a baseball diamond.

The first completed project of the Goals to Go, the Miami
University Art Museum, was dedicated on a golden autumn
afternoon, November 5, 1978, with ribbon cutting by John
Dolibois between donor Walter I. Farmer and Architect Walter Netsch. The opening exhibition from the richly eclectic
Farmer Collections ranged from ancient Roman glass, Lu-
ristan bronzes, and pre-Columbian terra cotta to 17th century
tapestries and rare pieces of furniture from more recent periods.
Two Farmer collections have been given to the university;

others, presently on loan, will come to the museum by eventual bequest.

Other distinctive holdings in the museum are the prints, textiles and ceramics collected by the late Miami art teacher, Orpha Webster, the unique Alma Pratt Collection of International Folk Art — acquired through untiring efforts of Miss Webster — and fine pieces of pre-Columbian art garnered by Theodore T. Foley '37, during a career of foreign service in Latin America and Egypt.

The Foley benefaction is a story in itself. During his years abroad, Ted Foley acquired a collection of 1,600 items, reviewed by six of the foremost American archaeologists and asked for by the Museum of the American Indian in New York and the Colombia Museo de Oro. One piece, a firegod effigy vase, was on extended loan to the Metropolitan Museum of Art. Some of Foley's treasures had been donated elsewhere but a substantial number remained when the Miami University Art Museum was created. He then began making annual donations to his own univeristy. Forty years earlier, John Dolibois and Ted Foley had teamed up in moving seasonal equipment at Akron's Camp Manatoc. Now, in a sequel beyond all foreseeing, they removed from crates and cartons exotic primitve treasures, including a gold Chibcha balsero and a classic stone Maya ceremonial hacha, which were soon featured in Miami exhibits. Some of the last of his rare pieces Foley gave to the museum during his 45th Miami class reunion in June 1982.

On the museum's opening day, President Willard L. Boyd of the University of Iowa spoke in Yager Auditorium. A university museum, he said, must nourish the artistic talent of teachers, the teaching potential of artists, and the learning capacity of students. This museum, he said, is more than a showplace; it is art itself. That perception is quickly shared by visitors from near and far. In striking contrast to the red-brick Georgian buildings across the way, its silver gray facade of stone and glass is akin to the weathered gray stone of Kumler Chapel and Presser Hall beyond the wooded glen. At the museum entrance, a reflecting pool mirrors the squares and folded circles of a sculpture in bronze, aluminum and steel, created by Fletcher Benton '55. Like architect Netsch, he works in geometric forms. The five triangular galleries of the museum invite displays ranging from fine prints and ceramics to the largest works of painting and sculpture. On that November afternoon, President Boyd concluded: "Though art is created in private, its consequences are public. In a university museum, the artist addresses the largest audience with the greatest results." Within four years after that dedication, the Miami University Art Museum had attracted 100,000 visitors and had been pictured in art journals from Germany to Japan.

That winter night in Cincinnati, John Dolibois spoke of another Goal — the relocation, enlargement and modernization of Miami Field. Almost a century old, the playing field dated back to 1895 and the stands to 1916, the smallest and oldest in the Mid-American Conference. In some places, a stadium would have the first priority, but at Miami it yet remained unrealized. "We have a lot of sentimental people here," said the grounds superintendent. Despite the impatience of many athletic fans, there was a general reluctance to abandon the old area in the heart of the campus that had produced enviable track-and-field records and a remarkable roster of coaches. In the mind of John Dolibois, a new stadium was less urgent than certain other goals. Two months after his departure, however, state funds were allocated to Miami for a new Art Education building, a Biological Science building, and the re-location and construction of a multi-faceted sports complex including a football stadium. Located between Millett Hall and the Tallawanda, the stadium was completed in time for the football season of 1983. A Biological Science building is planned on the site of old Miami Field.

With the hectic pace of mid-20th century technology, a new phrase — continuing education — is often heard in business, professional and university circles. In his travel and his correspondence, John Dolibois became increasingly aware of a need and an opportunity on the spacious Miami campus in its tranquil setting. To the dinner guests in Cincinnati, he told of unending requests from academic, professional, industrial and civic organizations that Miami space be made available for conferences, workshops and seminars. Except in summer months and short periods of academic recess, Miami could not schedule such meetings. Countless opportunities, he said, were being lost for want of suitable facilities. There was, however, an idle empty building, a commodious structure on spacious grounds at the eastern edge of the campus. Historic Fisher Hall was an ideal site for conference gatherings, but, with sinking foundations and fractured masonry, the romantic old building was unusable. Architectural and engineering studies declared it beyond reclaiming. To the regret of countless alumni and many Oxford residents, the landmark building was slated for demolition so that a conference center could be erected in its place.

When a Hamilton, Ohio family with ties to Miami made a handsome endowment, the Timothy Marcum Memorial Conference Center was staked out beside the Conrad Formal Gardens. After long deliberation, an architectual design emerged, a three-story brick building with twin wings, its central roof capped by a slender cupola with an airy 1981 weathervane. It is modeled upon the Wren Building of William and Mary College in Virginia, the oldest extant academic structure in the nation. A memorial to a recent Miami undergraduate, this new building calls to mind the foremost graduate of Old Miami. Among graduates of the Williamsburg College was Benjamin Harrison, a James River planter, governor of Virginia and signer of the Declaration of Independence. His son, William Henry Harrison, went west to Ohio and became the nation's ninth President; his great-grandson, Benjamin Harrison, Miami 1852, was the 23rd President. In addition to lecture and demonstration halls, the building includes lodging and dining rooms, lounges, library and seminars. A Memorial Room contains the military memorabilia of four-star General John Edwin Hull '15, and the honor roll of all Miamians who have given their lives in defense of the nation.

While the building took shape, the Marcum family added endowment for a nature trail in the virgin woods that slope down to the Tallawanda, an expression of the late Timothy Marcum's love of unspoiled nature. The family of Verlin Pulley '25, former Oxford mayor and university trustee, planned an outdoor Pulley Pavilion near the head of the Marcum Nature Trail. A substantial grant from the Kellogg Foundation enabled a director to publicize the conference facilities and to plan 1982-83 scheduling. The director, Jack DePree, with broad experience of continuing education in Michigan,

soon announced twenty conferences booked for the fall of
1982. In the first year of operation more than sixty
professional, business, cultural and social gatherings, totaling
some five thousand conferees, assembled there for periods of a
single day to one or two weeks. Academic seminars, discussions and exchanges were held by the College English Association

the American Studies Association
the American Chemical Society
the Ohio College Health Association
the Lilly Fellows
the Ohio Board of Regents
the Association of Spanish Teachers
Financial Aid Counsellors
the Commission on Adult Development and Aging

Demonstrations and discussions centered upon Electron
Microscopy, Clinical Psychology, Economic Botany, Management Supervision, Systems Techniques, Information Storage
and Retrieval, and other provinces of technology and research.

On that night of February 1, 1978, the unveiled projects
seemed uncertain and the campaign formidable. But John
Dolibois revealed that study, discussion and planning had
begun more than a decade past. That preparation and the commitment of alumni like Fred Yager and Walter Farmer gave
immediate momentum to the campaign. On schedule, the goals
ahead became goals achieved. The campaign formally ended
on February 1, 1981, three years after its beginning, with
closing ceremony on Charter Day, February 19. Over $15 mil-
lion had been raised for Goals for Enrichment. In a concluding
address to the campaign cabinet, Charles Mechem thanked
"the thousands who made the program a success" and John
Dolibois thanked the many colleagues and volunteers who had
shared in the effort. Both men stressed the value of goals un-
seen, the endowment for academic projects, faculty development, alumni scholarships, and the enhancement of resources
that will touch an untold number of lives.

Chapter XXIX

SLANT WALK MEDLEY — 1984

FOR many years the Slant Walk was bordered by Benton Hall, Brice Hall, Thobe's Fountain, Hepburn Hall, Old Main, Alumni Library, Herron Gym, and ended at Old North and Old South dorms. Where are they now? Gone, replaced, removed, renamed; only the Slant Walk endures unchanged.

The naming and renaming of buildings, a puzzle to Miami alumni of recent years, has vexed faculty veterans who still say Old Benton when referring to Hall Auditorium and Old Library in preference to Alumni Hall, a name sometimes confused with Murstein Alumni Center. Why Van Voorhis rather than long-standing Herron Gym? And why Hughes Laboratories when laboratories still function in the old Hughes — now Kreger — Hall? Like Biblical Pilate they ask — and do not wait for an answer.

Hall Auditorium was named when plans for expansion of King Library dictated the removal of Benton Hall. To retain on the campus the name of an outstanding Miami president "Benton" was transferred to the new Psychology building. When it developed that King Library would not be extended over the site of the former Benton, some people recalled that Miami's Civil War president, the Reverend John W. Hall from Huntsville, Alabama, had never been memorialized — on account of his Confederate background plus the fact that "Hall Hall" sounded either forced or funny. But there was nothing unsuitable about "Hall Auditorium". Old Main was renamed half a century ago for the nation's 23rd President, Benjamin Harrison, who had recited Greek and Logic there; his name survived though the twin-towered historic building was replaced at the time of the University's sesquicentennial. Old North and Old South dorms, renovated in the 1930s, were then named Elliott and Stoddard for two of Harrison's venerated professors.

The commanding new Chemistry building seemed the proper place for the name of President Raymond M. Hughes, Miami's first professor of Physics and Chemistry. The old Chemistry building then took the name of a later chemist, and university vice president, C. W. Kreger. Miami's first gymnasium, Herron Hall, named for a distinguished trustee who was father-in-law of U.S. President William Howard Taft, became Van Voorhis for a breezy director of intramural sports, when the Herron name was transferred to the new women's gymnasium built in 1962. With the growing feminist movement of the 1970s, Herron's name gave way to that of Margaret Phillips, head of women's physical and health education for forty years.

One name that caused no confusion or question came in 1981. The announcement of President Shriver's resignation as soon as a successor could be found was climaxed by disclosure of trustees' action; henceforth the University Center would be known as Phillip R. Shriver Center. It set off an ovation.

With the 142nd Annual Commencement on May 10, 1981, President Shriver was concluding 16 years in office; only Alfred H. Upham, with 17 years, had a longer tenure. In these 16 years Shriver conferred 43,221 degrees, 61 percent of all Miami baccalaureates. On that Commencement platform he was flanked by honorary designates Congressman Clarence J. Brown, Trustee Barry J. Levey, Dr. Robert A. Hefner, the Rev. Martin Luther King, Sr., and alumnus Harold L. Kohlmeier. With TV cameras panning the podium and the convocation, this was the first Miami Commencment to be video-taped. The retiring president was too much occupied to ponder the past. But some in the 12,000 audience reviewed the change and accomplishment that marked those 16 years.

Aside from the merging of Western and Miami, the Shriver years had seen the construction of Millett Hall, Tappan, Emerson and Morris Halls, Hughes Laboratories and the Marcum

Center. Entirely new were the branch campuses of Middletown and Hamilton and the establishing of a European Center in Luxembourg. More significant than physical growth was the heightened stature of Miami University with more than forty Masters programs and full accreditation of the Ph.D. in ten fields of study. Untallied but significant were new measures of student involvement in university governance while maintaining the no-car rule and regulation of social life in forty residence halls. An increasing number of student applications allowed and required selective admission. By his own request President Shriver had taught one History course each year. His chosen "early retirement" would now involve half-time teaching as a member of the History department.

When the Shriver family moved to Oxford in July, 1966 they took residence in Grey Gables, then on the site of present Tappan Hall, while workmen renovated Lewis Place. On summer evenings the president played softball with five children; the oldest was on college vacation, the youngest would soon begin the third grade. Now, in 1981, about to vacate Lewis Place were the Shriver parents whose new generation were mostly married and gone, with six grandchildren among them. Only rarely, again, would the long table in the Center's 1809 Room fill up for Sunday dinner of the Shriver clan.

At the close of his tenure President Shriver spoke of problems confronting his successor and the challenge to maintain the quality of Miami programs in an austere time. Yet, he concluded, "I am optimistic because of my high regard for Dr. Paul G. Pearson. With his leadership Miami can respond affirmatively and effectively to the demographic and economic pressures that lie ahead."

Dr. Pearson was a past president of the American Institute of Biological Sciences, an executive vice president of Rutgers University, and a former acting president there. His wife, Winifred Pearson, after graduation from Florida State, had taught English and Spanish in secondary school and, along with family duties had served as administrative assistant to the president of Florida State University. The Pearsons were not strangers to problems and responsibility.

At his inauguration in October President Pearson shared the platform with the man he had succeeded as Provost at Rutgers,

Henry M. Winkler, president of the Univrsity of Cincinnati. These two, coming to Ohio from New Jersey, recalled the 1788 Symmes Purchase of land between the two Miami rivers which opened the wilderness of southwestern Ohio. Its leading settlers were, like Symmes himself, colonists from New Jersey. President Pearson saw Miami University as a source of strength for the people of Ohio as well as for the people of the region and the nation. In assuming office he said "With pride and humility I accept your designation as the 18th president of Miami University. We come with expectations of continuity as well as change."

Continuity was valued at Old Miami and change was already evident. In a seven-month span in 1982 Miami had acquired a new president and three vice presidents as well. Resignation of John E. Dolibois, to become U.S. Ambassador to Luxembourg, of Lloyd Goggin, for retirement, and of David Brown as president-elect of Transylvania University, occasioned the appointment of C. K. Williamson as Provost, Douglas M. Wilson as Vice President for University Relations, and Edward J. Demske as Vice President for Finance and Business Management. Williamson's move took him just next door, to Roudebush from Upham Hall where he had been Dean of the College of Arts and Sciences. Demske came from New York state with high marks for business management at SUNY Binghampton. Wilson traveled farthest, returning to Miami from Eugene, Oregon after two years of accomplishments as Director of the Oregon University Fund.

On his inauguration day President Pearson was presented with a handsome Scroll of Greetings from the Miami University Alumni Association — greetings and pledged support.

Greetings on Behalf of the
Miami University Alumni Association

Dr. Pearson, as you have experienced already, Miami's alumni can be characterized by three words; "concerned"—"generous"—and "loyal." "Concerned" . . . . . for the future of their alma mater as one of the nation's and midwest's best state universities. "Generous" . . . . with their financial support, their time and their talents to make Miami a better university, and "loyal" . . . . fiercely loyal — always willing to stand up and be counted as a Miamian.

Although I am only one Miami alumnus, I can speak for all Miamians who are aware that today, we put her in your hands. We ask of you but four things:

First, keep her sound! In the 1980's, the university will face resource challenges of several kinds — financial, human, and physical. Keep her sound financially, filled with challenged students, and well maintained. Miami's sons and daughters are available to help — as they always have been.

Second, keep her personal! Each of the 75,000 living alumni can easily name a professor, staff member, or support person who walked that extra mile to make Miami different. Surround yourself with those who know that Miami is special, and that her students are her lifeblood. The phrase "Miami Family" is not a cliche.

Third, keep her traditions alive! Miamians are scattered all over the globe. Each might have a particular way to describe his or her experience at Miami. One word which might continue to surface would be "unique". A great deal of Miami's scuccess results from her long, proud history. The fact that you are only the 18th president in its long history tells us something.

And lastly, keep her great! There is a pride in Miami that swells among its graduates. Miami quality is reflected in an outstanding faculty,

and in the bright, eager students who become
its products. This pride is reflected in the
esteem with which a Miami degree is held by
others because we are proud of our degrees.

Dr. Pearson, alumni interest and support is one
of those long-standing traditions to which I
referred. Miami's alumni formed their alumni
association in 1832, the first at a state university.
As the representative of those alumni, I offer
you our help in keeping Miami great, our
support, and our warm welcome as you begin
your administration.

W. Perry Brown '52
President, Miami University Alumni Association

While setting up in Oxford the Pearsons made it clear that
they belonged there. In Lewis Place they hung portraits and
collected literature of Old Miami. During a June visit their son
Andy, a pre-med student in Pennsylvania, joined the 4-mile
Alumni Fun Run, crossing the line in a close second place. On
travels from coast to coast and from Luxembourg to Korea
and Japan, Paul and Winnie carried a warm sense of belonging
to the Miami community in Oxford and at large. In Columbus
President Pearson voiced Miami hopes and fears with candor
and resolve.

A new era was begining, with new problems and new
prospects. While a depressed economy curtailed enrollment in
many American colleges, the Miami roll stood fast with superior students. In the face of increased tuition cost financial
support from private sources provided additional scholarship
funds and grants for faculty improvement and research. The
alumni quarterly took a new name, MIAMIAN, with sharp
focus on the current scene. Successive issues carried cover
themes: Change at Miami, Challenges to Education, Computer Literacy. In separate interviews the new officials repeated a respect and regard for the art of teaching. President
Pearson recalled a biology instructor who shaped his professional career. "My interest in and compassion for students," he

said, "result from her example." Another influence had come
from a professor who related the laboratory to the changing
world. "I intend to lead Miami University," Pearson declared,
"to a sharing of ideas with the business and industrial community . . . A broad and firm foundation prepares a college
graduate to consider change, adapt to change, and prosper
with change." Provost Williamson set up a goal of quality
teaching, even superb teaching. "Miami," he said, "is made up
of many impressionable young people whose lives find direction from one magnetic professor." As a director of development, Douglas Wilson was acutely aware of the current economic cruch. "Miami University," he stated, "has survived
other crises, and It will survive this one." Beyond survival he
foresaw new stature in its challenging academic standards and
superior teaching. Vice President Etheridge viewed the 1980s
as a time of testing, to which Miami University can bring its
humane residential character, inspiring traditions, and goals of
academic excellence.

Change and continuity . . . . more perhaps than they were
aware these leaders in the final decades of the twentieth century
were in key with the past. In 1928 President Upham made "The
Art of Teaching" his inaugural address. He saw teaching as an
original and individual art, always dissimilar, in keeping with
personal mind, character and style. What he said finds continuity in a Commencement poem by a member of the English
Department 53 years later. Describing "Faculty Procession
1981" Marilyn Throne pictured those

Who walked before us under shadowed trees . . .
Some witty or intelligent or wise,
Some merely stubborn for the things they loved,
Their faith in what the human mind might teach,
Belief in what humanity might reach.

A generation earlier than Upham, President Hughes had said,
"A great college is a college with great teachers. Our problem is
to increase the number. Miami's future will grow from superior
teaching and concern for individual students." His words
echoed old deep memories of Miami, going back to President
Bishop who stood before the students, 68 in number, saying
"My young friends —"

Old and new jostled on the 1980s campus, where male students donned smocks and aprons in Home Economics nutrition courses and women pressed into Laws Hall lectures in Marketing and Accounting. On Cook Field it was commonplace to see mixed softball teams, boys and girls together rounding the bases and shagging outfield flies. On tennis and volleyball courts women had their own intramural and inter-collegiate competition. In 1982, with an 11-1 basketball record, the female Redskins won a State championship. Mary Ann Myers, having scored 1595 points, joined the sports immortals by having her No. 20 jersey permanently retired.

Any thought of Miami change and continuity soon leads to Fisher Hall. Although the venerable vine-clad hall is now replaced by the Marcum Conference Center, the vanished building remains fixed in Miami memories. Located on an edge of the campus between formal gardens and primeval Tallawanda woods, its history is varied and eventful. Since its construction as Oxford Female College in 1856, it had been a health resort, a sanitorium, a Miami dormitory, a war-time Naval Training Station, a University theater, and a ghost-haunted landmark that fascinated generations of students. During its Miami years it housed five thousand students and some fifty faculty. With shared nostalgia they still say "I lived in Fisher Hall."

During the summer of 1978 when Fisher Hall was being demolished a hundred-foot crane swung a wrecking ball against the grand old tower. As one blow after another battered the massive brickwork the last dispossessed blackbirds fluttered into the Tallawanda oaks and sycamores. From a woven wire barrier a few observers watched the Fisher Hall demise. Among them was a gangly youth in dusty jeans and a Miami T-shirt, jotting figures on a clipboard. When the crane fell silent he straddled the barrier and approached the hard-hat foreman, following him from one mound of rubble to another.

When the youth returned, an observer asked what business brought him there.

"Buying bricks," he said.

"What for?"

"Five thousand dollars," he pointed to his clipbord, "for 15,000 bricks."

"You mean you're scrambling around this rubble with 5,000 bucks?"

"Oh, no. I'll pay for them next month, when the new term begins. I'll sell them for a dollar a-piece. There's no student who won't pay a dollar for a brick from Fisher Hall."

As it developed, the contractor declined the young man's offer, but told him to come back after 5 o'clock and pick up whatever he could haul away.

A month later when the campus streamed with new-term students a table outsdie the Shriver Center was piled with battered bricks under a sign:

SAVE A PIECE OF FISHER HALL
SUPPLY LIMITED
A BRICK FOR A BUCK

Toward the semester's end, four months earlier, a protest petition — PRESERVE FISHER HALL — had in a few days' time garnered four thousand signatures. Now, in a week of marketing, this deflated youth collected a scant forty dollars. Student zeal swings like a weathervane. In the new year Fisher Hall was out of sight and out of mind. Alumni have longer memories. Now thousands of Miami graduates prize the Marston Hodgin paintings of Fisher Hall in sun and shadow, and for Conference visitors the legends on that site enhance the distinctive character of the Marcum Center.

When John Dolibois at the 1978 Goals for Enrichment rally envisioned a conference center on the site of storied Fisher Hall, he sprang the biggest surprise of the evening. The proposal prompted question and misgiving as well as upbeat expectation. Some faculty, who should have known better, asked "What good is a conference center? Who needs sales meetings on this campus?" Questions continued as the handsome building rose amid new landscaping with garden plazas, the inviting Pulley Pavilion, and the Marcum Nature Trail. Under direction of Jack DePree, a veteran of continuing education programs in Michigan, the Center was booked solid for its first year of operation, 1982-83, while the office file filled with inquiries and applications. Some of the first year's conferences, serving business organizations, built bridges in the regional economy. Others comprised civic, social and academic gatherings. The idyllic setting on the edge of a university community and the modest conference cost (while urban hotel rates soared) were unfailing attractions. In a single week of April 1982 the Marcum Center hosted the Great Lakes American Studies Association, the American Society for Environmental History, the Applied Science Advisory Council, the annual session of Ohio Geology Chairmen, and the Ohio Board of Regents. Such meetings enlarged the influence and enlivened the spirit of Miami University.

The memorial character of the Marcum Center is most evident in two westward-facing rooms that look toward the Conrad Gardens and Dogwood Pond — the John E. Hull Memorial Room and the Robert B. Sinclair Memorial Library.

A first impression of the heroic Hull Room is of far places and momentous events. There is a feel of history unfolding, the making and breaking of nations, the testing of war and peace. From flags, swords, cordons, medals and medallions there emerges a single word — the title of the poem cast in bronze on the wall beside the western windows. The poem was written in 1942 by Louise McNeill, M.A. '38, in Middlebury, Vermont, while General Hull in North Africa was mapping strategy that threw back Rommel's Afrika Korps in Kassarine Pass. The poem is called "Dedication."

In years to come many themes, problems, and conceptions will be deliberated in the Hull Room. No doubt, in this changing world, they will range beyond present keeping and foretelling. But the spirit in the room will encourage patriotism, so that all the deliberations there will somehow be touched by duty, honor, country.

Tall as General Hull himself are the flags of Vice Chief of Staff, of Four-Star General, and of Commander-in-Chief of United Nations Forces in the Far East. Between is a scroll

CALLIGRAPHY
For General John Edwin Hull
by President Syngmun Rhee
"A Righteous War Always Wins"

A nacreous shield bearing crossed flags is inscribed

to J. E. Hull
by
General Chung Il Kwon
Chief of Staff, ROKA

Beneath the shield rests an exquisite silver box etched with a map of Indo-China, and engraved

To John E. Hull
Commander-in-Chief
United Nations Command
From the Thailand Korean Veterans Association
Under His Majesty's Patronage
25 January 1955

Among U.S. medals — Silver Star, Legion of Merit, Distinguished Service Medal with three oakleaf clusters — are other awards and decorations:

Commander of the Order of the British Empire
Grand Officer of Military Merit (Brazil)
Grand Cordon of Yun Hui (China)
Commander Philippine Legion of Honor
Commander Military Order Ayachuco (Peru)

and a large jade-inlaid silver key "Presented to General Hull with Warmest Regards of the Citizens of Seoul. 2 October 1953"

Encyclopedia of World War II records: "HULL, John E. (1895 - 1974) U. S. Army Officer, Chief of the European Section of the General Staff and a distinguished strategist. No West-Pointer but a graduate of Miami (Ohio) University, Hull became an Army careerist in World War I.... Later a four-star general, he was Supreme Commander, Far East. Extremely modest "Ed" Hull was highly popular with his fellow soldiers."

Amid the valor and the laurels of the Memorial Room, one may picture the Miami stalwart, a Chemistry major, president of his class, a 4-letter man in track and football, where he played beside "Red" Blaik and "Monk" Pierce. His class of 84 members was graduated in June, 1917, two months after U.S. entry into war, but Hull's degree came in absentia. Already beginning his Army career, he was a recruit in Officer Training School. In brisk sequence he became a platoon, company, and battalian commander, moving into combat on the French front with the 4th Infantry Division. As Far East commander in the 1950s he was quartered on a baronial estate in the western outskirts of Tokyo, where, in a garden setting, in the company of forty high-ranking military and civilian guests, on June 21, 1954, President Millett conferred the LL.D. degree. In response General Hull said, "My standard of character was built while a student at Miami University, and I owe the university a debt of gratitude."

Returning to Miami fifteen years later, on Miami Field, October 8, 1969, he was claimed by the athletic Hall of Fame. On that visit he made an endowment to accompany his bequest of military laurels to Miami Univerity. The general's life-long modesty explains the immaculate condition of his trophies — decorations rarely worn and medals still in their presentation cartons. The collection was never on display until it came to this room in Marcum Memorial Center.

For years a Miami University War Memorial, recognizing all whose lives were given to their country, had been discussed and projected without deciding its form and location. Should it be a garden, a monument, a plaza or rotunda, within a building or in the open air? At last, with a Conference Center under construction and the Hull laurels stored in the Alumni building, the answer was at hand. A Memorial Room, distinguished with the emblems of a historical career, would be the ideal place for a Book of Remembrance, an honor roll of three hundred names from Old and New Miami.

Adjoining the Hull Room is the Robert B. Sinclair Memorial library. It is a place of repose. With shelves of books and a few cherished pictures, it invites contemplation. On the inner wall a calligraphy tablet pays tribute to the life, learning and dedication of a Miami professor who loved books and music and for forty years lived among students in the residence halls. Many of his books are in this room that fosters both conversation and reflection, as did Robert Basil Sinclair. "A teacher," wrote Henry Adams, "can never tell where his influence stops."

Change and continuity . . . . A new tradition was begun on a bright spring day of 1982 with dedication of a Scholar-Leader Room in Stoddard Hall. The specially furnished and decorated room is assigned, rent-free, to an undergraduate who combines superior scholarship with campus activity. The first such room honors the late Dean W. E. Smith, a leading historian and educator during faculty tenure 1926-63, and its current occupant Martha Tanner, '83. Present at the dedication were the donors L. Scott and Margaret T. Bailey, '48, Mrs. Ophia D. Smith, author and collaborator with her husband, and son Joseph W. Smith a California business-historian, along with university officials and faculty colleagues. Five months later, in Elliott Hall, the W. F. Cottrell Scholar-Leader Room was presented to President Pearson by Robert L. Cottrell, '54, in honor of his father the late Dr. W. Fred Cottrell, a long-time leader on the Miami campus and in national associations of Sociology and Political Science.

It is anticipated that other Scholar-Leade rooms, with residents chosen by the Miami University Alumni Scholarship program, will be created in Stoddard Hall for women and Elliott Hall for men. In the past 150 years Miami men studied Latin, Greek and Logic by candlelight, where their successors study French, German, Russian, along with Personnel Management, International Business, and Systems Analysis. As Scholar-Leader endowments accrue, the Honor halls become an enduring bridge between Miami's past and present. In the *Diamond Anniversary Volume,* 1899, we can read: "Age is an element of power and usefulness to an institution like this. The moss-covered foundations and ivy-twined walls have a history which in itself is a liberal education. The boy who sits in a room which for many years had been filled with men who became honorable or famous . . . is fired with an ambition and ardor that add immeasurably to the power of teachers and books."

Coninuity and change. . . . As the Miami campus has developed, the Beta Bell Tower, erected half a century ago, has become its central image. Halfway between the Tallawanda and Collins Run, the chimes reverberate from Millett Hall to Peffer Park, and from Slant Walk Gateway to the Pines. Recalling its construction, then on the edge of the central campus, one pictures its deep foundation and the tons of steel-ribbed concrete that underlay the first brick courses at ground level. Said to be unique — a Georgian companile — its lines are clean, simple, and upreaching. *Prodesse Quam Conspici* finds expresion there.

A south wind carries the Beta chimes all the way to Yager Stadium. In 1895 a cowpasture corner, where High Street ended at Patterson Road, became the "Miami Athletic Grounds" enclosed by a high board wall with a shedlike ticket office. Continuity there spanned 88 years in which Miami Field acquired wooden bleachers, roofed brick gateways, then steel stands eventually seating 15,000, and a nonpareil roster of football coaches. Two of them, Paul Brown '30, and Ara Parseghian '49, became University trustees. In 1982 a nostalgic last game on Miami Field brought football stars from 56 classes, all the way back to 1909. After the game—a Miami win—these team representatives passed a pigskin from hand to hand, spanning the decades on the trampled field.

At Miami, Parseghian became head coach in 1951, succeeding Woody Hayes. He went on to head-man jobs at Northwestern and then at Notre Dame for eleven years before resigning after a one-point victory over Alabama in the Sugar Bowl of 1973. Ten years later, in Cincinnati for a dinner benefitting the Multiple Sclerosis Society and the local Notre Dame Club, he told the press he had another errand — "a little matter thirty miles up the road to a little school [Miami had not quite reached 5,000 enrollment in his time] that left a lasting impression on my life."

In those last words Coach Ara was speaking for the Miami Hall-of-Famers — Blaik, Pierce, Hull, Ewbank, Dietzel, Pont, Cozza, Pagna, Schembechler, Root, McVey, Fry, Mallory, Reed and many more. How does Miami do it? sportswriters asked — little Miami with its mini-stadium and recruiting ruled by academic as well as athletic talent. Parseghian had given an answer in Oxford at the All Sports Banquet of 1958. "Because of its tradition, environment, athletic ability and academic standing, I am proud to be associated with Miami University."

Saturday, October 1, 1983 — a day long anticipated and destined to be long remembered. Flags flying, banners billowing, pennants rippling, crowds cheering, a mounting excitement in the air as the red-and-white team ran onto the virgin field. Actually it had begun the day before, when Weeb Ewbank '30 brought sportscaster Howard Cossell to Oxford where his first appearance was in a classroom, giving an academic lecture to an overflow Communications class. The ubiquitous Cossell, believe it or not, is an adjunct Professor of Communications at Yale. That evening in the quick autumn dusk the band marched onto Millett parking area trailing thousands of football fans for a pre-game rally — shades of old Cook Field. After words from President Pearson, Coach Tim Rose, and Redskin co-captains, came the pronouncements of gravel-voiced Cossell. Beside a red-and-white tent the band struck up German *um-pah* and the fans rollicked in Oktoberfest of food and drink while the band played on.

Next morning highway traffic coverged on Oxford — cars, vans, station wagons, buses, including caravans from the branch campuses in Middletown and Hamilton — filling up the acres of Millett parking.

While university officials and designated guests sat down to a ceremonial luncheon dedicating the new sports complex, crowds swarmed around the red-and-white "wigwam" and streamed down the broad curved ramp to the stadium gate-ways. The stands were filled when Cossell at field level spelled out a symbolism. The football used in the final play of the last game on Miami Field, ten months past, would be presented by the co-captains for the first play in the Yager Bowl. Following the game attention would fix upon a formal opening of the "Cradle Room" under the main stand. There, amid football memorabilia, the book *Miami of Ohio — Cradle of Coaches* would be autographed by co-authors Robert Kurz '58, and Bob Howard, former sports information director.

Now, in a surprise action, a new Redskin mascot, replacing the long-familiar foot-stomping "Hiawa-bob" was about to appear. On a galloping horse a Miami feathered Indian with an upraised spear dashed in. Pulling up on the 50-yard line he launched his spear into the ground where a huge egg burst open, releasing a new-fledged Tom O Hawk. While that crea-ture beat its wings the marching band blared out the Miami Fight Song, and cheering filled the 12-acre compound. From now on Tom O Hawk would emerge at the start of every game — a new tradition begun.

After the coin toss the "last ball" was set up for kickoff and the whistle called for play. At the first down that ball was retrieved for permanent exhibit in the "Cradle" — a room filled with trophies honoring Miami men who have made history in the coaching profession. Three hours later while lines of traffic crept out of town a few reluctant alumni lingered in the dusk of old Miami Field. A smooth green lawn, awaiting construction of an academic building for the Biological Sciences, it was as calm and quiet as a cowpasture.

Continuity and change . . . . The news headline for 15 May 1983 was COMMENCEMENT LARGEST EVER. The 2932 degree candidates included Catherine Ann Kiel of Penn Valley, Penna., whose grandmother on that day presented to the university a pair of French vases that had come from the home of William Holmes McGuffey whose schoolbooks carried literacy across the expanding nation. In 1983 President Pearson set a goal of computer literacy for all Miami graduates who, he said, "are entering an information age in a technocratic era. Students from art to zoology, including business, education, languages, music, nursing, philosophy, psychology or science will be handicapped without some basic computer skills." F. G. Rodgers, remembered on the campus as "Buck" Rodgers, class of 1950, is IBM vice president in charge of world-wide marketing. In an arresting article for the MIAMIAN, January, 1983, he wrote: "Despite tight budgets the influence of computers on American education continues to accelerate." Already, in Oxford, in the basement of Hughes and Hoyt halls microcumputers were tirelessly coping with massed financial, curricular and environmental data.

Oxford's oldest and most enduring thoroughfare was never planned, marked or designated. First known as the Slanting Path, it was the students' bee-line from the old college to the High Street taverns and the Church Street sanctums. Muddy, dusty, leaf-strewn and ice-crusted, it was trodden in all seasons. The first improvement was a surface of sand and a grilled crossing to keep livestock out of the hedged campus. The first gateway was a pair of iron posts at the portal. As years passed, the Slant Walk landmarks kept changing. In 1902 the college well was boarded over and its tilted sweep removed. A 1909 Centennial Gate gave way to a Williamsburg-style entrance in

1973. Old Main itself was replaced by the new Harrison Hall in sesquicentennial 1959. After forty years of bubbling in the shade of huge old elms, Thobe's fieldstone fountain was supplanted by the stone circle bench of Kappa Kappa Gamma sorority. A few steps farther the six-sided Delta Gamma Kiosk flutters with books for sale, rooms for rent, roommates needed, bicycles for sale, picnics in Peffer Park and Dogwwod Grove, Skating Club rehearsals, Recensio subscriptions, and rides wanted to Columbus, Toledo, Buffalo, Akron, Chicago, Philadelphia. Ninety years ago the Slant Walk ended at Elliott and Stoddard Halls. It lengthened when Alumni Library and Irvin Hall arose, and a jog or two attached it to Spring Street with the Chapel and the Shriver Center. From there they way leads on across Patterson Avenue to Bachelor Hall and Patterson Place. Beyond the old apple orchard it crosses the long bridge to venerable Peabody Hall and the remote beechwoods where slate-gray trunks are hatched with 130 years of Western and Miami initials and the copper beech leaves mulch over prehistoric Indian artifacts.

College fads and fashions, modes and manners, go on changing as in generations past. In the 175th year the Slant Walk parade wears blue jeans, T-shirts, blue-striped tennis shoes, and shoulder bags in many colors. The garb is unisex without distinction. Along with soft drinks, lite beer, and pizzas, the T-shirts advertise colleges — Penn State, Rutgers, Purdue, Cornell, Dartmouth, Tulane and Colorado mixing with Miami. The shoulder bags, mostly made in Taiwan, have outdoor names — Sierra, Shasta, Aspen, Key West, Caribou, Lookout Mountain, Adirondack, Yellowstone. Inside King Library all shoes come off — study dictates stocking feet —and the shoulder bag dispenses a pocket calculator along with books and manuals of sixty majors, from Accounting and Aeronautics to Urban Planning and Zoology. In fall of 1983 a reappearing book was George Orwell's somber *1984*. The assigned Freshman summer reading, it was discussed in hundreds of informal groups under volunteer staff members.

The first formal Commencement of Miami, in academic dress with processional and recessional, came in 1903. President Benton, who liked ceremony, led the march from Old Main Hall to a wooden platform facing chairs and benches under the campus trees. When old Benton Hall was built in 1908, Commencement moved inside. In 1930 the procession was longer, ranks forming in front of Brice Hall and marching down Bishop Street to Withrow Court. That gymnasium, converted for convocation, proved too small in the early 1960s while Millett Hall was under construction. One might think that as it grew from the 300 convocation in 1903 to 12,000 in 1983, Commencement would become more formal. In a sense it did — with marshals, pageantry, choral music and rehearsed candidates. At the same time it grew crowd-festive. Polite applause was appropriate in Old Benton. It swelled to cheers, whistles and ovations in vast Millett.

The financially apprehensive year 1982-83 ended in a heartening Commencement. Malcolm S. Forbes, president and editor-in-chief of *Forbes Magazine, Inc.* gave a racy, offhand, up-to-date address, telling his young classmates that few of them could foresee the careers ahead. Most would be engaged with knowledge and services rather than in traditional business enterprise. They were on the threshold of a technocratic computer age that will bring unmatched productivity, widespread prosperity, and longer and more fruitful lives. His final counsel, "Do what you enjoy, and you will succeed at it," brought a standing acclamation.

A few in that huge audience found themselves pondering Forbes's bright scenario alongside Orwell's dismaying prediction of *1984*. Though set in the future when it was written (on a windswept island of the Hebrides in 1949) Orwell's fable is not futuristic; no scientific marvels or space technology remove it from our world. His bleak Utopia, now at hand, is not a prophecy but a warning of humanity crushed by the will of the collective state — the political steam roller of the East and the business behemoth of the West. Read by millions in many languages, since 1950, the book is now fearfully contemporary.

Occasionally, even in 1983, an old-line professor speaks to his class as "my fellow students" — suggesting that teacher and learner are on common ground and that education is unfinished business. But students know the difference. They know, despite their status, that they are one-up on the professor. He has found his viewpoint; life has measured his character and talents. Anything he does now will not really change him. What he is at 55 he will still be at 60; he is all set. But they are 18, with a whole world to discover. They can stretch and grow.

In his essay on *Travel,* four centuries ago, Francis Bacon wrote: "Travel, for the older is a part of experience; for the younger it is a part of education." So it is. When a retired person — that dimly viewed senior citizen — goes abroad, something is added to his observation; while the youthful traveler is altered and enlarged. The young have the advantage. What a student sees and thinks and feels becomes a part of him forever.

In *1984* these Miami freshmen, at the starting gate, have a grim, almost forbidding introduction. The Slant Walk leads them to library, laboratory, and lecture hall, to discoveries they cannot foresee in a world that daunts their most seasoned teachers. Some books will interest and enlighten them. Others, like the Orwell fable, may frighten and appall. Most of the book learning will soon be forgotten, so that one cannot measure what was garnered from a text or reference book, or often from a course of study. Yet there is a residue, an enduring remainder. Names go, scenes fade, situations and examples blur. But the true schoalrship, which goes too deep to be summoned up at will, is an enlargement of comprehension. Eighteenth century Jonathan Swift, to whom the mordant Orwell is akin, gave an enduring definition of liberal knowledge. "If a rational man reads an excellent author with just application, he will find himself exremely improved, and perhaps insensibly led to imitate that author's perfection, although in a little time he should not remember one word in the book, nor even the subject it handled." The reading of Orwell surely leaves a lifeline question: In this world where social and political issues press upon us with terrible urgency, how can one preserve a private self?

With all the bread and circuses — the Greek Week bicycle races and tug-of-war, spectacles in the ice arena and the ultra Yager stadium, Homecoming parades and quadrangle picnics — Miami students still live in the midst of great issues. The pursuit of knowledge has no end, but for every generation of Miami youth the Slant Walk has been a path toward insight and understanding. "I come back to reunion," an alumnus writes, "for quite personal reasons. A part of myself was formed here, and I want to reclaim it. I believe it is the best part of myself, the best ever."

BIBLIOGRAPHICAL NOTES

T HE PRINCIPAL SOURCES drawn upon are listed with reference to specific chapters of this book. Manuscript and pamphlet materials, as well as most of the printed volumes, are in the Miami Collection of the Miami University Library. Some folders of pertinent correspondence, clippings and photographs are on file in the University archives.

CHAPTER I.   BEGGAR ON HORSEBACK

The James McBride Manuscripts Relating to Miami University, edited by John Ewing Bradford (Cincinnati, 1909), were published as a part of the observance of the Miami Centennial. This volume contains the Reverend John W. Browne's account of his Eastern tour while seeking donations for the University, the entailing of a college township in the Symmes Purchase and the locating of Miami University, and sketches of the original members of the Board of Trustees. The formal report of Browne's mission, which came to light after more than a century, was printed in the *Miami University Bulletin* (Alumni News Letter), May 1937. Adoption of the University motto, *Prodesse Quam Conspici,* is recorded in the Board of Trustees records, September 26,

1826. In the *Diamond Anniversary Volume* (Miami University, 1899), edited by Walter L. Tobey and William Oxley Thompson, the Symmes patent and the Act of 1794 are reprinted from *Laws of the United States*, Vol. 1, p. 497. Jane Knox Skinner's bound typescript *Background of Oxford Town and Township* (1946) contains copies of the Act of 1792, the patent of John Cleves Symmes and an account of the origin of Oxford township in lieu of the College township entailed in the terms of the Symmes Purchase; also copies of James McBride's manuscripts, sketches of early Oxford settlers and notes on the first roads in the township. The *Journal of the Historical and Philosophical Society of Ohio* (Columbus, 1838; reprinted Cincinnati, 1872) includes James McBride's "Sketch of the Topography, Statistics and History of Oxford, and the Miami University," which described the survey of Oxford and its early settlement, the construction of the University's first buildings, the organizing of the Board of Trustees and the first faculty, and the University's income in its early years.

CHAPTER II.   FOUNDATION STONE

The effort to remove Miami University to Cincinnati is detailed in the *Diamond Anniversary Volume*, pp. 352–59. McBride's speech arguing that the University was permanently fixed in Oxford is included in *The James McBride Manuscripts Relating to Miami University*, pp. 45–79. A brief report of the infant Miami University and its enrollment appeared in the *Philadelphia Register and National Recorder*, June 12, 1819. Thomas J. Porter's *History of the Presbyterian Church of Oxford, Ohio* [1902] contains a biographical sketch and a silhouette of James Hughes. Francis R. Gilmore's M.A. thesis *James McBride* (Miami University, 1952) contains a chapter on the important services that McBride performed for the early University. Verna E. Harcourt's M.A. thesis *Pioneer Days of Oxford Township* (Miami University, 1953) traces the development of the community to 1860. An account of James Dorsey and the "Rational Brethren of Oxford" by Ophia D. Smith appeared in the *Miami University Bulletin,* January 1946. The booklet *Oxford Town,* by R. J. McGinnis (Oxford, Ohio, 1930), contains sketches of early settlers, an 1828 list of householders and an account of the incorporation of the village. A reference to the former Indian mound on the site of present Stoddard Hall appears in the *Miami Journal,* May 1889.

CHAPTER III. INAUGURAL PROCESSION

John Scott's *The Family History of Robert Hamilton Bishop* (1951) follows Miami's first president from his native Scotland to southwestern Ohio. Various volumes of R. H. Bishop's sermons and addresses are in the Miami Collection. James H. Rodabaugh's *The History of Miami University from its Origin to 1845* (Miami University, 1933) is a close study of the first Miami years. This M.A. thesis was expanded and extended in James H. Rodabaugh, *The History of Miami University from its Origin to 1885* (Ph.D. thesis, Ohio State University, 1937). Virginia Steele Young's M.A. thesis, *Times and Life of Joel Collins* (Miami University, 1953), includes an account of the locating of Miami University, the first sale of college lands and the construction of the first college buildings.

CHAPTER IV. SHADOW OF A MAN

Robert Hamilton Bishop's intermittent journals and letters, covering the entire period of his life in Ohio, 1824–55, are in the Miami Collection. James H. Rodabaugh's *Robert Hamilton Bishop* (Columbus, 1935) describes the early years of Miami University and the tensions within the Board of Trustees and the faculty. *The Correspondence of Thomas E. Thomas* (1909) contains a number of letters to early Miami faculty relating to the anti-slavery movement and Presbyterian doctrine. James H. Rodabaugh's "Miami University, Calvinism and the Anti-Slavery Movement" in the *Ohio*

State Archaeological and Historical Quarterly, XLVIII (1939), 66–73, gauges winds of doctrine in early Miami. Thornton A. Mills reviewed "The Life and Services of Rev. R. H. Bishop, D.D.," in the *Presbyterian Quarterly Review*, December 1855. The origin of the old stone (telescope) pier was detailed by R. W. McFarland in the *Miami Student*, November 1904, and the account was reprinted in the *Miami University Bulletin*, October 1931.

CHAPTER V.   PRIMER FROM A GREEN WORLD

The *Miami Journal*, March 1888, featured reminiscences of McGuffey by four Miami alumni—Charles Anderson, J. W. Caldwell, B. W. Chidlaw and John I. Covington; Chidlaw's sketch includes his being paid five dollars for copying one of McGuffey's rough manuscripts. A thorough account of early Oxford journalism is given in Jesse H. Shera's "An Eddy in the Westward Flow of Culture: The History of Printing and Publishing in Oxford, Ohio, 1827–1841," in the *Ohio State Archaeological and Historical Quarterly*, XLIV (1935), 105–37. In *William Holmes McGuffey and His Readers* (New York, 1936), Harvey C. Minnich traced the life of McGuffey and the influence of his textbooks. The second volume of Mark Sullivan, *Our Times* (New York, 1927), begins with a chapter on McGuffey. James H. Rodabaugh's "McGuffey: A Revised Portrait," appeared in the *Oxford Criterion*, Winter 1933. A letter by John M. Gordon of the Class of 1837, published in the *Miami University Bulletin*, November 1929, tells of an early student tilt with the faculty. An extensive collection of McGuffey letters is preserved in the Miami University McGuffey Museum, along with some seven hundred copies of the *Readers* in their various editions.

CHAPTER VI.   VOICES ON THE THIRD FLOOR

The voluminous records of the Erodelphian, Miami Union and Eccritean literary societies are in the Miami Collection. A detailed study of the Literary Societies is made in the

M.A. thesis of Virgil Davis, *The Literary Societies of Old Miami* (Miami University, 1950). Ralph L. Treichler's typescript *Miami Union Literary Society* (1926) is a briefer history. The *Miami Journal* in its issues of 1887–89 included alumni reminiscences of "Old Miami"; the literary societies are prominent in these memories. The Literary Halls in the 1830's are recalled in B. W. Chidlaw, *The Story of My Life* (Philadelphia, 1890), and N. R. Johnston, *Looking Back from the Sunset Land* (Oakland, California, 1898). The student diaries and journals of David McClung, Isaac Anderson, Joseph Brady and Abner Jones contain numerous references to the literary societies in the years between 1843 and 1858.

CHAPTER VII.   FORTUNES OF THE GREEKS

The beginnings of the Miami fraternities are recorded in Francis W. Shepardson, *The Beta Book* (Menasha, Wisconsin, 1927); Walter B. Palmer, *The History of the Phi Delta Theta Fraternity* (Menasha, Wisconsin, 1906); Robert M. Collett, *The Centennial of Sigma Chi Fraternity* (Evanston, 1955); and Jack L. Anson, *The History of Phi Kappa Tau Fraternity* (Oxford, Ohio, 1957). Hinckley Smith traced the development of fraternities at Miami in his *Kappa Chapter of the Delta Kappa Epsilon Fraternity* (Hamilton, Ohio, 1903). The "snow rebellion" is recorded in the Board of Trustees records and the minutes of the Faculty for 1848. That event was nostalgically narrated by Alfred H. Upham in *Old Miami* (Oxford, Ohio, 1909), pp. 110–14. An eyewitness account appears in Joseph Brady's student journal, January 12–22, 1848.

CHAPTER VIII.   MORNING PRAYERS AND MIDNIGHT REVELS

The diary of Joseph Brady reflects undergraduate life at Miami, 1843–48. The journal of David W. McClung covers the college year 1852–53. Isaac Anderson's student diary spans the first six months of 1854. Abner Jones' journal treats the years 1854–58. Chapter 34 of E. N. Clopper's *An Ameri-*

can *Family* (1950) draws upon the diary of Edward W. Clopper, Miami, 1861, for an account of college life, 1858–61. A sketch of "Old Miami" by David Swing appeared in the *Chicago Alliance*, July 14, 1877; the account describes his college years, 1848–52. Joseph Fort Newton's *David Swing, Poet-Preacher* (Chicago, 1909), describes Swing's years in Oxford, 1848–67, as student and teacher, and his notable Class of 1852. J. W. Scott's own account of the origin and early history of the Oxford Female College appears in the *Miami University Bulletin*, January 1930. Professor Stoddard's lecture notes are in the Faculty File of the Miami Collection. The ceremonial "Burial of Logic" is described in Abner Jones' student diary; it was recalled by Waldo F. Brown in the *Miami Student*, May 1899. A printed program of the ceremonial burial by the Class of 1856 is in the Miami Collection.

CHAPTER IX.   A COLLEGE DIVIDED: 1861–65

To the *Diamond Anniversary Volume* (Oxford, Ohio, 1909) Colonel David W. McClung, Miami, 1854, contributed a chapter, "Miami in the War." James B. Falconer's diary pictures Miami student life 1861–63. A description of Oxford in 1862 by Richard Butler, editor of the *Oxford Citizen*, is included in R. J. McGinnis, *Oxford Town* (Oxford, Ohio, 1930). Edwin W. Brown's "Reminiscences of an Ohio Volunteer," edited by Philip D. Jordan and Charles M. Thomas, in the *Ohio State Archaeological and Historical Quarterly*, XLVIII (1939), 304–23, is the narrative of an Oxford youth who joined the "University Rifles," which became Company B of the 20th Ohio Infantry. The first volume of Whitelaw Reid, *Ohio in the War* (2 vols.; New York, 1868), includes biographical sketches of Miami men who held high military rank: Robert C. Schenck, Minor Millikin, Ben P. Runkle and R. N. Adams; the second volume contains the roster of the 20th Ohio Infantry, along with other Ohio regiments. R. W. McFarland's narrative of the pursuit of Morgan's raiders appears in the *Ohio State Archaeological and Historical Quarterly*, XVII (1908), 243–47. The account of McFarland's student who had been one of Morgan's men appears in the *Miami University Bulletin*, January 1930. Robert N. Adams' "My First Company," an address read April 11, 1905, tells of the forming of the University Rifles, of farewell ceremonies in Oxford and of entraining for Hamilton, where the Northern volunteers parted from their Southern companions and classmates. An address to the Alumni Association, "Miami in the Civil War," by Stephen Cooper Ayres of the Class of 1861, was printed in the *Miami University Bulletin*, October 1906.

CHAPTER X.   INDIAN SUMMER

The student diary of W. D. Hancock gives some glimpses of Miami life in 1868. The *Miami Student* was published 1867–73, and after a fifteen-year interval resumed publication in 1888; the burlesque ceremony of the Peace Pipe during Commencement season is described in the issue of June 28, 1871. "Miami in the 1870's" is idyllically pictured in Chapter 12 of Ophia D. Smith's *Fair Oxford* (Oxford, Ohio, 1947). President Stanton's 1867 inaugural address, "The Present Conditions and Wants of Miami University," is in the bound volume *Inaugural Addresses, 1835–1928*. The Board of Trustees records show the growing financial problems of the old college which led to the decision, in June 1873, to close the institution until its debts could be paid off and a balance accumulated for the future. The privately operated "Miami Classical School" with its gathering of boys from distant places is described in Carl R. Greer, *Old Oxford Days* (Oxford, Ohio, 1947), pp. 18–20. Robert B. Stanton's *Down the Colorado*, edited by Dwight L. Smith (Norman,

Oklahoma, 1965), describes Stanton's pioneer survey of the Grand Canyon. Historical addresses delivered by spokesmen for the alumni in connection with the Centennial Commencement exercises, June 12–17, 1909, were printed in the *Miami University Bulletin*, September 1909.

CHAPTER XI.   AGE AND YOUTH

During plans for the reopening of Miami University an account of Old Miami appeared in the *New York Tribune*, August 13, 1884, and was reprinted in the *Oxford Citizen* eight days later. "An Old College Campus," by Jennie Brooks, in the *Western Christian Advocate*, April 17, 1912, is an idyllic picture of Miami University in the 1880's. A biographical sketch of Jennie Brooks is included in Jane Knox Skinner, *Background of Oxford Town and Township* (1946). The reopening of Miami University and the rivalry of Mc-Farland and Hepburn are described in Ophia D. Smith's *Fair Oxford*, pp. 178–86. Bertha Boya Thompson's M.A. thesis, *The History of Miami University from 1873 to 1900* (Miami University, 1954), treats men and events of the Warfield administration and gives an account of the first state aid to Miami. Edwin Emerson's 350–page typescript *An Old College Town* recalls the college years of a spirited undergraduate in 1887 and 1888; Edwin Emerson's career is sketched in the *Miami University Bulletin*, October 1935. The beginnings of football at Miami are recalled in Carl R. Greer, *Old Oxford Days* (Oxford, Ohio, 1947), pp. 52–53. The first Miami vs. University of Cincinnati football game is reported in the *Miami Journal*, December 1888; a fuller account of that historic game is given in the *Miami Alumnus*, September 1948. Reminiscences of the "Dude Faculty" appear, with pictures, in the *Miami University Bulletin*, October 1940 and January 1941. Reference to the attempt to interest Herbert Spencer in the Miami presidency is made in Ophia D. Smith, *Fair Oxford* (Oxford, Ohio, 1947), p. 188.

CHAPTER XII. WIND FROM THE WEST

William Oxley Thompson (Columbus, 1955), by Professor James E. Pollard of the Ohio State University, gives a full account of the life of President Thompson. Oxford and Miami University at the turn of the century are recalled in Carl R. Greer, *Old Oxford Days* (Oxford, Ohio, 1947). "Miami in the 1890's" is the final chapter of Ophia D. Smith's *Fair Oxford* (Oxford, Ohio, 1947). The Lybarger Bill is referred to in the *President's Report* (Miami University, 1906) and in the *Miami University Bulletin*, August 1916. The life of R. H. Bishop, Jr., who died in 1890, was reviewed in the *Miami Student*, March 1891, with reminiscences by Charles Anderson, B. W. Chidlaw, John Shaw Billings and John I. Covington. William J. McSurely's "History of the Library of Miami University" appeared in the *Miami University Bulletin*, February 1908; beginning with John Browne's collection of books in 1811 it traced the growth of the Library to its catalogue of 24,500 volumes in 1908. The typhoid epidemic of 1900 is referred to in a reminiscence by Stephen Riggs Williams in the *Miami University Bulletin*, July 1930.

CHAPTER XIII. "THE SPIRIT OF THE INSTITUTION"

Alfred H. Upham described "the Centennial of Miami University" in the *Ohio State Archaeological and Historical Quarterly*, XVIII (1909), 322–44. In an M.A. thesis, *Guy Potter Benton: His Effect on Miami University* (Miami University, 1950), Peter Joseph Vogt treated the years 1902–11. Fielding H. Garrison's *John Shaw Billings, A Memoir* (New York, 1915), contains Billings' account of keeping bachelor's hall in the old dorms and his memories of the Miami library in the middle 1850's; once during a vacation period he made a burglar's entrance by way of a trap door in the roof and had a whole library to himself. The *Autobiography of Andrew Carnegie* (Boston, 1915) recounts Carnegie's response to John Shaw Billings' suggestion that he use his fortune for the creation of public libraries. The history of Lewis Place, since

1903 the home of Miami presidents, is told in Ophia D. Smith, *Old Oxford Houses* (Oxford, Ohio, 1941). Helen Benton Minnich's memories of Lewis Place appeared in the *Miami Alumnus*, January 1967. The typescript diary of Katherine Shideler pictures the life of a Miami coed 1904–5.

CHAPTER XIV. A FULL-GROWN COLLEGE

The life of President Hughes is recorded in Arthur C. Wickenden, *Raymond M. Hughes* (Oxford, Ohio, 1966). Wickenden's *The Miami University Y.M.C.A., 1889–1964* (Oxford, Ohio, 1964), deals especially with the years 1910 to 1940. *President Hughes' Addresses to the University Staff, 1911–1927*, are in the Miami Collection. R. M. Hughes, "The Next Ten Years at Miami, 1925–1935," appears in the *Miami University Bulletin*, December 1925. In *Education, America's Magic* (Ames, Iowa, 1946), R. M. Hughes brought together his ideas on education and vocational guidance. A detailed account of Miami in the First World War appears in the *Miami University Bulletin*, February 1918. The Miami unit of the Students Army Training Corps is described in the *Miami University Bulletin*, August 1918 and in a *Supplement* dated July 1918. The Whaling bequest is the subject of an article in the *Miami University Bulletin*, May 1915, and is described in detail in the President's Report, June 8, 1915. A Miami chapter of Phi Beta Kappa was in prospect in 1848 when the "snow rebellion" crippled the college; *Phi Beta Kappa, Iota of Ohio Chapter* (Oxford, Ohio, 1945), tells how the chapter was eventually installed in 1911 under sponsorship of R. M. Hughes and other eminent alumni.

CHAPTER XV. ARTIST-IN-RESIDENCE

The *Miami University Bulletin*, February 1922, notes the wide attention given to Miami University for the establishment of a Fellowship in the Creative Arts. Percy MacKaye's article, quoting Robert Frost's letter regarding artists' fellowships, appeared in *The Forum*, June 1921; it was reprinted in the *Miami University Bulletin*, August 1921. The *Oxford Criterion*, Fall 1933, contains articles on Ridgely Torrence by Alfred H. Upham, Mrs. Wade MacMillan and R. J. Mc-Ginnis. The Winter 1933 number of the *Oxford Criterion* includes essays by and about Percy MacKaye. MacKaye's career following his Oxford residence is traced in the *Miami Alumnus*, July 1950. Ridgely Torrence is the subject of an article in the *Miami Alumnus*, January 1951.

CHAPTER XVI.   DEATH OF THE ELMS

Alfred H. Upham's inaugural address, "The Art of Teaching," is included in *Inaugural Addresses 1835–1928*. The Upham inauguration on Homecoming Weekend, 1928, was featured in the *Miami Student*, October 23, 1928. The merger of Oxford College with Miami University was reported in the *Miami Student*, October 9, 1928. Dedication of the Caroline Scott Harrison Memorial is described in the *Miami University Bulletin*, May 1930. Dedication of Withrow Court was reported in the *Miami University Bulletin*, January 1932. An account of the Freshman Adviser System in its first year appears in the *Miami University Bulletin*, November 1929. Sketches of H. S. Thobe appeared in the *Miami University Bulletin*, March 1931 and January 1939. Early development of the formal gardens near Fisher Hall is described in the *Miami University Bulletin*, October 1934. Reconstruction of Elliott and Stoddard halls is reported in the *Miami University Bulletin*, January 1936, January 1937 and October 1937. President Upham's around-the-world tour is engagingly recorded in his *Rhyming Round the World* (Boston, 1939); the reception for the Uphams on their return was described in the *Miami University Bulletin*, May 1938. Arthur F. Conrad's "Miami's Magnificent Trees," in the *Miami Alumnus*, October 1962, tells of great old trees on the campus and of new plantings that have helped to replace the vanished

elms. The Beta Theta Pi centennial celebration and dedication of the Beta Bell Tower are reported in the *Miami University Bulletin*, May 1939 and October 1940.

CHAPTER XVII.   "ANCHORS AWEIGH!"

"The University and National Defense" was discussed in
the *Miami University Bulletin*, May 1941. The first steps in
a War Emergency Program in the university are described
in the *Miami University Bulletin*, January 1942. The *Report
of Civil Aeronautics Administration, War Training Service
Program, Miami University*, covers the period 1942–44. The
beginnings of military training and arrival of the first Naval
trainees are recorded in the *Miami University Bulletin*,
October 1942. A report on the WAVES at Miami appears in
the *Miami University Bulletin*, March 1943. Naval training
in Oxford is reviewed in the *Miami University Bulletin*,
January 1945. A breezy fortnightly newspaper named *The
Pines* (1942–43) and then *The Dispatch* (1943–44) reported
on activities and personnel of the U.S. Naval Training School
(Radio), Miami University. A record of Miami's part in
World War II, text and pictures, constitutes the *Miami Uni-
versity Bulletin*, June 1946. A summary of *Regulations and
Organization of the Naval ROTC Unit, Miami University*,
was published in 1948.

CHAPTER XVIII.   ON THE G.I. BILL

"The Veteran on the Campus" was discussed by E. N.
Albaugh and Robert T. Howard in the *Miami Alumnus*,
September 1947. *Student Life at Miami University in World
War II* was studied in an M.A. thesis (Miami University,
1947) by Martha Francis Church. Charles W. Meinert,
*American College Life and the Influence of the Korean War
as Seen in Student Life at Miami University*, is an M.A.
thesis (Miami University, 1954). The *Alumni News Letter*,
published in the Miami University Bulletin Series beginning
December 1911, made its final appearance in July 1947; in

September 1947, the *Miami Alumnus* began publication with an account of the Alumni Association project of an advisory Long Range Program for the university, under the leadership of J. Paul MacNamara, '29, and C. Ray Wilson, '26. The eventual report of the Long Range Program Committee was printed as a supplement to the *Miami Alumnus*, September 1949. The opening of Upham Hall was described in the *Miami Alumnus*, March 1949. The end of "Veterans' Village" was recorded in the *Miami Alumnus*, January 1959.

CHAPTER XIX. THE LIBERATING ARTS

The inauguration of President Millett was featured in the *Miami Alumnus*, November 1953. A preliminary report on the Common Curriculum was presented in "Plan for a Common Curriculum at Miami University" by a University committee, 1955. *The Common Curriculum at Miami University*, published in the Miami University Bulletin Series, June 1963, described the aims and scope of the program and concluded with a discussion of General Education by President Millett. In his wide-ranging *The Liberating Arts* (Cleveland, 1957), John D. Millett discussed the dual needs of the undergraduate: to grasp the intellectual heritage of Western civilization while seeking preparation for a professional career. Wallace P. Roudebush (1890–1956) is the subject of ten pages of memorial in the *Miami Alumnus*, May 1956. The newly opened University Center was described in the *Miami Alumnus*, September 1957 and November 1957.

CHAPTER XX. THE AVENUES OF LEARNING

The experimental project in teaching by television was reported in the *Miami Alumnus*, January 1956. A report on *Experimental Study in Instructional Procedures* (Miami University, 1957) gave results of the project under grant from the Fund for the Advancement of Education. The end of the historic old Main Building was lamented in the *Miami Alumnus*, May 1957, and was pictured in the *Miami Alum-*

nus, November 1958. A *History of the College Curriculum of Miami University*, by S. Chester Parker, was issued as a Miami University Bulletin, October 1910. In *The Academic Community* (New York, 1962), John D. Millett described the component elements of the university—faculty, students, alumni and administration—and concluded that "consensus in action is the test of both freedom and responsibility." The career of Raymond M. Hughes (1873–1958) was featured in the *Miami Alumnus*, November 1958.

CHAPTER XXI. THE SESQUICENTENNIAL YEAR

The Congressional Resolution (H. Con. Res. 185) extending felicitations to Miami University appears in the *Congressional Record*, House Doc., May 25, 1959, p. 8128. The *Miami Student* issued a Sesquicentennial Supplement on Charter Day, February 17, 1959. The *Miami Alumnus*, June 1960, reviewed in text and pictures the events of the anniversary year. The Sesquicentennial booklet *Miami, Her 150th Year*, lists anniversary events and presents, chiefly in pictures, the University of 1959. *What Is a College For?* (Washington, 1961), with foreword by John D. Millett, comprises papers given by R. M. Hutchins, Max Lerner, August Heckscher, David A. Shepard and Mark Van Doren at a Sesquicentennial symposium sponsored by the Humanities Center for Liberal Education.

CHAPTER XXII. MIAMI MURAL

Accounts of the painting and placing of the Miami Mural are given in the *Miami Alumnus*, July 1963 and May 1964. The first experiment with a trimester schedule is noted in the Board of Trustees records for 1867 and in the *Miami Student*, December 30, 1867. Articles on Miami in the Coaching Field appeared in the *Miami University Bulletin*, January 1941 and March 1941, and in the *Miami Alumnus*, November 1958 and November 1959. The two designations of

"Coach of the Year" were reported in the *Miami Alumnus*, January 1959. During November 1967 the *Miami Student* ran a series of columns, "25 Years of Winning Football." A column, "End of an Era," summarizing the athletic traditions of Withrow Court, was featured in the *Cincinnati Enquirer*, March 6, 1968.

CHAPTER XXIII. A SENSE OF MISSION

President Shriver's inauguration and his inaugural address were featured in the *Miami Alumnus*, December 1965. The *Report of the President, 1964–1967*, gives a comprehensive account of developments in the university in the mid-1960's. Pros and cons of the trimester calendar were presented in the *Miami Student*, September 12, 1967. The trimester schedule occasioned not only discussion and debate but also an M.A. thesis: James G. Williams, *Oxford, Ohio: Time, Trade and the Trimester* (Miami University, 1966). The legends of Fisher Hall were first recorded in the *Miami Student*, November 20 and 24, 1953, and April 16, 1954. The "Save Fisher" campaign was reported in the *Miami Student*, March 29, 1968. *Miami University Programs for Superior Students* (Oxford, Ohio, 1963) described the Advanced Placement program, the Honors program, Undergraduate Fellowships, Scholarships, Prizes and Awards.

CHAPTER XXIV. HORIZON

The *Provisional Master Plan for Public Higher Education in Ohio* was published by the Board of Regents in April 1965. Fifteen months later, in June 1966, after hearings and consultations, the Board of Regents published a *Master Plan for State Policy in Higher Education. The University at the Service of Society* (New York, 1966) comprises a discussion held by trustees of the Carnegie Foundation for the Advancement of Teaching on the public service responsibilities of American universities. The *President's Newsletter* (Miami

University) issued to the faculty and staff beginning in 1966 takes note of developments in the entire range of Miami University activities and affairs. A feature of the *Miami Student*, March 29, 1968, was a page of articles describing the projected Miami program in Luxembourg.

CHAPTER XXV. BRANCHING OUT

Local history in both Hamilton and Middletown is sketched in *Memoirs of the Miami Valley,* Chicago: Robert O. Law Company, 3 vols. 1919, and in William E. Smith *History of Southwestern Ohio,* New York: Lewis Historical Publishing Co. 3 vols. 1964. The full text of McBride's argument that even before its material construction Miami University was permanently fixed in the as yet unbuilt town of Oxford appears in John Ewing Bradford, ed., *The James McBride Manuscripts Relating to Miami University,* Cincinnati, 1909. The Miami University Office of Information has issued annual booklets on each of the branch campuses and their relation to the respective communities. Details of the planning and development of the European Center in Luxembourg appear in Walter Havighurst *The Dolibois Years 1938 - 1981,* published by the Miami University Alumni Association in 1982. *Middfest* magazine, published 1981 by the citizens of Middletown, gives a detailed illustrated account of the annual Middletown International Celebration and of the relationship of Middletown, Ohio, to Luxembourgville in the Grand Duchy of Luxembourg. A very readable account of civic and industrial development is given in George Crout, *Middletown U S A, All-American City,* Middletown, Ohio 1960. Its author is a Miami graduate of 1938.

CHAPTER XXVI. CAMPUS CRISIS

Details of the events of April 15 - June 14, 1970, at Miami University are recorded in a 52-page typescript "Diary of Disruption," compiled by the Miami University Office of Public Information. This chronology eschews subjective interpreting and evaluation. A brief "Report on the Closing of Miami University," comprising news media accounts, was issued as a Newsletter of the *Miami Alumnus,* dated May, 1970. Interpretation and evaluation are included in the 30-page "Report of the President's Commission to Investigate the Events of April 15, 1970" and in the 26-page SCAR report "Findings of the Select Committee on the Abuse of Rights." Various viewpoints are represented in the concurrent minutes of the University Senate, Miami University Faculty Council, Miami University Council of Deans, Miami University Council of Student Affairs, and the Miami University Student Senate. Soon after the Kent State tragedy *Reader's Digest* sent researchers and editors to Kent to gather information on the events of the first week of May, 1970. Interviews with students, faculty, University officials, and the Ohio National Guard were followed by visits to other Ohio institutions — Ohio State University, Ohio University, and Miami University — that had experienced campus disruption. Author James Michener was called in three months after Kent's violent weekend. From his own interviews, observations and researches, along with the accumulated mass of information, came his volume *Kent State,* New York: Random House, 1971. (n.b. While the Thomas Hume epigraph on the title page of *The Miami Years* seems contradicted by this chapter, one may reflect that times are always trying, and no path of life can be free of obstacles.)

CHAPTER XXVII. MIAMI WESTERN UNION

The Miami University Archives contain an accumulation of press clippings, reports from the President's office, and of working papers of the planning team on The Western College of Miami University. The formal report of that committee was published as a special issue of the in-house periodical MIAMIAN, vol. 2, no. 9, Nov. 12, 1973. A detailed review of the first ten years of the Shriver administration at Miami University, written by Phillip R. Shriver, was published as a preface to the customary Annual Report of the President, in September 1975. After summarizing a current self-study of the university, this 35-page account culminates in reporting the visit of an evaluation team of the North Central Association of Colleges. The resulting evaluation was the highest possible accreditation for the longest possible period. "The Western Idea," an attractive informal brochure containing viewpoints of the Western faculty members and highlighting the campus community, the individualized major, and Senior projects, is Miami University Official Publication Series 78, No. 8, January 1980. A colleague's memories of Joseph M. Bachelor are recorded in The MIAMIAN, Nov. 8, 1979. Other Bachelor references appear in the MIAMI ALUMNUS October 1979 and January 1980. The letter from "thirty years after his death" is quoted in the MIAMI ALUMNUS October 1979, p. 3. The student diary of Abner Jones, 1854-58, is in the Special Collections of the King Library. A file of the OXFORD CRITERION, 1933-35, is in the King Library Special Collections.

CHAPTER XXVIII.   THE ROAD AHEAD

The "Million Dollar Campaign" of 1919-20 was announced in the *Alumni News Letter* of May 1920, with follow-up reports in August 1920 and May 1921. The "Goals for Enrichment" brochure is preserved in the Miami Collection shelves of the Special Collections in the King Library. Recurrent articles in the MIAMI ALUMNUS track the progress of the "Larger Usefulness" campaign from its launching in February 1978 to its successful conclusion in the spring of 1981. Dedication of the Miami University Art Museum is the leading matter of the MIAMI ALUMNUS of January 1979. This article, along with photographs, includes the dedication address, "Crucible of Change," given November 5 at the museum by President Willard L. Boyd of the University of Iowa. Photos in this issue include the principal donors and both exterior and interior views of the building. The continuing growth of the Presidents Club and its vital support of Alumni Association projects is reported in a 6-page feature of the MIAMI ALUMNUS, Summer 1981. Ribbon-cutting and formal opening of the Marcum Conference Center are recounted in MIAMIAN of January 1983. The same publication, p. 21 and p. 30, pictures progress in construction of the Yager Stadium. Removal of the old Spring Street power plant, beside Gaskill Hall, is pictured in the MIAMIAN, January 1983.

CHAPTER XXIX.   SLANT WALK MEDLEY — 1984

The Shriver presidential years are reviewed with text and photo in the *Miami Alumnus,* Summer 1981, and Fall 1981. The Pearson inauguration and the first one hundred days of Pearson administration are pictured and narrated in the first ten pages of the *Miami Alumnus,* Winter 1981. A James Langley article in MIAMIAN, September 1982, characterizes the new vice presidents in the Pearson regime. A framed reproduction of the Alumni Association "Greetings" to President Pearson now hangs in the upper lobby of Murstein Center. The Marilyn Throne poem appears in the *Miami Alumnus,* Summer 1981. The MIAMIAN January 1983 reports on two successive women's basketball championships. The *Diamond Anniversary Volume* (Miami University, 1899) portrays student life in the old North and South dorms, now Elliott and Stoddard halls. The *New York Sunday News,* October 25, 1959, featured football history at "Miami of Ohio." Construction of Yager Stadium and the new sports complex is reported and pictured in MIAMIAN, January, 1983, and in the *Oxford Press* April 14, 1983. The Parseghian quote appeared in *Cincinnati Enquirer,* February 11, 1983. "Miami Field, End of an Era" is a double-page spread in MIAMIAN, April, 1983. The MIAMIAN, January 1983 is given almost entirely to computer education. "Miami University in Age of the Computer" is surveyed in a column of the *Cincinnati Enquirer,* August 22, 1982. Details of the John E. Hull Memorial Room with a biographical profile of General Hull appear in the *Miami Alumnus,* February 1970 and Summer 1981. The Commencment of 1983 is reported in *Oxford Press,* May 19, 1983. The Special Collections of the King Library contain a George Orwell collection of some two hundred titles, including all of Orwell's books, in several languages, and a number of critical appraisals.

ACKNOWLEDGMENTS

I N this third edition of *The Miami Years* I continue in debt to present colleagues and others of years past. Of the earlier volumes the first was occasioned by the University's 150th anniversary in 1959, and the "revised edition," ten years later, was called for by the remarkable growth and development in the 1960s — development that made the sesquicentennial publication seem out-of-date. This "175th Anniversary Edition" seeks to portray an institution not so much enlarged as of added standing and accomplishment. In the fifteen years recounted in the final chapters, Miami has become more sophisticated and resourceful, and more attuned to changing culture and society than most of us could foresee.

For kind assistance I am grateful to to Douglas M. Wilson, Vice President of University Relations, Kathryn Y. Wiley, Assistant for Public Relations, Robert T. Howard, Director of Public Information, Richard M. Engle, Director of Physical Plant, William G. Slover, University Secretary, Myron D. Macechko, Director of Alumni Affairs, John E. DePree, Director of Marcum Memorial Conference Center, David A. Young, Director of Sports Information, Gordon D. Wilson and Charles W. Butler, University Archivists, James M. Langley, Director of News Bureau, Richard W. Sollmann, News Service Coordinator, Kay Foster, Coordinator of University Events, Sue Frazier of the Office of Student Affairs, Robert A. Wilkin, Alumni and Development Editor, Kaye York, Assist-

ant Editor of Alumni Affairs, Jacqueline Wallace, Director of
Western College Alumnae Association, Jean Perry, Western
College Alumnae Association Archivist, Sterling Cook, Cu-
rator of Collections of University Art Museum, and Edwin H.
Meador of Audio-Visual Service. In casual conversations
former presidents John D. Millett and Phillip R. Shriver, without their awareness, have given grist for my mill. Although
they are now four thousand miles away, I still gain perspective
and insight from Ambassador and Mrs. John E. Dolibois of
Luxembourg. For helping hand with countless searches, iden-
tifications and clarifications, I am happily in debt to Mrs.
Helen Ball and Mrs. Frances McClure of the Special Collections Library.

Finally a wholly personal word. As the years pass I frequently recall Psalm 16: "The lines are fallen unto me in pleasant places" — pleasant, above all, because of personal ties that
span almost a lifetime. Old friends to cherish — more than I
can number — but saying that I think of two whom I first knew
in residence hall and classroom. After fifty-five years of wide-
ranging experience, they are now my nearest neighbors. Great
riches in a small domain. We rarely reminisce, but there is a
mingled past and present in our friendship. To Ed Brown and
Anne Amos Brown this book is (*sub rosa*) dedicated.

WALTER HAVIGHURST

352 King Library
August 1983

INDEX

INDEX